Teaching Writing in Diverse Classrooms, K–8

ENHANCING WRITING THROUGH LITERATURE, REAL-LIFE EXPERIENCES, AND TECHNOLOGY

Margaret A. Moore-Hart
Eastern Michigan University

Boston New York San Francisco
Mexico City Montreal Toronto London Madrid Munich Paris
Hong Kong Singapore Tokyo Cape Town Sydney

Executive Editor: Aurora Martínez Ramos
Editorial Assistant: Jacqueline Gillen
Executive Marketing Manager: Krista Clark
Production Editor: Janet Domingo
Editorial Production Service: Omegatype Typography, Inc.
Composition Buyer: Linda Cox
Manufacturing Buyer: Megan Cochran
Electronic Composition: Omegatype Typography, Inc.
Interior Design: Omegatype Typography, Inc.
Cover Designer: Elena Sidorova

For related titles and support materials, visit our online catalog at www.pearsonhighered.com.

Library of Congress Cataloging-in-Publication Data

Moore-Hart, Margaret A.
Teaching writing in diverse classrooms, K–8 : enhancing writing through literature, real-life experiences, and technology / Margaret A. Moore-Hart.
p. cm.
Includes bibliographical references and index.
ISBN-13: 978-0-13-513526-6 (pbk.)
ISBN-10: 0-13-513526-5 (pbk.)
1. English language—Composition and exercises—Study and teaching (Elementary) 2. English language—Composition and exercises—Study and teaching (Middle school) 3. Multicultural education. I. Title.
LB1576.M67 2010
372.62'3—dc22

2009002920

Printed in the United States of America

Credits appear on page 312, which constitutes an extension of the copyright page.

www.pearsonhighered.com

ISBN-10: 0-13-513526-5
ISBN-13: 978-0-13-513526-6

Dedications

To my mother, Doris Binnion, and in memory of my father, John Binnion, who gave me an everlasting, treasured gift—my education.

To my caring husband, Tom, and our supportive children—Chad, Tiffany, Chris, and Allison—whose boundless love encircles me and fuels inspiration.

About the Author

Margaret A. Moore-Hart, a former codirector of the Clemson National Writing Project, is currently a professor and coordinator for the Reading Program Area at Eastern Michigan University. Writing has always been an area of intrigue and interest for her as a classroom teacher and educator. This focus on writing became a journey as she has explored ways to effectively teach writing and help students become successful writers. After testing Donald Graves's and Lucy Calkins's ideas in her own classroom, she began to investigate how technology might further enhance writing for elementary students. Influenced by Calkins and Graves, she also began to work closely with teachers and students in kindergarten through middle school classrooms. Using a collaborative approach to inquiry allowed her, as well as the teachers, to discover ways to improve student writing. Detecting ways to promote more effective writing continues to energize and stimulate her as she continues her journey.

Dr. Moore-Hart is the coauthor of *Multicultural Literacy: Mirroring the Reality of the Classroom.* In addition, she has published numerous articles on writing, multicultural literacy, technology and literacy, and parents and literacy. She has also been an invited guest speaker on writing and technology for state organizations and has made numerous presentations on writing and technology for state, regional, national, and international organizations.

Over the years, she has been the recipient of numerous awards. First and foremost, she received a teaching excellence award at her university. She was also the corecipient of the Christa McAuliffe Showcase of Excellence Award in research for a multicultural literacy program (MLP). The MLP was later validated by the U.S. Department of Education Program Effectiveness Panel and became part of the National Diffusion Network. Building on the successes of this program she became the director of an AmeriCorps tutoring program designed to increase reading/writing performance of elementary students, especially those who live in poverty or who are culturally diverse. This grant was a finalist for the Michigan Governor's Service Award.

Indeed, the experience of working with multiple teachers and students over the years has helped her extend her understanding of writing and how to teach writing effectively. This text is a record of her journey—a journey that will continue to evolve.

Contents

Chapter Five
Integrating Multicultural Literature with Writing and Word Processing 103

Chapter Six
Using Writing in an Integrated, Interdisciplinary Curriculum 138

Foreword

All students have the right to high-quality writing instruction. And what a joy to read this interesting and informative text filled with exciting ideas for helping students learn the craft of writing. In *Teaching Writing in Diverse Classrooms, K–8: Enhancing Writing through Literature, Real-Life Experiences, and Technology,* Margaret Moore-Hart takes us on a journey from the theoretical perspectives of a writing program to a wealth of strategies for enhancing writing across the curriculum. She culminates the volume with a thorough treatment of how to organize and manage a successful writing program. This highly engaging treatment of writing development K–8 is on the cutting edge of current knowledge.

With this book Margaret Moore-Hart has given teachers and their students a wonderful gift. Each chapter in this book provides research-based practices on the teaching and learning of the writing craft. Teachers understand the importance of being able to write well and are committed to helping their students become creative and proficient writers. This book is firmly rooted in the belief that, with good instruction, all students can learn to read and write effectively.

Two characteristics make this book unique and essential for K–8 teachers. First, the book emphasizes making our teaching practices relevant to culturally and linguistically diverse students. Second, this book pushes our thinking about writing instruction forward to include technology and how technology can be incorporated effectively into our writing curriculum so that our students are prepared for their roles in a global, computer-mediated society.

This text will inspire teachers and get them excited about helping students become joyful and lifelong writers. Teachers will have access to ideas for providing instruction that will help students see their potential and continually improve in their writing ability. The examples of student writing and the Teaching Tips make the text "come alive" for the classroom teacher. I was particularly impressed with the motivating qualities of the writing strategies, as well as the emphasis on authentic writing experiences. The final part of the book, Organizing and Managing a Successful Writing Program, provides educators with strategies for organizing, managing, and monitoring a successful writing program. This section is a "must read" for both teachers and administrators who are interested in implementing and maintaining high-quality writing instruction.

Finally, I want to thank Margaret for her beautiful prose. A book about writing instruction *should* be beautifully written. Often, that is not the case. This text is a pleasure to read and it is filled with valuable ideas for improving writing instruction. It will provide teachers, administrators, staff developers, and teacher educators with a very practical and powerful research-based instructional model that will help to empower both teachers and their students.

Linda B. Gambrell
Distinguished Professor of Education
Eugene T. Moore School of Education
Clemson University

Preface

A sea of ongoing changes requires that competent, knowledgeable, and courageous teachers continuously use problem solving and thinking to respond to evolving challenges in teaching and learning. One of those challenges is the teaching of writing. Donald Graves tells us that children can acquire the conventions and tools that writers use to rework their texts if we provide them instruction in reading and *writing.* This belief mirrors my own experiences with teachers and students within numerous classroom settings. Young writers can acquire the conventions and tools they need to write and rework their written text into a message that expresses meaning. And while there is no one formula for the effective teaching of writing, we can learn from others and use their experiences and research to guide us to new levels of understanding.

In order for "best practice" to flourish and for students to learn to write confidently and well, we need to look at ongoing research and professional readings. We also need to draw on teachers' experiences. Teachers have learned to think, question, and reflect on what works in classroom settings. I hope my own evolving journey of experiences with teachers in classroom settings reflected in this text models a way for us to become lifelong learners who think about our practice while drawing on research and theory. Inspired by giants in the field of writing—Lucy Calkins, Jane Hansen, Gail Tompkins, Regie Routman, and Roy Peter Clark—this text mirrors the best of their research and what we currently know about teaching children to write. Uniquely, the text also shares ways technology tools can be used to enhance students' writing in a global, computer-mediated world.

Rationale for the Text

In his 1983 book, *Writing: Teachers and Children at Work,* Graves demonstrated that young children can write. He further showed that young children learn to write by going through developmental stages. Students just need the opportunity to write daily and to learn about the writing process. My text shows you how to give all students the opportunity to write daily and how to help them learn about the writing process. Specifically, the text models how to (a) address the needs, interests, varying abilities, and cultural and linguistic backgrounds of young writers; (b) guide and facilitate students as they analyze, synthesize, and evaluate ideas through writing; (c) use technology tools to enhance and facilitate writing; and (d) coach students as they access, retrieve, interpret, and apply information from multiple sources, including the Internet.

Although we have made great strides in literacy learning and teaching during the past two decades, we need to push our thinking forward to include technology. Since our lives are entwined with technology, we need to ponder our teaching practices related to writing and technology. Word processing, databases, spreadsheets, electronic mail, the fax machine, PowerPoint, and the Internet dominate the working environment of industry and large and small businesses alike. Computer software, videodisks, video games, word processing, email, and the Internet are also a significant part of our children's play environment. To prepare our youth for their roles in a changing world dominated by new technologies, we need to incorporate computers and technology into the writing curriculum.

As writing continues to have a larger impact on our way of living and working, students also need opportunities to interact and function with writing in their learning environment. As knowledge rapidly expands and transforms, teachers become facilitators of knowledge for students. They further need to coach students as they use writing to analyze, synthesize, and evaluate information that they access and retrieve using technology tools.

To address these compelling issues, the text combines writing theory with teaching practice. Infusing technology perspectives throughout the text may inspire you to integrate technology with your writing curriculum to empower your students, enabling them to become critical and active thinkers, readers, and writers in our changing world. The vignettes provide models for coaching and guiding students as they use technological tools to access, retrieve, interpret, and apply information from multiple sources.

Organization of the Text

This text, which emerges from 20 years of classroom research in K–8 settings, includes theoretical underpinnings and extensive research on writing within diverse classroom settings. Its content reveals an integration of research with my experiences while working with teachers and students, helping them learn more about writing, technology, and multicultural literacy.

Part One: Theoretical Perspectives of a Literacy Program Integrated with Technology

Chapter 1: Literacy as a Process. This initial chapter provides in-depth considerations of literacy as a process. The chapter begins with an overview of writing theory, showing how writing evolves for young children within the home environment. Illustrating how this natural way of learning can become patterns for literacy learning within the school, the chapter further focuses on the importance of emphasizing meaning in writing development. This fundamental principle leads to theories of the relationship between reading and writing. The chapter concludes with a review of the research related to writing as a process and its role in literacy development.

Chapter 2: Using Technology to Enhance and Extend Literacy Learning. This chapter presents a rationale, need, and purpose for integrating technology within the language arts curriculum. The chapter lays the foundation for using technology to enhance and extend literacy learning by identifying the theoretical perspectives for integrating technology with the language arts curriculum. Through the use of a classroom vignette, you will see how technology becomes a tool to enhance and support literacy.

Part Two: Strategies for Enhancing Literacy across the Curriculum with the Use of Writing and Technology

Chapter 3: Getting Writing Started. This chapter addresses the sensitivity of writing and how to create an atmosphere that is caring and supportive so that writing will grow and develop for students of all cultural and linguistic backgrounds. It shows how teachers help preschoolers and kindergarten children become young authors. As the chapter continues, you will view specific teaching strategies for helping students gain fluency in their writing through the use of journals, learning logs, or lifebooks. The chapter also reveals how journaling helps students learn the content of math, science, or social studies. Throughout the chapter, you will gain insight on how to help learners of all ages and cultural backgrounds become comfortable with their writing and technology.

Chapter 4: Real-Life Experiences in Writing. Chapter 4 describes how to use real-life experiences to promote writing within classroom settings. Through the use of vignettes, the chapter models a process approach to learning that emerges from the daily lives of students. The vignettes reveal innovative ways to use observation, description, interviews, and the collection of information with students of varying age levels and cultural backgrounds. The chapter concludes with a vignette that models how to implement writing response groups.

Chapter 5: Integrating Multicultural Literature with Writing and Word Processing. This chapter examines how culturally and linguistically diverse students become authors when their cultural heritage, traditions, beliefs, and values are reflected in their reading and writing. You will perceive how writing can be a way for all students to discover and appreciate the similarities and differences among people. Specifically, vignettes depict how writing can sharpen sensitivity toward differences as students learn to acknowledge and affirm students' cultural and linguistic heritages. These vignettes further reveal how reading and writing about multicultural literature can become a way to study social issues and take actions to solve problems as students begin to perceive social issues in a global society with "inside eyes."

Chapter 6: Using Writing in an Integrated, Interdisciplinary Curriculum. After discussing the theoretical issues related to interdisciplinary learning, Chapter 6 focuses on ways to create effective connections between the core subjects through writing. You will gain an understanding of how students can practice language arts skills within a content area while using writing to gather and present information. Informational literature offers many new opportunities for adding breadth, depth, meaning, and interest to the learning environment.

Chapter 7: Using Information and Communication Technology Tools in an Integrated, Interdisciplinary Curriculum. In Chapter 7, you will recognize how the Internet can be integrated with the language arts and social studies curriculum in a meaningful, purposeful context. Distinctively, this chapter illustrates how teachers and students combine their efforts to explore the Internet and construct a home page about changes in their school and community. Throughout the chapter, you will perceive how technology can become a wonderful tool to publish students' writing, inspiring them to become lifelong readers and writers.

Chapter 8: Generating Meaning through Electronic Learning. Certain strategies provide effective links between technology and reading, writing, social studies, science, and mathematics. This chapter illustrates how students of varying ages and abilities learn to become authors as they apply the writing process in electronic learning environments. You will learn ways to use hypertext, databases, and word processors to promote higher level thinking skills as students access, retrieve, process, and evaluate information.

Chapter 9: Fostering Respect and Appreciation through the Use of Technology in an Inclusion Environment. Teachers can use specific strategies to promote students' respect and appreciation of one another, sharpen their sensitivity toward differing abilities and strengths, and foster self-esteem of all students through the use of writing in an inclusion learning environment. The chapter begins by describing how two teachers—one a teacher of children with physical and mental impairments and one a teacher of culturally diverse fifth graders—use team teaching in an inclusion classroom. After emphasizing the need to first acknowledge and affirm students' self-identities, the chapter models activities that build on the use of technology and multicultural literature to help all students become successful learners. While gaining an understanding of how students' knowledge and understanding emerge within a technological learning environment, you will also read about new ways to address the needs of students of varying ability levels so that they *will not be left behind.*

Part Three: Organizing and Managing a Successful Writing Program

Chapter 10: Organizing and Managing Assessment in a Writing Program. Underscoring the need for an organizational framework for developing a successful writing program, this chapter highlights ways to organize and manage the content and social context of the writing program while addressing the changing national standards for reading and writing, high-stakes testing, and expanding information in an age of technology. To maintain a successful program that is consistent with the National Standards in writing, you will learn how to use multiple assessment processes to evaluate student learning on an ongoing basis.

Special Features of the Text

This text, which is designed for preservice and in-service teachers who work with students in kindergarten through middle school, can be used as an invaluable resource to discover effective teaching practice in the field of writing. Special features that increase the book's usability include:

- **A strong, theoretical, research base** that permeates the text and grounds the real-life classroom practices, offering you an understanding of the connections among literacy, language, culture, and technology.
- **Specific teaching strategies,** modeling and demonstrating how to infuse writing and technology across the curriculum.
- **Step-by-step directions,** helping you understand how to implement these strategies successfully within your own classroom.
- **Vignettes** that examine what works and what doesn't work in classrooms. The vignettes illustrate what is discovered as a result of teacher problem solving, questioning, thinking, and reflection. The names of teachers are included for authenticity as well as to acknowledge the teachers' expertise and willingness to share their students and classrooms with us.
- **Samples of students' work** and, in particular, samples of students' writing. I share these to illustrate the possible responses that evolve when using the teaching strategies offered in this text.
- **Comments and quotes** from teachers and students, illustrating their viewpoints and perspectives.
- **Figures, tables, graphic organizers, and Teaching Tips** to help you perceive the theoretical and practical issues of teaching and to highlight information.
- **Questions teachers frequently ask** and responses to these questions, integrated at the conclusion of each chapter.

The Ultimate Goals of This Text

As a result of reading this text, I hope you will be inspired to help students become lifelong writers who experiment and take risks with their writing. In this way, students will begin to see their potentials and improve their writing. Just as writers experiment and take risks with their writing, I hope you will feel empowered to take risks in your teaching, modify what isn't working and use what is working through self-reflection. Importantly, I anticipate that the text will help you embrace technology and its potential to increase writing appreciation and performance.

Acknowledgments

This book is a tribute to the many students and teachers whose voices emerge from each page of the text. I am deeply grateful for the warmth and trust with which they welcomed me to their classrooms. There are many others to whom I wish to express my appreciation and gratitude—those who supported, assisted, and sustained me through the process of writing the book. I especially owe a debt of gratitude to many educators, administrators, and parents. Even though the words in the text are my own, the ideas emerged through continuous sharing, interaction, and collaborations with these people.

I especially would like to thank the Ann Arbor, Ypsilanti, Wayne-Westland, Brighton, Howell, and Hartland school districts in Michigan. Specifically, the following administrators, teachers, and staff have all provided their time, support, and expertise in the creation of this book.

I am deeply appreciative of the support and trust of the administrators within the various school districts I worked over the years. In particular, they include Deanna Birdyshaw, Lynnette Blocker, Lana Callihan, Lee Cole, Pauline Colemen, Jacquilyn Dudley, Paul Kacanek, Ruth Knoll, Noni Miller, Pat de Rossett, Ann Schmidt, Tulani Smith, Sally Stavros, Nancy Voght, Karen Zokas, and David Zuhlke.

The following teachers in the Ann Arbor School District kindly gave their time and support by opening their doors to me, allowing me to work with them in their classrooms. I would like to thank Gerard Antekeier, Basil Babcock, and Beth Caldwell.

I would also like to thank the following teachers in the Wayne-Westland School District: Aileen Balatico, Pam Cusumano, Nathan Dolbert, Lois Egeler, Sue Florida, Tracey Franklin, Diane Heiss, Jeanie Lawrence, Stacy McBroom, and Sandi Schutte.

I am equally thankful for these teachers residing in the Brighton, Hartland, and Howell School Districts: Emily Mihocko, Erin Minnis, Kim Nichol, and Kellie Wood.

In addition, I am deeply appreciative of the following teachers in the Ypsilanti School District: Charlotte Andrews, Trish Archibold, Jack Bauer, Judy Benns, Elaine Bortz, Mandy Church, Barbara Cornish, Andrea Cousins, Barbara Dykman, Susan Fenker, Kim Ferrell, Monica Haddock, Merrell Harkema, Alexa Hoylman, Beth Hurdle, Bette Jessee, Eloise Johnson, Bill Madden, Mary Manchester, Kathy Micallef, Kelly Newton, Lynne Raglin, Beth Ramsey, Candy Reaume, Shari Simpson, Venetia Sims, Linda Skinner, Alicia Stowe, Mary Streeter, Vonnie Taylor, Sima Thurman, Sandy Todd, Margaret Trapp, Beverly Tyler, Sue Weeks, and Connie Williams.

Finally, I am grateful for Michaele Rae's and Michelle Cox's willingness to allow me to work with them and their students at Summers-Knoll School. I also owe a special thanks to David Wayne in the Plymouth-Canton School District.

I would also like to thank the following professors for their thoughtful reviews: Dr. David Adewuyi, Albany State University; Bonnie Armbruster, University of Illinois at Urbana-Champaign; Anna Bolling, California State University–Stanislaus; Deanna Gilmore, Washington State University; Linda Kleeman, Harris-Stowe State University; and Amy Thornburg, Queens University of Charlotte. Certainly, they helped me find ways to strengthen my writing.

I am deeply indebted to Linda Gambrell for her thoughtful insights, expressed within the foreword. Certainly, she has continuously inspired and nurtured my professional development as a researcher and writer.

For all her endless hours in facilitating the publishing process, I am most appreciative of Linda Bishop, who supported me through all stages of the book. Her flexibility, knowledge, suggestions, and continuous words of encouragement have been invaluable. I anticipate that the success of this book will be due to her ongoing efforts.

I am indebted to students who took the risk to share their writing and wonderful ideas with me over the years. They have enriched my life and led me down a path of amazing learning experiences. Without their guidance, I would not be able to share this information with others. Nor would I be able to offer others clues and suggestions for promoting their writing. The students are the ones who educate us all about writing.

Ultimately, I would not have been able to complete this book without the support and love of my friends and family. I am deeply grateful for their love and cheers along the way. I know I could not have succeeded without their love and patience throughout the whole process. They include my husband and editor, Tom Hart; my children, Chad, Tiffany, Chris, and Allison; my mother, Doris Binnion; and my brother and sisters, John Binnion, Ginny Bettendorf, and Lee Binnion.

In closing, I believe that this book is truly a collaborative effort, made possible by the talents, support, commitment, and openness of many people. To each and every one of them I am most thankful. I have accomplished far more than I ever dreamed.

chapter ONE

Literacy as a Process

Poems are hard to make
Even without writers' block
I've tendered it watered it,
But still it will not grow.
So I switched to a bigger pot
And gave it new soil,
But still it will not grow.
I've watered it, I've tendered it.
But still it will not grow.
Wait a minute.
What's this?
Have I written a poem?
And finally it grew!

by Jenny

Writing as a Thinking Process

Jenny, age 10, realizes that writing is not magical. She understands that writing must be carefully molded and shaped to express a message. While molding and shaping her poem over three days, she experimented with words and phrases in her journal. She crossed out, deleted, and inserted words and phrases; sometimes she crossed out the whole draft of the poem and started over, switching to a bigger pot and giving it new soil. As she struggled with her poem, she shared drafts with her peers, trying to convey her message. Just as an artist shapes a piece of sculpture from a piece of wood, Jenny crafted a poem. Jenny gained a sense of authorship.

According to Calkins (1994), authors are artists every single day of their lives as they take hold of their writing and make something of it. The richness of Jenny's poem comes from her effort to take hold of her poem and layer it with meaning. Just as Calkins (1994, p. 8) takes "a moment—an image, a memory, a phrase, an idea, holds it in her hands, and declares it a treasure," Jenny took an idea and molded her idea into a poem. This is the essence of writing.

Writing is communicating, planning, thinking, imagining, remembering, collecting information, accessing information, or storing ideas in memory. According to Calkins (1994), writers represent their experiences through writing, reclaiming them for the reader. She suggests that this is why early people inscribed stories on cave walls. Similarly, this is why young children use magic markers, pens, and pencils to leave their marks on paper.

Writing as a Process of Communicating Meaning with Young Children

Young children use magic markers, pens, and pencils to convey messages just as early people created messages with pictures. For example, at age 18 months, Tiffany watched her mother write lists, letters, thank-you notes, phone messages, or notes on the refrigerator. She, too, wanted to write her own "lists, letters, and messages." Seeing her natural interest in writing, her mother gave her some paper and a pencil, showing her how to write on the paper—not the walls, tables, or chairs. In a natural way (Sulzby & Teale, 1991), Tiffany began conveying her messages through prephonemic spelling (see Figure 1.1 for the stages of temporary spelling), using scribbles, lines, dots, and circles that mimicked her mother's own writing.

As Tiffany continued to invent and reinvent forms of written language with pencil and paper, she began to notice that her brother, age 4, was writing on his chalkboard. He wrote his name, Chad, all over the chalkboard. He also experimented with lines, trying to form the shapes of the alphabet letters scattered around his chalkboard. Watching him form the shapes of the alphabet on his chalkboard, Tiffany began to explore making letterlike forms (Miller, 2000) on her paper and the chalkboard when Chad was not there.

Before long, she wanted to learn to write her own name, just like Chad. So her mother showed her how to make a *T*. With practice, Tiffany also learned to write the letters *T-I-F-F*, her nickname. Through play, experimentation, and a natural interest in representing her experiences, Tiffany began to communicate meaning (Sulzby & Teale, 1991; Teale & Sulzby, 1986).

Chad simultaneously continued to explore the process of communicating meaning, expressing a desire to learn to write "I love you," "Mom," and "Dad." After being shown how to write these messages, he mimicked writing these words over and over on his chalkboard and paper. Through play, he gradually learned how to spell the words and write them on his own, using conventional spelling. His natural interest in conveying messages directed his early writing development.

Andrew similarly followed these natural inclinations of representing experiences. At an early age, Andrew expressed an interest in drawing. Drawing, which began with scribbles, became a way for him to express his experiences and interests. After finishing his drawings, he would talk about his drawings, pointing to the pictures while sharing the meaning of the pictures. Andrew's early interest in drawing directed his understanding of print as he began to record the first letter of his name, *A*, next to his pictures. Over time, the *A* grew into *Andrew* (see Figure 1.2).

While Andrew drew his pictures, his mother would simultaneously draw pictures, representing experiences they had shared together. As she drew pictures, she would also talk about her pictures and ask him questions about his pictures, helping him discover that the pictures communicate a message. As Andrew got older, his mother enlisted his knowledge of letters and sounds to help him relate to the beginning sounds of words in her pictures. As he told her the beginning sounds, she recorded the words under her pictures. Soon Andrew began to try this with his own pictures, recording the first letter of some words next to his pictures. Sometimes he asked his mother to finish the word (see Figure 1.3). Other times, he scribbled his message next to his pictures. Over time, Andrew's attempt to write became sentences.

The social relationships that Tiffany, Chad, and Andrew experienced evolved within their home environment. These playful experiences largely shaped their literacy development and their understanding of written language. Their natural ways of learning (Butler & Clay, 1987; Dyson, 1993; Graves, 1983; Graves & Stuart, 1987; Teale & Sulzby, 1986) provided a foundation for reading and writing to emerge for these children.

Figure 1.1

Stages of Temporary Spelling

Stage 1: Prephonemic Spelling

Children scribble, form shapes or letterlike shapes, draw pictures, and form numbers or letters to create a message. They are not yet aware that letters represent speech sounds or phonemes. As young as 18 months, children begin experimenting and exploring writing through prephonemic spelling. Preschoolers, as well as many kindergarteners, continue to represent their messages through prephonemic spelling. If we continuously ask them, "Tell me about your writing," they will begin to associate written language with the spoken word.

Example:

Translation: This is me with my mommy and my grandpa.

Stage 2: Phonemic Spelling

Children begin to represent phonemes in their messages with letters during this stage. At first one letter, usually the first letter, is used to represent each word in their message. Gradually, children represent the first and last sounds of words in their messages, often omitting spaces between words. Over time, they also begin to represent the long vowel sounds of words, as well as other consonants they hear in messages. If we continue to ask them to tell us about their writing, they will take more risks, trying to represent more of the phonemes in the messages with phonemic spelling.

Example: WIWABABEICKBLDLOVRT

Translation: When I was a baby, I scribbled all over it.

Stage 3: Letter–Name Spelling

Children begin to represent short vowel patterns within the words in their messages. They realize that words have vowels and that the vowels are frequently between the consonants. They often represent the *i* as an *e* in *deg* (dig); or short *e* as an *a* in *slad* (sled); or short *o* as an *i* in *clik* (clock). Even though the spellings seem odd to adults, they are based on phonetic relationships (Read, 1976). Children will often begin to spell some of the words using conventional spelling during this stage. As emphasized, the children continue to take risks if we ask them to read their messages to us. They need to know we can read their messages using their temporary spelling.

Example: The pig levd on a fom he lic the mud.

Translation: The pig lived on a farm. He likes the mud.

Stage 4: Transitional Spelling

In this stage, children begin to internalize more information about spelling patterns and the words they write become similar to the way they look. All syllables and sounds are represented in the words within their messages. The syllables also follow certain spelling patterns, but often the pattern children apply doesn't always work with the word they are spelling. In addition, many children tend to overgeneralize spelling rules within their words at this stage. Children still need to hear teachers affirm their temporary spellings so they will continue to explore and experiment with spelling patterns during this stage.

Example: My favrite caricter in wy muskeydoes buzz in peepuls ears. The caricter is the Igwona beecus he looks funny with the stics.

Translation: My favorite character in *Why Mosquitoes Buzz in People's Ears.* The character is the Iguana because he looks funny with the sticks.

Stage 5: Conventional Spelling

When children advance to this stage, they spell most of their words correctly. Children have begun to build a repertoire of spelling patterns and even begin to learn to spell homonyms, contractions, and irregular spellings. They have internalized rules that govern more difficult vowel and consonant combinations, word endings, and prefixes or suffixes. However, they will continue to resort to earlier stages when writing more difficult words. Children continue to use temporary spellings whenever needed and require validation for their efforts. This validation encourages them to use the best word possible to express their message rather than only use words they know how to spell.

Example: Well how about this frog? It won't crack any dishes and it won't get any water on the floor.

Tiffany, Chad, and Andrew never heard anyone say that they didn't make the letter correctly or that they didn't spell the word perfectly. They saw that people were interested in what they were doing. Their family members celebrated their first attempts at forming the letters or writing. Learning evolved through delightful experiences as they played with print, experimented with lines and shapes, and explored how to form words.

Figure 1.2

Andrew Progresses from Writing Beginning Letters to Writing His Name

(a) Andrew begins writing letters, including the letter *A* to represent his name. (b) Andrew writes more of his name on his pictures. (c) Andrew writes his name on his picture.

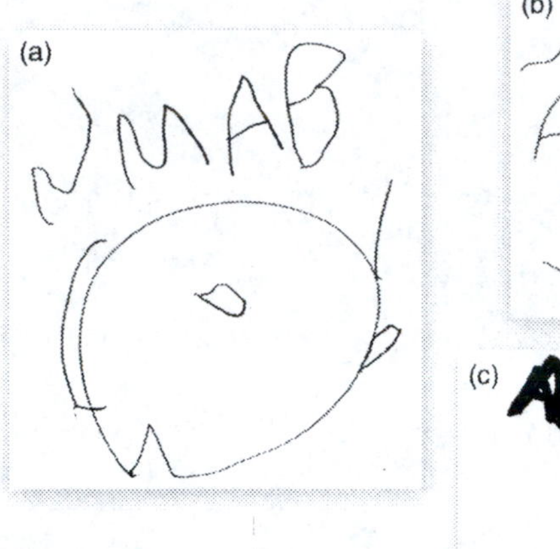

Figure 1.3

Andrew Gives the Beginning and Ending Sounds of Words

Andrew writes the word *cow* underneath his picture. He recorded the *c* on his picture; then his mother told him the ending sound of *ow,* which he wrote on his paper.

Writing as a Process of Communicating Meaning in the Elementary Classroom

We can capture these natural ways of learning—these natural ways of representing experiences that occur in the home environment—within the classroom. Writing in school settings needs to be self-sponsored, emerging from children's interests and evolving from real-life purposes and the life experiences of students, just as it grew out of real-life purposes and the lives of Tiffany, Chad, and Andrew.

As teachers, we need to celebrate the beginnings of students' writing just as parents, grandparents, and relatives cheer children's writings. Writing flourishes when we recognize the significance of everyday happenings in students' lives and how they express these happenings in their drawings and writing. Instead of viewing students' writing as a "line that moves haltingly across the page, exposing as it goes all that the writer doesn't know," we can show respect for what students know and celebrate their early attempts at writing. When we honor their ideas, students won't feel like they are put on the line, showing us what they don't know (Shaugnessy, 1977, p. 7). Rather, students will feel like their writing ideas are treasures (Calkins, 1994; Graves, 2004).

One place for early childhood students to transform their experiences into written language is the writing center. Through playful experiences, young children can invent ways to draw, scribble, form letters, or write words and texts. The more they explore various writing tools (markers, chalk, pencils, pens, crayons) and materials (lined and unlined paper, cards, envelopes, whiteboards, chalkboards, Post-its, note pads, notebooks), the more they learn about literacy and written language. As they discover real-life purposes for writing, they begin to master the conventions of writing.

Integrating writing tools and materials into all learning centers further stimulates mastery of the conventions of writing. Through trial and error, young children reconstruct ways to generate messages and texts. These approximations gradually become closer to conventional forms. Offering opportunities for young students to explore writing in learning centers further fosters an understanding of two types of writing experiences—practical writing and personal writing.

According to Burrows (1984), one of the pioneers in the writing movement, practical writing fulfills a purpose for writing and includes an audience. Tiffany's first explorations with print included practical writing as she wrote notes, grocery lists, or letters, following her mother's example. Other examples that include practical writing might consist of thank-you letters, memos, reports, or captions.

Personal writing, in contrast, is spontaneous, with the writers becoming their own audience. Andrew's first attempts at writing were examples of personal writing as he communicated his ideas and experiences. Young writers also share their emotions, triumphs, or hardships in life through personal writing. Placing writing tools and materials in multiple settings enables children to discover their own entrance into literacy. They can begin to invent and reinvent written language according to their own interests similar to the way literacy emerges in the home environment.

Writing as a Process of Representing Life Experiences in the Elementary Classroom

According to Clark (1995), students of all ages become clearer thinkers and stronger communicators when they write about themselves and their worlds. Showing a genuine interest in students' experiences helps students realize that writing is generating meanings about their lives and experiences. Through the act of writing, they begin to understand themselves, learn about others in the community, and think about issues that affect their lives.

Many young writers naturally begin writing about themselves and their lives, representing their experiences through drawing and writing. Since students of all ages are experts on themselves, writing emerges more easily when they write about their own lives or experiences. Gradually, writers become more comfortable with writing and move from this first circle of ideas, which is centered around themselves, to the second circle of ideas, centered around the family (see Figure 1.4). Over time, more experienced writers advance to the outer circles centered around the school, community, nation, and world (Clark, 1995).

Through the lens of their writing, students begin to see the world as a place where they can learn (Clark, 1995). As they write, students think about their lives and their worlds; they begin to ask questions, ponder, observe, learn, and grow. Writing provides the tool for learning to occur. Students' choices provide the direction for their learning to evolve.

If we focus on students' natural fascination with print, as in the emergent writings of Tiffany, Chad, or Andrew, students begin to realize that authors generate meanings about their experiences and their world through writing. Showing a respect for what they know and expressing an interest in their ideas, rather than their attempts to spell or form letters, helps students begin to feel like authors. After the ideas are composed, students spontaneously share their writing with others. Sharing their message with others fosters an avenue for social interactions to evolve. These social interactions help writers discover that they create meaning from the printed words for themselves, as well as their audience. Through this natural, ongoing process of writing, reading, and sharing, young learners discover the relationship between reading and writing (Sulzby, 1985; Teale & Sulzby, 1986).

> ***teaching* TIP 1.1**
>
> Children want to write. Our job is to see that they retain an "I-am-a-writer" spirit.

Promoting the Reading and Writing Relationship

When Donald Graves, a well-recognized researcher and author on writing, completed his seminal research study on writing in a second grade classroom, professor Margaret Salter asked him, "And what did you find in your research about the relationship between writing and reading?" (Graves, 2004, p. 88). At the time, Graves replied that he had found nothing. However, this important question spurred Graves to examine this relationship in future studies with Jane Hansen. Their work, as well as that of many other researchers (Calkins, 1994; Hansen, 1987, 2001; Shanahan, 1988; Shanahan & Lomax, 1988; Stotsky, 1983; Sulzby & Barnhart, 1992; Tierney & Pearson, 1983; Tompkins, 2004) demonstrated that reading and writing are active processes as readers and writers construct meaning. In reading, students

Figure 1.4
The Circle of Ideas

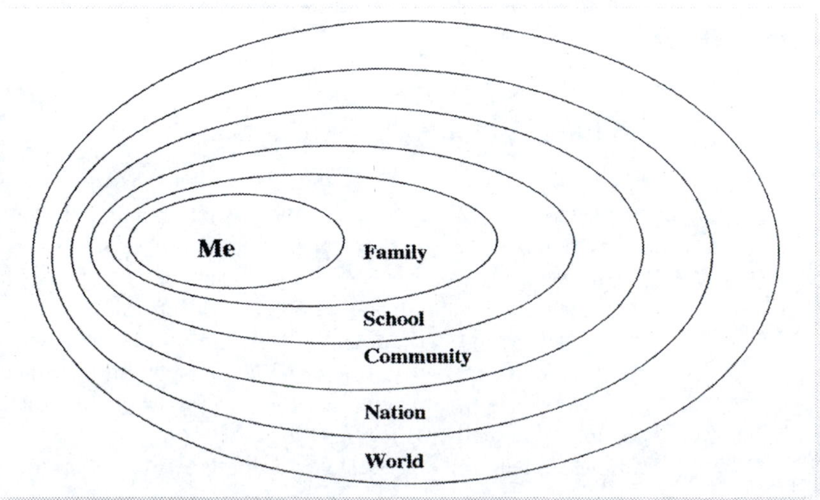

create meaning from a given text. In writing, students *generate* texts in order to make meaning. At first, writers create and generate meaning for themselves; later, while sharing their writing with others, they begin to construct meaning for an audience. Using similar thought processes as they read and write, students prepare themselves to read by drawing on their background experiences to create meaning; likewise, they prepare themselves to write by drawing on their background experiences to generate meaning.

Reading and Writing Relationships Emerge from Oral Language

Importantly, reading and writing are both grounded in oral language (Goodman, 1976; Moffett, 1982). In its beginning stages, writing emerges from this talk. By talking about his drawings, Andrew began to figure out how to get his speech onto paper. Recall that when Andrew first drew pictures, he used them to talk about his experiences. At first his speech was pictures on the paper. These pictures often portrayed experiences he had with others. For example, trains fascinated Andrew early on. He loved to ride the train at Greenfield Village, close to his home. In addition, he had toy trains at home. As a result of his fascination with trains, many of his early drawings included train tracks. While drawing the tracks, he spontaneously talked about his experiences riding the train or playing with trains. Later, as he began to use symbols to write about his experiences, the talk became written print on the paper. These conversations about the pictures became prephonemic and phonemic writing. While reading the print about his experiences, Andrew naturally began to associate print with the spoken language.

The more children write, the more they begin to read their writing. Gradually they learn to judge what they have written, edit their text, share their work, and read the works of others (Calkins, 1983). In fact, students zigzag back and forth, moving from their writing to their reading and from their reading to their writing.

Reading and Writing Relationships Emerge from Social Interactions

teaching TIP 1.2

Revising is how we shape our writing to deliver our message clearly.

As Jenny zigzagged back and forth between her reading and writing, for example, she discovered her intention for writing the poem, as well as her purposes and probable meanings for the poem. Since the words did not at first convey her purposes and meaning for the poem, she kept revising the poem until her purposes and meaning emerged from the words. Just as this recursive process helped Jenny achieve objectivity while reading her poem, this process helps all writers gain objectivity in their work and the work of others (Tierney & Pearson, 1983).

Jenny's work on her poem shows us the thinking that reading and writing demand as one analyzes, synthesizes, and evaluates one's own writing. Importantly, sharing her writing with her peers helped Jenny discover what she wanted to say and how to say it so that others would understand her meaning and purpose. These social interactions, in turn, affected the meaning she generated through repeated attempts to shape her poem.

Similarly, social interactions among students, their teacher, or peers affect the meaning students generate through their writing (Dyson, 1993; Langer, 1986). As students tell stories, explain how things work, predict what will happen, or guess why people behave the way they do, they rehearse ideas for writing. Students also test their ideas with others while sharing their writing with teachers and peers. When Jenny discussed her ideas for the poem, she checked out her ideas with others; she also got ideas from them to help her explain her message more clearly.

If we want our students' writing to flourish, we need to capitalize on positive, respectful social interactions that reflect the responses from parents, grandparents, and relatives within the home environment. Creating an environment within our classrooms that is caring, supportive, and affirming for all writers is one way to accomplish these respectful social interactions. Responding in thoughtful, helpful ways, peers and teachers might praise the ideas of the writers or ask questions to clarify the writers' meaning and intentions for writing.

Creating Links between Reading and Writing through Guided Reading and Writing

We can draw on the relationship between reading and writing to enhance reading and writing growth and development. The two reinforce and support one another (Hoyt, 2003; Mooney, 2003; Shanahan, 1987; Shanahan & Lomax, 1988; Stotsky, 1983; Tierney & Pearson, 1983). For example, asking students to write a paragraph that includes a topic sentence and detail sentences can strengthen their understanding of main ideas and supporting details in reading. This is especially true if we point out connections between writing a paragraph and reading paragraphs found in informational texts together within the classroom.

Forming Links between Reading and Writing through Guided Reading

Judy Benns, a Title I teacher of second graders, applied these principles while teaching her students concepts about topic sentences and detail sentences in paragraphs. Following her students' natural interest in animals, Judy and her second graders read several informational books, as well as selected magazine articles from *Zoobooks,* about cheetahs.

Reading the books and magazines with her students provided them models for their own writing, especially as Judy pointed out how authors include many detail sentences about various topics related to the cheetahs during her guided reading lessons. Using guided questions, Judy supported her second graders' understanding of how authors record information in books. For example, Judy asked:

- Where does the author tell us cheetahs live?
- What does the author tell us about their habitat on the next page?
- Now what did the author share on this page? Yes, the author describes how cheetahs hunt.
- Who can tell me how cheetahs hunt?
- How do cheetahs move? What words did the author use to show us this movement on the next page?

Continuing with guided questions, Judy helped her students discover how some pages show them what the cheetahs looked like, while still other pages explain what they ate or how they moved.

Following these guided explorations of text, Judy pointed out that some authors write several facts or details related to a specific topic on a page or in a paragraph. Showing how one author recorded different information about the cheetah on each page helped the second graders begin to see how authors write. Consistent with Hoyt (2003), students simultaneously learned about cheetahs and the author's craft as they explored and compared informational texts about cheetahs in various books and magazines.

After the guided reading lessons, Judy reinforced what the second graders had learned by having them create their own books about cheetahs. Through guided writing lessons, Judy showed her students how to gather their ideas for writing by forming a web about the cheetah from their readings. After they made their webs, she showed them how to create a draft from the web with pencil and paper, type their drafts on the computer, revise their computer drafts, and finally edit the drafts for publication.

Forming Links between Reading and Writing through Guided Writing

To begin the guided writing lessons, Judy drew on her earlier lessons, reinforcing how the authors place specific information about a topic related to cheetahs on separate pages. She then helped her students craft their own paragraphs about cheetahs by applying the model seen in their books. First she demonstrated how to form a web about an animal—its habitat, what it ate, or how it moved—by creating a web about tigers on her chart paper (see Figure 1.5). Following this minilesson, students developed their own webs about cheetahs.

The next day Judy modeled how to draft a page about what a tiger looks like, using information from her web about the tiger. Following her example, the second graders then lifted information from their webs to create their own detail sentences about cheetahs.

Throughout the process, Judy's students received support as she circulated among them, providing guidance, giving them praise for their efforts, and asking or answering questions as they wrote. Specifically, the guided writing kept the focus on the "how" of writing through all stages of the process, ensuring that the meaning would be clear to the reader (Mooney, 2003).

Thus, the informational books provided both the raw material and the model for Judy's student, Crystal, to write about cheetahs (see Figure 1.6). Crystal and her peers learned how we select and gather facts and details from informational texts and how we organize the information by placing specific facts and details about a topic on pages or in paragraphs. Using word processing tools to type her rough draft, as well as revise and edit the draft, helped Crystal understand the process authors follow when they write books. She, too, became an author as she crafted, illustrated, and published her own book.

Figure 1.5

Judy Models How to Insert Information about Tigers into a Web for Her Students

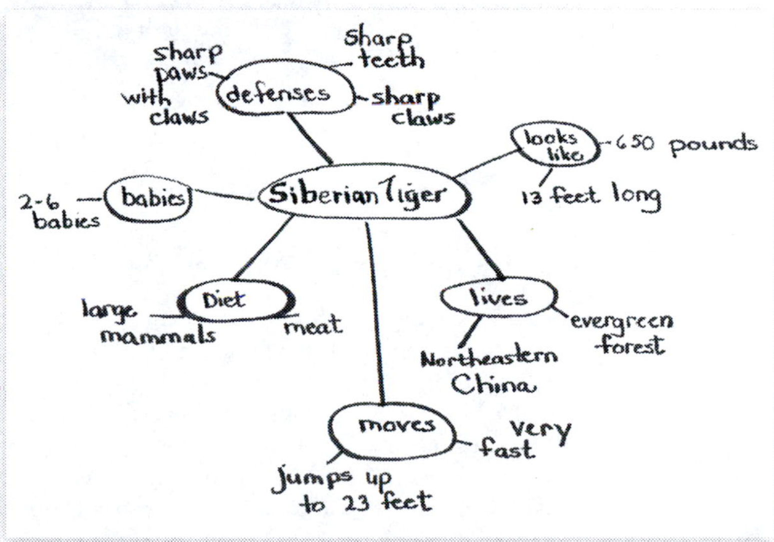

Figure 1.6

The First Three Pages of Crystal's Book, *The Cheetah*

The cheetah

The cheetah lives in Africa and Asia. Their favorite places are dry grasslands and woodlands and bushlands. They like lots of space so that they can chase their prey.

The cheetah is orange and yellow with black stripes. The cheetah attacks and eat other animals, like the antelope and wildebeests and zebras.

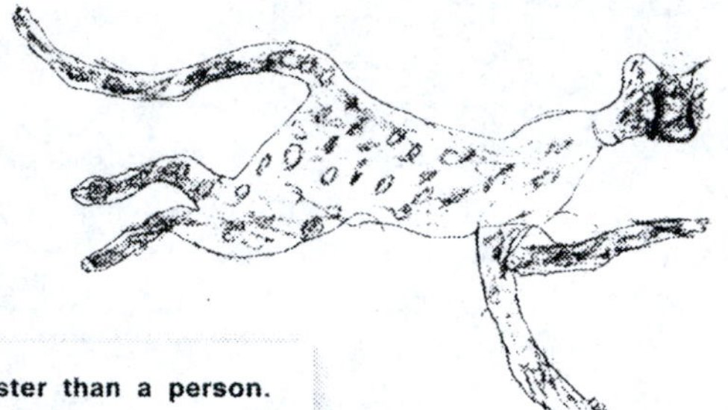

The cheetah runs 3 times faster than a person. They chase their prey down at high speeds. Cheetahs live in Africa and Asia.

Forming Links between Reading and Writing through Narrative Fiction

Similarly, reading and talking about the story elements—characters, setting, problem, events, and resolution of the problem—will help students learn to incorporate these elements in fictional stories they write on their own (see Chapter 5). For example, if we teach particular concepts about setting during guided reading and then teach them during guided writing, students have the opportunity to apply the principles in their writing. This application of concepts reinforces and strengthens understanding of the ideas so that students actually remember them (Hoyt, 2003). The explicit instruction—modeling, demonstrations, guidance, support, and encouragement—that occurs during guided reading and guided writing results in quality writing that students and teachers enjoy. Specifically, explicit instruction (Mooney, 2003, p. 16) enables students to

- Receive feedback and support on their performance.
- Receive support while working independently.
- Practice strategies and skills while receiving encouragement.
- Explore and experiment with newly acquired strategies and skills.
- Extend their understanding of known strategies and skills.
- Apply their understanding of strategies and skills through guidance.
- Listen and respond to the opinions and ideas of others through sharing.

Forming Links between Reading and Writing through a Variety of Reading Experiences

Creating links between reading and writing also includes multiple opportunities for students to read independently. Students need numerous experiences reading both fictional and nonfictional texts (Dreher, 2000; Duke, 2002, 2003; Kletzien & Dreher, 2004). With the influx of information that informational technology brings to people, there is a greater need for students to have many experiences with informational text early in their developing literacy so they will be able to understand, evaluate, and synthesize information from a variety of sources as they grow older (Leu, 2000; Kletzien & Dreyher, 2004). People who read frequently have an easier time writing; people who read a variety of genres have an easier time writing different types of genres. Through reading, students begin to acquire the style of language they need for their writing; they begin to gain a sense of how to write particular kinds of texts (Hiebert & Raphael, 1998; NCTE, 2004; Stead, 2001).

Reading quality literature aloud to our students is also an important way to help students begin to incorporate the writing styles of authors and the syntactical language of literature into their own stories (Calkins, 1994; Graves, 1994, 2004), especially if we talk about what authors do when they write while we read stories aloud. In her book, Calkins (1994) shares the example of Byrd Baylor, the author of *I'm in Charge of Celebrations,* a book commemorating important occasions in one's life. Byrd Baylor drew on her life experiences to describe a "Green Color Day" in her story. While driving her pickup truck along the Arizona highway one day, she decided to take a longer route because the skies were so picturesque that day. She'd never seen such skies—the clouds overhead appeared to be green. Desiring to capture this moment to memory, she stopped her truck to view the scene. Others who were driving by similarly stopped. Before their eyes appeared a green cloud in the shape of a parrot. Byrd Baylor exclaimed, "No one in the entire universe has seen what we are seeing today" (cited in Calkins, 1994, p. 4). Hearing this story helps students see that writing allows us to hold precious memories within our hands so that we can preserve them forever.

Fostering Links between Reading and Writing through Authors' Stories

Students need to hear other authors' stories as well. These stories help them begin to discover how great writing emerges. For example, students need to hear how authors get their ideas for books. When I interviewed Verna Aardema, I asked her how she became interested in writing African folktales. She explained that she always had an interest in African folktales and researched them in depth while she was teaching second grade. After researching the folktales and learning them by heart, she began telling the stories to her second graders. Later in life, many folktales she had been sharing with her second graders became picture books—*Why Mosquitoes Buzz in People's Ears* and *Who's in Rabbit's House?* The folktales she had researched and retold over the years transformed into books for more children to read and enjoy. Knowing this story might empower students to think of themselves as authors, too. We all have stories we love to share with others.

When visiting a school in Michigan, Arnold Adoff, an author and poet, brought a poem with him that he had recently written on a roll of paper towels. He became so inspired to write a poem that he grabbed whatever he could find to compose the poem. As he held up the finished poem on the roll of paper towels, Arnold Adoff asked the students how many times they thought he had reread and revised his poem. Students guessed 5, 7, 10, and 15. Arnold noted that their guesses weren't even warm. So other students estimated 20, 25, 30, and 35 times. Again, he emphasized they weren't even warm. Trying again, students guessed 40, 55, and 60. Arnold shook his head, saying he reread and revised his poem 77 times. To emphasize how many times he revised the poem, he unrolled the paper towels one by one. This story shows students that writing is not magic. Writing is complex, requiring thought and hard work if we want it to be published.

I have told Arnold Adoff's story to students in many classes. Students immediately became more willing to revise their own writing once they realized that real authors revise over and over again.

Similarly, to help young writers learn about the process of editing, I bring in the galleys of my own published writing to schools. I show them how I use proofreaders' marks to insert punctuation or capitals, change letters to lowercase, delete punctuation, insert paragraphs, or correct spelling on the galleys. Students are amazed that authors need to edit their work. Once they realize that authors and adults have to reread their work slowly and carefully in order to edit their works, students are more willing to tackle editing themselves.

Relating Authors' Stories to Real-Life Writing

When students see that the writing activities they are doing in school are related to what authors do, they realize that there is meaning and purpose for what they are doing in school. Seeing how authors and adults use reading and writing to shape and mold their writing eases the challenges that writing often presents to writers of all ages. Publishing students' writing further motivates young writers to consider revising and editing their writing just like real authors.

Overall, conversations about the connections between reading and writing are helpful to students. Through these conversations, students begin to understand more about the structure and craft of writing itself. They also begin to understand why authors select a particular genre for a particular writing piece, as well as how a particular genre conveys a message in a particular way and what its rhetorical constraints might be. Through these ongoing discussions, students will learn how to produce a variety of genres and become familiar with their features (NCTE, 2004).

Describing Writing as a Process

The writing process, which involves thinking, feeling, and communication, is a dynamic, complex process (Daiute, 1985; Graves, 1983). Moffett (1982) suggests that writing is a discovery process as writers expand and master inner speech. Through talking, emerging writers form links to their prior knowledge and experiences so they can generate their messages. As young writers transform their experiences and knowledge into written language, they gradually learn to make judgments about their readers' backgrounds; they make judgments about how to express their ideas so that readers think or act in a certain fashion in response to their writing (Flower & Hayes, 1981).

In the opening poem of this chapter, Jenny used problem-solving strategies to plan, select, combine, arrange, monitor, and evaluate her writing so that her poem met the needs of her intended audience. She selected and combined, rearranged, and replanned her poem so that it would show the writing process to her peers and teacher. Her published poem illustrates the artistic nature of writing to her peers and teacher. However, what was challenging for Jenny can become alarming to other writers. Helping fearful writers discover the ideas they wish to express and what form or structure they will use to translate their ideas into written language often becomes a challenge for teachers. The pioneering work of Graves (1983), Emig (1971), and Flower and Hayes (1981) confirms the importance of using a process approach to writing to ease students' concerns and fears about writing.

This process approach to writing includes five subprocesses—the stages of composing that authors follow in order to communicate effectively. Although researchers use various labels to describe the subprocesses of composing, most teachers use the following labels to describe these subprocesses: (a) prewriting, (b) drafting, (c) revising, (d) editing, and (e) sharing (see Figure 1.7). Even though the labels describe the subprocesses in a linear fashion, the process is recursive as writers move back and forth among the stages. The labels are only aids for identifying and discussing writing activities (NCTE, 2004; Tompkins, 2004). Authors eventually personalize the process to meet their needs; many authors even vary the process according to what they are writing.

Prewriting

During the prewriting stage, writers discover their ideas for writing, set goals, organize their ideas, and generate content through prewriting and rehearsal activities. Another way to consider the process suggests that writers discover their ideas and topics, collect information to use with their writing, rehearse and think about their plans, and gather a focus on the important points of their writing (Clark, 1995; Murray, 1985). Through this process of thinking and problem solving, authors open up their minds and imaginations to see things others may ignore. Prewriting and rehearsal activities often help transform the writers' ideas and thoughts into written language.

Examples of prewriting activities might include modeling, daydreaming, sketching, doodling, making lists or clusters of words, outlining, reading, conversing with a partner, or writing in personal journals (see Figure 1.8 on p. 14). By using multiple prewriting activities, writers discover possible directions for their writing. Students need to learn a variety of strategies for prewriting so that they can select what works best for them as they write

Figure 1.7

The Stages of Writing That Writers Follow to Communicate Their Ideas

Prewriting	Drafting	Revision	Editing	Publishing
• Recalling ideas • Brainstorming • Discovering ideas • Planning spelling • Rehearsing • Organizing • Observing • Collecting information • Notetaking	• Getting ideas down before they get away • Developing ideas • Writing/composing • Thinking • Making meaning	• Reseeing the writing • Rethinking the writing: Does it say what you want to say? • Questioning writing • Clarifying: Does it make sense? • Seeking feedback from peers • Reorganizing writing	• Inspecting writing • Checking mechanics in context of writing (i.e., capitals and punctuation) • Checking accurate spelling • Communicating courteously to readers • Proofreading • Peer editing	• Going public with a piece • Sharing your writing with others • Displaying writing • Celebrating writing • Publishing writing

Figure 1.8

Examples of Prewriting Strategies Used by K–5 Students

(a) Janine, age 5, creates a web to organize her ideas before writing about her parakeet. (b) A fifth grader webs her ideas for a poem about lightning. (c) A first grader lists ideas for writing about magnets. (d) A fourth grader uses notes to collect information for his story.

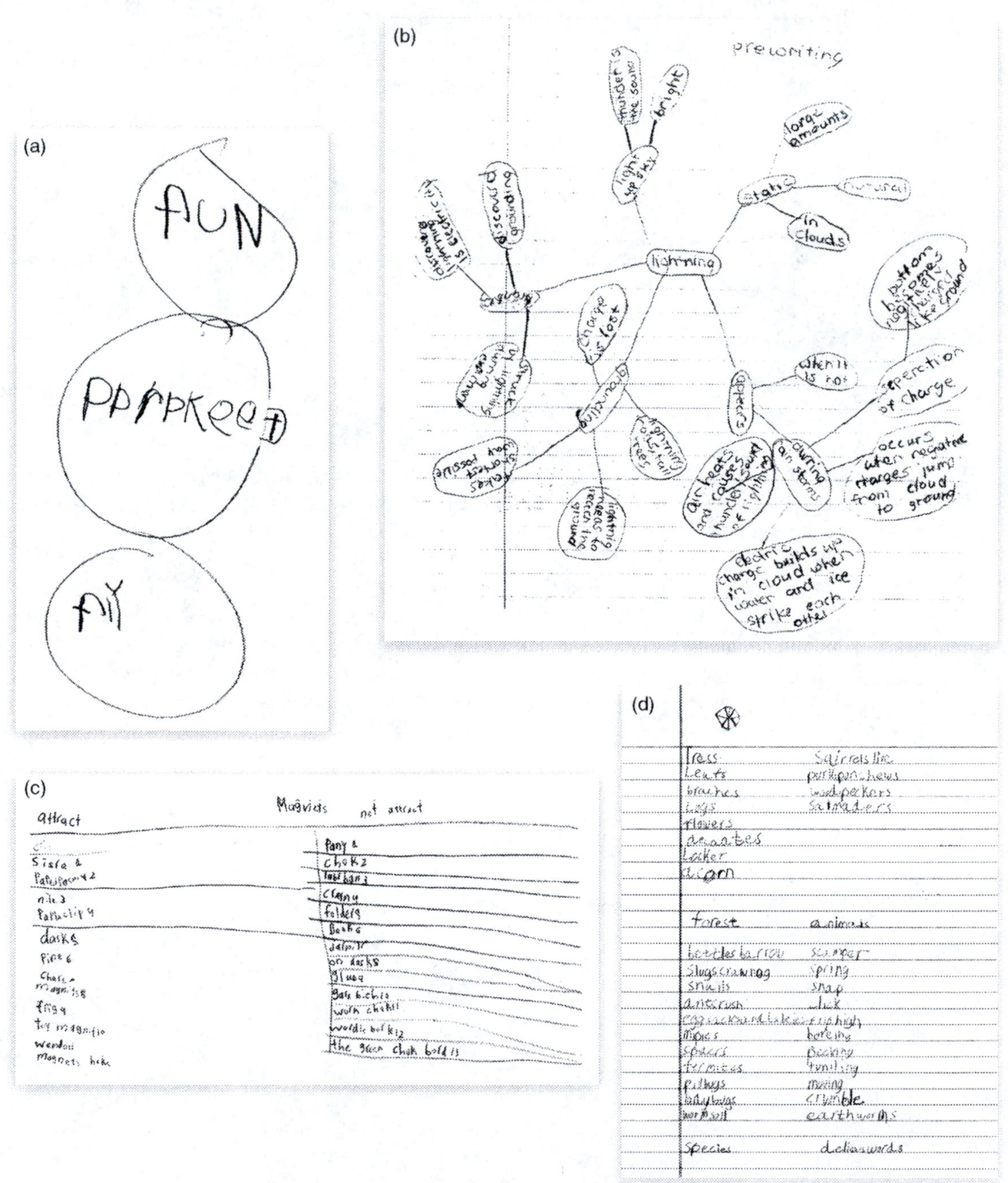

independently. Sometimes what works best depends on the genre of the writing piece. As shown earlier, Judy modeled webbing to her second graders to help them collect ideas about cheetahs and then organize these ideas in their drafts. Specifically, the prewriting helped Crystal and her peers see where to place similar details about cheetahs in their writing.

According to Murray (1985), 70 percent or more of writing time should be spent in prewriting or rehearsal activities; this is the stage where students begin to gain control over their inner speech. Using several prewriting activities helped Judy's students gain control over their ideas. First, Judy read several books and magazines to help her students gather information about cheetahs for their writing. She also used the literature to talk about how writers organize information into paragraphs. Then she modeled how to create a web and encouraged her students to apply the technique of webbing.

In particular, Peregoy and Boyle (1993) and Jalongo (2003) emphasize that task-directed talk about writing often helps linguistically diverse learners and students from oral traditions develop their own thinking and discover their ideas. Simultaneously, they expand their language proficiency in oral and written language. Since Judy's class included linguistically diverse learners, she used task-directed talk through guided reading and writing lessons over several days. Her guided questions and references to authors helped her students see how writers organize their ideas. Her modeling and demonstrations showed how authors collect information for writing. Equally important, Judy offered multiple opportunities for her students to talk about cheetahs and share the information with others so that Crystal and her peers could successfully transform their talk into written language.

Figure 1.8 includes examples of prewriting strategies used by students of varying ages.

Drafting

Once students have gathered their ideas for writing, they are ready to develop their writing by composing a draft. Drafting places huge demands on writers' cognitive processes. Writers must simultaneously record their ideas and thoughts while dealing with the conventions of writing—structure, spelling, handwriting, typing, punctuation, and grammar (Humes, 1983). To alleviate these cognitive demands, teachers need to emphasize that writing is temporary and that writing is messy. They must also remind their students that the information and content are more important then the correct spellings of words and the neatness of their handwriting.

Similarly, Judy consistently reminded her students to use their temporary writing while creating their webs and drafting their writing. She did not emphasize spelling or neatness at this point. She encouraged them to take the ideas they collected during the prewriting stage and to put them down on their paper. By focusing on her students' ideas, Judy helped her Title I writers feel more comfortable with their writing. They began to take more risks, experimenting and exploring written language and ways to express their ideas. With repeated opportunities to write, Judy realized that her students would slowly gain control of the conventions of written language. If we only offer limited opportunities to write, students' understanding of the conventions of writing will not advance.

Revising

The subprocess of revising is sometimes characterized by backward movements as students reread to determine "whether or not the words on the page capture the original sense intended" (Perl, 1979, p. 331). The complexity of writing emerges full force during this stage as students reread, reexamine, delete, shape, and correct the written message to meet

teaching **TIP 1.3**

Revising, which is a separate stage from editing, is frequently omitted from instruction. This critical stage helps students learn to shape, mold, and refine their ideas so that readers easily understand their message.

the needs of their readers. The ability to resee one's writing emerges more easily when students view words as temporary and information as manipulative (Calkins, 1994; Graves, 1983; Lane, 1999). Gaining the objectivity to resee one's writing takes practice as one revises his or her drafts over time.

Since her students were just beginning to learn to write, Judy began this stage of the process with simple revisions. As students typed their rough drafts on the computer, some of her students began to resee their writing. Many discovered that they accidentally forgot a word on their draft. While typing their drafts, some students spontaneously inserted the missing word. Others who accidentally left out a word discovered the missing word when Judy asked them to share their writing pieces. The missing word was later easily inserted with word processing tools.

After students finished typing the drafts, Judy used the friendly nature of the computer screen, easily viewed by the teacher and student, to conference with them. As students shared their writing with her, she asked them questions about their writing to help them see how to add more information to their drafts. For example, Alex's draft pointed out that the cheetah runs fast. To help him elaborate on this, Judy asked, "Alex, do you remember how fast cheetahs run?" When Alex explained that cheetahs can run up to 60 miles per hour, Judy showed him how to insert this sentence next to the sentence about the cheetah running fast. In this way, students experienced the revising process and how to insert more information into their drafts.

Judy's students will need many more opportunities to revise their writing before they gain the objectivity to rethink their writing. Through Judy's questioning, however, they begin to learn about objectivity. Just by sharing their writing with their peers, young writers will begin to resee their writing more objectively.

Figure 1.9 displays an example of how a fourth grader revises his writing.

Editing

During this stage of writing, the focus shifts from content to mechanics as writers polish their writing by correcting their spelling, punctuation, capitalization, grammar, and word usage. According to Clark (1995), writers learn the mechanics of writing—commonly accepted conventions of written standard English—within the context of writing. Editing in pairs is usually most effective during this stage. However, writers must complete the corrections *themselves* as they apply the mechanics of writing to their own writing or the writing of their peers.

Consistent with Clark (1995), Judy used her students' writing to help them learn about the conventions of writing. To facilitate their understanding of spelling and mechanics, Judy had her second graders print out a triple-spaced copy of their writing. Triple-spacing their drafts left room for students to insert their edits.

First, she asked them to look for words they wanted to know *how* to spell and circle them. Most of the second graders could find words they wanted to spell as they knew they had used their temporary spelling for the drafts. Looking for words that they wanted to know how to spell, however, removed criticism from the exercise. Once they circled the words, Judy spelled the words for her students, explaining she was a resource for spelling just like a dictionary or the Word Wall. Then, they went back to the computers and used the arrow and delete keys to change their temporary spelling (Judy had turned off spell check on her computers so that her students would not be hindered in using their temporary spelling when drafting their writing).

Figure 1.9

A Fourth Grader Revises His Story about a Polar Bear

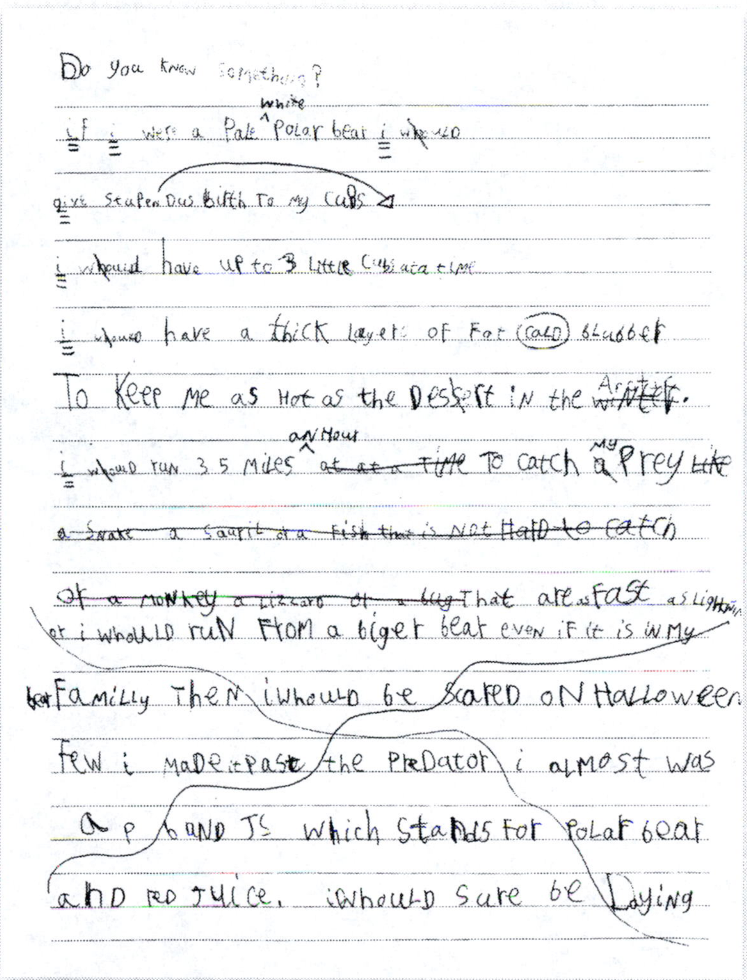
Do you know something?
if i were a Pale ^white Polar bear i whould
give stupendous birth to my cubs
i whould have up to 3 little cubs at a time
i whould have a thick layer of fat (cold) blubber
To keep me as hot as the desert in the Arctic ~~winter~~.
i whould run 35 miles ^an hour ~~at a time~~ to catch ^my ~~a~~ prey ~~like~~
~~a snake a squirrel a fish that is not hard to catch~~
~~or a monkey a lizzard or a bug~~ That are as fast as lightning
or i whould run from a biger bear even if it is in my
family Then i whould be scared on Halloween
Few i made it past the predator i almost was
a p and J's which stands for polar bear
and red juice. i whould sure be laying

The next day Judy helped her students find missing capitals and ending marks in their writing. Using a minilesson, she modeled this process on an overhead transparency of Laura's piece. As they talked about where to add capitals or periods, she showed them the editing marks for capitals and how to use the caret to insert periods. Following the minilesson, students applied these skills to their own writing pieces. Using editing marks this way helped them learn to find and correct their own mistakes. Judy served as the "top editor," similar to the editor-in-chief of a newspaper. As students used word processing tools to complete these edits on the computer, she circulated among the students, conferencing with them individually. As needed, she pointed out lines that had missing capitals or periods. Using her *cues,* students identified the missing capitals or periods and then easily inserted them on the computer.

By following this process, Judy helped her students maintain ownership of their writing while learning how to edit their pieces through guided teaching. Teachers' red ink pens merely show students what they don't know or what they can't do. In contrast, these second graders gained powerful tools to help them polish their own writing through Judy's guidance. If students retain ownership of their editing, they will be more likely to remember the skills and apply them when editing future writing pieces. Figure 1.10 displays examples of students' editing.

Publishing

Sharing, one way to publish writing, should occur during all stages of the process. This is the time to celebrate students' successes. Whether sharing lists of ideas for writing, the opening sentences for their lead, a revised ending for a poem, or a published writing piece, students begin to receive encouragement from their listeners. Sharing becomes the catalyst for more writing to evolve. As students learn what is pleasing about their writing, they are willing to take new risks and experiment and explore written language in more depth.

When we allow students to share their writing with their peers, teachers can change students' viewpoints about themselves as writers. The spontaneous laughter, the natural praise for ideas or for ways to express ideas, the murmurs of excitement in anticipation of events to come, and the unprompted applause from the audience encourage writers. Similarly, seeing their writing published in formal ways stimulates a desire to write more and more. Publishing, whether done formally or informally, helps young writers begin to perceive themselves as authors.

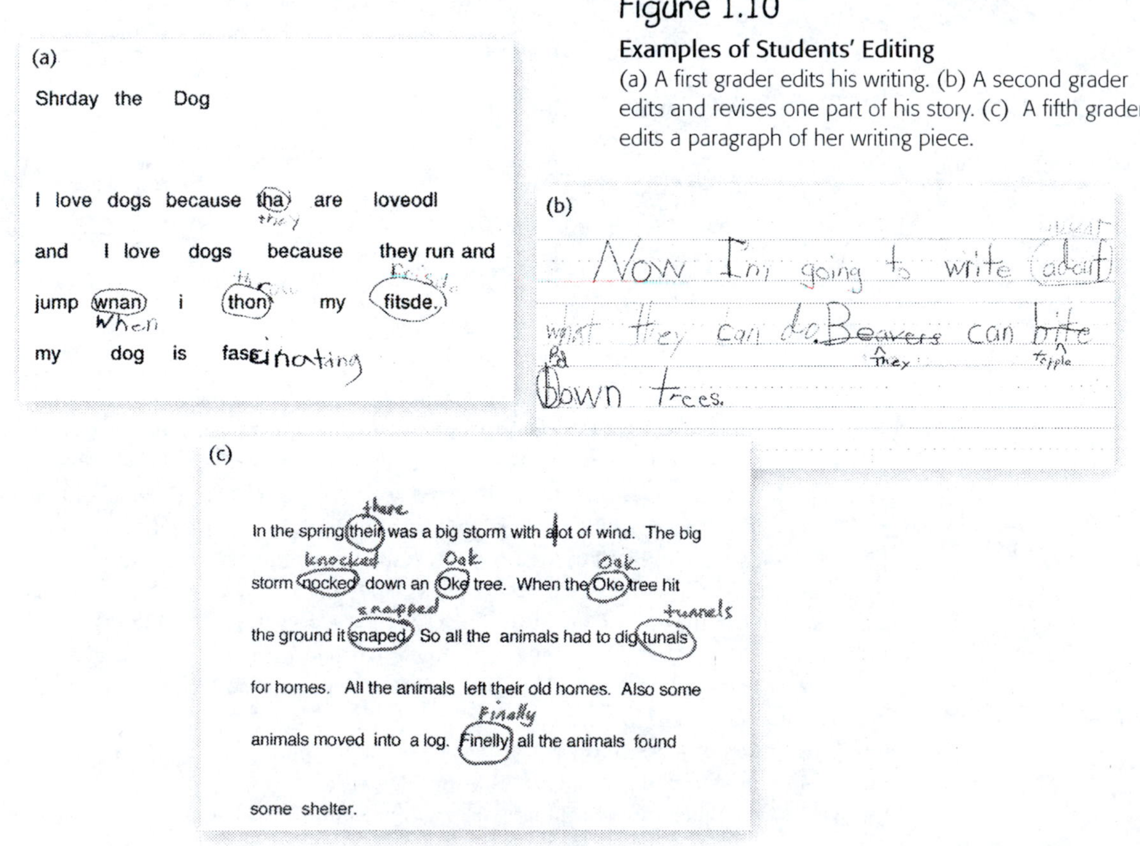

Figure 1.10

Examples of Students' Editing

(a) A first grader edits his writing. (b) A second grader edits and revises one part of his story. (c) A fifth grader edits a paragraph of her writing piece.

Jason proudly watches as the printer publishes his final draft.

Supporting Young Authors through the Writing Process

When writers know the steps that lead to a desired result, even when they are tired, happy, lazy, or troubled, they can write (Clark, 1995). According to Graves (2004), we underestimate what students can do. Having the knowledge and ability to use the writing process, which is mechanical, reliable, predictable, versatile, yet mysterious, gives writers confidence so they can write. Having the opportunity to practice and use the writing process provides opportunities for self-knowledge and self-discovery to evolve so that writing ventures become more desirable.

This process approach to writing is as important as the products students produce (Tompkins, 2004). The process gives students ways to solve problems they encounter as they write. Future chapters will describe and model the subprocesses in more depth and provide examples of how teachers use the process to make writing exciting and challenging for students of all cultural and linguistic backgrounds and abilities.

Closing Thoughts

Through the act of writing, writers of all ages discover themselves and the world around them while communicating their ideas, thoughts, and feelings to others. Even though writing anxiety never disappears completely, students gradually realize that they can use the writing process to access their ideas, record their ideas on paper, clarify and rework their ideas to meet the needs of readers, and then polish the mechanics of their writing for publication to share with others. In order for this realization to occur, writers need to write daily and practice what they are learning. This fosters writing growth and development.

While students practice writing, we continuously orchestrate and facilitate their writing development. We also assess how we guide and coach students' writing through ongoing monitoring, conferencing, and reflection. Consistent with Graves (2004), we must ponder our teaching practice to see whether we

- Show a personal interest in our students' lives and writing.
- Recognize and support students' ownership of their learning.
- Instill a sense of responsibility in our students by facilitating their choices in writing, their evaluation of their work, and their sense of audience.

- Maintain high expectations for our students so that they might live up to their potentials.
- Model writing by using our own writing or the writing of students.
- Maintain our own learning by reading voraciously and by continuing our professional development.

Finally, as shown through the vignettes, we must remember to be supportive of students, sprinkling words of praise and encouragement as they write. If we follow these guidelines, students will gradually meet our expectations. In fact, I have found that students learn to create pieces that exceed my imagination.

Teachers' Questions

1. How can I get my students interested in writing?

Students become interested in writing when they have ownership and choice in what they write. Using personal journals (see Chapter 3) is a good way to give writers this ownership and choice in what they write. In addition, students need to know that they can use their temporary spelling to record their ideas. If they think that we will "red ink" their writing, correcting their spelling or handwriting, students quickly lose interest in writing. They need to know that we value their ideas over spelling or handwriting. We can show them that we treasure their ideas by giving them praise and encouragement as they write. For example, after they begin writing, we might say, "What an interesting way to begin your journal entry!" if they have an unusual beginning; or we might say, "You like football? That's my husband's favorite sport, too!" when we see what they are writing about.

In addition, we need to leave time for students to share their writing every day. As students share their writing, we need to continue praising them for their ideas, leads, endings, word choice, or topics. If we listen carefully, we can find at least one thing they are doing well. Our specific praise lets them know how they are successful so they can build on this accomplishment the next time they write. Hearing praise from their peers is also motivational.

2. At what grade level should teachers introduce the writing process?

Students in kindergarten and first grade can begin to learn about the writing process as we do language experience stories or shared writing (see Chapter 3). For example, they can learn about prewriting strategies if we create a web or a list of ideas before writing a language experience story or shared writing on chart paper. Later kindergarteners and first graders can apply these prewriting strategies before writing in their journals or during focused writing. They can also learn about revising and editing if we revise and edit the language experience story or shared writing activity. Once they become comfortable with writing, they can apply revising and editing strategies with writing pieces they plan to publish later in the year. They can also apply revising strategies if we have them go back to a writing piece after a few days and add to the writing piece. This is the beginning of revising—adding more information. Similarly, we can have them practice editing by having them go back to a writing piece and circle three words they want to know how to spell. Then we can write the correct spelling of the words for them above the words. This is the beginning of editing.

Then, of course, first graders and kindergarteners love sharing their writing. Hearing specific praise about their writing becomes motivational, inviting them to write more and more.

3. What is the difference between the writing process and Writing Workshop?

The writing process and Writing Workshop are related. The writing process is a process we follow whenever we write, especially if we plan to publish what we write. Writing Workshop (see Chapter 4), which is a predictable time for writing instruction, is a place and time to apply the writing process as we write.

4. When do students use the writing process?

Students of all ages use the writing process whenever they record a message. Since the writing process is a recursive event, students naturally move back and forth among the stages as they write. Before they begin writing, they may use brainstorming to gather their ideas for writing and then begin to draft their ideas. Sometimes they change their mind about the topic and erase or cross out the first sentence or two, applying the revising stage. Then they may do some more brainstorming before they begin drafting their ideas once again. Periodically, students change the spelling of words as they draft their ideas, applying the editing stage. Then they continue drafting the message.

The example above is an informal application of the writing process, which can even happen as students journal. More formal applications of the writing process occur when a writing piece is to be published. We must remember, however, that students do not need to publish everything they write. If we publish too often, students quickly begin to experience burnout. The enjoyment for writing soon is extinguished for our students and us. Usually, I think about publishing one or two writing pieces per marking period.

There are even times when students may only use prewriting strategies without drafting. For example, students might take notes while listening to a story about skeletons. This is an example of informal writing. Using notetaking, in this case, may be a tool for learning about skeletons.

Children's Literature

Aardema, V. (1975). *Why mosquitoes buzz in people's ears.* New York: Dial.

Aardema, V. (1977). *Who's in rabbit's house?* New York: Dial.

Baylor, B. (1986). *I'm in charge of celebrations.* New York: Macmillan.

References

Burrows, A., Jackson, D., & Saunders, D. (1984). *They all want to write.* Hamden, CT: Library of Professional Publications.

Butler, D., & Clay, M. (1987). *Reading begins at home: Preparing children for reading before they go to school.* Portsmouth, NH: Heinemann.

Calkins, L. (1983). *Lessons from a child: On the teaching and learning of writing.* Portsmouth, NH: Heinemann.

Calkins, L. (1994). *The art of teaching writing.* Portsmouth, NH: Heinemann.

Clark, R. (1995). *Free to write.* Portsmouth, NH: Heinemann.

Daiute, C. (1985). *Writing and computers.* Reading, MA: Addison-Wesley.

Dreher, M. (2000). Fostering reading for learning. In L. Baker, M. Dreher, & J. Guthrie (Eds.), *Engaging young readers: Promoting achievement and motivation* (pp. 94–118). New York: Guilford.

Duke, N. (2002). *Reading to learn from the very beginning: Informational literacy in early childhood.* Paper submitted for publication.

Duke, N. (2003). Informational text: The research says, "Yes!" In L. Hoyt, M. Mooney, & B. Parkes (Eds.), *Exploring informational texts: From theory to practice* (pp. 2–7). Portsmouth, NH: Heinemann.

Dyson, A. (1993). *Social worlds of children learning to write in an urban primary school.* New York: Teachers College Press.

Emig, J. (1971). *The composing processes of twelfth graders* (Research Report No. 13). Urbana, IL: National Council of Teachers of English.

Flower, L., & Hayes, J. (1981). A cognitive process theory of writing. *College Compositions and Communication, 32,* 21–32.

Goodman, K. (1976). Behind the eye: What happens in reading. In H. Singer and R. Ruddell (Eds.), *Theoretical models and processes of reading* (pp. 470–496). Newark, DE: International Reading Association.

Graves, D. (1983). *Writing: Teachers and children at work.* Portsmouth, NH: Heinemann.

Graves, D. (1994). *A fresh look at writing.* Portsmouth, NH: Heinemann.

Graves, D. (2004). What I've learned from teachers of writing. *Language Arts, 82,* 88–94.

Graves, D., & Stuart, V. (1987). *Write from the start.* Portsmouth, NH: Heinemann.

Hansen, J. (1987). *When writers read.* Portsmouth, NH: Heinemann.

Hansen, J. (2001). *When writers read* (2nd ed.). Portsmouth, NH: Heinemann.

Hiebert, E., & Raphael, T. (1998). *Early literacy instruction.* New York: Harcourt Brace.

Hoyt, L. (2003). Linking guided reading and guided writing. In L. Hoyt, M. Mooney, & B. Parkes (Eds.), *Exploring informational texts: From theory to practice* (pp. 120–134). Portsmouth, NH: Heinemann.

Humes, A. (1983). Research on the composing process. *Review of Educational Research, 53,* 201–216.

Jalongo, M. (2003). *Early childhood: Language arts.* Boston: Allyn & Bacon.

Kletzien, S., & Dreher, M. (2004). *Informational text in K–3 classrooms: Helping children read and write.* Newark, DE: International Reading Association.

Lane, B. (1999). *Reviser's toolbox.* Shoreham, VT: Discover Writing Press.

Langer, J. (1986). *Children reading and writing: Structures and strategies.* Norwood, NJ: Ablex.

Leu, D. (2000). Literacy and technology: Deictic consequences for literacy education in an information age. In M. L. Kamil, P. B. Mosenthal, P. D. Pearson, & R. Barr (Eds.), *Handbook of reading research* (Vol. 3, pp. 310–336). Newark, DE: International Reading Association.

Miller, W. (2000). *Strategies for developing emergent literacy.* Boston: McGraw-Hill.

Moffett, J. (1982). Writing, inner speech, and meditation. *College English, 44,* 213–246.

Mooney, M. (2003). Thinking as a reader and writer of informational text. In L. Hoyt, M. Mooney, & B. Parkes (Eds.), *Exploring informational texts: From theory to practice* (pp. 115–119). Portsmouth, NH: Heinemann.

Murray, D. (1985). *A writer teaches writing.* Boston: Houghton Mifflin.

NCTE. (2004). NCTE beliefs about the teaching of writing. [Online]. Available: www.ncte.org/about/over/positions/category/write/118876.htm [June 13, 2005].

Peregoy, S., & Boyle, O. (1993). *Reading, writing, and learning in ESL.* New York: Longman.

Perl, S. (1979). The composing process of unskilled college writers. *Research in the Teaching of English, 13,* 317–336.

Shanahan, T. (1988). The reading-writing relationship; Seven instruction principles. *The Reading Teacher,* 635–647.

Shanahan, T., & Lomax, R. (1988). A developmental comparison of three models of the reading-writing relationship. *Research in the Teaching of English, 22,* 196–213.

Shaugnessy, M. (1977). *Errors and expectations.* New York: Oxford University Press.

Stead, T. (2001). *Is that a fact? Teaching nonfiction writing K–3.* York, ME: Stenhouse.

Stotsky, S. (1983). Research on the reading/writing relationships: A synthesis and suggested directions. *Language Arts, 60,* 627–643.

Sulzby, E. (1985). Children's emergent reading of favorite storybooks: A developmental study. *Reading Research Quarterly, 20,* 485–481.

Sulzby, E., & Barnhart, J. (1992). The development of academic competence: All our children emerge as readers and writers. In J. Irwin & M. Doyle (Eds.), *Reading-writing connections: Learning from research* (pp. 120–144). Newark, DE: International Reading Conference.

Sulzby, E., & Teale, W. (1991). Emergent literacy. In R. Barr, M. Kamil, P. Mosenthal, & D. Pearson (Eds.), *Handbook of reading research* (pp. 727–757). New York: Longman.

Teale, W., & Sulzby, E. (1986). *Emergent literacy: Writing and reading.* Norwood, NJ: Ablex.

Tierney, R., & Pearson, D. (1983). Toward a composing model of reading. *Language Arts, 60,* 568–580.

Tompkins, G. (2004). *Teaching writing: Balancing process and product.* Upper Saddle River, NJ: Merrill.

chapter TWO

Using Technology to Enhance and Extend Literacy Learning

Jerusalem

A place where
Sharp eyed eagles glide
Sidewinder rattlesnakes
Move quickly across loose sand
Where some people live in thatch houses
People speak different languages
Lots of people go to the Wailing wall
David's tower built 2500 years ago

Zimbabwe

Integrating Technology with Literacy

Zimbabwe, a second grader in a Title I program, composed this poem (Diamond & Moore, 1995, p. 251) using word processing technology. This was not Zimbabwe's first draft of the poem; this was his revised poem. While participating in prewriting activities to help him discover his ideas for the poem, he discovered that he did not know very much about Jerusalem, which was part of his Jewish heritage. With the help of his teacher, Vonnie Taylor, he got books from the library to help him learn about Jerusalem and complete his prewriting. He used this information to compose the first draft of his poem. Then he used word processing tools to help him revise and edit his poem for publication. Not only did Zimbabwe learn more about his cultural heritage, but he learned how computers can help him write, revise, edit, and publish his work.

Using Technology to Support and Enhance Literacy

This is but one example of how technology can be used to support and enhance literacy. Technology offers an exciting, fresh approach to literacy learning for Zimbabwe. The personalized nature of the computer screen enables Zimbabwe and his teacher Vonnie to talk about his writing as he writes. While viewing his writing, Vonnie can ask him questions as she points to specific words, lines, or paragraphs. Since the print font, which can be enlarged for easier reading, is neat, Vonnie and Zimbabwe can read and reread his writing without having to ask, "What's this word?"

As Zimbabwe continues to move through the writing process, Vonnie can continuously guide his writing. Fortunately, the revising and editing stages will seem less frustrating to him; the word processing tools will help him insert, delete, or rearrange text without the penalty of having to recopy the poem.

The following vignette shows how Zimbabwe and his teacher use technology as a learning tool. According to Bork (1987), the real value of computers lies in their effectiveness as learning tools. Consistent with Daiute (1985, 1986) and Newman (1984), the word processor and its powerful editing tools offer Zimbabwe the opportunity to explore written language as he revises and edits his poem. He can rearrange text and experiment with his choice of words once he drafts his poem. He can also use spell check to verify his temporary spelling of words. While the powerful editing tools of the word processor facilitate Zimbabwe's writing, the computer screen enables Vonnie to consistently guide his writing.

> ***teaching* TIP 2.1**
>
> The recursive nature of the word processor enhances writing, especially during the revising and editing stages.

Using Technology as a Learning Tool

The user-friendly screen provides a natural environment for Zimbabwe to discover language and grammar in the meaningful context of writing. At the same time, the user-friendly screen promotes social interactions between Zimbabwe and his teacher as they read his poem, talk about the poem, and use problem solving and thinking to revise the poem. As the two begin editing the poem, they continue using word processing tools, especially spell check, to search for words that they need to respell. When they resume editing the poem, Zimbabwe and his teacher reread the poem searching for words that need to be capitalized. Next, they reread the poem a third time, determining where the lines of the poem begin and end, using word processing tools to insert or change where the lines of the poem begin and end.

Similarly, the computer screen can facilitate learning among students as they read and write. As students collaborate with one another while they write, they can provide one another support, assistance, and feedback (Daiute, 1986; DeGroff, 1990; McKenna, Reinking, Labbo, & Watkins, 1996; Moore, 1987; Moore-Hart, 1995, 2004). For example, they can share what they are writing with a neighbor, inquire about the spelling of a word, or ask a neighbor to help them think of a new word. According to Fox and Mitchell (2000), this high level of social interaction and mutual support is almost essential for developing writing abilities. As students collaborate with one another, they also learn to read their text more critically in order to revise the text (Moore-Hart, 1995, 2004). Active reading, discussion, and interpretation enhance students' problem-solving and thinking skills when drafting, revising, editing, or publishing their writing.

What happens with technology depends on how we interpret and respond to it, how we use it in our daily lives or teaching practice, and how we alter it to meet our needs (Bruce, 2003). Just like Vonnie, we need to consider ways to use technology with our teaching practice. As technology presents new ways of communicating with one another—word processing, email, hypermedia, PowerPoint, CD-ROMs, the Internet—we have many choices available to us. New choices will emerge within the next few years.

Rationale for Integrating Technology with the Language Arts Curriculum

Zimbabwe uses word processing technology to draft, revise, edit, and publish his poem. As his poem about Jerusalem emerges, Zimbabwe learns more about his cultural heritage.

Prior to writing the poem, he did not know much about Jerusalem. By going to the library in order to find books about Jerusalem, Zimbabwe extends his knowledge about Jerusalem, influencing him to refine and shape his poem to reflect this new knowledge.

As a result of this writing experience, Zimbabwe might want to learn even more about his Jewish heritage. He might want to learn more about the people in Jerusalem, their language, and their homes. By using the Internet, Zimbabwe can easily find more information. He can also email a school in Jerusalem to discover information about their schools. After accessing this information, Zimbabwe can publish what he has learned on his own website. He might include additional poems, stories, or articles about Jerusalem. Using a PowerPoint presentation, he can then share what he has learned about Jerusalem with his class.

Technology Transforms Our World and Learning in the School

Technology, which offers many learning tools for students to use (Bork, 1987; Jonassen, 1996), is rapidly transforming our society—the workplace, our homes, and our schools. The evolving technology has, in fact, profoundly impacted the social, economic, political, and cultural conditions in which we live (Snyder, 1999). New communication and information processing technologies—whether the technology is word processing, electronic mail, CD-ROMs, hypermedia, the Internet, or PowerPoint—have also changed our conception of literacy (Anderson & Speck, 2001; Bruce, 2003; Leu, 2001; Leu, Leu, & Coiro, 2004; Reinking, 1998). According to Costanzo (1994, p. 11), "computers are altering the way many of us read, write, and even think. Not only have the tools of literacy changed, the nature of texts, of language, of literacy itself is undergoing crucial transformations. From the home and the classroom to the market and the workplace, computers are reshaping the environments in which language is learned, produced and practiced."

As can be seen, these new forms of information and communication technology (ICT) change how Zimbabwe and his peers read, write, and think; they also transform how their teachers define literacy. If Zimbabwe begins to use the Internet to learn about his cultural heritage, for example, his literacy experiences begin to extend beyond textbooks and chalkboards to include technological literacy (Labbo, 1996; Leu, 1997; Leu, Jr., 2001; Leu et al., 2004; Reinking, 1995; Snyder, 1999).

Vonnie, as well as Zimbabwe's future teachers, will need to provide him literacy experiences that include multiple modalities of print and a variety of ways to read. For example, if he uses the Internet to learn more about his cultural heritage, Zimbabwe will need to know how to navigate through several forms of information, including images, sounds, animation, or ongoing discussion groups online (El-Hindi, 1998; Henry, 2006; Sutherland-Smith, 2002; Wepner & Tao, 2002).

When Zimbabwe continues through school, he will also need to learn how to use a variety of technological and informational resources—libraries, databases, computer networks, websites, presentation software, and video. Gradually, his understanding of texts will expand beyond print to include nonprint forms of communication. As a reader and writer, he needs to begin thinking about the physical design of text, the appropriateness of visual images, the integration of sound with reading, and what medium authors use to convey a particular message for their particular purpose and audience (Henry, 2006; International Reading Association, 2001; NCTE, 2004; Sutherland-Smith, 2002; Wepner & Tao, 2002).

While using alternate forms of communications to investigate various topics of interest to him, Zimbabwe will need to learn how to access and retrieve information from the Internet, how to analyze and synthesize the information he finds, and then how to evaluate the information for its authenticity. These activities require that Zimbabwe use problem solving and higher level thinking skills. After accessing, analyzing, and synthesizing the information, he might later discuss the information with his peers, possibly seeking more information about his topic with a friend or reflecting about the information he has found with a friend.

Technology Transforms Literacy Teaching

Vonnie, as well as her peer educators, will need to regard literacy as a social process that is dependent on both cultural and electronic contexts (Anderson & Speck, 2001; Flood & Lapp, 1995; Leu, 1997; Leu, Jr., 2001; Reinking, 1998; Snyder, 1999). This social process includes the active construction of knowledge as Zimbabwe and his peers access, retrieve, analyze, synthesize, and evaluate information with the use of technology tools. Once students access the information, they will then collaborate with others, discussing, debating, and inquiring about the concepts and ideas. These ongoing collaborations will then support Zimbabwe and his peers as they write about the information using sound, graphics, or animation to enhance the message. Sometimes Zimbabwe's peers might assist him as he begins to learn how to link text with sound, graphics, or animation. Through collaborations and discussions in writing response groups, Zimbabwe and his peers will also begin to see and hear how their text impacts an audience and how their text supports or hinders understanding of the message.

As a result of rapidly changing forms of technology, Vonnie and her peer educators must understand how technology changes their literacy practice and their roles as literacy teachers. In fact, their roles will transform; they will become learners among learners, striving to remain informed about innovative technology (Leu, 1997, 2000; Leu et al., 2004; Reinking, 1998). Equally challenging, Vonnie and her peers will need to consider new ways to integrate the changing forms of technology and communication with their literacy curriculum (IRA, 2001; NCTE, 2004). If they do not actively consider ways to embrace the use of technology, they will risk marginalizing their students and limiting their literacy learning (Leu et al., 2004; Li, 2005; Snyder, 1999).

teaching TIP 2.2

Technology tools offer new and exciting ways to publish our writing through the use of pictures, sound, graphics, or animation.

Certainly, the ever-changing possibilities for technology present an immense challenge to us. How we proceed becomes an ongoing experiment. We must be willing to take risks in our teaching so that we embrace technology as a learning tool, a tool that enhances lifelong teaching and learning.

Integrating Technology with the Language Arts Curriculum

Communication and technology tools, which often motivate reading and writing (Becker, 2000; Carroll, 2004; Diamond & Moore, 1995; Moore-Hart, 1995, 2004), add breadth, depth, meaning, and interest to the language arts curriculum. Travers (1999) reminds us that integrating communication and technology tools with the language arts curriculum will be a large, expensive, and long-term experiment that will simultaneously offer ongoing, exciting possibilities.

Although many view technology as a tool to support, facilitate, and enhance lifelong learning, others view technology as a partner in the process of knowledge construction. Applying both these views represents an effective and efficient way to integrate technology with the curriculum, particularly when we consider technology as an evolving tool that may develop and transform literacy in unforeseen ways.

However, integrating technology with the language arts curriculum only becomes successful if we teach reading and writing as a process. This implies that we no longer deliver knowledge; we serve as collaborators and audiences for reading and writing. As teachers, we further become facilitators who guide and coach literacy learning through monitoring and conferencing. Technology then becomes a (1) tool to support, facilitate, and enhance students' reading and writing and (2) a partner in the reading and writing processes as students use technology to access, store, or retrieve information.

Using Mindtools in Technology Environments

Michaele Rae's class, a multiage classroom of students ranging in age from 7 to 10, provides a snapshot of how technology may be integrated with the language arts curriculum. It may seem a little noisy in the room, but the noise is not misdirected, off-task noise. It's just the hum you hear when people are working alongside one another or when people become involved in different tasks.

Over in the far corner, Alayna and Nada are looking at a book about slavery. As they read *Follow the Drinking Gourd,* by Jeannette Winter, a story about the Underground Railroad, they talk about Molly and James's escape to freedom. After reading the book, they plan to use the software, *Young Harriet Tubman: Freedom Fighter,* to learn more about the Underground Railroad. Using what they learn from the book and the software, they plan to write and illustrate their own book about a family's escape from a plantation.

At a nearby table, Nicky is writing about the Civil War in his journal, pretending to be a soldier from the North. As he writes, Nicky tells his teacher he can't imagine why someone would be for slavery. He questions how another person could own another person, adamantly exclaiming that no one has the right to own another person.

Andrew and Josh are researching the Underground Railroad on the Internet. They have discovered the location of some homes that were part of the Underground Railroad. They want to see if the class could go on a field trip to visit these homes. They plan to email some of the sites to determine what some of the costs might be.

Keisha, Haley, and Mariah are working at the computer station on their newspaper about the Civil War. Haley is using word processing tools to edit her editorial on the prohibition of slavery; Keisha is writing a draft for an article about the Confederates who have burned homes, destroyed crops, and killed innocent people in Campbellsville, Kentucky; Mariah is cutting and pasting historical pictures of clothing and food items from the Internet for her advertisements to be displayed in the newspaper.

Working at another computer station, Brianna and Kevin are taking notes while working on the Internet. They are reading about the Battle at Tebbs Bend, a crucial battle for the Union due to its location by the Lebanon-Campbellsville-Columbia Turnpike. Later they will use their notes to describe the battle in detail for the newspaper. While collecting their notes, they talk about how the Union soldiers used the terrain to their advantage. Talking about what they read helps the learners understand the information so they can determine which ideas to include in their article.

Over in the corner, Andrew, Olivia, and Leah are huddled close together, listening to Randall share his diary entries. Randall is pretending to be a Union officer, keeping an account of the daily events on the battlefield in his diary. As they listen, they jot down notes of things that Randall has done to make the diary entries interesting, stimulating, or lifelike. They also record any questions they may have about his writing. After he finishes sharing his first two entries, Olivia first gives him praise on his lead for the first entry; Leah compliments him on his use of strong verbs to tell about the battle. Andrew wants to know how many soldiers died that day; Olivia wants to know how long the battle lasted. Hearing his

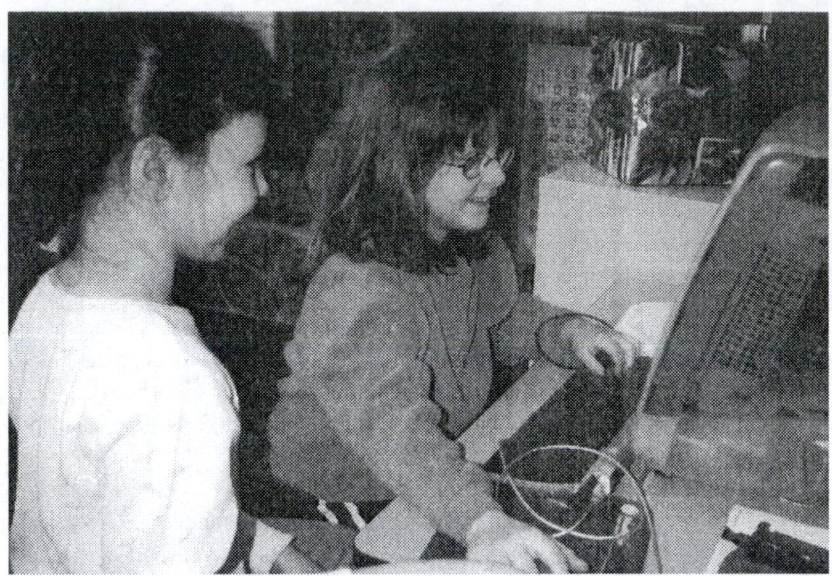

Haley and Mariah work together to edit their newspaper about the Civil War.

peers' words of encouragement becomes motivational to Randall. He also understands that he may need to insert additional information in his diary entries. After thanking them for their feedback, Randall explains that he got the ideas from an American Civil War website that includes information about other battles as well.

David and Mitch have found some poems about the Civil War. After reading several poems in *Hand in Hand: An American History through Poetry* by Lee Hopkins, they share the poems with one another and talk about composing their own poems. David wants to compose his own poem about a Confederate soldier who died on the battlefield. Mitch wants to compose a poem about a 15-year-old boy who ran away from home to fight for the Union.

Christine is emailing a history professor to learn more about women in the Civil War. She just read about Mary Edwards Walker, a surgeon during the Civil War, who received a Medal of Honor for her accomplishments while assisting with Union and Confederate casualties. She wanted to know the names of other women and their accomplishments during the Civil War. Before sending the email, Christine creates a list of questions for the professor.

This snapshot of Michaele's class shows how her students use technology to extend their learning about slavery, the Underground Railroad, and the Civil War. As her students pursue their own inquiries about these topics, Michaele continuously circulates among her students. She guides and facilitates their learning by periodically asking questions to stimulate their thinking; by giving them praise for their leads, choice of words, or use of examples and details to show what is happening in their writing; or by helping them find a website or book for their inquiry project. Importantly, her students follow a process as they use the technology for their writing: they locate information, collect information, create lists or webs of their ideas, draft their ideas, revise their writing, edit their writing, and then plan how to publish their inquiry projects.

While working on their projects, her students use technology as a tool—a tool that helps them do powerful things. Each student has a real-world outcome in mind, some purpose for his or her inquiry,

teaching **TIP 2.3**

Writers need to know what's "working" with their writing first. Specific praise gives them this information. Next, they need to know what additional information readers need in order to understand the message or enjoy the message. Questions provide this information.

Christine emails a professor to learn more about women and their accomplishments during the Civil War.

beyond just "getting it finished" (Duke, Purcell-Gates, Hall, & Tower, 2007). When they share their published projects with one another, all students will gain a better understanding of this historical time period.

Orchestrating Literacy Learning in Technologically Rich Learning Environments

Similar to Michaele, we must all mediate literacy learning of our students within a technologically rich learning environment. Students have many skills and strategies they must acquire in order to use new forms of technology. To help her students acquire these skills and strategies, Michaele uses minilessons to model and demonstrate the process before students begin working with the technology tools independently. For example, she plans a minilesson on how to read information from a text, take notes on the ideas, and then draft a paragraph about the information (see Chapter 6). Acquiring strategies to use with communication and technology tools takes time. Learning is an ongoing process that emerges from her students' needs as they work on a variety of small, intermediate projects.

Michaele realizes that she must project ahead, thinking about what communication tools they will be using and what skills and strategies they might need while using the tools. For example, before students use the Internet, she must model how to navigate hypermedia formats, using hypertext links. Once they learn to navigate hypermedia formats, she then demonstrates how to access, store, and retrieve information through notetaking procedures. Through the use of minilessons, Michaele shows students how to analyze, synthesize, and evaluate information through critical and creative thinking strategies while they read. For example, she shows them how to look at the sources authors use on websites to be sure the information is accurate and authentic. She then models how to apply these same strategies as they revise and edit their own writing.

Students gradually begin to reflect on what they know, assess what they know, and determine what they need to know as they read and write, using both print and nonprint sources. Throughout, her students practice collaboration, discussion, questioning, and inquiry. With each new literacy learning experience, they develop and refine these strategies, acquiring new ways to apply the strategies with new communication tools.

Just like Michaele, we need to recognize the developmental aspects of literacy learning and devise learning experiences to help our students move to higher forms of literacy learning as they use the communication tools available to them. Her classroom begins to reflect real-life work environments where people access information from multiple media sources (Duke et al., 2007; Mann, 1998) and where people learn how to function in a world integrated with changing technology tools and resources (Balajthy, 1989, 2000; Leu et al., 2004; Valmont & Wepner, 2000; Wepner & Ray, 2000).

If we view technology as an evolving tool with ongoing *exciting* possibilities for literacy learning, our students will begin to pick up our own enthusiasm for learning. They will embrace innovative technologies and learn how to become independent lifelong learners who constantly update their skills, knowledge, and experiences from our model.

The Components of Literacy Learning in Technologically Rich Learning Environments

When we consider the components of literacy learning in technologically rich learning environments, we must remember Bork's (1987) words. He reminds us that the real value of technology lies in its effectiveness as a learning tool. Similar to Michaele, we need to consider technology as a tool that supports, facilitates, and enhances reading and writing. Consistent with Jonassen (1996), we also need to cultivate an environment that supports the use of cognitive and technology tools—mindtools—to help students learn how to analyze, synthesize, and evaluate information. Simultaneously, we must make judgments about what students currently know and what instruction they will need to advance to new levels.

This snapshot of Michaele's classroom demonstrates how technology tools may enhance and facilitate literacy learning. Viewing literacy as a process, Michaele integrates technology with her curriculum while orchestrating the literacy learning of her students. Her own energy and enthusiasm about technology becomes contagious to her students as they read and write, using mindtools. Consistent with the International Reading Association's position statement on integrating technology with the literacy curriculum (IRA, 2001) in her classroom, Michaele

- Integrates information and communication technology (ICT) with her instructional program.
- Provides instruction on how to access information on the Internet and how to analyze, synthesize, and evaluate the information for her students.
- Assesses her students' ability to read on the Internet and to write using word processing software.
- Provides instruction on safe and responsible use of ICT for her students.
- Provides equal access to ICT for all her students.
- Continuously increases her knowledge of effective ways to use ICT for teaching and learning.

Similar to Michaele, we need to create technologically rich learning environments for our students. As we all move forward in a biotechnology age, we must continuously ponder our own roles in preparing our youth to function in a world transformed by evolving technology. Ignoring our roles will only marginalize literacy learning of our youth (Li, 2005).

As previously stated, our own enthusiasm and interest in technology and writing set the tone for literacy learning. Just as Michaele's students lived literacy, trying new ideas, techniques, and technology tools, we need to foster students' exploration and experimentation of technology tools. Our students need to feel safe in a risk-free environment, knowing if they don't succeed, they can try again.

Reflecting on Our Teaching Practice. Whether we use technology or pencil and paper, we need to reflect on our current teaching practice to determine whether our literacy curriculum will promote effective writing. Technology and communication tools only become successful when our teaching practice is grounded in theory and based on research and experience. Consistent with Graves (2004), we need to assess our writing curriculum to determine if we

- Offer our students time to write daily.
- Provide our students choices about their writing.
- Follow the writing process.
- Supply our students with ongoing praise and encouragement as they write.
- Provide our students ongoing responses, coming from us as well as their peers, about their writing.
- Offer opportunities for our students to publish their writing, both formally and informally.
- Provide minilessons for our students to learn strategies authors use during the prewriting, drafting, revising, and editing stages of writing.
- Include ongoing assessment through the use of writing folders and portfolios.

Closing Thoughts

In order to create a technologically rich learning environment for literacy learning, we must be sure that our teaching practice is consistent with theory. Effective literacy instruction continuously draws upon research and practice. To accomplish our goals for literacy learning, we need to draw on the research related to quality teaching (McIntyre & Pressley, 1996; Spiegel, 1998). According to this line of research, we need to determine whether we

- Enhance literacy learning through the use of communication and technology tools.
- Respect and honor the cultural heritage and traditions of our students.
- Refine and shape our teaching through reflection.
- Believe in our students' ability to write.

As shown, word processing tools, the most common application of technology (Becker, 2000), can easily be integrated with the writing process. Comparatively easy to learn and use, word processing technology may be a good place for teachers to begin integrating technology with the literacy curriculum.

As we explore, expand, and develop ways to effectively use technology, we need to begin where we feel safe. Routman (2000) reminds us that the struggle in teaching is inherent. As a result, we need to be reasonable and gentle with ourselves as we consider implementing innovative practices. We can't struggle with everything. Instead, we need to focus and take small steps—taking risks, exploring, collaborating, thinking, and reflecting as we modify our instruction. Once we are comfortable with this change, we can refocus and take small steps as we consider another way to integrate technology with our literacy curriculum.

Certainly, literacy educators continuously face new challenges as they explore and experiment with ways to integrate technology with the literacy curriculum. Intertwined with many aspects of our daily lives, technology does not yet play the same natural role in our

teaching TIP 2.4

Even kindergarteners and first graders can learn to use word processing technology. In fact, the kinesthetic, tactile keyboard often helps them learn the names of letters and their sounds more easily. Many young writers can also write more easily because they just have to press a key rather than form a letter.

classroom teaching that it plays in our daily lives (Li, 2005). Even though the reasons for this phenomenon are complex, we must all participate in the preparation of our youth for the real world; we must actively explore new ways to integrate technology with the literacy curriculum. At the same time, we must continuously remain open-minded and flexible, seeking innovative ways to use technology and communication tools that enhance and support literacy learning for all our students.

Just embracing communication and technology tools will not promote the literacy learning of our students. We must still follow the literacy process, using a balanced approach and applying the principles of quality teaching that lead to improved literacy learning of our students (Routman, 2000; Tompkins, 2003). Specifically, we need to continuously assess whether we

- Provide instruction in reading and writing for our students, while showing them connections between reading and writing.
- Organize our literacy environment so that quality literature, including multicultural literature, is at the heart of our program.
- Use minilessons to teach our students skills and strategies they would apply in their reading and writing.
- Provide reading instruction for our students, including word recognition and identification, vocabulary, and comprehension.
- Provide writing instruction for our students, including strategies for expressing a message using the writing process and strategies for using conventional spelling, grammar, and punctuation to express the ideas.
- Integrate reading and writing across the curriculum, often using a thematic approach to learning.
- Create a learning environment that consists of opportunities for varied grouping arrangements, including whole-group learning, cooperative learning, guided, small-group learning, and independent learning.
- Maintain a learning environment that inspires our students to become lifelong readers and writers.

How we proceed will be an ongoing experiment. Time-tested teaching and learning strategies will change; new teaching and learning strategies will evolve as the new capacities of technology emerge. Therefore, teachers' beliefs, rather than technology, will influence how we proceed with our instruction (DeGroff, 1990).

Teachers' Questions

1. I don't feel comfortable with computers. What should I do?

Technology is advancing so rapidly that we all become quickly overwhelmed. In order for us to begin integrating technology with the curriculum, we don't have to know everything about computers, word processing, the Internet, or email. We need to find where we are most comfortable and begin slowly. Once we find a comfortable place to begin (often word processing), we can use this as an entry point. For example, maybe we want to begin with having a computer center, a place for students to informally write on the computer. Then gradually, we can introduce using the computer during journaling, having one or two students write on the computer for their journals.

Usually, one or two students are already comfortable with computers. They can become our computer experts, students who help students having problems while using the computer. Of course, we will need to meet with our computer experts first, showing them how to help others who are experiencing difficulty. Once they receive training, they become invaluable assistants so that we can continue circulating, helping all students as they write. Chapter 3 explains how one teacher began using computers with journaling.

What's most important is to remember that we are learners among learners. We don't have to be experts. We are facilitators of knowledge.

2. I only have one computer in my classroom. How can I use computers with my writing curriculum?

Whether we have one computer or six computers in our classroom, we can begin integrating computers with the curriculum. Students love using technology, because technology is such a large portion of their lives at home and in the community. One easy way to begin integrating computers with the curriculum is to integrate the computer with journaling. If we put up a schedule, all students can rotate to the computer. Students eagerly look forward to their rotation and provide the motivation to integrate computers with the curriculum in other ways before long. Chapter 8 shares how one teacher (Elaine Bortz), who only had one computer, integrated computers with her reading, writing, and social studies curriculum.

3. How can I begin using computers with my kindergarten children? Are they too young to use computers?

Kindergarteners are not too young to use computers! Many have already been using the computer at home. They see their parents using the computer daily and naturally want to use it as well. Frequently, kindergarteners' early experiences with computers begin with educational software or computer games. We can build on these early experiences by helping them learn how to write on the computer. Just as preschoolers' and kindergartners' early forms of writing begin with scribbling, their first experiences with word processing may be randomly pressing the various keys. If we ask them to tell us about their writing, the random letters become a message. Gradually, they will begin to type their names, their friends' names, or words they know. Through play and experimentation, they begin to learn more about the symbols and sounds and how to link these into a message. Notice that this process is also the way they learn to write with a pencil. Chapter 3 explains how a teacher in a multiage classroom (kindergarten and first grade) helped her young writers begin to use computers with journaling.

4. Do I need to teach my students keyboarding skills before they begin using computers?

The research is divided related to keyboarding skills. In my own experiences, I have found that it is helpful to show students the location of the home keys (*ASDF* and *JKL*) and show them how they can stretch their fingers to the various keys from the home keys while using two hands. I often use color-coded keyboards for this, modeling the process as part of a minilesson (see Chapter 4 for more about minilessons). Then, by using exercises found in keyboarding instructional texts, I have them practice stretching to other keys (i.e., *fgf, fgf, fgf* or *lol, lol, lol*). After they practice these simple exercises, I have them apply the strategy of stretching their fingers to nearby keys as they spell simple words like *dad, mad,* or *sad;* or *leg, beg,* or *peg;* or *did, hid,* or *lid.* Once students understand that they can type easier using two hands as they stretch to the nearby keys, typing becomes quicker and easier for them. I have also found that they are so motivated to use the computer as they publish their writing that they learn the locations of the keys. The more students word process, the easier it becomes to find the keys.

Certainly, students can also rotate to the computer on a scheduled basis to practice keyboarding, using keyboarding software as well. This will reinforce the use of two hands as they type. However, I don't want them to feel like they have to use "perfect" keyboarding skills as they type. If they just remember to leave their fingers on the home keys, they seem to learn to type fluently and more quickly.

5. Do I need to teach my students word processing skills before they begin using computers?

The research on word processing skills is also divided. I have found that it is very useful to show students the location of the return key, the delete key, the shift key, the space key, and the arrow keys during a minilesson. (Using color-coded keyboards is helpful for this as well.)

Once they learn the location of these keys, they can practice using them as they type, "My name is . . ." and their first name, using the shift key and the space key. After typing this short sentence, they can practice inserting information by adding their last name, using the arrow keys. Next, they can delete their name and type the name of a friend, practicing the use of the delete key.

After practicing these simple exercises, students become comfortable using the essential word processing strategies. In addition, I show them how to begin a new document, how to save, and how to print. Once students begin publishing their writing, they begin to learn other word processing skills. In fact, students show one another how to change the print font or use colors with the fonts. Other skills such as centering or spacing can easily be taught through minilessons.

Having "computer experts" is also helpful. They can always help students when they become stuck or when they forget.

Children's Literature

Hopkins, L. (1994). *Hand in hand: An American history through poetry.* New York: Simon and Schuster.

Winter, J. (1988). *Follow the drinking gourd.* New York: Alfred Knopf.

References

Anderson, R., & Speck, B. (2001). *Using technology in K–8 literacy classrooms.* Upper Saddle River, NJ: Merrill.

Balajthy, E. (1989). *Computers and reading: Lessons from the past and the technologies of the future.* Englewood Cliffs, NJ: Prentice Hall.

Balajthy, E. (2000). Is technology worth my professional time, resources, and efforts? In S. Wepner, W. Valmont, & R. Thurlow (Eds.), *Linking literacy and technology: A guide for K–8 classrooms* (pp. 203–218). Newark, DE: International Reading Association.

Becker, H. (2000). Internet use by teachers. In *The Jossey-Bass reader on technology and learning* (pp. 80–112). San Francisco: Jossey-Bass.

Bork, A. (1987). *Learning with personal computers.* New York: Harper & Row.

Bruce, G. (2003). *Literacy in the information age: Inquiries into meaning making with new technologies.* Newark, DE: International Reading Association.

Carroll, M. (2004). *Cartwheels on the keyboard: Computer-based literacy instruction in an elementary classroom.* Newark, DE: International Reading Association.

Daiute, C. (1985). *Writing and computers.* Reading, MA: Addison-Wesley.

Daiute, C. (1986). Physical and cognitive factors in revising: Insights from studies with computers. *Research in the Teaching of English, 20,* 141–159.

DeGroff, L. (1990). Is there a place for computers in whole language classrooms? *The Reading Teacher, 43,* 568–572.

Diamond, B., & Moore, M. A. (1995). *Multicultural literacy: Mirroring the reality of the classroom.* New York: Longman.

Duke, N., Purcell-Gates, V., Hall, L., & Tower, C. (2007). Authentic literacy activities for developing comprehension and writing. *The Reading Teacher, 60,* 344–355.

El-Hindi, A. (1998). Beyond classroom boundaries: Constructivist teaching with the Internet. *The Reading Teacher, 51,* 694–700.

Flood, J., & Lapp, D. (1995). Broadening the lens: Toward an expanded conceptualization of literacy. In K. A. Hinchman, D. J. Leu, & C. K. Kinzer (Eds.), *Perspectives on literacy research and practice* (pp. 1–16). Chicago: National Reading Conference.

Fox, B., & Mitchell, M. (2000). Using technology to support word recognition, spelling, and vocabulary acquisition. In S. Wepner, W. Valmont, & R. Thurlow (Eds.), *Linking literacy and technology* (pp. 42–75). Newark, DE: International Reading Association.

Graves, D. (2004). What I've learned from teachers of writing. *Language Arts, 82,* 88–94.

Henry, L. (2006). Searching for an answer: The critical role of new literacies while reading on the Internet. *The Reading Teacher, 59,* 614–627.

International Reading Association. (2001). *Integrating literacy and technology in the curriculum: A position statement of the International Reading Association.* [Online]. Available at www.reading.org/resources/issues/postions_technology.html [March 21, 2005].

Jonassen, D. (1996). *Computers in the classroom: Mindtools for critical thinking.* Englewood Cliffs, NJ: Merrill.

Labbo, L. (1996). A semiotic analysis of young children's symbol making in a classroom computer center. *Reading Research Quarterly, 27,* 185–201.

Leu, D. (1997). Caity's question: Literacy as deixis on the Internet. *The Reading Teacher, 51,* 62–67.

Leu, D. (2000). The convergence of literacy instruction with networked technologies for information and communication. *Reading Research Quarterly, 35,* 108–127.

Leu, D., Jr. (2001). Internet project: Preparing students for new literacies in a global village. *The Reading Teacher, 54,* 567–585.

Leu, D., Jr., Leu, D., & Coiro, J. (2004). *Teaching with the Internet: New literacies for new times* (4th ed.). Norwood, MA: Christopher Gordon.

Li, L. (2005). No child left behind: Enhancing literacy education through technology. *Michigan Reading Journal, 37,* 6–12.

Mann, D. (1998). Using telecommunications to link homes and schools. Paper presented at the 43rd Annual Convention of the International Reading Association, Orlando, FL.

McIntyre, E., & Pressley, M. (Eds.). (1996). *Balanced instruction: Strategies and skill in whole language.* Norwood, MA: Christopher-Gordon.

McKenna, M., Reinking, D., Labbo, L., & Watkins, J. (1996). Using electronic storybooks and beginning readers (Instructional Resource No. 39). Athens, GA: University of Georgia, National Reading Research Center. (ERIC Document Reproduction Service No. ED 400 521).

Moore, M. (1987). The integration of word processing technology into the Developmental Writing Program. In *Seventh yearbook of the American Reading Forum.* Muncie, IN: Ball State University.

Moore-Hart, M. (1995). The effects of Multicultural Links on reading and writing performance and cultural awareness of fourth and fifth graders. *Computers in Human Behavior, 11,* 391–410.

Moore-Hart, M. (2004). Creating learning environments that invite all students to learn through multicultural literature and information technology. *Childhood Education, 81,* 87–95.

NCTE. (2004). *NCTE beliefs about the teaching of writing.* [Online]. Available at www.ncte.org/about/over/positions/category/write/118876.htm [June 13, 2005].

Newman, J. (1984). Language learning and computers. *Language Arts, 61,* 494–497.

Reinking, D. (1995). Reading and writing with computers: Literacy research in a post-typographic world. In K. Hinchman, D. Leu, & C. Kinzer (Eds.), *Perspectives on literacy research and practice: The 45th yearbook of the National Reading Conference* (pp. 17–33). Chicago: National Reading Conference.

Reinking, D. (1998). Introduction. In D. Reinking, M. McKenna, L. Labbo, & R. Kieffer (Eds.), *Handbook of literacy and technology: Transformations in a post-typographic world* (p. xi). Mahwah, NJ: Lawrence Erlbaum.

Routman, R. (2000). *Conversations: Strategies for teaching, learning, and evaluating.* Portsmouth, NH: Heinemann.

Snyder, I. (1999). Using information technology in language and literacy education: An introduction. In J. Hancock (Ed.), *Teaching literacy using information technology: A collection of articles from the Australian Literacy Educators' Association* (pp. 1–10). Newark, DE: International Reading Association.

Spiegel, D. (1998). Silver bullets, babies and bathwater: Literature response groups in a balanced literacy program. *The Reading Teacher, 52,* 114–124.

Sutherland-Smith, W. (2002). Weaving the literacy Web: Changes in reading from page to screen. *The Reading Teacher, 55,* 663–669.

Tompkins, G. (2003). *Literacy for the 21st century.* Upper Saddle River, NJ: Merrill Prentice Hall.

Travers, J. (1999). Everything is connected: An information technology program comes together. In J. Hancock (Ed.), *Teaching literacy using information technology* (pp. 66–77). Newark, DE: International Reading Association.

Valmont, W., & Wepner, S. (2000). Using technology to support literacy learning. In S. Wepner, W. Valmont, & R. Thurlow (Eds.), *Linking literacy and technology* (pp. 2–18). Newark, DE: International Reading Association.

Wepner, S., & Ray, L. (2000). Using technology for reading development. In S. Wepner, W. Valmont, & R. Thurlow (Eds.), *Linking literacy and technology* (pp. 76–105). Newark, DE: International Reading Association.

Wepner, S., & Tao, L. (2002). From master teacher to master novice. Building responsibilities in technology-fused classrooms. *The Reading Teacher, 55,* 642–651.

chapter THREE

Getting Writing Started

I live a pretty exciting and a different life from some of the kids still I live a normal life. When I was age two was one of my exciting years and a war was going on. I would have a feeling that my family and me would never be free cause my family and me were kept by the thai soldiers and there would be a river near the village where my family were kept on. One day my family was saying they were going fishing to one of the guards, but really they were trying to get across from the river. Cause that river leads to freedom and there would be my dad's brother across the other side of the river. My parents would give me a sleeping pill so I wouldn't make any noise cause there were guards and soldiers on ships. This is the time and they have to do it. They would swim underwater and manage to escape. But I wish I could go back in the pass and see how it felt like. Being kept in thai and don't have freedom but I kind of know how it felt. I call that river freedom river. I really miss loas. I had never seen most of my relatives cause they live in loas. Someday I would go back to my country. But most of all I want to learn about loas history. How they felt like in the way and learn their culture and see my relatives.

Vangchai, Grade 5

The Sensitivity of Writing

When I work with teachers in the classroom, they frequently ask me, "How do I get writing started with my students?" These teachers explain that their students groan and moan whenever they hear the word *writing.* They add that some students say they find writing boring; others say they don't like to write. Students' reluctance to write or their anxieties about writing are not uncommon, especially if they have had limited experiences writing. Clark (1995), in fact, states that these anxieties, which are common among many adults and children, can probably be traced back to childhood. He believes that either something happened, or failed to happen, when these adults and children wrote in school. Even though we continue to make great strides in the teaching of writing in the elementary school, we still have miles to go.

As shown by Vangchai's journal entry (Diamond & Moore, 1995, p. 147), writing is a very sensitive activity because it evolves from our lives and our experiences, often highlighting its triumphs or hurdles. For this reason, writing becomes like our skin, which is sensitive to the sun's rays. Writing, however, is sensitive to the reactions and responses of others. If we want Vangchai to write freely and naturally, we must cultivate an atmosphere of acceptance and respect for his ideas, as well as those of his peers. We must create a comfortable, safe environment where students can experiment and explore language, where they can have multiple opportunities to talk and express their ideas. We must create a risk-free environment.

Creating a Risk-Free Environment

A risk-free environment recognizes students' strengths as teachers affirm and acknowledge their thoughts and language. Rejecting the language or the culture of our students, in contrast, jeopardizes future writing performance. Vangchai's teacher, Elaine Bortz, validated his language, his linguistic strengths, and his cultural heritage. This affirmation enhanced his writing performance and the writing performance of his peers (Cummins, 1986; Diamond & Moore, 1995; NCTE, 2004; Reyhner & Garcia, 1989).

Once we recognize and affirm all students' ideas—whether expressed in oral or written language—we can use the writing process to help them record their message in conventional language during the editing stage of writing. When Vangchai saw his story in print and heard himself read the printed message within the supportive atmosphere of his classroom, he discovered that he was an author. When he saw his peers listening attentively to each word, he learned that his message was far more important than correctly spelled words or punctuated sentences.

Interestingly, Vangchai returned to his seat after sharing his journal entry and began to insert words he had accidentally left out. He still had more to say. He also added an *s* to the verb *lead* and the noun *guard,* words that didn't have the correct suffixes in his first draft. Reading the journal entry aloud helped Vangchai see how to change part of his message into conventional language.

Most importantly, Vangchai gained momentum and motivation to write from his teachers and peers when they spontaneously clapped when he finished reading his piece. Without prompting, students' hands shot up the minute he finished reading his piece. They eagerly began asking him questions: "How did you breathe under water?" "Did the guards hear you?" "How did you and your family escape from the guards?" These genuine questions affirmed and recognized Vangchai's ideas and thoughts.

In fact, his peers' natural interest in his experiences encouraged him to continue writing about his family's escape to freedom. Each day his class eagerly anticipated hearing more about the escape. They also wanted to know more about his life in Laos. Swayed by his peers' interest in his story, Vangchai later revised and edited his journal entries for publication. His teacher then submitted the story to a Young Authors Conference held at a nearby university.

Fostering Fluency in Writing

Once we create a climate for writing, students become less reluctant to write. However, students also need the opportunity to write daily in this warm, accepting environment. The more Vangchai practiced his writing in his journal, the more fluent he became. As he experimented and explored print, spelling, and writing styles, he learned how to write in conventional English. At the same time, he gradually became more comfortable with this new language.

If students believe that we are pleased with their writing—whether it is a single line of temporary or invented spellings, a mixture of Spanish and English symbols and sounds, or scribbling—they begin to experiment with written language, naturally learning about writing conventions and how to express their ideas. This spontaneous way of learning is the same way they acquire language as an infant.

As students discover the features of written language through trial and error, they simultaneously gain more fluency in their writing. Using notebooks, journals, or lifebooks—books to write about their lives or experiences—is one way to foster experimentation and exploration of written language.

While writing in their journals, students have the opportunity to practice writing about topics of their choice. They frequently choose to write about their lives or experiences, just like Vangchai. Since Vangchai knew about his topic, he could concentrate on how to tell his story. The more he practiced writing, the easier it became to put the story into words. This is how he began to improve his writing fluency. Similarly, all students begin to increase their fluency as they practice writing on a daily basis.

As one might imagine, thinking about his ideas while attending to the conventions of writing was challenging for Vangchai. This also happens with young writers and struggling writers. During the beginning stages of writing, emergent writers must think about how to form letters, how to spell words, and how to express their ideas clearly while using correct grammar and mechanics. They cannot simultaneously monitor their ideas and attend to all the conventions of writing (NCTE, 2004). Forcing conventions of language too early would stifle Vangchai's expression of the ideas; forcing conventions similarly stifles young writers' and struggling writers' thought patterns (Graves, 1983). Vangchai slowly began to learn about the conventions of language through trial and error. While preparing his story for publication, he learned about many other conventions of language.

Responding to Students' Ideas First

For these reasons, we need to respond to students' thoughts, feelings, or beliefs when they write in journals, notebooks, or lifebooks. Just as Vangchai's peers naturally responded to his family's escape to freedom, we need to show an interest in the messages our students write. If Vangchai's teacher had used a red pen to correct his writing, Vangchai would have begun writing less and less so that he would be safe from the red marks on his paper. When we respond to the conventions of language, many students begin to leave their pages blank or compromise their message in order to say something that is easy to spell.

Even when we respond to their ideas, some students will initially fear the red pen's marks on their journals. Their past experiences often influence how they write. For example, when Mandy Church responded to Jason's sentence, "I have a black cat," she exclaimed, "You are so lucky to have a cat! What's your cat's name?" Jason innocently replied, "I don't have a black cat." Jason knew how to write these words. He felt safe writing this sentence in his journal. He believed that a red pen would not touch his paper if he spelled words correctly.

Nurturing Positive Feelings about Journal Writing

Mandy wanted Jason to communicate his ideas fluently, so she created a safe environment for him to write his ideas—a place where he could use temporary spelling on a daily basis. We, too, can stimulate a warm, supportive environment if we

- Give students many opportunities to make choices in their writing.
- Provide an atmosphere rich with environmental print (i.e., chart stories, poems, songs, KWL charts, semantic maps, etc.).

- Become a positive role model for reading and writing.
- Provide an environment that emphasizes learning to read and write naturally.
- Give students multiple opportunities to share their writing orally with their peers.
- Focus on the writing process, not the writing product.
- Eliminate criticism and minimize highlighting students' mistakes.
- Avoid premature emphasis on mechanical skills.
- Model respect for students' ideas.
- Show an ongoing interest in students' ideas.

Not only will students gain fluency in recording their ideas and thoughts in journals within the context of this caring environment, they will begin to look forward to writing. Some additional suggestions for nurturing positive feelings about writing include the following:

- Use encouraging words and specific praise when you respond to students' writing.
- Help writers think "I'm O.K.," even when they make errors.
- Give students a variety of writing tools, including computers, that are readily available.
- Create opportunities for students to write collaboratively in mixed ability level groupings.
- Surround students with multicultural literature, literature, drama, art, music, dance, and play to stimulate ideas for writing.
- Use multicultural books with a variety of languages, language patterns, and dialects to model respect for different ways of expressing ideas.
- Emphasize meaning over the conventions of writing.
- Avoid punitive writing interactions as this negative experience may become associated with writing later.

Thus, we must consistently allow students to practice expressing their feelings, experiences, or beliefs in their journals. Our evaluations of their journal writing, if used, must similarly reflect a response to the message. Jason and his peers do not need to see red pen marks, noting spelling errors, missing punctuation, or incorrect grammar; they need to see Mandy's spontaneous responses and her genuine interest in their ideas in their journals.

Students of all ages generate their own excitement for reading and writing within a nurturing atmosphere. Having students share their writing orally is one way to refuel this excitement for reading and writing. If their peers' responses reflect the responses Vangchai's peers gave him, students will become eager to write more and more. The more they write, the more opportunities they will have to practice writing. Through practice, their writing will grow and develop.

Using Personal Writing Adventures in Preschool Settings

This supportive atmosphere is especially important for emerging writers. We need to respond positively to their early forms of print, even the scribbles and wiggly marks that race across the paper. For example when a young child exclaims, "Me cookie," or "I want a cookies," we might respond by saying, "Do you want a chocolate cookie or vanilla cookie?" Just as parents respond positively to infants' creative forms of language, we need to respond to the scribbles and wiggly marks by saying, "Tell me about your writing."

Preschool Writing Opportunities in Literacy Centers

Graves (1994, 2004) continuously emphasizes that we underestimate what children can do with writing. Melissa Wood wanted to test this theory in her preschool setting. Similar to many preschool teachers, Melissa enjoys setting up literacy centers, which revolve around themes, for her 4-year-old preschoolers. Writing materials, however, were missing from her centers.

Following the ideas of Tompkins (2004), Melissa added a variety of colored pens, pencils, markers, index cards, writing pads, and Post-its to her centers to see if her young learners might begin to do more writing. To her disappointment, the writing materials remained unused. During circle time, some of her preschoolers even shared that they want to use them, but they forget.

Determined, Melissa decided to modify her centers slightly; she decided to create centers that evolve around real-life writing experiences. Picking up on her children's interests in trains, Melissa set up several literacy centers revolving around trains. One of these centers was a dining car, equipped with dinner plates, eating utensils, glasses, cups and saucers, and play food, as well as various writing materials.

This time, Melissa models being a waitress in the literacy center. With her pencil and writing pad in hand, she goes to one table in the dining car and asks the children what they want to eat. As they share what they want, Melissa writes down each item on the pad. When Andy asks for a Coke, Melissa does a think-aloud. She stretches out the word *Coke,* explaining, "Mmm . . . Coke . . . that begins with a 'kuh' sound like *k* or *c,* and I think it's a *c.*" Then she continues to write the word *Coke* on her pad. Jordan says he wants milk. Melissa similarly models how *milk* begins with an *m* and records the *m* and then the rest of the word on her pad.

Modeling how to use the writing materials in the center became important. After she moves to another center, the young learners begin using the writing materials, following her lead. Some children merely scribble what their friends order; others draw pictures; still others write random letters. Her preschoolers are beginning the prephonemic stage of writing (see Figure 1.1 in Chapter 1), the stage where children record sounds and letters by scribbling, drawing pictures or shapes, or writing random letters.

As the preschoolers continue to experiment with written language, they will eventually move to the phonemic stage of writing where they will begin to use the first and last letters of words to record their messages. An example of one child's writing at the prephonemic stage of writing is found in Figure 3.1.

Modeling Writing with Morning News during Circle Time in Preschool

To help her young learners continue to think about the written language, Melissa also models writing with the Morning News during Circle Time. Morning News becomes a special time of the day for one preschooler to share his or her news for the day. On Tuesday, Maria shares that she went to her grandmother's house for dinner. After Maria shares her news, Melissa restates the news—"Maria went to her grandmother's house for dinner."

As Melissa begins recording Maria's news, first she asks Maria how to write her name. As Maria slowly spells her name, Melissa records the letters of Maria's name on the chart paper. Then Melissa asks her children what the first letter of *went* would be, slowly stretching the word out for all to hear. Alex recognizes that *wagon* and *went* have the same sound, so he responds that *went* begins with *w.* Melissa then records the *w* and proceeds writing the rest of the word for all to see. Then she slowly says the word *to,* asking what the first letter of *to* would be. Thomas knows that *to* begins like his name and quickly shares *t.* Melissa then records the word *to* on the paper. Similarly, Melissa asks her children to give her the first letter of *grandmother's, house,* and *dinner.* Choosing these words for her students to give the first letter of the words allows her to quickly record the message without tiring her students. She also briefly talks about some of the conventions of language as she writes.

Figure 3.1

Four-Year-Old Dennis Begins to Use Prephonemic Spelling

For example, she explains that we always use an uppercase letter for a name, or she notes that we end our sentences with a period.

After the news is recorded, Melissa then reads the sentence aloud, pointing to each word as she reads. Then she asks the group to reread the news chorally with her. Next Melissa rereads the news, stopping at the words *Maria* and *house,* encouraging her students to supply the words when she pauses. Through this process of reading and writing, her preschoolers begin to associate the sounds of written language with their spoken language; they also learn that written language has a message to convey.

> ***teaching* TIP 3.1**
>
> This process can also be used to help English language learners begin to acquire a new language system, its symbol–sound relationships, and its vocabulary.

Recording the news for the day also helps her children begin to learn how to write the first letters of words on the notepads or Post-its at the various centers. Even though most of her young learners are at the prephonemic stage of writing, some children gradually begin to write the first letters of words on their notepads in the literacy centers.

Stimulating Preschoolers' Understanding of Written Language

After introducing a literacy center revolving around the train, Melissa creates a new center two weeks later. The new center is the doctor's office. Once again, Melissa models how to record prescriptions and notes about one's temperature or weight on the writing pads or Post-its. She is even able to get prescription pads from a local office for the children to use. As the children visit the centers, they begin to follow her model. Melissa observes that a few of her children are beginning to write the first letters of some words. Others continue to record their messages using prephonemic spelling—scribbling, random letters, or shapes. Still others write their names or the names of their friends.

Providing opportunities for preschoolers to practice using the symbols and sounds of written language is an important addition to Melissa's curriculum. As her young learners begin to listen for the relationships of sounds to letters, they begin to acquire a sense of phonemic awareness, an awareness of the sounds of letters, and a foundation of the relationship between symbols and their sounds (Chapman, 1996; Griffith, Klesius, & Kromrey, 1992; NCTE, 2004). They also become familiar with certain conventions of language such as beginning sentences with a capital or ending sentences with a period. Creating centers related to real-life experiences of her children, as well as modeling how to record our spoken language, is critical if her preschoolers are to advance in their writing development.

Personal Writing Adventures in Kindergarten Settings

Similar to Melissa, Jackie Sperling creates literacy centers that revolve around themes in her kindergarten classroom. In addition to providing writing materials and writing tools for her kindergarten students to use at all her centers, Jackie added a writing center close to the computer in her classroom. She encourages her students to rotate to the writing center so that they might become more independent while writing. Locating the writing center close to the computer allows her students to explore and experiment with written language using a variety of writing tools, including the computer.

To help her students become comfortable writing with the computer, Jackie models this first. She models how to write her name on the computer and how to write her own Morning News on the computer. She also shows how to type random letters or the words on the labels (i. e., labels for the table, lights, flag, whiteboard) scattered across the room. Importantly, this center gives her students a variety of choices on what they want to write. Consistent with Graves (1983), Jackie believes her emergent writers need to learn to make choices and decisions about their writing. Figure 3.2 displays examples of students' writing on the computer.

Using Lifebooks to Foster Personal Writing in Kindergarten

In addition to using centers, Jackie plans time for her kindergarten students to write daily during the first 20 minutes of the day. In fact, on the very first day of class, Jackie demonstrates how her students would use their "lifebooks," books about their lives and experiences, to record their daily writing. Following the suggestions of Calkins (1994), Jackie creates a lifebook for each student, using unlined papers stapled together with a construction paper cover. She explains to her students that they are all going to be authors this year.

Modeling Temporary Spelling. To help her young authors know how to use their lifebooks, Jackie models how they can write during Circle Time. She asks her students if they remember how they first began to write when they were younger, even 1 or 2 years old. Brianna shares that she scribbled when she was 1. Jackie models scribbling on chart paper for all to see, explaining that this is one way we can all write. T'Dell comments that he drew pictures, so Jackie draws a picture of a cat, adding that this is another way we can write. Isabelle shares that she knew how to write *cat,* so Jackie asks her to spell *cat* as she records the letters on the chart. Similarly, Mike explains he could write his name when he was 3. Again, Jackie asks him to spell his name as she records the letters, *M-i-k-e.*

Next, Jackie asks, what if you want to write the word *pumpkin?* Darrell responds that he would write the letter *p* because it begins like his friend Patrick. Jackie records the *p* on the chart and explains that she knows this is the word *pumpkin* because of the *p,* which is the first letter of *pumpkin.* Isabelle adds that she would write *pn.* After recording her response on the chart, Jackie validates that she also knows this is *pumpkin* because it has the first and

Figure 3.2

Example of Students' Writing on the Computer

(a) Travis uses prephonemic spelling to write a message on the computer. (b) Travis types words from the Word Wall, his friends' names, letters, and, numbers. (c) Jason begins to write stories using temporary spelling. (d) Ginny and Crystal begin to write stories using their temporary spelling.

(a)

UEDEQ7SYDDRYHSHDDGYRDYEE64363634E6EETUEURFFUFHF

YRRYRFHFDGSYTERRTE7WSYDDW7W3W637822309WW044364WFDFHFSJSKYSEGRFYEHESYGWH

FWFYWSGE3EEEEE55RQASDCGF123DIERF;FIRYRTR12345A

DYRRTTEERRTTRTY512333345666666666666666666666666666666666666666666666666

66666666666666777777777777777788888888888888999999999999999999111111111

112222222222222233333333333444444444555555555666666666677777777799999999

(b)

TRENT MARTIN CAT DOG FISHH PIG SUN BED BIRD BEE
STOP GO DUCK TURTLE PIGS CAMEYESRIDE LITI TRENT 6 LITA 1988
ABCDEFGHIJKLMNOPQRSTUVWYZ 12345678910 TRENT 6 MARTIN P

CHRISTYKEELIN.123456789APPIEIIETATADDISKECIACHAPTER1985SHIFTINUSE

DRIVE22017991004CATDOGFISHPIGSUNBEDRUIESCRAYDIA

(c)

10/14/88

the travis was play footbool.

a bug was play in grass.

buffy and mack was play bool in

bool. a biu grass in a big

10/14/88

The travis was play footbool.

A bug was play in grass.

Buffy and mack was play bool and

bool. A big grass a big rat

was play in a taw bug.

(d)

ME and MY Mama

Me and My Mama go sopg

sum tims and wen I cum

hom frum schll and I hav sum

schll wurc tn My Mama ruvus

it wet Me . 10-3-88

this hailween

10-7-88 one day i was up i said it

is haliween day it was a good day to

me it was hallween girls and boys are

trick or treat i said the witch was

at the door boo i went home

the end

teaching **TIP 3.2**

Demonstrations or minilessons model how we record messages in written language and how we use tools to record our messages.

last letter of *pumpkin.* DeJuan then explains that he would write *pkn.* Again, Jackie writes down the letters, explaining how these letters help her read the word *pumpkin.*

As Jackie reviews the different forms of writing with the group, she explains that all these forms are ways we can write in our lifebooks. She continues, sharing that we call this our temporary spelling for what we want to say. By using temporary spelling, we can read what we write; others can read what we write, too. Figure 3.3 shows examples of students' temporary spelling.

Brainstorming Topics for Writing in the Lifebooks. After modeling different ways to write, Jackie asks her kindergarteners what they can write about in the lifebooks. Annaleisha says she can write about her family; DeJuan comments that he can write about football; Mike adds he can write about his pet dog; and Arianna shares she wants to write about her birthday party.

Figure 3.3

Jackie Models How to Use Temporary Spelling to Write Messages in Lifebooks

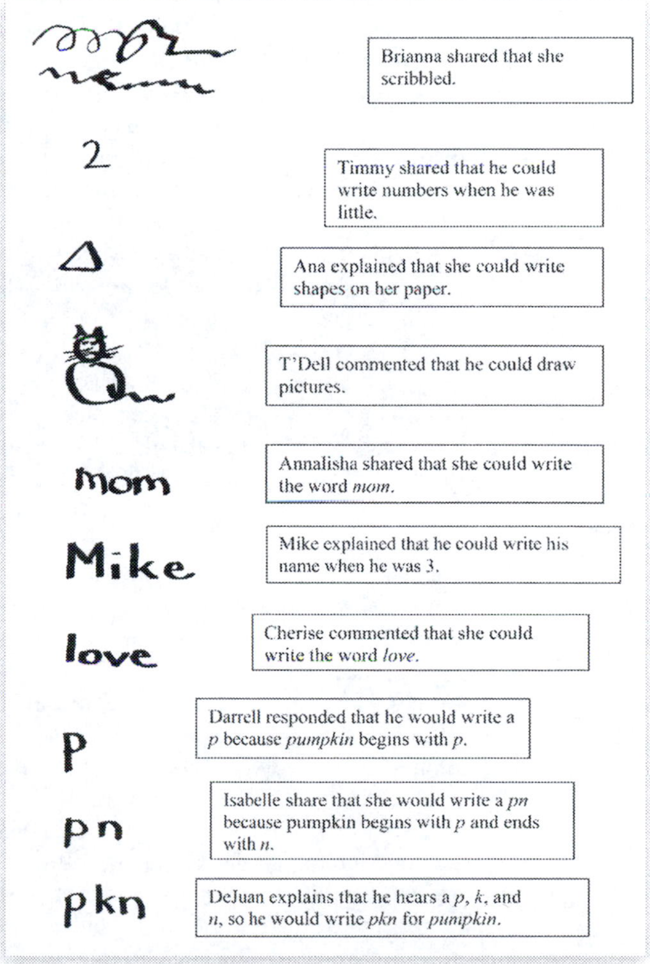

Brianna shared that she scribbled.
2
Timmy shared that he could write numbers when he was little.
Ana explained that she could write shapes on her paper.
T'Dell commented that he could draw pictures.
mom
Annalisha shared that she could write the word *mom*.
Mike
Mike explained that he could write his name when he was 3.
love
Cherise commented that she could write the word *love*.
p
Darrell responded that he would write a *p* because *pumpkin* begins with *p*.
pn
Isabelle share that she would write a *pn* because pumpkin begins with *p* and ends with *n*.
pkn
DeJuan explains that he hears a *p*, *k*, and *n*, so he would write *pkn* for *pumpkin*.

As students share their ideas, Jackie affirms all their ideas by responding with interest and enthusiasm for their thoughts. Then she reemphasizes that everyone can write about anything they would like in their lifebooks, explaining that lifebooks are about our lives and us. She further adds that they can use any of the forms of writing from the chart when writing in their books. To help them formulate their thoughts, she notes that they will usually draw a picture about their topic first. When we hear our class bell ring, she explains, we will begin writing about the topic.

Before sending them to their tables, she has each student tell a partner what they will draw and write about in their lifebooks. This additional prewriting activity helps them begin thinking about their topics. Now they are ready to return to their tables and begin drawing a picture.

Using Drawing and Talking to Help Generate Ideas for Writing. Following these approaches, Jackie validates all the different forms of writing she sees in her class. She further affirms their ideas for drawing by showing interest in their ideas. Naturally, the kindergarteners draw pictures related to their lives. Consistent with Calkins (1994) and Graves (1994), her students feel more comfortable drawing and writing about their lives or experiences.

Having her young writers draw pictures first helps them organize their ideas for writing, which takes time and thought. Then when they begin thinking about the forms of the letters or shapes and what letters or shapes to use as they write, they can more easily concentrate on this, as well as their message. To support her students as they form the letters while writing, Jackie tapes alphabet strips to the tables for easy reference.

While children draw their pictures, Jackie circulates, asking them to *tell* her about their pictures. Talking about their writing helps them understand that written language is like the words we speak. Early experiences with writing need to include multiple opportunities for students to explain orally what is in a text, whether in written symbols or drawn. Writing, in its beginnings, exists in a nest of talk (Goodman, 2005; Goodman & Smith, 1987; NCTE, 2004). Talking about their writing supports students who are unsure about their ideas for writing, especially when we show our interest in their thoughts.

After the children have drawn for about 5 minutes, Jackie then has a few children share their pictures, further giving them opportunities to talk about their topics or ideas. Once a few students have shared their pictures, Jackie has them continue drawing for about 4 minutes. Then she rings the class bell, signaling that it is time to begin writing about their topic, using their own form of temporary writing.

Using Temporary Spelling to Record a Message. To further support them in this transition, Jackie has a few children share what they will write in their lifebooks. T'dell shares he will write, "I am playing ball. My dog caught the ball." Arianna replies she will write, "I had a cake for my birthday. I am 5 years old." Then, everyone begins writing. After about 4 minutes, Jackie has a few more children share what they wrote with the class. When Jackie notices that some students use the first letters of words or the first and last letters of words, she points this out to the children so that everyone will gradually transition to beginning and ending sounds. Talking about the use of first and last letters also reinforces concepts about written language's symbols and sounds.

Similarly, Jackie strengthens these concepts about print with the Morning News (modeled by Melissa) during Circle Time. She also highlights the concepts when modeling writing with language experience stories or chart stories (see Chapters 4 and 6). Sometimes she even has the children use these concepts as they interactively write language experience

Figure 3.4

Violet Writes a Story about Kim and Then Copies a Poem from the Story Chart Hanging on the Wall

stories or chart stories with her. An example of writing at the kindergarten level is shown in Figure 3.4.

Supporting Kindergarten Writers' Emergent Writing

Modeling how to write is important. What's most important is providing time to write daily. As noted earlier, the more young writers write, the easier it becomes to generate the beginning and ending sounds of words and to form the shapes of the letters. Slowly, emergent writers advance to other stages of spelling such as the letter–name or the transitional stages of writing (see Figure 1.1 in Chapter 1). Without daily writing opportunities, however, young writers will not advance through these stages in kindergarten.

Using Praise to Encourage Writing Development. Young authors also need to hear encouraging responses from their teachers as they write. As Jackie circulates, asking her students to tell about their drawings and their writing, she spontaneously praises her children, validating and affirming their writing attempts. Her specific praise for using beginning or ending sounds further encourages the young writers to take risks and try to spell the sounds they hear. Her model of praise and enthusiasm soon becomes contagious. The children begin to praise their peers for writing the first letter of *pet* or spelling the word *cat* on their papers.

> ***teaching* TIP 3.3**
>
> Students of all ages need this supportive context for their writing. When we emphasize the message over the conventions of writing, students become more joyful communicators.

Others might praise a friend for showing how she fell and hurt her arm ice skating. Just like Vangchai, young writers need to know that others are interested in what they have to say.

Sharing Writing as a Way to Support Emergent Writing. Another way to stimulate a caring, supportive environment for young writing is through the use of an Author's Chair or a microphone as students share their writing. When sharing their writing, young authors like to go to the Author's Chair while reading their piece; others enjoy using the microphone so everyone can hear their story. Using the microphone amplifies young writers' voices so everyone can easily hear them read their pieces. Calkins (1994) suggests we can also have a Notebook Museum where everyone opens their journals to a particular page and lays out their journal for everyone to view. All authors then circulate to see the different ways their peers use their journals. Spotlighting students' writing in these ways makes writing become even more motivational.

Of importance, whenever writers share their writing, Jackie insists that all students listen attentively. She explains to her children, "This is just good manners! We need to be respectful of others when they share."

Using Personal Writing Journals in the Elementary Grades

According to Clark (1995) and Graves (1983), ideas for writing first evolve from the students, their interests, and their experiences. Clark (1995) further emphasizes that real-life writing enables students to learn about themselves, about others in the community, and about issues that influence their lives. Lifebooks and personal journals—informal journals used for writing about topics of choice—are wonderful tools for helping writers discover ways to communicate their ideas and feelings to others.

Interestingly, as I work with students in a variety of classrooms, I have observed that writing frequently emerges from students' lives and experiences. Students are able to express their ideas more easily and freely when writing about themselves. The following section provides examples of how teachers use expressive writing—writing about students' lives and

Caitlyn shares her writing with her peers.

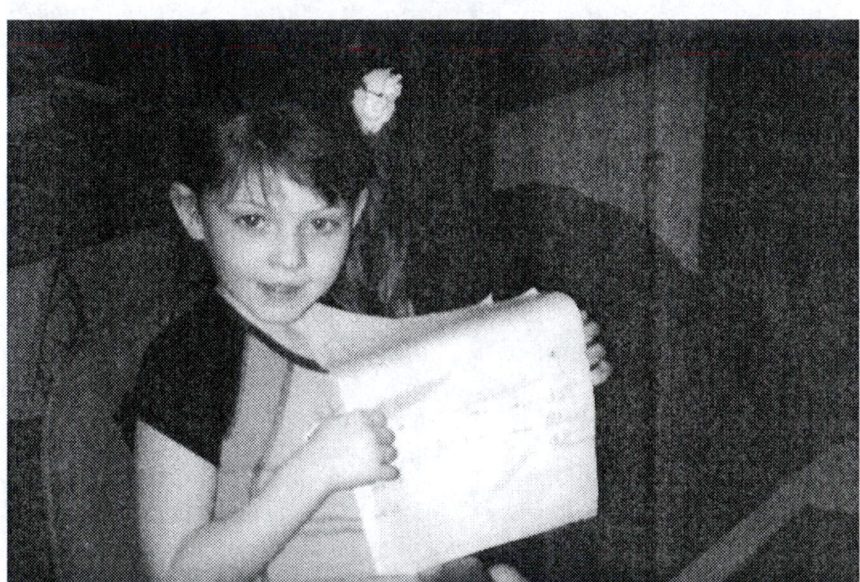

experiences—in journals. As stated previously, expressive writing helps students become comfortable with writing and facilitates the formation of positive experiences with writing.

Using Personal Journals in Fifth Grade

Similar to many teachers, Elaine Bortz finds it important to begin the school year with personal journals so that her students become comfortable with her and with writing. When she first introduces journals to her students, she explains, "Today we are going to write in our personal journals. You may choose your own topic for writing in your journal. It's your choice." Her students' interest is usually piqued at this moment, because they like having a choice when they write.

Using Brainstorming to Generate Ideas for Writing in Journals. To help her students uncover their ideas for writing before they begin, she asks her students to brainstorm what they'd like to write about. Matt says he will write about football or basketball, while A'Jada comments that she will write about her family. Bryant shares that he will write about the Olympics, while Erica remarks that she will write about Black history. As students share their ideas, Elaine records the ideas on chart paper for all to see. Additional ideas that emerge from the brainstorming session include pets, animals, the park, friends, games, movies, television shows, or science. Elaine reminds her students that they can choose a topic from this list or come up with their own idea for their topic, reminding them that this is their choice to make.

After brainstorming, Elaine talks to her students about recording their ideas. First, she emphasizes that personal journals are a place for us to record our ideas—a place where we can thrive in our own thoughts and dreams. At this point, she reminds her students to just record the ideas quickly and not worry about grammar and spelling. She explains that looking the word up in a dictionary, or asking for the spelling of the word, may cause us to forget our ideas and thoughts. If we want to use a word and are not sure of the spelling, she explains, we can use temporary spelling. Then she notes that if they want to publish what they have written, they will use the writing process to help them revise and edit the piece.

In this way, Elaine confronts the fears and anxieties her students might have about writing. She lets her class know that the conventions of writing are secondary in their journals. Beginning each school year this way enables Elaine to reinforce these points right away. She wants her students to take risks with their writing and to feel comfortable expressing their ideas with minimal concerns about the conventions of writing.

Helping her students understand that conveying the message is the primary goal is especially important for struggling writers and for students who come from culturally and linguistically diverse backgrounds. Letting them know that she will not use the red pen with their journals allows them to have positive experiences with writing. Elaine knows that all her students will have daily opportunities to practice writing; and practice will gradually help them learn more about the conventions of writing. Through minilessons, lessons focused on their ongoing needs, she can also model how we express language in conventional ways.

Before students begin writing in their journals, Elaine has everyone share their topic and what they plan to say with a partner for a few minutes. She realizes that writers frequently need to talk about the content—what they are going to say—before writing; this conversation often provides an additional impetus for writing (NCTE, 2004). After having time to rehearse their ideas with a partner, students begin writing.

Creating a Supportive Environment for Journaling. Similar to Jackie Sperling, Elaine circulates among her students while they are writing. Sometimes she comments:

- "What a good topic to write about! I enjoy watching football."
- "I like how you began your piece—'Shopping is fun because you can buy anything you want.'"
- "What an interesting word to use here—*pounce.* The word shows me just how the cat moves when it's hungry."

These comments help her students feel comfortable with their writing. They also affirm that Elaine is looking at the ideas, not the spellings of words.

If someone is still having trouble coming up with a topic, Elaine stops by to brainstorm some more possible topics with the writer. If another is having trouble thinking of what to say, Elaine asks them questions like

- "What happened next?"
- "How did you feel?"
- "What is your favorite part so far?"

These questions, which deal with the message of the writing, validate students' writing. They also give ideas for continuing the thought pattern of the writing.

After students have been writing for about 7 minutes, Elaine usually asks if anyone would like to share his or her writing with the class. Sometimes she invites someone who has a good beginning or an interesting use of describing words to share his or her writing first.

Having students share their writing with their peers provides more opportunities for positive feedback related to their writing. As Elaine listens to them share their writing, she always gives them specific feedback about their writing. She might comment about the choice of topic, word choice, interesting leads, or good examples or details that show readers what's happening. These comments show students what good writers do and what works in their writing piece (Graves, 2004). After three or four students have shared their writing, everyone begins writing again.

Promoting Writing through Ongoing Sharing Experiences. After her students have written for 15 or 20 minutes, Elaine then allows them to share their pieces with partners. Each partner reads his or her piece while the partner listens. After the author finishes sharing, the partner tells the author one or two things he or she likes about the piece. Then the partner, in turn, shares his or her piece. Next Elaine encourages a few students to share their writing with the whole class. Again, Elaine provides each volunteer specific feedback about his or her writing.

The following entries show the variety of topics her students choose to write about.

You know how people say a dog is a man's best friend. Well how about a dog is a kid's best friend. When I was 9 I had a pitbull named Blaze. Me and Blaze would all ways chase people and play. When I would feed Blaze he would all ways push me down and jack me for food. Blazes faviort [favorite] meal was chicken bones a dog food. Blaze would all ways have my back and I would always have his back. So rember [remember] a dog can be any bobidys [anybody's] best friend.

Christian, grade 5

Electronics are very powerful. If you are wet do not touch anything electronics because you will get shocked. You can probly die. If you got hit by a hericane [hurricane] and the cords nock down don't touch them! When you turn on a light you never leave it on unless it's battery powered. Or you will have a high electric bill. Never, ever flick a switch on and off—a whole bounch [bunch] of times. You will blow a fuse.

Michael, grade 5

Black history means a lot to me. Like what my great untis done for me. Like Harrit tubman done she freed the black slaves. now Put yourshelf in their shatawation [situation] it would be hard. Now liten to what some people went throw. . . . My teacher told us a story about a black woman who was try to get away she had a baby the baby would cry she held it to her chest and when thay go across the border her baby died. Now put yourshelf in the shitwaytion [situation]. What would you do? Think of what they went throw. Think of what I told you even thow I am a 11 year old child I still understand.

Erica, grade 5
(Diamond & Moore, 1995, p. 147)

Fostering a Community of Learners through Personal Writing. As one can see from these examples, these students are learning about their lives, their interests, their past history, and their cultures as they write in their journals. New opportunities for cultural understanding and sensitivity to cultures and languages naturally emerge in class through their writing. Specifically, Piazza (2003, p. 109) states, "when students are invited to freely express feelings, concerns, thoughts, and observations, a tapestry of diverse abilities and backgrounds emerge among the members of the class." She further adds that an interdependent relationship forms between the individual and the social group, which becomes "the driving force behind personal writing, expressive communication centered on student likes, dislikes and experiences."

Not only does Elaine foster the driving force, she also creates a caring environment for writing, a community of learners. Gradually, she sees her students' voices emerge and their messages flow. Through daily writing, she observes that her students' temporary spelling advances to new stages. The conventions of writing also evolve when students carry some of their writing through all stages of writing, including revising and editing. As shown earlier, Vangchai, a member of Elaine's class, became motivated to publish his writing due to his supportive environment.

Specific Ways to Foster Writing Development with Culturally and Linguistically Diverse Learners

As the numbers of children from linguistically diverse backgrounds continue to escalate (Diamond & Moore, 1995; Jalango, 2003; Thomas & Collier, 1997), teachers face the challenge of how to help these students move from their first language to English. The essential starting point is respecting and validating the languages and cultures of all students (Diamond & Moore, 1995). Language and its symbols can be spoken, written, typed, or signed in many ways. We must affirm all these forms of language (Jalango, 2003; NCTE, 2004). We must also build respect and a sense of community among all the members of our class; everyone's cultural heritage and language has to be valued and respected.

One concrete way to communicate this respect is to celebrate the differing forms of language that appear in our classrooms. For example, on her first days in a U.S. school, Alana wrote her journal entries in Greek. After she completed her journal entry, her teacher, Sandy Whitcomb, asked her to share her writing with the class. While Alana read her journal in Greek, Sandy's students began to learn about Greek, its sounds, its intonations, and its prosody. Their natural enthusiasm and interest in her language encouraged her to continue writing. See Figure 3.5 for one of Alana's journal entries. The translation into English is given in the following paragraph. As she began to learn English, her journals included a combination of English and Greek. Then, toward the end of the year, she began to write all of her journal entries in English. Her teacher's and peers' validation and respect for her language gave her the energy to make this transition.

My name is Alana. I go to school. I have a lot of friends. I like to play games. Every summer I go to Greece. I have a lot friends there too. Every day I go swimming. Grandma has a small house close to the sea that way I swim all the time. My Grandma she buys me everything. Every night we go out and eat souvlakia. I like them very much. The thing I don't like is that you have to fall asleep every afternoon. That is what everyone does there.

Similarly, Zen, age 5, writes in both English and Chinese during journal time. After recording a message in English, he uses his journal to write his numbers in Chinese (see Figure 3.6). His kindergarten teacher, Jodie Marsh, celebrates his ability to write in two languages in his journal.

Just as we show interest in multilingual students' language, we need to show interest and respect in students' cultural traditions and heritage. After Abdul wrote about Ramadan in his journal, his teacher, Meghan Keith, showed her interest in his cultural traditions by helping him publish the story in a book for him to share with the class. Similarly, when Niki wrote about Nourooz, the most important holiday in Iran, she and her mother typed up the journal entry into a book for her to share with the class. As Niki shared her book, her peers learned more about her cultural traditions and heritage. This genuine interest in her book validated her cultural heritage and motivated her to write more about her cultural traditions. Figure 3.7 (p. 54) shows a page from her book.

Publishing Students' Personal Journal Entries

Whether we call them journals, day books, lifebooks, or notebooks, Piazza (2003) emphasizes that journals are places for us to rehearse our writing. Calkins (1994) further adds that they are seedbeds out of which rough drafts grow; they are a place for bits of life.

Periodically, Susan O'Donnell, a second grade teacher, has her students go through their journals to find something they might want to publish. With some guidance, her students select their pieces for publication. After taking these drafts through the writing process, students then publish their writing. With the help of parents, children then type the pieces on the computer. Depending on the author, some of the drafts become books. For example, Okirah's draft became a diary about her and her life. Figure 3.8 shows how she illustrated the pages of her diary.

Figure 3.5

Example of a Journal Entry Written in Greek by Alana

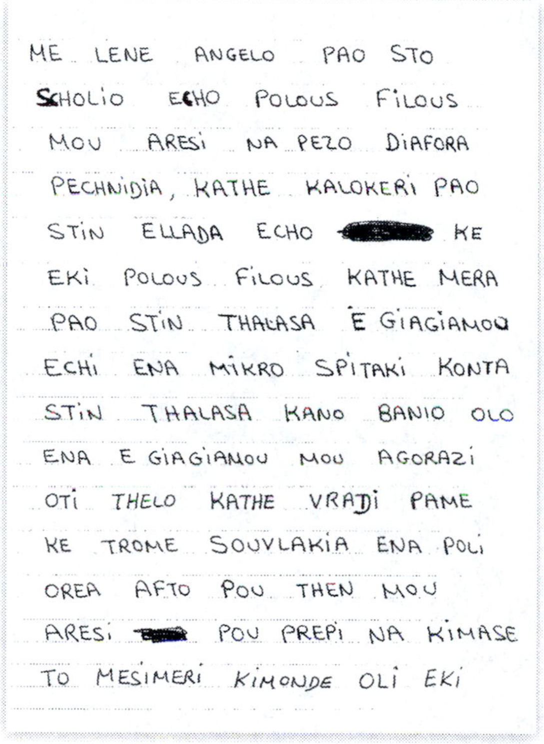

ME LENE ANGELO PAO STO
SCHOLIO ECHO POLOUS FILOUS
MOU ARESI NA PEZO DIAFORA
PECHNIDIA, KATHE KALOKERI PAO
STIN ELLADA ECHO [illegible] KE
EKI POLOUS FILOUS KATHE MERA
PAO STIN THALASA E GIAGIAMOU
ECHI ENA MIKRO SPITAKI KONTA
STIN THALASA KANO BANIO OLO
ENA E GIAGIAMOU MOU AGORAZI
OTI THELO KATHE VRADI PAME
KE TROME SOUVLAKIA ENA POLI
OREA AFTO POU THEN MOU
ARESI [illegible] POU PREPI NA KIMASE
TO MESIMERI KIMONDE OLI EKI

Figure 3.6

Example of a Journal Entry Written by Zen

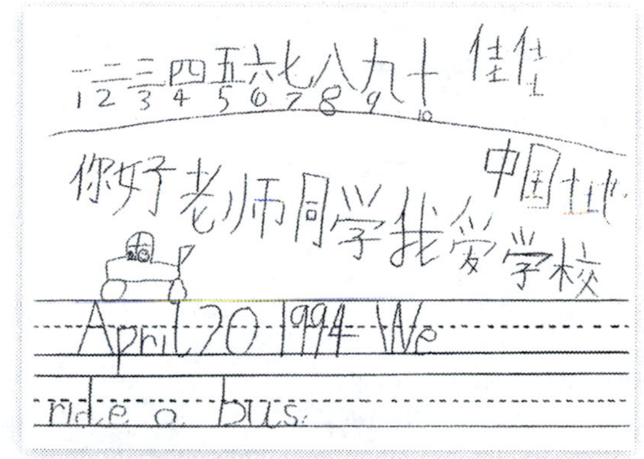

Alternative Ways to Use Journals in the Elementary Grades

As seen through the various scenarios presented, personal journals offer opportunities for students' strength and creativity to evolve within a community of learners. Certainly students of all ages thrive in an environment that celebrates the uniqueness of each child.

However, if we use personal journals day after day, students' enthusiasm and interest may dwindle. Periodically, we need to take a break and use journals in other ways and in different content areas. When students discover that journals and notebooks serve many functions, they begin to see a purpose and need for journals in their daily lives. At the same time, they learn that journals are a safe place to explore writing because the journals are informal and unstructured.

Dialogue Journals as a Way to Guide the Development of Writing

Candy Reaume, a first grade teacher who uses personal journals, periodically responds to her students' journal entries in the form of a dialogue. Candy uses dialogue journals—a two-way communication between a teacher and student or a student and peer—to ask her students questions, share additional information about a topic, or to add information about her own personal experiences. Responding to students' journal entries allows

(a)
I would like to tell you about Nourooz which is the most important holiday of my country Iran.
Nourooz means "New Day" and it starts on the first day of spring. It is the start of the awakening of nature.

Figure 3.7

Niki Writes about Iran's National Holidays

(a) Niki writes about her special holiday, Nourooz. (b) Niki continues to share more information about her special holidays.

(b)
The last Wednesday of the year is called Chahar Shanbeh Suri. On this night people light fires outside and jump over them. This is especially fun for the children.
Then the children put long sheets on their heads and go door to door in their neighborhoods to collect candy. It is almost like Halloween.

Candy to model effective conventions of language. Through her responses, her young writers begin to learn what a sentence looks like, how to use questions marks when we ask questions, how to spell a word, or how to use capitals and ending marks. Even though she does not criticize their written responses, their misspellings, or their missing capitals and periods, her first graders begin to imitate her model of spelling, punctuation, and capitalization in future journal entries. Through her model, they begin to learn the conventions of language.

Candy further reports that her students are more motivated to write when she responds to their writing. Within a short time, she observed that the entries became longer and more elaborate because children had an audience for their writing. Consistent with Piazza (2003), she notices that the journals help her learn more about her students' lives and experiences. At the same time, the dialogue journals help her observe their growth and development in their writing over time. Figure 3.9 displays an example of a child's journal entry with her response.

Similarly, Marc Flynn, a special education teacher, likes to keep his own dialogue journal so he can write with his students for a few minutes each day. In addition, one student responds to his journal entry each day of class. An example of his journal entry (Diamond & Moore, 1995, p. 149) with the accompanying student response is on page 56.

Figure 3.8

Okirah Illustrates Her Diary Entry, Which Will Be Published as a Book

On the weekend, I will go to my friends house and play. We will play like we are at a buffet with my food seat. We will go to Walmart, Dollartree, and Best Buy on our bikes. Oh, we will go to a play ground. Oh and we will pack two apples, three boxes of gum, four boxes of juice and one big bottle of water. Then we will go back to her house and take a nap but we won't stop there. Then we will eat again there. Then we will eat again then we will go to bed.

Figure 3.9

Example of How Candy Responds to AnneMarie's Dialogue Journal

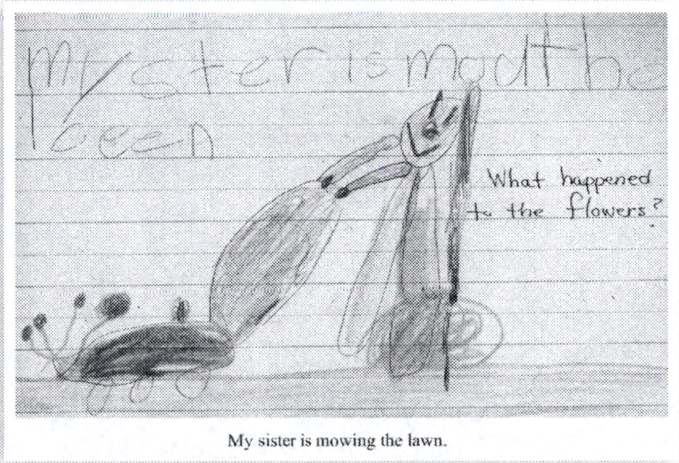

My sister is mowing the lawn.

9/17/92
I am really excited today. I am going bowling tonight. I bowl every Thursday night with my friends. It's really the only night that I really get to see my friends.

9/17/92
It sounds like fun to go bowling. So who are your friends? Hope you have a good time.

One can see that Marc's students are reflecting his model of responding to their writing. They react to his ideas. They also enjoy asking him questions, just as he asks them questions about their writing.

Peregoy and Boyle (1993) report that dialogue journals are particularly effective with students from diverse linguistic backgrounds. Students acquire the conventions of book language naturally from their teachers' model, which includes elaboration and expansion of English. In fact, the format of the dialogue journal provides a genuine way to guide and assist written language development. Through questions, modeling, and elaborations, students of all ages, abilities, and backgrounds learn about the conventions of language. The spontaneous flow of interpersonal communication further makes the experience meaningful to the learner as they have an audience for their writing.

Using Computers with Focused Journal Entries

Michelle White, a teacher of a multiage class (K–1) occasionally likes to have her students use their journals to write about a specific topic. This allows her students to practice rehearsing their ideas about a topic through prewriting activities. For example, one day she has her students write about a dream they had. To help her students think of a dream, she first has them close their eyes and think about dreams they had had. Next she has them think about a favorite dream and pauses to allow them to think about this dream. To further stimulate their thinking while their eyes are closed, she asks them, "What happened first? Then what happened? What happened next? How did your dream end?" After helping them think about their dreams, she asks her children to draw pictures of their favorite dream.

Since this is their day to work in the computer lab, she has them bring their pictures to the lab and complete their journal entries on the computer. As the students begin writing on the computer, she quickly reminds them they cannot change the font style, color, or size until they finish writing about the dream. Once they finish their drafts, they can choose their favorite font style, color, and size to publish their journal entry. Having learned from experience, Michelle knows that her young learners need this restriction or they will continuously experiment and play with the fonts while drafting on the computer.

The writing samples below show how the young learners transform their dreams into a journal entry.

Once upon a time I dreamed it ws snowing and there was a fairy. It piced [picked] a flower. And it gave it to a ciled [child]. When the chilled [child] woke up she fond it and put it in a vase she like it.

Gabrielle, age 6

One nite I had a dreme ubawt [about] a little kittin and the litl kittin crold [crawled] awt [out] uv [of] my dreme a lttl noys [noise] kame frum the bed a cat wus in my bed it krld [crawled] up bimy [by my] side adremecumtroo [a dream come true].

Caitlyn, age 5

Since Michelle's students have had multiple experiences with computers, she further allows two students to do their journal entries on the computer every day in her classroom. She finds that using computers adds new excitement and interest to journal writing. Her students love to write on the computer and can hardly wait for their turn.

Using Literature Response Journals

Another way to help students gain fluency with their writing is through literature response journals, journals where students write their thoughts about and reactions to a novel they are reading. Using booklets of paper stapled together with construction paper covers, Mary Streeter encourages students to reflect on information about the story elements—setting, characters, problems, events or actions, and the resolution of the problem—in their literature response journals.

Reinforcing Information about the Story Elements in Literature Response Journals. Using the book *Search for Delicious,* by Natalie Babbit, for example, Mary has her students keep a list of each character in the story, descriptions about the character, and each character's definition of the word *delicious* as she reads the story aloud to her class. To further help her students listen more carefully to character descriptions while reading the novel aloud, she has them illustrate the characters in their journals (see Figure 3.10). As the story unfolds, the illustrations become more elaborate.

Other days, Mary asks her students to respond to a favorite part of the story, an interesting character, or a perplexing problem. In this way, the literature response journal leaves

Nyasha reads her draft and then types the words on the computer.

Figure 3.10

Jason's Illustration of "A Woldweller" from the Book *Search for Delicious*

choices for her students. When her class read *Sounder,* by William Armstrong, Casey shares her feelings about the judge's penalty for the boy's father, who had stolen some meat to feed his family, in her journal (Diamond & Moore, 1995, p. 150). She adamantly exclaims:

I think that it was a harsh decision to give him a severe penalty. I think he sould have a penalty but not a sever penalty. I don't like that Judge. He would be stipid to do that because he stole some [meat]. And if a white person would have stole the meat they would of said nothing and let him take the meat that to me is not fiar because every [body] is the same nobody is or has more athoraty than anybody.

Casey, age 10

Learning about Point of View with Literature Response Journals. When reading *The Sign of the Beaver,* by Elizabeth Speare, Mary's students learn about Native American traditions and points of view as they used their journals like a diary, pretending that they were Matt, who must try to survive on his own while his dad returns to their cabin in Maine to get his mother and baby sister. Melissa's diary entry (Diamond & Moore, 1995, p. 150) describes how Matt learns to survive through the help of his Native American friend, Attean.

Today I put the seventh notch on my last stick. My family would be back soon. Attean took me out to the woods and taught me about the sign of the beaver on the tree and that when Indians go through the woods they leave secret signs like broken twigs and rocks standing certain ways. These things wore very interesting to me

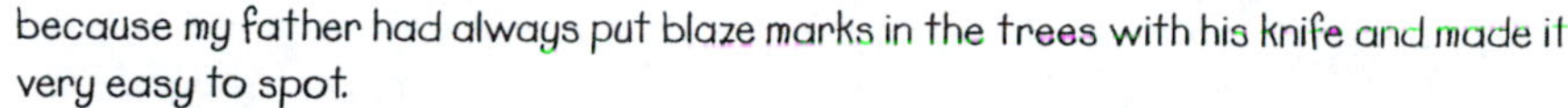
because my father had always put blaze marks in the trees with his knife and made it very easy to spot.

Melissa, age 10

In one of his diary entries (Diamond & Moore, 1995, p. 151), Jeremy describes Matt's encounter with a bear.

All of a sudden I heard a thing in the bush and I am scared to death. I want to run but I didn't I just stood their. The Bear came out and it saw me. I hit the bear with my rabbit so I would disstaced [distract] him. Attean took his bow and arrow and shot him.

Jeremy, age 10

By giving her students choices on what they write about, Mary provides more interest in the writing. She also plans time for her students to share their journal entries. According to Mary, sharing gives her students time to discuss the book and the story parts in more depth. As emphasized earlier, sharing also provides opportunities for students to receive positive responses and feedback on their writing. Importantly, no one knows who misspelled a word or who forgot a period when they share their journal entries. Responses and reactions are about the ideas, thoughts, and feelings conveyed through their writing.

Reflecting about Stories through Reader Response Reactions. Mary Manchester uses the literature response journal in a different way. She calls her format "reader response reaction," a format that stimulates more focused reflections about a story. After reading an exciting part of the story *Sadako and the Thousand Paper Cranes* by Eleanor Coerr, for example, Mary asks her students to record their thoughts and feelings about this incident in their journals. Places where she stops for students to record their thoughts or feelings include (1) when Sadako found out that she had leukemia; (2) when Chizuko make Sadako a golden crane, reminding her of the traditional story about the crane that grants one's wish; (3) after she learned that her friend, Kenji, died; and (4) after her visit home with her parents. Examples of students' entries (Diamond & Moore, 1995, p. 151) follow:

I would feel very sad and down that I didn't teel anyone that I was feel week and dizzy. And now I found out I cought a disease from the atom bomb and for ten years and never knew about it. I would feel very poorly how would you feel if you had leukemia for ten years and just found out and you mit die? And I would feel very lonely and miserable just like she is and if I wanted to do something before I dies I would put something throo the window and climb down and go hang some cranes on the beig statgue that is just like me and build the best statgue of all call the golden grane.

Daniel, age 9

But I gust wont her to live. I fell so sad because she is kind of a pen-pal to me. I also feel she is kind of like a siether [sister]. But she died. I think it is very importo to have dreams because if you didn't have dreams you wod [would] have no hope that you

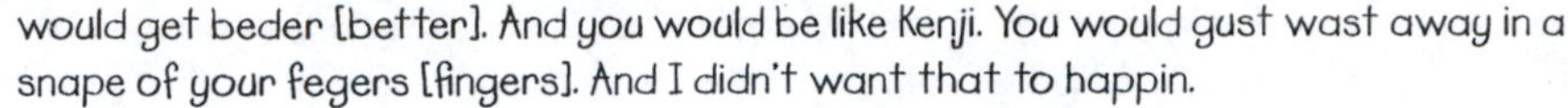
would get beder [better]. And you would be like Kenji. You would gust wast away in a snape of your fegers [fingers]. And I didn't want that to happin.

Katie, age 9

Using Electronic Dialogues with Journals

Another exciting way to use journals is through computer communications or email. By teaming fifth graders with undergraduate students who were taking a reading course called Teaching Reading in the Elementary School, Lynne Raglin provided opportunities for her students to dialogue about the book *The Best Christmas Pageant Ever,* by Barbara Robinson, with college students. After each fifth grader and his or her college partner introduced themselves, they began a general discussion of *The Best Christmas Pageant Ever,* exchanging their reactions and feelings about the story with one another. Tony independently began to make a comparison (Moore, 1991) between the book *Superfudge,* by Judy Blume, and *The Best Christmas Pageant Ever:*

My teacher is reading a new book called the Best Christmas Pageant Ever. The book is about a play that some children put on around Christmas. I especially like the Herdmann family and all the boys who smoked cigars. I like the book because it reminds me of Fudge and Daniel and Jimmy Fargo and Alex because ther [they're] all bad. All the characters talked back. I wish I lived in Connitcut because it gots lots of dogs.

Chapter 8 includes more details about electronic dialogues and additional samples of dialogue exchanges.

Using Simulated Journals with the Social Studies Curriculum

Charlotte Andrews, a fifth grade teacher, enjoys using simulated journals with her students during her social studies curriculum. When reading biographies or studying a historical period, she encourages her students to assume the role of a historical character. For example, while reading Jean Fritz's *Where Do You Think You're Going Christopher Columbus?* she has them assume the role of Christopher Columbus through a series of simulated journal entries. By writing these simulated entries, her students gain new insights into the lives of the crew and the Native Americans during this time period. As they weave information about Columbus with historical events, arranged in chronological order, her students begin to critically view this historical period. The simulated experience helps many students even change their viewpoints about the explorers and their relationships with the Native Americans.

Similarly, Mary Streeter has her students assume the role of a pilgrim child aboard the *Mayflower.* Students choose their pilgrim name from the list of the pilgrim children on the *Mayflower.* These are examples of students' journal entries:

September 5, 1620—My family is packing whatever they can in a small chest. I'm nervous about going over the great ocean because we might be attacked by a sea monster or something. I am sad because I am going to miss my friends and grand parents. But this way we will be able to worship God as we like.

John Cook

October 10, 1620—I am sick of the rocking boat. Nobody can go up on the decks because of the storms. The water is spoiling and we have to drink beer. It's crowded more than ever. We haven't taken a bath in a long time. I'm getting sick of the food and there's bugs everywhere. It's a treat when we get to have warm soup.

John Cooke

Michaele Rae likewise uses simulated journals while studying about the Civil War and slavery. As students write in their simulated journals, they intertwine information from their social studies text, picture books, and videos with their journal entries. In this way, the simulated journals help them gain multiple perspectives from multiple sources in their social studies curriculum. Writing also helps students remember and retain facts about history (Langer & Applebee, 1987; Moore-Hart, Ligget, & Daisey, 2004). Nick's journal entry shows how he learned to integrate information from the social studies text and picture books with his writing.

Day 4

One day I was looking out the window and I saw the confadarates break into our nebgor's [neighbor's] house and take food and clothes. I was very scared. Fifteen days ago a runaway slave was found at our nebgor's cellar and they were arrested and went to jail. I hope that the confaderates don't break in our house.

Nick, age 8

Using Science Journals to Reinforce Science Concepts

Theresa Cyrnavich, a fourth grade teacher, believes that science journals are a great way to help her students increase their observation skills. When studying food chains and webs, Theresa has her students keep a science journal. Some students create pictures of the food chain in their logs. Others write about the activities they do in class during science time. Still others create fictional stories that illustrate how the food chain works. Theresa finds that giving students choices when they write in their science journals adds motivation to writing.

teaching TIP 3.4

Using journals in the content areas is a way to reinforce concepts students are learning. Teachers also gain insight into students' understanding of the concepts being taught.

While sharing their journal entries, everyone benefits as this provides a review of the information they are learning. The journal entries displayed below show her students' deep understanding of complex science concepts, illustrating the importance of writing to learn (Glenn & Muth, 1994; Moore-Hart et al., 2004; Richardson & Morgan, 1994).

I learned that salt can damage animals and plants. I also learned that when you put a potatoe in saltwater it can change. Another fact I learned is that diffusion can change the size of something. However, the most important thing I learned is that salt can be damgaeing to plants and animals.

Kylie

The grass is a producer. the grasshopper is a consumer and the grasshopper gets eaten by the mole and the mole is a consumer. The mole gets eaten by the snake the snake is eaten by the hawk. And it go back to the decomposers. Thet is the Food Chain about Animals.

Kari

Using Math Journals to Reinforce Math Concepts

Bonnie Lin, a fourth grade teacher, likes to use math journals with her fourth graders. She finds that the math journals help her students think about the math concepts in more depth. As they write about what they learned during math class, she also finds that the journals become a record of their acquired knowledge. Sometimes her students like to go back to reread some of the journal entries. Rereading the journal entries provides students a quick review of concepts they are learning over time. In the journal entry below, Cedric explains what he learned about calculators.

Today and yesterday we worked with calculators. You had to press the buttons it says on the sheet. Today my partner was Robbie. We got all the problems right! Today I learned that I shouldn't pay attention to whatever people say like "Your's is diffent than mine so your's is wrong." It turned out that [both] our's were right.

Rachel's journal entry, displayed in Figure 3.11, shows what she knows about calculators.

Closing Thoughts

Helping students overcome their reluctance to write begins with the creation of a classroom environment that is supportive and nurturing. Through teachers' modeling, the classroom soon transforms into a community of learners who validate and affirm one another's writing. Calkins (1994) describes the classroom as a place where students write about what is alive, vital, and real for them. She adds that other writers in the room listen, extend, guide, laugh, cry, and marvel when writers share their writing. Consistent with Piazza (2003), these person-to-person interactions change the dynamics of our classrooms.

Writing also takes practice in order for students to gain fluency and control over the conventions of writing. Whatever one calls journals—lifebooks, personal journals, day books, or notebooks—they are great ways for students to gain control over their writing. The journal entries provide further insight into what our students know about writing—how to express their ideas, how to spell words, or how to apply grammar and mechanics with their writing. By keeping track of students' writing over time, we can see their growth in writing as well as what areas need additional focus through minilessons.

Importantly, students can easily become bored with doing the same thing day in and day out. Using dialogue journals, literature response journals, reading response journals, electronic dialogues, simulated journals, or science journals adds variety to our writing curriculum. The differing formats simultaneously integrate writing across the curriculum and provide more opportunities for students to practice writing. While writing in these alterna-

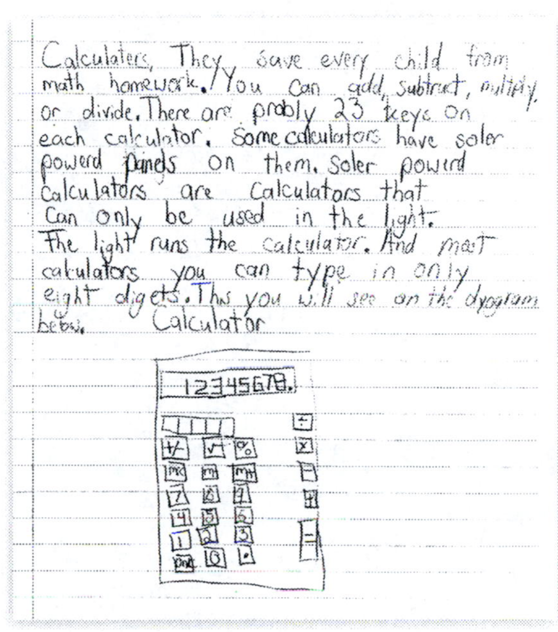

Calculaters, They save every child from math homework. You can add, subtract, multiply, or divide. There are probly 23 keys on each calculator. Some calculators have soler powerd panels on them. Soler powerd calculators are calculators that can only be used in the light. The light runs the calculator. And most calulators you can type in only eight digets. This you will see on the dyogram below. Calculator

12345678.

Figure 3.11

Rachel Shows What She Has Learned about Calculators in Her Math Journal

tive formats, students begin to apply higher level thinking and problem-solving skills while demonstrating their knowledge and understanding of concepts.

Just as reading needs to be taught daily, writing needs to be taught on a daily basis (NCTE, 2004). As teachers, we need to be well versed in writing theory and practice; we need to be knowledgeable of effective practices that support the developing writer and understand how to most effectively deliver this instruction. Teaching writing well is a lifetime process. Giving students time to learn about writing and opportunities to practice writing helps writing grow and develop.

Teachers' Questions

1. My students don't seem to enjoy writing. What should I do?

When I visit classrooms, teachers often say the same thing. The first thing I ask them is, "Do your students choose their topics for writing or do you use prompts?" I find that many teachers give their students prompts because they feel that their students don't know what to write about. Students, however, seem to enjoy writing more when they can select their own topics for writing. What we may need to do is brainstorm possible ideas for writing topics. Once we do this, students eagerly select their own topics. This gives them ownership.

If teachers give students a chance to select their own topics for writing, the next question I ask them is, "Do you give your students an opportunity to share their writing daily?" Many teachers explain that they just don't have time to write and share daily. Leaving time for at least three to four students to share their writing is crucial. Sharing is motivational, especially when students hear praise about their writing. Sometimes I "steal" additional time for sharing just before lunch, just after lunch, or just before we go home. Students look forward to these sharing sessions, so I have to be sure to allow time for different people to share; everyone needs to have a turn. I have also found that students also enjoy sharing in pairs or in small groups. This way everyone gets a turn to share.

If teachers give students a chance to select their own topics and an opportunity to share daily, the next question I ask them is, "Do you vary how you have students write?" I find that students get tired of writing personal journals every single day. If I rotate how I use journals, I find I am able to maintain their interest. Usually, I switch from personal journals to literature journals, science journals, simulated journals, dialogue journals, or math journals monthly. I find that changing how I use journals sparks renewed interest in writing. At the same time, students continue to have opportunities to practice writing and gain fluency in their writing. They also begin to explore new topics for writing. When I rotate back to personal journals, many students begin to write about what they do in various subject areas; others discover new interests or hobbies to write about.

2. My first graders keep writing about the same topic day after day. What should I do?

When young writers first begin writing, they often write about the same topic day after day, especially in kindergarten and first grade. They have so many things to learn and think about when they write: how to form the letters, how to spell the words, how to use beginning sounds and ending sounds, how to form sentences, how to use the conventions of writing like capitals and periods. For this reason, they write about topics that are very similar to them, topics that are part of their life and experiences. Once they become more comfortable with the formation of letters and temporary spelling, they will begin to explore new topics for writing.

We can support young writers' early attempts to write by taping an alphabet strip to their desk. This helps them remember how to form the letters and think about which letters they hear at the beginnings and endings of words. We can also reinforce the symbols and sounds during phonics and reading. Pointing out the connections between reading and writing further reinforces these concepts and strengthens understanding of the symbol–sound relationship.

One way to encourage them to explore new topics for writing is by keeping journals for math, science, or social studies later in the year. Periodically brainstorming possible topics for writing may also encourage them to write about new topics. If they still continue to write about the same topic, they may not feel safe writing yet.

3. Should I use personal journals with my students every day, all year long?

As mentioned above, students become bored if we do the same thing day after day. Integrating journaling with the content areas adds variety to the writing curriculum. This is also a way to save time. When we integrate two subject areas, we gain time for writing in our busy schedules.

4. I don't have time for writing in my curriculum. I barely have time to cover reading, math, science, and social studies each day.

Having time to teach all the subject areas in today's crowded schedule is overwhelming to us all. One way to gain time in our busy schedules is by looking at ways to combine subject areas, using thematic teaching (see Chapter 6).

In addition, we tend to find time to teach the subjects we value and enjoy. If we are not comfortable with a subject area, we often fail to find time to teach it. Some teachers take courses in this subject area at the university so they can become more comfortable with the material. Others try to attend workshops or inservices related to the subject area; still others enlist the help of peer teachers.

If we want our students to improve their writing, we must provide them instruction in writing, as well as reading. Students need to learn how to write, and they need an opportunity to practice writing. This will only happen if we teach writing daily. If you find you are not comfortable with writing, be sure to consider taking additional classes in the teaching of writing and attending workshops or inservices related to the teaching of writing.

5. My students don't know what to write about. Should I use prompts instead of letting them choose their topics?

Students need to learn strategies to help them select their topics for writing. As mentioned earlier, periodically we need to brainstorm possible topics for writing as a class. Posting these ideas on chart paper will help students begin to refer to the chart when they have trouble thinking of a topic for writing, especially if we display the chart in the classroom. Some teachers also set aside one or two pages in the journals for students to record their ideas for writing topics. Once students become familiar with the writing process, they also begin to independently use prewriting webs, lists, or charts to discover their writing topics.

Using prompts for writing takes away from students' ownership of their writing. They begin to write just what they know or what they think their teacher wants them to write. If we feel that some of our students need additional assistance in selecting their topics, we can brainstorm with them individually or we can post two or three prompts on the board for them to choose. By giving them choices, we preserve their ownership of the writing.

6. My students often write one or two sentences in their journal. How can I help them expand their journal writing?

Whenever I visit classrooms I especially find this happening in kindergarten and first grade classrooms. We need to maintain high expectations for all our students, regardless of their age or ability.

Once students become comfortable writing and using their temporary spelling to draft their ideas, we can help students expand their writing by asking them questions. As I circulate, I usually find something positive to say about their writing, and then I pose a question. For example, if a student writes, "I have five people in my family," I may say, "You have *five* people in your family! What are their names?" This question shows my interest in his or her writing and my desire to learn more about his or her family. Once the student gives me an answer, I help him or her see where they can add this information on their paper. Before leaving I share, "I'll come back in a few minutes to see how you're doing." When I return to the student's desk, I celebrate his or her writing. Depending on the grade level, I may even share how she or he added more sentences, filling up the page. This usually motivates others to write more.

Children's Literature

Armstrong, W. (1969). *Sounder.* New York: Harper & Row.

Babbitt, N. (1969). *Search for delicious.* Toronto: Farrar, Straus, & Giroux.

Blume, J. (1981). *Superfudge.* New York: Dell.

Coerr, E. (1977). *Sadako and the thousand paper cranes.* New York: Dell.

Fritz, J. (1980). *Where are you going, Christopher Columbus?* New York: Coward-McCann.

Robinson, B. (1988). *The best Christmas pageant ever.* New York: Harper Collins.

Speare, E. (1983). *The sign of the beaver.* New York: Dell.

References

Calkins, L. (1994). *The art of teaching writing.* Portsmouth, NH: Heinemann.

Chapman, M. (1996). The development of phonemic awareness in young children: Some insights from a case study of a first-grade writer. *Young Children, 51,* 31–37.

Clark, R. (1995). *Free to write.* Portsmouth, NH: Heinemann.

Cummins, J. (1986). Empowering minority students: A framework for intervention. *Harvard Educational Review, 56,* 18–36.

Diamond, B., & Moore, M. (1995). *Multicultural literacy: Mirroring the reality of the classroom.* New York: Longman.

Glenn, S., & Muth, K. (1994). Reading and writing to learn science: Achieving scientific literacy. *Journal of Research in Science Teaching, 31,* 1057–1073.

Goodman, K. (2005). Making sense of written language: A lifelong journey. *Journal of Literacy Research, 37,* 1–24.

Goodman, K., & Smith, F. (1987). *Language and thinking in school: A whole-language curriculum.* New York: R. C. Owen.

Graves, D. (1983). *Writing: Teachers and children at work.* Portsmouth, NH: Heinemann.

Graves, D. (1994). *A fresh look at writing.* Portsmouth, NH: Heinemann.

Graves, D. (2004). What I've learned from teachers of writing. *Language Arts, 82,* 88–94.

Griffith, P., Klesius, J., & Kromrey, J. (1992). The effect of phonemic awareness on the literacy development of first-grade children in a traditional or a whole language classroom. *Journal of Research in Childhood Education, 6,* 85–92.

Jalongo, M. (2003). *Early childhood language arts* (2nd ed.). Boston: Allyn & Bacon.

Langer, J., & Applebee, A. (1987). *How writing shapes thinking: A study of teaching and learning* (NCTE Research Report No. 22). Urbana, IL: National Council of Teachers of English.

Moore, M. (1991). Electronic dialoguing; An avenue to literacy. *The Reading Teacher, 45,* 280–287.

Moore-Hart, M., Liggit, P., & Daisey, P. (2004). Making the science literacy connection: After-school science clubs. *Childhood Education, 80,* 180–186.

NCTE. (2004). NCTE beliefs about the teaching of writing. [Online]. Available at www.ncte.org/about/over/positions/category/write/118876.htm [June 13, 2005].

Peregoy, S., & Boyle, O. (1993). *Reading, writing, and learning in ESL.* New York: Longman.

Piazza, C. (2003). *Journeys: The teaching of writing in elementary classrooms.* Upper Saddle River, NJ: Merrill Prentice Hall.

Reyhner, J., & Garcia, R. (1989). Helping minorities read better: Problems and promises. *Reading Research and Instruction, 28,* 84–91.

Richardson, J., & Morgan, R. (1994). *Reading to learn in the content areas.* Belmont, CA: Wadsworth.

Thomas, W. P., & Collier, V. T. (1997). *School effectiveness for language minority students.* Washington, DC: National Clearinghouse for Bilingual Education.

Tompkins, G. (2004). *Teaching writing: Balancing process and product.* New York: Macmillan College Publishing.

chapter FOUR

Real-Life Experiences in Writing

My trip to Florida was nice. I had a nice trip on the plane. We went to the Red Barn. It was like a shopping mall. My Aunt Amy is going to have a baby. She's due in a couple of weeks. We got to go in a swimming pool. The weather was nice and warm, the weather here was 10 degrees. While I was there I got to color, we read the Brown Bear book. I had a good time with my Grandma! I'm glad to be back to school to see my teacher. I missed her while I was gone. I wrote a letter to my Grandma this weekend! I am glad to see my dad. I really miss him a lot. My Grandmother was very happy to see me also.

Time to go,

Kim

Kim, a 9-year-old Physically and Otherwise Health Impaired (POHI) student, is learning that writing evolves from her experiences. Although Kim is not able to record her ideas with pencil and paper due to her physical limitations, she can dictate her message to one of her fifth grade peers, Alicia. After Alicia records Kim's words, Kim can type her journal entry on the computer by herself, using one or two fingers.

This year Kim and her POHI peers were placed in an inclusion classroom, a room where a fifth grade teacher, Mary Streeter, and a POHI teacher, Kathy Micallef, combined their classes, using a teaming approach (see Chapter 9). Immersed in this inclusion classroom, Kim and her POHI peers wrote with the fifth graders during Writing Workshop. Gradually the classroom became a community of learners who began to enjoy writing as they shared their writing and responded to one another's writing. Following the model of the fifth graders, Kim and her POHI peers learned to write about their own lives and experiences. This collaborative learning opportunity allowed the fifth graders and their POHI peers to discover that their lives and experiences bring interesting information to their writing pieces. Through the use of concrete details, observation and description, and narrative lines, they learned to craft and shape their writing.

Managing Writing Workshop in an Inclusion Classroom

Gathering Time for Writing

Consistent with leaders in the field of writing (Atwell, 1987, 2003; Calkins, 1983, 1994; Clark, 1995; Graves, 1983, 1994; Routman, 1994, 2005), Mary and Kathy set aside *predictable time* for Writing Workshop each day. If their students are to become deeply invested in their writing, Mary and Kathy realize they need to commit at least an hour to Writing Workshop daily. By providing the luxury of time, they allow their students' writing ideas to grow and gather momentum. The investment of time further provides opportunities for students to draft, revise, edit, and share their ideas in partnership with their peers and their teachers who offer genuine, interested responses to their writing. This investment also gives students opportunities to just practice writing and gain fluency in their writing. Many times students just write drafts, without taking their writing through the whole process. Kathy and Mary realize that students do not need to publish everything they write.

Conducting Minilessons

Similar to many teachers, Mary and Kathy usually conduct minilessons, which last approximately 15 minutes, at the beginning of Writing Workshop. They structure these lessons to introduce a strategy, demonstrate authors' crafts, or illustrate techniques all writers need to use with their writing. Sometimes they conduct minilessons for the whole group; sometimes they provide minilessons for small groups of students who have similar needs or interests.

Although the minilessons vary in the amount of teacher support and student independence, many of the minilessons include teacher modeling or demonstrations. For example, one day they may use the write-aloud strategy as they model their thinking process and verbalize how to develop a lead for a writing piece on the overhead transparency; another day they may demonstrate how to use graphic organizers to web their ideas for writing; other days they may show a small group how to edit one's writing for commas, using a student's writing piece as an example. On other occasions, Mary and Kathy may work with a small group, creating a group story together, using the interactive writing strategy (teachers and students write together, sharing the pen). Sometimes the minilessons include guided writing strategies where the students create their own writing pieces through teacher prompts and guides. The format for these minilessons, which vary according to the students' needs, abilities, or development, enables students to move from dependence on the teacher to independent writing (Cooper & Kiger, 2003; Higgins, Miller, & Wegmann, 2007).

> ***teaching* TIP 4.1**
>
> Minilessons can be structured around any of the stages of writing. Lasting only a few minutes, the minilessons demonstrate or model a strategy that students will apply in their own writing.

Guided Writing with Students

After the minilesson, all students begin to write during guided writing. Although their students are frequently at different stages of writing, this is the "heart" of Writing Workshop; this is where students apply what they are learning about writing. As they write, Mary and Kathy—as well as their paraprofessionals—circulate among the students, conferring with them about their writing. When Mary and Kathy glance at their students' writing, they understand that the writing shows them what their students know about writing.

Due to the varied levels of ability within their class, these glances also reveal that their students require different levels of assistance and support. Through the use of miniconferences—conferences that last a minute or two—the two teachers *guide* and *nudge* individual students to new levels of writing as they circulate. They determine what to say or do during the miniconferences according to "what may be beneficial for the writer" rather than "what may improve the writing."

These miniconferences are further focused on one or two points—for example, how to select a topic for writing or how to determine the sequence of ideas. Sometimes the miniconferences are just words of specific praise about a lead that a student used or the choice of words to describe an event. Figure 4.1 provides examples of specific praise teachers can give students as they write.

To further help manage writing during this portion of Writing Workshop, Mary and Kathy arrange their classroom to be in groups of four. They organize the groups to include students of mixed abilities, as well as groups of students who can work together well, supporting one another as they read and write. This arrangement facilitates opportunities for students to help one another as they write. Sometimes students meet with their group to revise their writing. Other times they meet in twos to edit their writing. Consistent with Dyson (1997), this arrangement further fosters writing in students' social worlds by allowing them to talk and discuss one another's words and worlds.

Clustering students into groups further allows Mary and Kathy to circulate among the groups and confer with the students more easily. The arrangement also facilitates continuous assessment of their students' progress in writing.

Helping Students Shape Their Writing through Conferencing

Mary and Kathy's classroom gradually becomes like an art studio where students who have different levels of proficiency can work side by side. As students share their writing, talk about their ideas, and support one another, they help one another continue their writing and solve problems with their writing.

Just like artists, students need to learn how to shape their writing in order to express their messages. By asking open-ended questions, Mary and Kathy nudge their students to new

Figure 4.1

Examples of Specific Praise Teachers Can Give to Students

- I especially like your title because it . . .
- What a great lead! It . . .
- Your beginning makes me feel . . .
- I love the way you describe . . .
- You use such colorful words to show . . .
- Your words help me see, hear, smell, feel, taste . . .
- What an effective way to explain . . .
- I love this part–it makes me laugh . . .
- I can just imagine that happening to . . .
- I can just picture the events in my mind . . .
- Your piece makes me feel . . .
- Your sense of humor is very effective because . . .
- Your use of dialogue makes me feel like I can hear the people talking . . .
- You tell the story with drama . . .
- Your writing reminds me of . . .
- You have a way with words . . .
- What an effective ending; you captured . . .
- Your ending makes me feel . . .

Figure 4.2

Examples of Questions Teachers Can Ask to Stretch Their Students' Writing

- What part do you like best?
- What is the most important part of the piece?
- What parts do you think the reader will want to hear more about?
- Are there any confusing parts? How will you fix this?
- Do you have any missing information?
- What additional information will you add to your writing?
- Are there places where you need to be more specific? Are there places where there is too much detail?
- What are some words or phrases you like?
- Do you see some words or phrases you might want to change?
- How do you feel about your lead? Is there another way to begin your writing?
- How will you end your piece?
- How do you feel about your ending? Is there another way to end your writing?

levels of writing, helping them to communicate their ideas. During a miniconference, they often ask questions like "What will you do next?", "How can I help you?", "What's your favorite part?", or "How did you feel when that happened?" These questions help students continue writing or solve a problem in their writing (Atwell, 2003; Clark, 1995; Wolf & Wolf, 2002). Hansen (2002, p. 459) further observes that writers change when others show interest in their writing. She adds, "They lean forward, their eyes become intent, and their voices come to life when others ask questions and want to learn from them." Figure 4.2 gives examples of questions teachers can ask to stretch their students' writing during miniconferences.

In addition, Kathy and Mary consistently maintain a high level of expectation for their students. Asking questions often helps students expand and develop their writing, leading them to new levels of writing. Through ongoing guidance and a supportive context, Mary and Kathy continuously stretch their students so they might gradually advance to a new level of writing.

Share Sessions

Writing Workshop always culminates with share sessions—times for authors to share their writing. Sometimes the class gathers on a corner carpet; other times they gather in a circle of chairs; still other times the author comes to the Author's Chair to read his or her piece. In order that everyone can hear, the two teachers often have the author use a microphone.

Mary and Kathy know that their students will learn from one another as they share their writing. For example, when Jonathan shares his poem about the Aviation Center, Mary and Kathy point out how he "showed" his readers sounds with words like *cranking* and *squeaking:*

Spooky cartoon noises
Wheeling and turning
Cranking and squeaking
I never heard such sounds
And then I look around
I see I'm in a group
And then nothing
I am in the Aviation Center

Reneice shares her writing piece during a share session.

Periodically, Writing Workshop includes time for authors to publish and celebrate their finished work. Publishing their work might be in the format of a book, a class book, a mobile, or a display of students' writing on a bulletin board, in the hallway, or in a formal exhibit. Sometimes the class celebrates their publications on a designated day, determined by the class. Other times the class celebrates their writing as a culminating event for a thematic study, a genre study, or a poetry unit. Inviting parents, grandparents, or guests from the community to the celebration makes this become a memorable experience for everyone.

Beginning Writing Workshop with Lifework

Sustaining interest and gathering rhythm for writing is the goal Mary and Kathy set for themselves at the beginning of the year. Consistent with Calkins (1994, p. 3), they recognize that writing does not begin with "deskwork but with lifework." They believe that young writers overcome their fears and anxieties about writing or selecting topics when they begin the year by writing personal narratives about their experiences—like Kim's trip to Florida. Using real-life writing, in contrast to fiction and fantasy, provides ideas for writing that evolve from their students' lives and experiences. Graves (1994) says that students write more when they have knowledge about a topic, and they write with voice when they feel an investment in their topic. Personal narratives provide an avenue for students' writing to evolve more easily and their voices to emerge.

Similarly, Calkins (1994, p. 6) explains that we can "tap the human urge to write if we help students realize that their lives are worth writing about, and if we help them choose their topics, their genre, and their audience." She further encourages teachers to put away the "boxes, kits, and manuals full of synthetic writing stimulants. At best, they produce artificial and short-lived sputters of enthusiasm for writing, which then fade away, leaving passivity" (Calkins, 1994, p. 4).

Gaining Independence when Writing Personal Narratives

Being immersed in this classroom—a classroom where writing evolves from life experiences—Kim soon discovers that writing evolves from the spoken word. Since she is unable to write with a pencil, her paraprofessional or one of her fifth grade peers records her words. When she later shares her writing with her classmates, she discovers that written language is like the words we speak. Hearing her peers share what they like about her trip and all the fun things she did in Florida helps Kim realize that she, like her peers, is an author.

After becoming engaged within this supportive context, she begins to take risks with her writing by writing her journal entries on the computer herself, using her temporary spelling. Even though she cannot write with pencil and paper, she can press the keys on the keyboard to write. An example of her journal writing is displayed below:

It is fun to rit ploms [poems] at school.
We rot [write] bot [about] joj wosh crbr [George Washington Carver] I like my fens [friends].
My can potr [I use my computer] with my relechins [reflections]. My techr hlps [helps] me with my reting [writing].

This initiative to write independently evolved because Kim had learned that a message was far more important than correctly spelled words or properly punctuated sentences. Kim consistently heard Mary and Kathy, as well as her peers, praise writers for their ideas and their ways of expressing these ideas. Once she began to experiment and write daily on the computer, she began to discover more about the symbols, sounds, and the conventions of the language. The more she wrote on the computer, the easier it became to type the symbols and sounds to express her message. Knowing all the letters and their sounds was not essential for Kim to write; she learned the letters and sounds by writing.

Real-Life Writing and the Three Circles of Ideas—The Family, the Classroom, and the School

In his book *Free to Write,* Clark (1995) shows how young writers become authors as they create personal narratives from three circles of ideas—the family, the classroom, and the school (see Figure 1.4 in Chapter 1). As shown in her writing, family life is important to Kim. Similarly, many kindergarteners and first graders begin writing about themselves or their family life. After drawing a picture of her mother baking a cake, Melanie, a first grader, describes how her mother celebrated the magic of fall while baking a cake for her family.

Lite [last] nite my mom maed a cake. it was a rainbow. it was good and she put some popcorn [pumpkin] kaby [candy] [on it].

Just as Kim wrote about her experiences at school, Jason, a kindergartener, writes about his experiences at school on Valentine's Day.

It is valin times we git cade [candy] and crds and on the crds we see happy valin times to you av[Have] you evr git [gotten] a crd yes I av [have] this is cade [candy] fum [from] valin time day [Valentine's Day].

Similarly, Marcus, a second grader, writes about Halloween in his journal. He spontaneously creates a poem:

Halloween

We put on costumes
We go to houses and say trick-or-treat
We decorate our houses with skeletons and pumpkins
You might see a black cat
Happy Halloween!

As one can see, holidays are favorite topics for students of all ages. Gemeke, a fifth grader, writes a poem about Easter in her journal.

Easter
Easter looks like women dressed up in dresses and hats
Easter sounds like kids playing, singing in choirs, and singing church songs
Easter smells like barbecue and dinner cooking
Easter tastes like jelly beans and chocolate eggs
Easter feels like warm sunny breezes and furry stuffed animals
Easter

Likewise, Aaron, a sixth grader, chooses to write about his class's Christmas tree.

The Christmas Tree

The Christmas tree brings jubilance and joy to our classroom. The tree looks like the norweigen wood tree that represents the imperfections and selfishness of the universe. But the stars represent warmth, light, peace, and hope. The lights on the Christmas tree look like the rainbow–a spiral of rainbow skittles. The tree is like an abstract of happiness, hope, and joy.

All these writers begin to care about writing because they can write with, for, and about people or things that matter to them. Even though thinking about the formation of letters, the spelling of words, or the use of capitals and punctuation is often overwhelming to emergent learners, the burden becomes easier as they write about topics related to themselves, their family, or school. Similarly, the conventions of language become easier for the older students as they have the opportunity to select their own topics and genres for writing.

During the beginning stages of writing, students cannot simultaneously monitor their ideas and the conventions of writing. Forcing conventions of language too early stifles expression. Just like Kim, these writers feel safe in their classroom environment—a place where others listen to their ideas and positively comment about the messages within their writing. These positive comments fuel new energy for writing during Writing Workshop. For example, when Melanie hears Alex spontaneously comment that he likes how she described the cake—like a rainbow—she becomes motivated to write more.

Real-Life Writing and Multilanguage Learners

These same principles apply to multilanguage learners. Georgette, whose family moved to Michigan from Romania just two years ago, also chooses to write about her family during

Writing Workshop. Similar to other students whose families immigrate to America, Georgette, age 7, is simultaneously learning to speak a new language and learning to read and write a new language. Having the opportunity to write about her experiences and family facilitates Georgette's writing, which is a complex process, involving the control of multiple skills and a new language.

Through daily writing and practice, Georgette gradually learns how to express her ideas, as well as use the English language and its conventions. Day by day, new writing pieces about her family emerge. Seeing this pattern in her writing, her teacher, Maria Boles, decides to help Georgette publish a book about her family, using the writing process. As she revises and edits her writing with the support of Maria, Georgette begins to learn more about the English language and its conventions. In the writing excerpt below, which is a page in her book, Georgette tells us about her dad.

My Dad

My dad goes to work almost every day. He drives a truck. Sometimes he drives at day time and sometimes he drives at night time. Sometimes he doesn't get to sleep. When I go with him it is very fun. Sometimes everybody gets to go inside the truck.

Since learning to write in a new language can be very challenging, English language learners (ELLs) need a safe environment and an opportunity to explore writing (Coppola, Dawson, McPhillips, George, & Maclean, 2005; Espinosa, 2006; Peregoy & Boyle, 1993). Rather than focusing on skills, Maria initially focuses on the writing process and Georgette's needs as an ELL. Instead of rewriting her words below her temporary spelling, Maria first helps Georgette become comfortable writing in a new language, showing her that she is pleased with her ideas—even when her early attempts include a mixture of Romanian and English symbols and sounds.

If Maria had correctly spelled the words below the temporary spelling, Georgette would become afraid to write, afraid she would misspell words. ELLs need for us to celebrate their acquisition of a new language by focusing on their messages first. Rejecting their language and culture (Cummins, 1986; Espinosa, 2006; Peregoy & Boyle, 1993; Reyhner & Garcia, 1989) might jeopardize their progress in learning to read and write English.

Similar to emergent writers, Georgette gradually learns the English language through experimentation and daily writing. Later, as she uses the writing process to publish a book about her family, she learns more about the conventions of English and ways to correctly spell the words while conferring with Maria on a one-on-one basis. The motivation of having her book published gives her the incentive to learn the conventions of her new language.

Bringing Life into Learning through Observation

Once writers feel their lives are worth writing about, they become more enthusiastic about writing. They are ready to explore writing as a tool to learn about the world around them. By tapping into this enthusiasm and eagerness, we can provide many natural opportunities for young writers to simultaneously learn about writing and their environment (Casbergue & Plauche, 2003; Clark, 1995).

Students' natural interest in the world around them sometimes emerges in journal writing. As seen here, Nickie, age 7, discovers that the weather and science can be topics for writing in his journal.

Maria and Georgette proudly show a draft of a page from Georgette's book.

Yesterday before it rained I saw stratus clouds they were a light gray color. I don't like stratus clouds because they look iky and I don't like that.

Similar to many boys, Nickie's journal entry shows a natural interest in learning about the environment. Through the use of observation, he begins to record information about the weather.

Likewise, Benjamin, a first grader, uses observation to show what he is learning about caterpillars.

One day me and my sister did find a clpiler [caterpillar]. We maed a chge [cage] for him. It had lots of leafs and stics. In the morning he did wake up. We did find out that he did eat sum leafs.

In fact, many young writers use their writing to record their observations about the world, artifacts, pictures, or informational text. When given the opportunity to choose their topics and genres for writing, they spontaneously discover new reasons to write and gain a desire to learn about a variety of topics (Casbergue & Plauche, 2003).

Clark (1995) and Graves (1999) also emphasize the importance of firsthand experiences in Writing Workshop. They claim that firsthand experiences, which spark new ideas for writing, can bring new life into learning and create a better understanding of a subject. Clark (1995) further advocates the power of linking hands-on learning experiences with observation.

Using Firsthand Experiences and Observation in Writing Workshop

Following Clark's (1995) suggestions about firsthand experiences and observation, Jeanie Lawrence encourages her students to observe Oreo cookies during Writing Workshop. During her minilesson, Jeanie uses guided writing to help her students learn how prewriting strategies can heighten awareness of sights, sounds, smells, rhythms, and patterns to be incorporated into poems. Using prompts and guides, Jeanie helps her second graders learn how to use prewriting strategies when writing poems.

Jeanie begins the lesson by placing two Oreos on each student's desk, asking them to brainstorm what the Oreos smell like, look like, feel like, taste like, and sound like. Jaime shares that they taste "sugary"; Ayesha comments that they feel "hard" and "bumpy"; Darrell adds that they look "yummy." After students brainstorm some of their ideas, Jeanie explains that they can record these observations about the Oreos on a five senses cluster observation sheet (Figure 4.3). This prewriting graphic, she adds, will help them collect their ideas about the Oreos so they can write a poem about the cookies.

Using Firsthand Experiences and Observation to Collect Ideas for Poems. Working in twos, the second graders then begin to record their ideas on the webs. After about 6 minutes, Jeanie has her students pause so they can share some of their words with one another. Kenya observes that the Oreos look dark brown; Marvin notes that they taste "chocolately"; and Nadia remarks that they sound crunchy. As students listen to their peers' observations, Jeanie encourages them to add these words to their own charts. She explains that they don't need to worry about where they place their words so long as the category makes sense to them. She further reminds them that it is important to collect as many ideas as possible before they begin writing their poems.

Students continue to observe the cookies in twos, considering additional ideas and recording the information on their charts. After about 6 more minutes, she asks them to pause and share their observations again. After listening to more students share their observations, Jeanie points out that they will use these ideas to create a poem about Oreos tomorrow. Naturally, she also allows her second graders to enjoy the chocolatey, sugary treats.

Using Poetry as Models for Writing Poems. The following day, Jeanie asks her students to gather in a circle at the front of the room. She begins this minilesson by reviewing what

Figure 4.3
Five Senses Web Chart

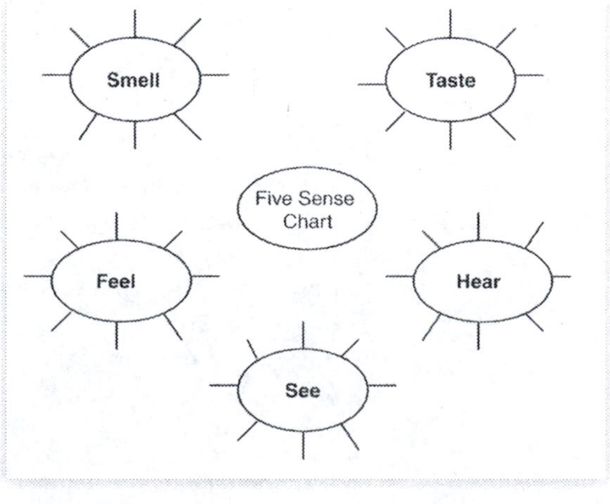

Smell
Taste
Five Sense Chart
Feel
Hear
See

they observed about the Oreo cookies yesterday. After allowing a few students to share some of their observations, she reminds her students that they will use these observations to write a poem about Oreos.

To help her students realize that they do not have to create poems that rhyme, she selects a few poems from *Eric Carle's Animals Animals* to read aloud to her students. By carefully selecting a few poems that use repetition, rhythm, or beat to read aloud, Jeanie uses literature as a model for writing poems about the Oreo cookies. Consistent with Harwayne (1992), she realizes that literature provides a model of how to say what we want to say. First, she reads "African Pygmy" (Carle, 1989, p. 10):

I throw myself to the left,
I turn myself to the right,
I am the fish
Who glides in the water, who glides,
Who twists himself, who leaps,
Everything lives, everything dances, everything sings.

As she reads the poem, she asks them to think about words they like in the poem. After reading the poem, she gives her students an opportunity to share words they like from the poem. Matt explains that he likes the word *glides* and makes a gliding motion with his hand; Ayesha notes that she enjoyed the word *twists,* while twisting her body around; Shawn adds that his favorite word is *leaps* because it reminds him of a frog leaping. Jeanie also points out how the author repeats the word *everything* in the last line—"Everything lives, everything dances, everything sings." By highlighting this technique, as well as the interesting words, Jeanie hopes to inspire her students to try similar poetic techniques in their own poems.

Second Graders Create Poems about Oreos. Following the same process, Jeanie reads a second poem from the book with her students. Once she feels they understand these poetic techniques, she encourages them to work in twos, composing their own poems. After they collaboratively draft their poems, Jeanie invites students to share them during her share session. As shown below, Dustin and Julie try repetition with their poem:

OREOS

Oreos look like a sandwich
Oreos smell sugree and chocolte
Oreos feel wle [really] roof [rough]
Oreos sound like a pop and a crush [crunch]
Oreos taste vary good and seet [sweet]
They are so good!

After listening to the two read their poem, Jeanie invites the second graders to praise their peers' poem. Laura comments that she likes how they compare the Oreo to a sandwich. Asama adds that he likes the word *crunch* to show what the Oreo sounds like when we eat it.

Austin and Adam, who read their poem next, also use repetition with their poem:

OREOS OREOS OREOS

Oreos brown.
Oreos yummy.
Oreos mushy.

Oreos choletу [chocolatey].
Oreos crunchy.
Oreos delish.
Oreos ruth [rough].
Oreos black.
Oreos round.
We love Oreos

After listening to their poem, Beth comments that she likes how Austin and Adam begin each line with *Oreos.* Michael notices that each line had two words. Jeanie affirms Michael's praise, explaining that many poets create a rhythm or beat for their poems by following a pattern or using repetition. Thus, Jeanie simultaneously supports the young writers' first attempts at poetry and reinforces understanding of poetic techniques that authors use in their poetry through praise.

By combining firsthand learning experiences with observation of the environment, Jeanie helps her second graders learn how to compose poems. She understands that young writers need opportunities to write in many genres (Piazza, 2003; Tompkins, 2004). As shown by their spontaneous responses to the poems, children naturally delight in the sounds of language and the magical powers of words that invite rhythm, dancing, or singing (Martin, 1972; Sloan, 2003).

Celebrating Children's Writing. The preceding example illustrates how observation became a prewriting activity to help young writers collect ideas for their poems. Listening to poems in Eric Carle's book gave the students a model for writing poetry, encouraging them to try the techniques of rhythm, repetition, or beat in their own poems. While sharing their writing with peers, the young writers began to discover that they were poets, just like Eric Carle. Although these poems were not published, sharing writing with another audience is also an important way to publish writing. Sharing can be very rewarding when the audience is receptive and encouraging.

Using Our Environment and Surroundings with Observation during Writing Workshop

Similarly, Tracey Franklin uses observation to help her students write poems about the school's playground and its surroundings. After calling her authors to the carpet area, Tracey begins Writing Workshop by explaining that today they will be using their writers' notebooks to gather observations of their school, the playground, and its surroundings.

Using a Minilesson to Model the Observation Process. To help her fourth graders think about words they can jot down in their notebooks, Tracey asks them to think about some observations from the classroom. Candise comments that she sees desks, chairs, and a whiteboard. Stephan adds that he sees a carpet, windows, and a clock. As she listens to their ideas, Tracey records her students' observations on chart paper.

After several ideas have been given, she asks her students to look at their observations and think of words to describe these words. Tiffany describes the carpet as "rust colored" and the clock as a "ticking clock." Shelby shares that the windows are streaked with dust and the whiteboard is covered with notes written in green. As her students note their descriptive words, Tracey records these ideas next to their observations. Through this interactive minilesson, Tracey models how to use writing as a notetaking activity (Indrisano & Paratore, 2005). Using accurate and precise observations in their notes will help the fifth graders simultaneously gather ideas for their poems.

Figure 4.4
Observation Chart

Senses Chart

See	Hear	Feel	Smell

After listening to their ideas, Tracey compliments her students for think [illegible] senses to help them describe their observations more fully. She reminds them t [illegible] also draw on their senses when they observe the environment in their science j [illegible] explains that today they will be just like scientists as they record their observa [illegible] school and the playground in their writers' notebooks.

To help them organize their observations, she encourages them to fold the [illegible] columns—see, hear, feel, and smell—and label the columns in their notebooks ([illegible] 4.4). Tracey also suggests that they focus on these four senses for the time being. She further explains they will be in groups of six, circulating around the school and the playground to record their notes with a parent volunteer. Tomorrow, she continues, they will use their observations to create a poem about their school, the playground, and its surroundings.

Using Observation to Collect Ideas for Poems. As the fourth graders observe and describe their environment in their writers' notebooks, they are beginning "to see the world as a place where they can learn" (Clark, 1995, p. 21). By linking adjectives to their notes, the young writers learn they can create a picture of what they see. These notes will also help them remember what the school, the playground, and the surrounding environment look like. Periodically, the parent volunteers, who were trained in the process the previous day, have the students gather in a circle to share their notes. By listening to their peers' ideas, the fourth graders see additional ways to use their senses while observing the environment.

When the groups return to their classroom, Tracey has students share their observations during the share session. As authors read their observations, Tracey encourages the listeners to add to their own notes. She explains that we want to collect as much information as possible about our environment, adding, "We never know which ideas we may use in our poems." As the fifth graders listen to their peers' ideas, they also begin to understand how to paint pictures through words.

Using Modeling to Help Students Compose Their Own Poems. The following day, Tracey begins Writing Workshop with another minilesson. Similar to Jeanie, she wants her students to begin thinking about a variety of ways to compose poems. In the past, she has found that too many students try to create rhyming poems that do not make sense. In order that her students might consider alternatives, she shares some poems written by her fourth graders last year. As she reads the students' poems, she asks her students to listen carefully to the poems and think about what each author does to help us "see" the environment. Tracey begins with Emma's poem:

Outside

Birds singing to a beat
Kids crying to their mommy
Rattling old rusty chains
What do you hear?

A new, red truck driving fast
A red and yellow drug free zone sign
A tall, silver basketball hoop
What do you see?

Brown, prickly grass
Hot sun burning
A black ant crawling on me
What do you feel?

Red roses fill the air.
Lawnmower cutting the grass.
Chlorine from the pool.
What do you smell?

After listening to the poem, Shelby explains that he likes how she organizes the poem around the five senses. Tiffany adds that Emma helps her feel the "brown, prickly grass" by using the word *prickly*.

Next, Tracey shares Daniel's poem:

The wind whistling through the swings
and through everything
The rough brown picnic table with the tiny red ants
Looking like little red polka dots alive
The birds making a sound like heaven bells ringing
Mary and I walking on the cemented walkway
In the dew of the morning

Mary notes that Daniel paints a picture of the wind by saying it "whistled through the swings." Stephan comments that Daniel helps him see the tiny ants by comparing them to polka dots. Jose points out that he can hear the birds' songs—they sound like heavenly bells ringing.

Supporting Students as They Compose Poems. After hearing these two poems, Tracey feels that her students are ready to use their observations to create their own poems. As she circulates, Tracey confers with her students, commenting about their choice of words or asking them questions to help them consider painting a picture so that the reader might see their observations. For example, when Stephan writes about the bushes "waving in the wind," she compliments him on his choice of words, explaining that she can see the bush waving in the wind. When Tiffany compares a trunk to "double chocolate chip ice cream dipped in chocolate syrup," she exclaims that she can feel the texture of the pine tree's trunk.

To stimulate Brian's use of descriptive words, she asks him, "Can you tell me how the grass felt? What did it look like?" Brian explains that the grass feels soft and tickly, and it looks like the emerald green crayon in his box. To help him see how to use these words in his poem, Tracey asks him to point to where he might place these words in his poem. After he inserts the words, she asks him to reread the line so that he can experience how these insertions enrich his poem.

Tracey's responses or feedback are critical in teaching her children to write effectively (Atwell, 1987; Routman, 1994, 2005; Wolf & Wolf, 2002; Wood & Dickinson, 2000). Using questions gives her students time to reconsider their writing and express their own ideas rather than those of the teacher.

After about 5 minutes, she encourages a few students to read their poems aloud, explaining that they can just share their poem's beginning if they aren't quite done. Motivated by her teacher's praise, Tiffany shares her poem with the group (Moore-Hart, 2005, p. 330). Spontaneously, everyone claps. Instinctively, Josh adds that he likes the message that her poem expresses—reminding us to take care of the environment.

The Brownest Tree

The pine tree looks as if it no longer survives in the wild any more
The tree's needles and trunk are as brown as a
Double chocolate chip ice cream,
Dipped in chocolate syrup.
It's needles are pointier than the sharpest knife.
I feel as if the tree should get another chance to live.
The tree used to offer us many privileges.

Through this experience, Tracey's students begin to realize that sensual observations enrich poems, narrations, or stories. According to Tracey, "If we look, listen, and wait, a small tree or patch of ground can become a beautiful poem."

Using Observations of Our Classrooms to Create Poetry

Similar to Jeanie and Tracey, Erin Minnis uses observation to help her students write poems. However, she wants her fourth graders to see that many topics for writing lie within the classroom. During her minilesson, she has her students list some observations about the classroom and then brainstorm some adjectives to describe their words. Just like Tracey, she records their ideas on chart paper.

After the shared writing activity, the students return to their desks and fold their paper into columns—see, hear, feel, and smell—placing labels above the columns. Once students complete their observations, they compose their own poems about their classroom, following the model of Erin's poem. Reading aloud her own poem provides her students a model of how to create a poem from the observations. Erin, who believes that her students need to hear and see her writing, hopes that her own poem might inspire her students to write a poem.

Following her model, Ryan composes the following poem about his classroom:

Ms. Minnis' Room

A lamp with a light as bright as the sun
A wall with lots of words like a swarm of bees
A big "Welcome" sign sticking out like a sore thumb

A chalkboard as black as coal
A red cowboy hat as red as an apple
A cow on top of the TV
Probably wanting to come down.

Using Observations of Our Home Environment to Create Descriptive Paragraphs

Mary Addison, a fifth grade teacher, takes a slightly different approach. Knowing that her students are very familiar with their bedrooms, she decides to have her students collect observations of their bedrooms. For homework, she has her students draw a map of their bedrooms and label the map as a prewriting exercise.

The next day students use their maps and their knowledge about their bedrooms to write a descriptive paragraph about them. Similar to Tracey, Mary first has her students list their observations by folding their paper into columns and placing labels above the columns in their writing notebooks. Then, they use these observations to create descriptive paragraphs about their bedrooms. Courtney's paragraph is displayed below:

Welcome to my Room

My room is pink, white, and blue. My room is the biggest one in the house. When you step inside you see some pictures. When you look to one side you see my closet. When you look to the other side you see my bed. I have a double bed with a white ruffled bedspread. In my room I have two dressers. One dresser is stained. My other dresser is white. One of my dressers has a mirror on it. I also have a mirror on the back of my door. I have two animals on it. When I sit on my bed I can look out my window. On my curtains are a flower stencil. I have a chairrail. Under my chairrail is wallpaper. The wallpaper is white with four little blue dots and pink hearts. My carpet is pink and my walls are white.

Japera takes a different approach when describing her bedroom. She captures the mood of her room and explains why it's so special to her.

Welcome to my Room

Welcome to my room, the most beautiful place in the world to me. You may not think so but I love it. I love my room from the ceiling down to my floor. The think [thing] that gets me is that it's all mine. No one else lives there but me. I'm in my own world. I love my posters because they express myself and how I feel. But the think that gets me is my music. It tells all my moods. When I'm happy I play it loud. When I'm sad I play it low. It changes everything, songs, tempos, styles, everything. I feel as if I'm in my own world. No one else matters. All my feelings go and I'm all alone. All alone is good when it's all you need.

Once her students complete their paragraphs, Mary has them type them on the computer so they can be published in a class book. After completing the book, Mary sends the book, enclosed in a large envelope, home to a different family each night. This strategy helps her parents remain informed about her writing curriculum. At the same time, students receive additional feedback on their writing.

To encourage parents to provide feedback to the children, Mary includes a page entitled "Readers' Comments," a page where parents can write down praise about the students' writing. The parents' responses and feedback to their writing provide another audience for students' writing.

To be sure that her parents will give positive responses and feedback to the fifth graders, Mary includes a letter to the parents, describing the activity and inviting them to respond to the fifth graders' writing, using praise and positive comments. The letter further explains how their responses and feedback, if positive, can be a way to motivate their children to write more.

Once students learn techniques to use in their writing, they often begin to apply these same techniques in future writing. For example, Silkya independently applied the use of observations to write a poem about her brother's room in her journal:

Troy's Disaster

My brother's room is dirty!
His underwear is all over the place.
Vido games on the bed and floor
Books under the rugs
Chicken on the dressers
My dog, Missy, hair is everywear
Under the bed is a disaster
My brother room is rally smelly
There's stains all over the carpit—juice and food stains—
And sometimes I think my brother
Really needs to clean his room!

Using Observations of Photos to Write Descriptive Paragraphs

Heather Chavez, a fourth grade teacher, similarly uses observation to help her students write a paragraph about a favorite photograph. To help her fourth graders collect their ideas for the paragraph, she has them begin by creating a web of their observations. As they record their observations on the web, Heather encourages them to add interesting and revealing details about the photograph, remembering to use their senses.

As can be seen, Azira brought the photograph to life through anecdotes, details, and dialogue:

Little ZZ

"Who's that little girl who's short, has on a pink dress, and is called little ZZ"? That's me, my full name is Azira Dane'e. At the time I was known as AAA, zipper, Poh Bear, Nae's Big girl. I was at White Hill, Detroit. I was visiting my granny. Behind the camera my cousins were being a nucense [nuisance]. They were making faces at me! I really, really wanted my favorite bunny in my arms but my mom wanted to hold it! I could smell the yellow roses behind me. My granny had planted them with love five years before. As the camera lense [lens] snapped my Mom put me down and I totled off with my Aunt calling, "where you go'n Nae"? I knew where I was going. I was going towards the friendly smell of my Granny!

Azira's piece recaptures this moment in time. We can see the yellow roses planted with love; we can smell Granny's friendly love.

Dumar's observation notes take an unexpected twist; they become the fuel to make his writing come alive for the reader as he expresses his feelings about a "gleaming sport."

Basketball

I like basket ball because [it] is important be me. Because I want to be a basket ball player when I grow up It is my dream. I be at the basket ball cort [court] mostlee every day It fun to play. I tell my friends it is not stuped. I love IT. It's a great sport to do it keep me away from troble [trouble] and other bad stuff. My mom says it's good for me I think so to. Basket ball is a gleming [gleaming] sport. It shines like the pretty stars and the sun shining to me.

The simple act of recording the observations permits both writers to create a sense of person and place. The observations and descriptions enrich and enhance the stories. Through their writing, both writers find meaning in their experiences and effectively communicate it to their readers.

Bringing Life into Learning through Interviewing

As they continue to explore topics for writing, students soon discover they can also write about people in their world, such as their teacher or an adult they know. According to Graves (1999), students want to know what we, as teachers, feel or what we're passionate about—books, current events, sports, or cars. He goes on to point out that students want to know how adults learn and what they do when things don't work. Students naturally have many questions; these questions often become a subject they can investigate in more depth.

Clark (1995) similarly adds that real-life writing permits young writers to learn about people in their community. Just as a journalist sees the world as a storehouse of ideas about people, the classroom is also a storehouse of ideas about people. Our community is filled with working and retired experts, homemakers, professional writers and journalists, and visitors from neighboring states and from abroad. They all have a story to tell; they are just waiting for an invitation to visit the classroom.

Students Interviewing Their Teachers

Teachers and parents know that young children are naturally curious. Wishing to tap into this reservoir of energy, Julie Pannell decides to let her first graders interview her. Given the opportunity, she knows that her young writers will have endless questions about her life at home.

Conducting the Interview. After inviting them to Circle Time, Julie begins her minilesson by permitting them to interview her. She explains that when we interview people, we ask them questions—things we want to know about them. Eagerly, the first graders begin to ask questions. Do you have any pets? How many children do you have? What do they like to do? What do you like to do? As they ask the questions, she records her responses on chart paper, using the web displayed in Figure 4.5.

Figure 4.5
Prewriting Web about Mrs. Pannell

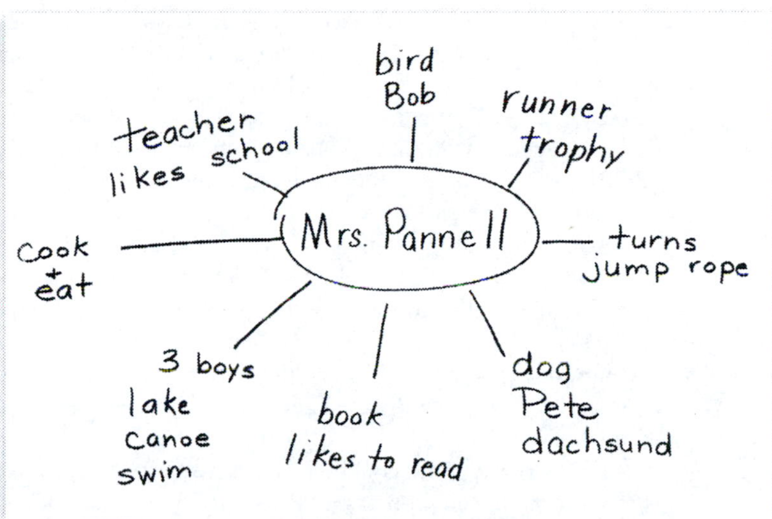

Once her students have finished asking the questions, Julie reviews the information on the web by asking them what they remember from the interview, for example, "What do I like to do?" or "How many children do I have?" As the children respond, she has them use the pointer to show where the information is recorded on the web. This activity provides a quick review of the information and simultaneously reinforces the first graders' word recognition skills.

After she finishes the minilesson, students return to their desks and begin writing in their journals. She invites them to consider writing about their own home life or things they like to do at home, adding that she loves to learn about their lives, their hobbies, and their feelings. Austin wrote about her feelings on the first day of school in first grade:

> On the frste [first] day of frste grade I was a little shie [shy]. I was shie fo [for] my techr. I rod the bose [bus] to school. I was glad t [that] sumr [summer] was ovr.

Writing a Story about Mrs. Pannell. The following day Julie does another shared writing activity with her class during her minilesson. Referring to the web she made the day before, she suggests that they write a story about her. First, she explains, we need to think about a way to begin our story. Mariam suggests they begin their story by telling who Mrs. Pannell is. Michael agrees and suggests that they say, "Mrs. Pannell teaches first grade at Concord." Then Gabrielle chimes in saying, "She likes to let us work. She teaches us to read books." Phil adds, "She's so nice to us."

Using a computer connected to an LCD projector—a device that displays the computer screen on the overhead projector so that all students can see the writing as it is word processed—Julie records the story, using their words.

To help her students organize their ideas, she stops periodically, asking her students to relook at the web and decide what they will

teaching TIP 4.2

Using the computer to record our writing during shared writing enables us to write the ideas down more quickly than when using a marker and chart paper. Furthermore, students remain more focused as we record their words, and they can more easily read the neatly printed page on the overhead screen.

write about next. For example, after they finish the first paragraph, Julie asks what they should write about next. Raneice comments that she thinks they should write about her children. Others nod in approval, so Julie explains that she will begin a new paragraph, because this will be about her children instead of her. To show that this is a new paragraph, Julie adds that she will indent. Then she has Raneice tell her what the first sentence would be. Raneice suggests, "She has three boys." As can be seen from the dialogue, Julie also teaches her first graders concepts about language conventions—ways to indent, use punctuation, or use capitals in sentences—as she records the story.

After completing the first two paragraphs, Julie recommends that they continue the story the next day. She does not want to lose her first graders' attention. Before stopping, however, she reads the story aloud to her first graders. Then she invites some students to read parts of the story independently. In this way, she uses reading and writing to strengthen and reinforce one another. Since the written language includes the children's language, they can more easily read the story independently, decoding some of the new words on their own.

The next day, Julie continues the shared writing lesson, following the same process. Her questioning and prompting models the process authors use to organize their ideas for writing. For example, referring to the web demonstrates how authors first use a web to gather information for writing and then later use this information to provide examples and details in their writing. Julie realizes that children need to see the process modeled if they are to become effective writers. The finished story is displayed below:

Mrs. Pannell

Mrs. Pannell teachers first grade at Concord. She likes teaching kids. She likes to let us work. She teaches us to read books. She is so nice to us.

She has three boys. She loves her boys. They like to swim and ride canoes and ride their bikes to friends' houses. They like to go fishing. They go to school at Concord.

Bob goes to Concord. He has all kinds of colors on him. He is a bird. Mrs. Pannell has a dog at home. She loves him. She likes to play with her dog. He is a dachshund and his name is Pete.

Mrs. Pannell likes to cook, because she likes to eat. She likes to run. Once, she won a trophy in a race. She won third place because there were only three ladies in the race.

And that's how Mrs. Pannell's life is.

Since this is a shared experience, built around the life experiences of their teacher, the first graders become engaged in the writing event. To extend the learning experience, Julie prints out copies for each of her first graders, who then illustrate the story at the bottom of the page. The children then take the stories home to read with their parents. In this way, technology becomes a tool to integrate reading with writing in a meaningful and purposeful way.

Students Interviewing Their Substitute Teachers

To help her first graders learn about interviewing, Emily Mihocko invites her substitute teacher back to her first grade classroom. Before Mrs. Dawson arrives, Emily has her students brainstorm questions they might want to ask Mrs. Dawson during a minilesson. Ben wants to know what other grades she teaches. Jayme desires to know what she does when she substitutes. Morgan prefers knowing if she has any pets. Caitlin is interested in knowing what she likes to eat. Similarly, Tracy is interested in finding out about her hobbies. As her first graders brainstorm their questions, Emily records the questions on chart paper for all to see. Then, when the first graders return to their seats, she has them record their favorite questions on Post-its.

Before Mrs. Dawson arrives on the following day, Emily reminds her students to quickly write down the answers to the questions on their Post-its. She also encourages them to just write down a word or phrase next to the question. Using Post-its helps her first graders write quickly. They remember to just use a word or phrase rather than a sentence during the interview, as there is only a small amount of space to record the information.

That afternoon, the first graders draw pictures of the interview with Mrs. Dawson. Underneath the drawings, they write down what they learned from the interview. Mesina's and Parker's writings are displayed below:

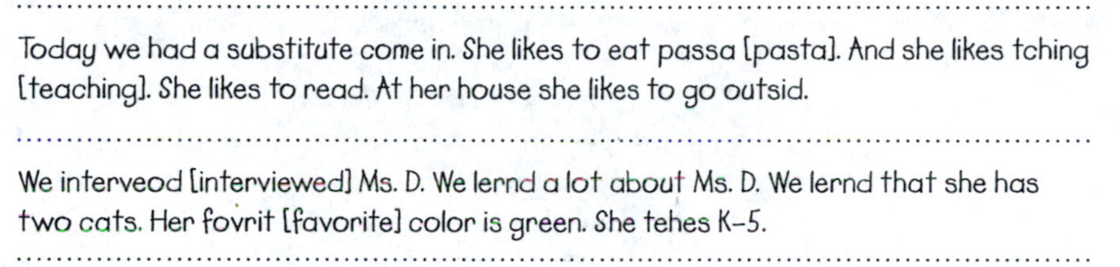

Today we had a substitute come in. She likes to eat passa [pasta]. And she likes tching [teaching]. She likes to read. At her house she likes to go outsid.

We interveod [interviewed] Ms. D. We lernd a lot about Ms. D. We lernd that she has two cats. Her fovrit [favorite] color is green. She tehes K–5.

Emily observes that her students are fully engaged during the interview. Even though the first graders know Mrs. Dawson, they want to learn more about her. As a result, they are eager to ask her questions and record their responses.

Emily further remarks that she likes this activity because students are responsible for their own learning—they have to develop the questions, ask the questions, listen, and record the responses. Because the students are responsible for their learning, Emily continues, they gain ownership of their writing.

Students Interviewing Parents

Diane Scott's third graders learn that listening, interviewing, and taking notes helps you understand and enjoy a person when Genisis's mother visits their class in the spring. Genisis and her family are from Costa Rica. Since more and more immigrants are settling in the area, Diane wants her students to learn more about people moving into the community. Through this interview experience, her third graders gain an understanding of how hard it is to leave your family and friends behind when you immigrate to a new country.

Similar to Emily and Julie, Diane prepares her students for the interview the day before Genisis's mother arrives. Explaining that Genisis and her family are from Costa Rica, Diane asks her students to think of questions they might want to ask Genisis's mother. Without prompting, questions emerge. Lynne wants to know what kind of food they eat in Costa Rica; Charlay is interested in learning about schools in Costa Rica; Tim wants to know about the games and sports people play; Aja is curious about learning a new language; and Abdul wants to know if it is hard to leave Costa Rica.

As children brainstorm their questions, Diane records them on chart paper for all to see. Following the process reporters often use, Diane has her third graders prepare their questions in advance. Next Diane has them relook at the questions and determine an order for asking the questions. To help them learn how reporters organize their questions, she explains that reporters usually begin with an easy question so that the interviewee becomes comfortable with the interview; they save the harder questions for the end of the interview. Once an order for the questions has been planned, Diane then has students sign up to ask the questions in twos so that everyone will feel part of the process.

Armed with questions, the third graders think that they are ready for the interview to begin, but Diane also wants to review strategies for notetaking. She reminds them to

- Listen carefully.
- Write quickly.
- Use temporary spelling.
- Use abbreviations when possible.
- Record the information, using words or phrases.
- Use manuscript or cursive, whichever is easiest for you.

To help them remember these strategies, she lists them on chart paper for all to see during the interview.

When Mrs. Mora arrives the following day, the third graders are ready to listen, interview, and take notes. The children quickly become fascinated with her story as she tells them how hard it was to leave her family and friends behind. They learn that coming to a new country can be lonely at first, especially when you can't speak the language well. Through the interview process they discover that Mrs. Mora acquired the new language with persistence and determination and that she attended school, learning how to become a chef. Gradually, she adapted to this new life, married, and had children. As they listen to her story while asking questions, the third graders become intrigued by the animals in Costa Rica—especially the monkeys who climb trees and steal food, the cobras, and pelicans. The graduation festivities on the last day of high school charm others.

When the students begin to write a thank-you letter to Mrs. Mora, they begin to empathize with her feelings about coming to a new country, learning a new language, and gaining an education. Writing a thank-you letter after the interview also helps them learn the conventions of letter writing, especially the use of commas for the greeting and salutation and the use of punctuation and capitals when addressing an envelope. Since they know that the thank-you letters will be mailed to Mrs. Mora, they become more motivated to edit their writing carefully. Ella's and Theo's letters are displayed below:

Dear Ms. Mora,

Thank you for coming into our classroom. We enjoyed learning about Costa Rica. I loved the stories. Especially the pelican story.

It's sad you had to give up a butiful rainforest, nice fruit, and neat trees. But it must have been worse to leave your friends and family behind?

But when you came to America you made a family, learned a new language, and made new friends. I think Genisis is one of the best friends I'll ever have. I mean shes nice, pretty, nice, did I menchun [mention] nice? Best of all shes fun!

I bet Costa Rica's great and fun! I wish you best of luck!

Sincerely,
Ella

Dear Ms. Mora,

Thank you for coming into our classroom. I'm sory you had to give up your family and friends to come here in North America.

When you came here you gained love, a family, a daughter and a son and new friends. I learned that the girls in Costa Rica couldn't leave the house until they got married and I also learned that you had bad monkeys in Costa Rica.

Have a great life in Costa Rica.

Sincerely,
Theo

Having an audience for one's writing often motivates a student to learn the conventions of language and grammar. Students further tend to remember and retain the skills when in a written context.

Students Interviewing People They Know

Deciding to test the ideas of Clark (1995) and Graves (1999) about interviewing people, I decided to let a multiage class (grades 1–3) interview me after experiencing an accident skiing. Hobbling on crutches as I entered the room, I knew the young learners would have lots of questions. Just as I imagined, the moment I stepped through the door, hands immediately shot up—three weeks ago I didn't have crutches.

Taking Notes While Interviewing. Knowing they had questions about my leg, I explained I would give them a few minutes to ask me questions, but I wanted them to also take notes as they listened. I added that we would later use their notes to write an article about my accident. Even though the class had taken notes before, we quickly reviewed the important points about taking notes during the minilesson, as discussed previously.

Next we talked about how they might record their notes. Christine suggested that people could write down the facts about the accident, placing each fact on a different line. Nathan recommended that they list the questions, followed by the answers. As a class, the students decided that either way would work. Michaele, their teacher, and I also reminded them to just record phrases or single words. Otherwise, they might not be able to write down all the information.

Once we reviewed the important concepts about notetaking, I let them begin asking questions. Christine asked me, "What happened to your leg?" Nathan wanted to know where the accident occurred. Heather asked when the accident happened. Nick wondered, "Who helped you?" As the children asked questions, I briefly paused so they could record their answers. Figure 4.6 shows how Nathan recorded his notes.

After about 20 minutes, they had asked over 20 questions. To help students complete their notes and review the information they had collected, I had them discuss their notes during our sharing session. As students spontaneously shared their notes, I encouraged their peers to add to their own notes if they did not already have this information. This also gave them an opportunity to clarify their notes or add details if needed. I was also able to help students be sure they had recorded the information accurately by explaining concepts that were not clear.

Figure 4.6
Nathan's Notes about the Skiing Accident

I concluded the sharing session by explaining that they were just like reporters today. Whenever reporters want to find out what happened after an accident or an exciting event in the community, they interview people to gather information for an article. To help them remember the facts about the accident or event, they record the information in their notebooks. Just like reporters, I continued, we will use our notes from the interview to write an article about me next week.

Additional Prewriting Activities. When I arrived the following week, I brought an article from the newspaper about a man who had lost his leg due to an accident. I used this article as a model for their writing during the minilesson. Once the students had gathered in a circle at the front of the room, I explained that we were going to use this newspaper article to help us write our own articles about my accident. As I read the article, I asked them to listen to the article in order to find out what the reporter did to help us understand the article. This experience gave us an opportunity to talk about titles, leads, and endings for an article. We also discussed the interesting details or examples the reporter used to show us what happened in the accident.

After sharing the article, I asked them to return to their desks and begin going over their notes while thinking about a way to begin an article about my accident or thinking about a title for an article. Nick decided he would begin his article by saying, "Peggy was skiing on February 11, at 2:30 at Mt. Brighton. As she was turning, she went into the air and fell. Crack! Her tibia and fibula were broken."

***teaching* TIP 4.3**

Just as literature provides a model for our writing, the newspaper provides a model for writing informational texts. In particular, they model motivational titles and leads, focus, and compelling endings.

He explained that his first sentences showed the reader what the article would be about and then answered the questions—who, what, when, where, and why. Sharing next, Leah commented that she would give her article the title, "Kids Can Be Good for Something," because she believed it was important that a young boy helped me.

Once a few students had volunteered their leads or titles, I asked them to look at their notes again and place a number one next to the first idea they might use for their draft. Similarly, I encouraged them to number each successive event or idea about the accident in their notes. Placing numbers next to the ideas might help them organize their notes before drafting their articles.

Drafting an Article from Interview Notes. As soon as students completed their numberings, I encouraged them to begin drafting their articles. To help them gather their ideas, I periodically asked them to stop (about every 6 minutes) and share their drafts with the class. Inviting students to share their articles right away helped those who were not sure how to begin or what to write next. Hearing their peers' ideas helped them discover what to say and how to organize their writing.

Whenever students shared their articles, I also sprinkled words of specific praise about their writing. For example, when Leah read her piece, I explained that I enjoyed how she integrated the part about the little boy who came to help me. I pointed out that this detail added interest to her article. When Randall read his article, I commented that I liked how he showed the reader how ski patrollers put a cardboard splint on my leg. This is information, I added, that many people might not know. Once the drafts were complete, several others had the opportunity to share their writing during the share session. Following my example, students then explained what they enjoyed about their peers' articles.

The next day everyone used word processing tools to type their drafts on the computer under Michaele's guidance. To help with revising and editing, she had her students triple space the drafts before printing them out.

Reseeing and Reconsidering Writing. When I returned the following week, I began my minilesson by explaining that reporters always revise their articles once they complete their drafts. After reviewing the writing process, we began to talk about the meaning of *revise.* Christine commented that she thought *revise* means to change your writing so that it makes sense. Nick shared that sometimes authors add to their writing—maybe they forgot some details. Heather explained that sometimes she adds adjectives to describe things in her writing. I added that some writers even delete or take out information if it's not related to the topic; others change information if the facts aren't correct.

After discussing what revision means, I explained that we can help authors know when to revise by asking them questions. Questioning, a technique that other reporters use to help one another revise their articles, helps authors relook at their writing or reconsider their writing. To help them think about possible questions to ask an author, I asked them to think of questions that would help authors relook at their writing. Nathan shared that we can ask someone what something looked like. Christine commented that we can ask, "When did the accident happen?" if the author forgot to tell when. Hannah similarly responded, saying we can ask, "What time did the accident occur?"

After pointing out what good ideas they all had, I emphasized that asking questions is a more "friendly" way of offering suggestions. I added that our writing is a part of us. As a result, we feel sensitive about our writing. If someone asks us questions, we don't feel like someone is

***teaching* TIP 4.4**

If we want our students to become effective writers, we must show them how to revise their writing. Using a minilesson to model how to revise will help them begin to modify their writing more effectively.

teaching TIP 4.5

When forming writing response groups, teachers should arrange the groups so that they include students of mixed ability levels and personalities. Students remain in these groups during the rest of the school year. Retaining group membership helps students gradually begin to feel safe with their group and trust them with their writing.

criticizing us. We feel like they are inviting us to relook at our writing. When we resee our writing, we can then shape the writing to be accurate and clear to other readers. Just like reporters, I explained, we need to shape our writing to be sure our message is correct and readable for those who read the article.

Using the PQP Process to Help Students Revise. Once the students had practiced asking questions, I continued with the minilesson, explaining that today we would be working in writing response groups to help one another revise the articles. Then I emphasized that we would follow the PQP process whenever we meet in our revising groups. As I wrote these letters on the board, I recorded the word *praise* next to the first *P*, *question* next to the *Q*, and *polish* next to the second *P* (see Figure 4.7). This is the process, I noted, we will use to help our friends revise their writing. To help them relate to the process, I reminded them that they already give praise to their peers during share sessions. Similarly, I reinforced that Mrs. Rae and I often ask them questions while they write. The last step, polish, is an opportunity for the author to share one or two ideas they might consider when revising their pieces. This, I added, is a way to thank the group for helping us relook at our writing.

Their teacher, Michaele, had already pregrouped students into writing response groups. She arranged the groups by placing students in mixed ability groups, including both leaders

Figure 4.7
The Praise–Question–Polish Process

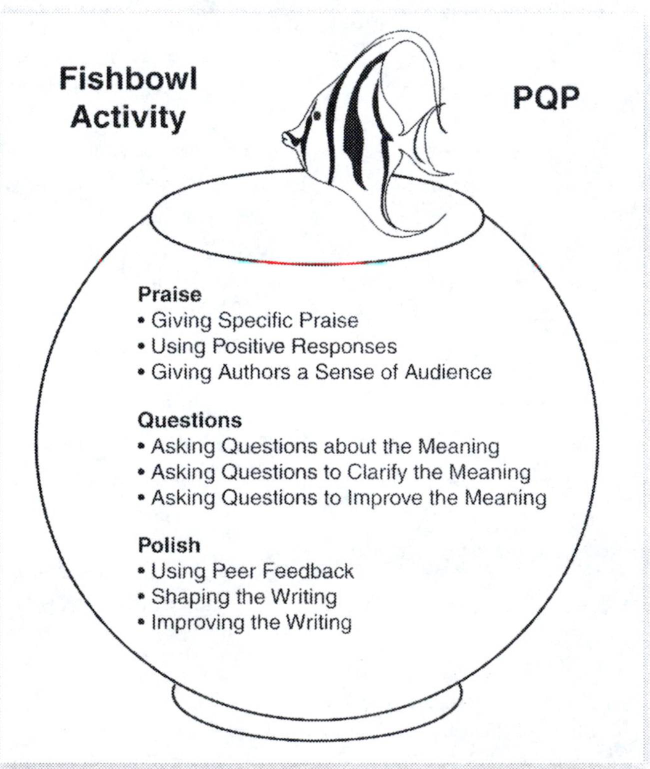
Fishbowl Activity
PQP
Praise
• Giving Specific Praise
• Using Positive Responses
• Giving Authors a Sense of Audience
Questions
• Asking Questions about the Meaning
• Asking Questions to Clarify the Meaning
• Asking Questions to Improve the Meaning
Polish
• Using Peer Feedback
• Shaping the Writing
• Improving the Writing

and followers in each group. She also placed students who could work well together within each group.

Modeling the PQP Process through the Fishbowl Technique. To help them understand the PQP process, we modeled the process with one group, using the fishbowl technique. It shows students how to work in revising groups using the PQP process. While students were at recess, Michaele arranged the class in a *U* shape, placing one table at the front of the *U,* or in the fishbowl. After recess, we explained that Mitch's group would practice the PQP process while the rest of the class took notes on how well the group implemented the process. All students sitting in the *U* shape would listen while recording the group's praise and questions in their notes. They would also record how Mitch, the author, would polish his piece.

Before Mitch's group began the PQP process, I explained that Mitch would read his piece first. After reading his piece, the group would begin to share their words of praise and then ask their questions. Finally, Mitch would explain some revisions he might consider. Figure 4.8 lists the steps for the PQP process.

As soon as everyone was ready to begin the process, Mitch, age 7, read his piece aloud to his reading response group:

Peggy Moore-Hart

Peggy Moore-Hart was sking on February 11. On a sunny day. Peggy Moore-Hart was sking and fell on Mount Brighton. A boy saw her fall. He helped Peggy Moore-Hart. The boy did somthing nice. He said are you okay. Peggy Moore-Hart told him to go to the ski patrel and he went and got them. Peggy Moore-Hart got on a tobggen that was atached [attached] to a snomobel [snowmobile]. The first people put her in a splint. It was 2:30 when she got to the hospital. The amlis [ambulance] came and took her to the University of Michigan. They gave her a crdbord [cardboard] splint with tape to hold it and crutes [crutches]. The splint was holding the bones togathr [together], so it woldn't hut [hurt] very much. Now, she is geting beter.

After he read his piece, Hannah shared that she liked how he explained that a splint is made of cardboard. Mariah added that she liked his ending—"Now, she is getting better." Max thought it was a good idea to tell about the weather on the day of the accident.

Figure 4.8

The Steps of the Praise–Question–Polish (PQP) Process for Writing Response Groups

1. Authors read their writing piece.
2. Peers listen, writing down examples of praise they might give the author or questions they might ask.
3. Peers give authors specific praise about their writing.
4. Peers ask authors questions about their writing to help them shape their writing.
5. Authors and peers brainstorm possible answers to questions or possible ways to revise piece.
6. As their peers offer praise and ask questions, authors take brief notes.
7. Once the group finishes offering praise and asking questions, authors share how they will polish their writing.

After participating in writing response groups, students polish their writing, using their peers' feedback.

Next, the group began to ask questions. Max asked if the cardboard splint was made before or after the ambulance came. Mitch replied that the ski patrol made the cardboard splint. To help Mitch understand how to change his writing, Michaele asked where would he put this part about the cardboard splint. Mitch pointed to the sentence, "The first people put her in a splint," and Michaele reaffirmed his decision, asking who the first people were. Mitch answered that it was the ski patrol. Hannah then asked where could he let the reader know that the first people were the ski patrol. After thinking, Mitch decided he could change the words *the first people* to *the ski patrol.* Mariah asked Mitch if the ambulance got to the hospital at 2:30. Mitch explained that this was right, adding that he could put this sentence after the sentence about the ambulance. Then Max questioned whether Peggy was skiing *on* Mt. Brighton or *at* Mt. Brighton. Mitch replied that he meant to say *at*.

After the group completed the praise and questions, Mitch shared that he planned to move the sentences about the splint next to the sentence about the ski patrol putting on the splint, change the words *first people* to *ski patrol,* change the word *on* to *at Mt. Brighton,* and move the sentence about the time they got to the hospital after the sentence about the ambulance.

Once the group finished the process, the class clapped for the group. Then they took turns sharing the words of praise they heard and the questions the group members asked. Thus, the fishbowl technique simultaneously modeled the revising process and reinforced the process of giving authors praise and asking them questions.

Applying the Revising Process. The following day students met in their writing response groups to share their drafts, using the PQP process. The accompanying picture shows one group as they applied the PQP process. As authors listened to peers' questions, they took notes in the margins to help them remember the changes they would make the following day as they revised their pieces.

Figure 4.9 shows some revisions Niki made in his article. To help the students become more enthusiastic about revising their pieces, Michaele distributed colored pens for authors to cross out, insert, or change information on their drafts. Since the drafts were triple spaced, students were able to insert the changes easily, using the colored pens. The next day, students made the changes on their drafts, using word processing tools to ease the burden

Figure 4.9

Example of Niki's Revisions for His Article

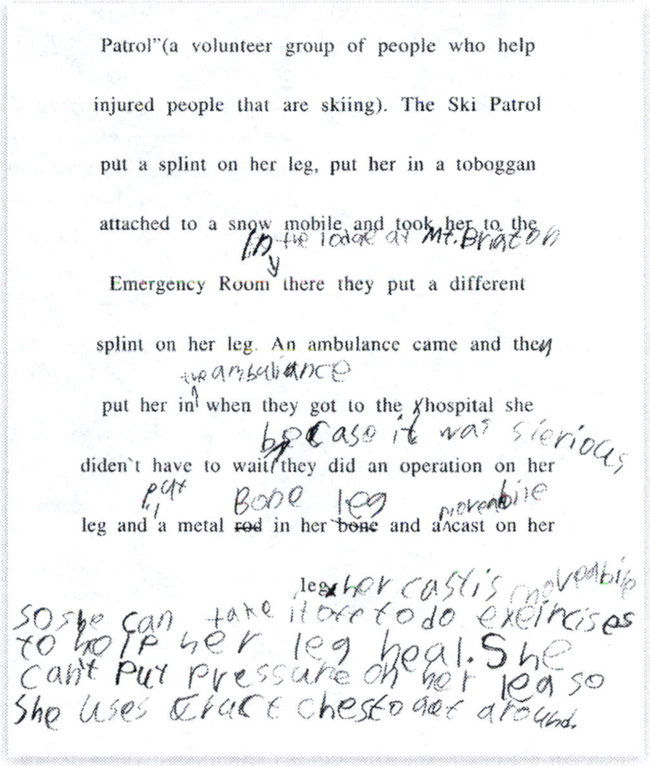

Patrol"(a volunteer group of people who help injured people that are skiing). The Ski Patrol put a splint on her leg, put her in a toboggan attached to a snow mobile and took her to the Emergency Room there they put a different splint on her leg. An ambulance came and they put her in when they got to the hospital she diden't have to wait they did an operation on her leg and a metal rod in her bone and a cast on her leg.

of revising because students did not have to recopy their pieces (Moore, 1989; Moore-Hart, 1995, 2004); they merely inserted new words, deleted words, or rearranged the text.

Using Peer Editing to Help Students Edit. When I returned the following week, I explained that reporters always edit their articles before publishing them. After quickly reviewing the writing process, we began to talk about the meaning of *edit*. Randall commented that he thought *edit* means to check the spelling of the words. If words are not spelled correctly, he added, readers will not be able to easily read the article. Mariah shared that sometimes authors check their writing to be sure that they have used capital letters for proper nouns or for the first word in a sentence. Heather added that authors also check their writing to be sure that all sentences have the proper ending marks. I shared that some writers may also check their writing to be sure that they inserted commas where necessary.

After affirming their ideas about editing, I emphasized that authors want to be courteous to their readers. For this reason, they edit their writing to make sure they have followed the conventions of our language, using appropriate grammar and mechanics as necessary. Since we were just beginning the process, I shared that today we would edit our articles for three things—the correct spelling of words, ending marks, and use of capitals.

Modeling the Editing Process. After discussing what editing involves, I explained that we would practice checking for the correct spelling of words, punctuation, and capitalization in Mitch's article. Michaele had made a copy of his triple-spaced article on an overhead transparency for us to use. To begin the process, I shared that we would have Mitch read his article aloud to us. Then we would give him praise on his newly revised article. After receiving this praise, Mitch would first self-edit his piece, beginning with spelling, then punctuation—in this case, ending marks—and last, capitalization. After he self-edited, we would help Mitch by peer editing his piece.

Before beginning the process, I shared that all authors find it very challenging to self-edit their writing. As authors, I continued, we sometimes overlook spelling, punctuation, or capitalization. We tend to "see" the words spelled correctly even if there is a typo. For this reason, authors and reporters have their peers edit their writing as well. Since we want to publish our writing pieces, I added, we want to follow the same process that reporters use when they edit.

Once everyone was seated comfortably to view Mitch's writing, we began.

Peggy Moore-Hart

Peggy Moore-Hart was sking on February 11. On a sunny day, Peggy Moore-Hart was sking and fell at Mount Brighton. A boy saw her fall. He helped Peggy Moore-Hart. The boy did somthin nice. He said are you okay. Peggy Moore-Hart told him to go to the ski patrel and he went and got them. Peggy Moore-Hart got on a tobggen that was atached [attached] to a sno-mobel [snowmobile]. The ski patrel put her in a splint. They gave her a crdbord [cardboard] splint with tape to hold it and crutes. The splint was holding the bones togathr [together], so it woldn't hut [hurt] very much. The amlis [ambulance] came and took her to the University of Michigan. It was 2:30 when she got to the hospital. Now, she is geting beter.

After giving him praise on his newly revised piece, Mitch began to self-edit his piece for spelling. To help him with this part of the editing, I gave him a blue marker to circle words that he wanted to know how to spell. Using the blue marker, he circled the words *sking, somthin, patrel, tobggen, snomobel, amlis,* and *crutes.*

After complimenting him on his careful edits, I asked his peers to suggest additional words we might want to circle. Randall thought we might want to circle the words *atached* and *crdbord.* Christine suggested that we might want to circle the words *togathr, woldn't,*

Jonathon and Jason peer edit each other's writing pieces.

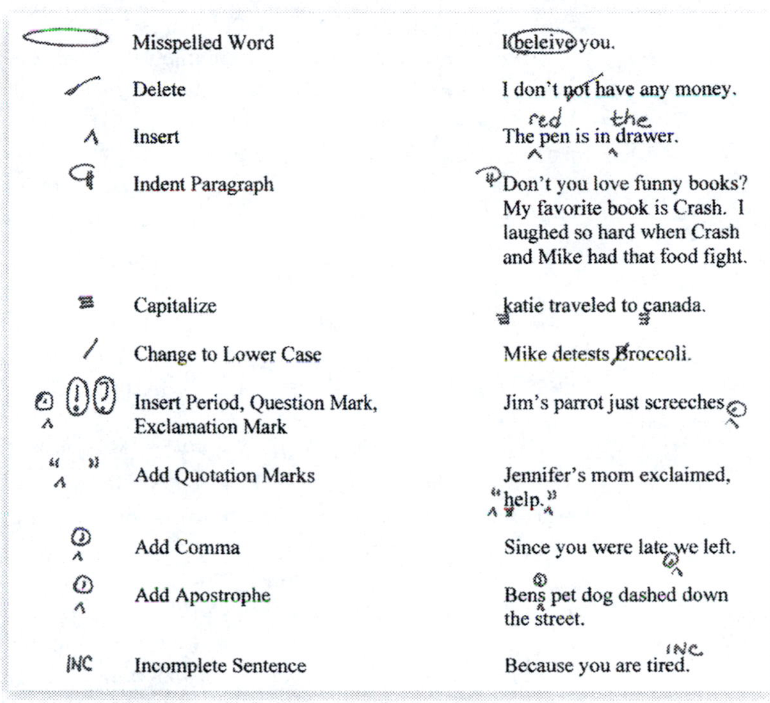

Misspelled Word
I beleive you.
Delete
I don't not have any money.
Insert
The pen is in drawer.
red the
Indent Paragraph
Don't you love funny books? My favorite book is Crash. I laughed so hard when Crash and Mike had that food fight.
Capitalize
katie traveled to canada.
Change to Lower Case
Mike detests Broccoli.
Insert Period, Question Mark, Exclamation Mark
Jim's parrot just screeches
Add Quotation Marks
Jennifer's mom exclaimed, help.
Add Comma
Since you were late we left.
Add Apostrophe
Bens pet dog dashed down the street.
INC
Incomplete Sentence
Because you are tired.
INC

Figure 4.10
Editor's Proofreading Marks

and *hut.* Nathan decided that we should also circle *geting* and *beter.* Once everyone had a chance to share their ideas, I asked if anyone knew how to spell some of the words, reminding them to only raise their hands if they were sure. Nathan correctly spelled *getting* and *better;* Heather correctly spelled *skiing, something, attached, wouldn't,* and *hurt;* Christine correctly spelled *cardboard* and *together.* Since no one was sure about the spellings of *patrol, toboggan,* and *ambulance,* Mitch and Nathan looked these words up in the dictionary together.

Next, I had Mitch check his article for ending marks. After carefully rereading the article, Mitch said that he believed he had all the ending marks for his article. However, he felt there should be quotation marks in the sentence "He said are you okay." Since several students had similarly used dialogue in their articles, Michaele decided to show them how to use quotation marks when someone is talking. First, she asked Mitch to show her where the boy was talking. Mitch pointed to the words "are you okay." After complimenting him, she showed him that we put the quotation marks at the beginning of this phrase and at the end, using the blue marker. Next she explained that we capitalize the first word of this phrase and then modeled how to make this change by placing three lines under the *a* (see Figure 4.10 for proofreading marks). Then she asked him if this phrase was a statement or a question. Mitch explained that it was a question, so she inserted a question mark inside the last quotation mark. Finally, Michaele showed Mitch how to place a comma just before the beginning quotation mark, to show that someone is speaking. After this demonstration, I asked his peers if they noticed any missing ending marks. No one found any.

After complimenting him on his careful edits for ending marks, I asked Mitch to check to see if there were any missing capitals. Again, Mitch carefully reread the article and announced that he thought all the capitals were correctly marked in his article. To verify his self-edits, I then asked the peers if they saw any missing capitals. No one noticed any, so I complimented Mitch once again on his work, noting that he even capitalized University of Michigan, Mount Brighton, and February.

To continue the process, I explained that everyone would work in twos to edit their writing after recess. First, I explained, everyone would carefully self-edit their writing just like Mitch. After checking for spelling, everyone would reread their article to check for missing ending marks; then everyone would reread their article to check for missing capitals. In addition, if they used dialogue, they could edit for quotation marks, capitals, and ending marks within the quotation marks. I reminded them that Mrs. Rae and I would help them with quotation marks as we circulated.

Students Assuming Responsibility for Their Own Editing. In this way, students began to take responsibility for their own editing. Students do not learn how to edit if teachers do this for them. They need to practice self-editing and peer editing themselves if they want to acquire the skills.

As students practiced these skills, Michaele and I circulated among the students, checking to see if they were self-editing and peer editing carefully. If students did not see words that were misspelled or where ending marks or capitals belonged, Michaele and I gave them cues by placing a dot next to a line that had a misspelled word or a line where ending marks or capitals belonged. If students were more advanced, we asked them to look at the beginnings, middles, or ends of their articles to find the required edits. With this additional prompting, all partners successfully completed their editing. Those who finished quickly, with few errors, became assistant editors. They, too, gave students cues by placing dots next to lines that needed to be edited more carefully. Michaele and I, however, did a final edit on all students' work.

Celebrating Students Writing. As shown by this example, an interview became the prewriting activity that helped the young writers collect ideas for their articles. Students further learned more about the writing process, in particular revising and editing their writing, through guided writing. If we want students to become authors who shape and develop their writing, we need to look for and think about guided writing activities that will make writing and its craft tangible for them (Atwell, 2003). According to Atwell (2003), these activities can help students begin to think about, talk about, and approach writing as authors for a lifetime of good writing.

To celebrate the efforts of these young authors, we showed them how to publish their articles, using digital pictures. The young writers then chose the style for their published articles. Some added a background for their articles; some published their articles in two columns, just as one sees in the newspaper. Figure 4.11 shows how Christine published her article.

Closing Thoughts

As students write about their lives and experiences, they become authors. Since their writing evolves from their prior experiences, the young writers become authorities on their topic. Their peers and their teachers often become their first audience, an audience who becomes fascinated by what they know (Hansen, 2002). The young writers, in turn, become motivated by the supportive feedback and responses they receive. As a result, they want to write again the next day. Hansen (2002) calls this process "e–value–ation." When others find value in the writer's message, the writers see possibilities in themselves.

Figure 4.11
Christine's Published Article

Peggy Moore-Hart's Accident

Peggy Moore-Hart, a reading and writing teacher, broke both her fibula and tibia when she was downhill skiing . She was skiing on Feb. 11th, at Mount Brighton and it was about 2:30 . Peggy got tired and something made her fall. A boy about eight or nine asked, "Are you okay?" She said, " No, I broke my leg and I need help.Go to the Ski lift and get the Ski Patrol." That is exactly what he did . The Ski Patrol put her in a toboggan and drove Peggy to the First Aid Room with a snowmobile. They gave her a splint and she was taken to the University of Michigan hospital. They gave her crutches and a cast and now her leg is getting better.

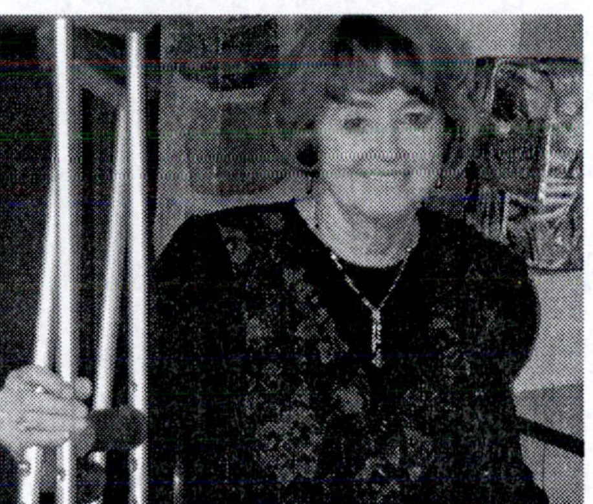

The vignettes or snapshots of classrooms within this chapter illustrate how to use personal narratives, observation, description, and interviews to gather and collect information for writing. As students within the various classrooms applied these strategies within their own writing, they learned how to craft their writing.

The teachers we viewed in the vignettes did not impose learning; they cultivated writing events for their students. Consistent with Chapman (1999), teachers created a classroom of learners where learners began to discover words and language through social interactions. As a result of these ongoing social interactions, students began to learn about written language and ways to use words to express their messages during Writing Workshop. What they learned about language was shaped by and developed through social encounters between teachers and peers.

Cultivating or shaping writing events to emerge from real-life experiences laid a foundation for learning how to write. The social interactions, combined with cognitive construction (Chapman, 1999), helped the students become authors. Through guidance and questioning during minilessons and miniconferences, teachers gradually cultivated students' writing. Writing was not a magical event. Students acquired the language of writers through

- Daily opportunities to write.
- Choices about their topics and genres for writing.

- Engagement and immersion in real-life experiences.
- Exploration and experimentation.
- Personal connections with writing events.
- Participation in a community of caring and supportive learners.
- The use of modeling and demonstrations during minilessons.
- The use of mentoring and coaching from their teachers and peers.
- Positive, thoughtful responses and feedback from their teachers, peers, or parents.
- Thoughtful questions that elicit the words, capturing the intended message of the author from their teachers and peers.
- Collaboration with their peers.
- Discussions, problem-solving activities, and thinking strategies.
- High expectations for what they can accomplish.

If we want our students to become authors, we need to make sure that we appropriately organize our instruction so that our students develop a self-image shaped by affirmation, efficacy, and trust (McCarthy & Watahomiggie, 1998).

Teachers' Questions

1. I teach first grade. When should I teach my first graders how to revise their writing?

With first graders and kindergarteners, our first goal is to help them become comfortable with writing and using their temporary spelling. Once we see this happening, we may explore revising their writing. One way to begin revising with the young writers is by collecting students' writing pieces and putting them away for a week or two. Then we can bring the writing out again, asking students to reread their pieces and see if there is additional information they may want to add.

Helping them understand how to add more information can be modeled through a minilesson, using one student's writing piece. For example, maybe a student wrote about going to a movie but didn't explain how he or she felt about the movie. After eliciting the student's feelings about the movie, we can model how to add a couple of sentences that show how he or she felt about the movie.

2. My students don't like to revise. How can I help them become more positive about revising?

One way to help students become more comfortable with revising is to share our own writing with students. For example, we might show them a letter we plan to send home to parents. We can invite students to give us praise about the letter and then ask us questions about the message. After listening to their questions, we can model how we will insert additional information to clarify the message in the letter. Students need to understand that all writers revise their writing. Once they see a value and a purpose for revising, they become less resistant.

Another way to help them appreciate how revising improves writing is to invite students to share their revisions. They can share a sentence before it was revised and then after it was revised. This helps them see, along with their peers, that revising perks up our writing.

3. Can kindergarten children edit their writing?

As emphasized, our first goal is to help young writers become comfortable writing and using their temporary spelling. Once we see this happening, we can ask students to circle two words they want to know how to spell, which we can spell for them. Kindergarteners enjoy this because they often want to know how to spell the words correctly. Using a parent to help us, we can easily circulate among the students, spelling the words. Students can write the correct spelling above the words they circled, using colored pens.

If we are going to have them publish a class book, we can also have them work in twos, checking to see that a sentence begins with a capital and ends with a period. Then we can ask a parent to type the sentences just like they would be in a book, finishing any additional edits that need to be made.

4. Do my students need to revise and edit everything they write?

As mentioned earlier, we don't need to publish everything students write. If we do, they become overwhelmed with writing, and so do we. If we publish about two pieces per marking period, students can learn about the writing process and how to apply the writing process to their own writing. Publishing in this way motivates students; they experience the joy of seeing their writing published for a larger audience.

Children's Literature

Carle, E. (1989). *Eric Carle's animals animals.* New York: Philomel Books.

References

Atwell, N. (1987). *In the middle: Writing, reading, and learning with adolescents.* Portsmouth, NH: Boynton/Cook.

Atwell, N. (2003). Hard trying and these recipes. *Voices from the Middle, 11,* 16–19.

Calkins, L. (1983). *Lessons from a child: On the teaching and learning of writing.* Portsmouth, NH: Heinemann.

Calkins, L. (1994). *The art of teaching writing.* Portsmouth, NH: Heinemann.

Casbergue, R., & Plache, M. (2003). Immersing children in nonfiction: Fostering emergent research and writing. In D. Barone & L. Morrow (Eds.), *Literacy and young children: Research-based practices* (pp. 243–260). New York: Guilford.

Chapman, M. (1999). Situated, social, active: Rewriting the genre in the elementary classroom. *Written Communication, 16,* 469–490.

Clark, R. (1995). *Free to write.* Portsmouth, NH: Heinemann.

Cooper, J., & Kiger, N. (2003). *Literacy: Helping children construct literacy.* Boston: Houghton Mifflin.

Coppola, J., Dawson, C., McPhillips, S., George, J., & Maclean, D. (2005). "In my country, we don't write stories, we tell our stories": Writing with English-Language Learners in the primary grades. In R. Indrisano & J. Paratore (Eds.), *Learning to write and writing to learn: Theory and research* (pp. 40–56). Newark, DE: International Reading Association.

Cummins, J. (1986). Empowering minority students: A framework for intervention. *Harvard Educational Review, 56,* 18–36.

Dyson, A. (1997). *Writing superheroes: Contemporary childhood, popular culture, and classroom literacy.* New York: Teachers College Press.

Espinosa, C. (2006). Finding memorable moments: Images and identities in autobiographical writing. *Language Arts, 84,* 136–144.

Graves, D. (1983). *Writing: Teachers and children at work.* Portsmouth, NH: Heinemann.

Graves, D. (1994). *A fresh look at writing.* Portsmouth, NH: Heinemann.

Graves, D. (1999). *Bring life into learning.* Portsmouth, NH: Heinemann.

Hansen, J. (2002). A teacher's development project: A cross cultural experience in Brazil. *The Reading Teacher, 55,* 456–462.

Harwayne, S. (1992). *Lasting impressions: Weaving literature into the writing workshop.* Portsmouth, NH: Heinemann.

Higgins, B., Miller, M., & Wegmann, S. (2007). Reading to the test . . . not! Balancing best practice and testing requirements in writing. *The Reading Teacher, 60,* 310–319.

Indrisano, R., & Paratore, J. (2005). *Learning to write, writing to learn: Theory and research in practice.* Newark, DE: International Reading Association.

Martin, B. (1972). *Sounds of language readers.* New York: Holt, Rhinehart and Winston.

McCarthy, T., & Watahomiggie, L. (1998). Language and literacy in American Indian and Alaskan native communities. In B. Perez (Ed.), *Sociocultural contexts of language and literacy* (pp. 69–98). Mahwah, NJ: Lawrence Erlbaum.

Moore, M. (1989). Computers can enhance transactions between readers and writers. *The Reading Teacher, 42,* 608–611.

Moore-Hart, M. (1995). The effects of Multicultural Links on reading and writing performance and cultural awareness of fourth and fifth graders. *Computers in Human Behavior, 11,* 391–410.

Moore-Hart, M. (2004). Creating learning environments that invite all students to learn through multicultural literature and information technology. *Childhood Education, 81,* 87–95.

Moore-Hart, M. (2006). A writers' camp in action: A community of readers and writers. *The Reading Teacher, 59,* 326–338.

Peregoy, S., & Boyle, O. (1993). *Reading, writing, and learning in ESL.* New York: Longman.

Piazza, C. (2003). *Journeys: The teaching of writing in elementary classrooms.* Upper Saddle River, NJ: Merrill Prentice Hall.

Reyhner, J., & Garcia, R. (1989). Helping minorities read better: Problems and promises. *Reading Research and Instruction, 28,* 84–91.

Routman, R. (1994). *Invitations: Changing as teachers and learners, K–12.* Portsmouth, NH: Heinemann.

Routman, R. (2005). *Writing essentials.* Portsmouth, NH: Heinemann.

Sloan, G. (2003). *The child as critic: Developing literacy through literature, K–8* (4th ed.). Newark, DE: International Reading Association.

Tompkins, G. (2004). *Teaching writing: Balancing process and product.* Upper Saddle River, NJ: Merrill.

Wolf, S., & Wolf, K. (2002). Teaching true and to the test in writing. *Language Arts, 79,* 229–240.

Wood, K., & Dickinson, T. (2000). *Promoting literacy in grades 4–9.* Boston: Allyn & Bacon.

chapter FIVE

Integrating Multicultural Literature with Writing and Word Processing

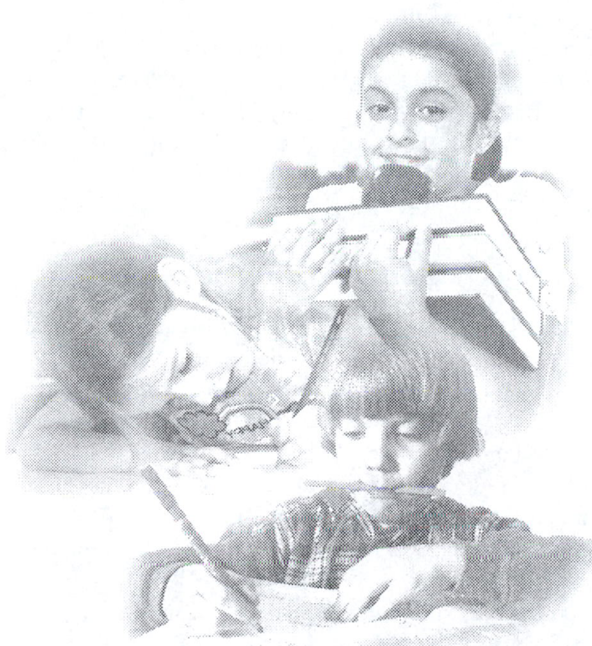

Many people are similar. Many people are different. My partners are similar because we all are girls. We all like music. We all like learning. In addition, we like summer, we like sleeping in, we all go to school, and we have homework. We all have moms. We all have hair. We all like French fries.

My partners are different from me because they all don't have glasses and we have different hobbies and different hair bows. We have different heights and different faces. We have different hair colors. We have different eye colors. We all don't wear jewelry, and we all don't like brussel sprouts.

All people are the same in many ways and different in many ways.

Samantha, an African American fifth grader, wrote this piece after hearing the story *People* by Peter Spier. Samantha and her peers were actively engaged in a variety of meaningful and authentic activities emerging from both their prior experiences and multicultural literature. Her teacher, Elaine Bortz, believes in providing her students challenging learning experiences that emerge from language, the foundation of reading and writing, and multicultural literature. To accomplish her goals, Elaine creates a community of learners who respect the language, culture, and identity of each member of the community.

Discovering and Appreciating the Similarities and Differences among People

The children in our schools are a microcosm of society. The intermingling of cultures, ethnic groups, religions, and languages creates a rich mosaic, a beautiful and balanced picture, with each piece of the mosaic forming a positive and distinct contribution to the whole (Diamond

& Moore, 1995). If parts of the mosaic become chipped away, devalued, or discarded, the mosaic begins to lose its inherent beauty and value (Diamond & Moore, 1995).

As teachers, we illuminate the mosaic when we celebrate the language, values, beliefs, and ways of learning that our students bring to the classroom. Samantha's fifth grade teacher, Elaine, believes that multicultural literature can become a tool to help illuminate the mosaic. As Samantha and her peers read multicultural books, they begin to see themselves, their friends, and their neighbors reflected in the books. While talking about and discussing the cultural features of the stories, the fifth graders discover more about one another, including their similarities and their differences. As they learn more about themselves and one another's cultural histories, they draw closer together. Gradually the mosaic becomes more illuminated as each piece of the mosaic highlights the inherent beauty of the picture.

As the fifth graders draw closer together, they gradually become a community of learners linked to one another and the world. The multicultural literature provides a mirror that reflects the rich diversity of their community, as well as the nation and the world. To be sure that the mirror accurately reflects the nation and world, Elaine carefully selects the multicultural literature she uses within her curriculum. Specifically, she considers multicultural literature to be literature that "focuses on specific cultures by highlighting and celebrating their cultural and historical perspectives, traditions and heritage, language and dialects, and experiences and lifestyles" (Diamond & Moore, 1995, p. 43).

Creating a Foundation for Respecting and Celebrating Diversity

Laying a foundation for a culturally sensitive classroom where all members respect and celebrate their cultural and historical traditions can be challenging. Elaine believes that Peter Spier's book *People* is a beautiful way to create this foundation at the beginning of the school year. The students in her class, who come from diverse backgrounds, include a large number of African American and European American students and a few Native American, Chinese, Japanese, Latino, Hmong, and Indian children. Her students are also economically varied, with numerous students receiving free and reduced lunches, and academically varied, with a large number of students receiving additional support through learning resource centers and special education teachers.

The book *People,* which reflects the diversity both within her class and society, offers an opportunity for cultural sensitivity to emerge within her class. To highlight the similarities and differences among people, Elaine starts the read aloud activity by asking her students to take a sheet of paper and fold it in half—the "hot dog way." Next she models how to label one side "Similarities" and the other side "Differences" (see Figure 5.1). Once the students have correctly labeled the sections of their paper, she has them list ways that people are similar and ways people are different. After writing for a few minutes, students stop and share their ideas. Marina shares that all people have hair and eyes. Shauntell adds that people have different colors of hair and different colors of eyes. Taking advantage of the teachable moment, Elaine points out that some words—like *hair* and *eyes*—may be in both columns. For example, we all have hair and eyes, but we have different colors and types of hair and eyes.

Raising her hand, Heather continues, pointing out that we are all people, we all go to school, and we all have the same teacher. Demario adds that we all have cells, and we all have blood. Next, Bryan points out that we all live in different homes, and we all enjoy different sports and games. Brittany chimes in next, sharing that some of us speak different languages, and many people in the world celebrate different religious beliefs.

After several more students share their ideas, Elaine points out that some of these ideas will be expressed in the book *People.* As she begins reading the story aloud, she encourages her students to add to their lists if they hear some new ways that people are similar or different.

Figure 5.1

Notetaking Chart for Similarities and Differences between People

Similarities	Differences

While listening to the story, her students hear many of the ideas that they have just shared. They also hear some new ideas like "We come in all sizes and shapes—tall, short, and in between." Or "People everywhere love to play. But not the same games everywhere" (Spier, 1990).

Spier's book also opens up opportunities to discuss ideas about diversity. For example, he shares, "All of us want to look our best. Still, what is considered beautiful or handsome in one place is considered ugly, and even ridiculous, elsewhere." This becomes a perfect opportunity for Elaine to share how women in some countries fashion their hair to be longer than men. However, in other countries men style their hair to be long while women shape their hair to be short. What is valued in one culture may not be valued in another culture.

Highlighting these differences among cultures helps her students become more sensitive to others' values and beliefs. At this point, Elaine emphasizes that laughing and giggling about what is considered beautiful or handsome would be disrespectful and hurtful to others. Thus, Elaine begins to model the importance of being sensitive to others' feelings and being respectful of others' values and beliefs.

Peter Spier's story also celebrates different ways to communicate and use language. Elaine's students are amazed to learn that there are 201 different languages spoken on earth. Seeing all the different alphabets and ways people write splashed across the pages fascinates her fifth graders.

Spier concludes the story by portraying how dreadfully dull our world would be if all the buildings, cars, signs, and people were exactly the same. Following a lifeless illustration of this world, Spier presents the readers with a new illustration, one that celebrates the beauty and richness of our world and nation—where "each and every one of us is unlike any other."

Through ongoing discussion, questioning, and dialogue, Elaine's students begin to view diversity differently. *People* laid a foundation for understanding how the people of our world and nation form a mosaic, with each piece of the mosaic forming a positive and distinct contribution to the whole.

Using Writing to Reinforce Cultural Values and Beliefs

Through writing, Elaine further instills these values and understandings about diversity the next day. She realizes that writing helps us recall and understand information at deeper levels (Langer, 1986). To begin the process, she asks her students to form groups of two or three. Next, Elaine explains that each group will fold a sheet of paper in half, labeling one side "Similarities" and the other side "Differences" once again. Since Samantha's group includes three students (due to the uneven numbers of students in the class), they list ways that the three of them are similar and ways they are different.

This exercise helps the fifth graders begin to examine the similarities and differences among themselves more closely. Elaine further uses this opportunity to extend their understanding about diversity, pointing out that there are similarities and differences within cultural groups, as well as across cultural groups, just like we see within our class.

Once the students complete their lists, Elaine has them write about the groups' similarities and differences. This is how Samantha's piece, displayed at the beginning of the chapter, evolved.

As can be seen, Samantha is beginning to perceive ways people are similar and different. Using her list of similarities and differences helps her organize her paragraphs about diversity. First she describes the group's similarities in one paragraph. She discusses their differences in a second paragraph, then she ends with a conclusion—"All people are the same in many ways and different in many ways." Through writing, Samantha's understanding of diversity begins to evolve.

Creating a Class Book about Diversity. To take cultural knowledge to an even deeper level, Elaine invites her students to create a class book about diversity, following Spier's model. When Elaine shares her idea with the class, the students decide that their class book would be about the students at George Elementary School.

Since her class has had limited experiences with writing, Elaine determines that her students will work on the book in groups so that they will become more familiar with the writing process. In order to facilitate positive working relationships within the small groups, Elaine forms the groups herself. She makes sure that the groups include students of mixed ability, both leaders and followers, and students who will work together well.

Once the groups are formed, students begin brainstorming what they want to write about. One group decides to write about pets; another chooses to write about games; still another selects holidays; another group decides to write about shoes. After selecting their topics, the fifth graders then create webs about their topic. Continuing the process the next day, the groups use their webs to create a draft about their topic.

Under Elaine's guidance, the groups revise their drafts a few days later, following the PQP process explained at the end of Chapter 4. Next they edit their pages in pairs.

By working in groups of mixed ability levels, her students become more comfortable with the writing process and more familiar with how to use the process to shape their writing. Samantha's group creates the following pages for the book:

Many people have pets like dogs, cats, birds, mice, or even snakes. Some people have two different animals together.

Birds are good pets to have around. Some birds can talk or sing, or do both. Birds can be different colors like blue, green, or red. While most birds fly, some spend their lives on the ground.

Dogs are fun, frisky animals. They are easy to train. You can train dogs to play catch or to play dead. Some dogs are trained to pull sleds.

Cats can train themselves. Though cats aren't as lively as dogs, they are still good pets. Cats love to play a lot. They are very clean pets. They lick themselves when they get dirty.

Some people have snakes for pets. Some snakes are poisonous. Rattlesnakes rattle their tails before they bite. There are some poisonous snakes in Michigan.

Some mice like cheese. Mice live in our school. Cats love to catch mice. There are different kinds of mice like field mice. Some people keep mice for pets.

As can be seen from this group's writing, Samantha and her peers learned to incorporate Spier's rhythmic writing style into their own writing. Reading the book multiple times helped them internalize his lively style of writing, which is interspersed with pictures.

Following Spier's example, Samantha's group also illustrates their pages. Their charming, colorful drawings add a "lookability" to their message—living harmoniously together by understanding and respecting different viewpoints and values.

Using Collaborative Writing. Having the opportunity to select their own topics for writing helped the fifth graders remain engaged and interested throughout the activity. Since the topics emerge from their personal experiences and lives, students easily gather information about their topics. While writing in groups renews their confidence in writing, students simultaneously acquire new strategies for expressing their ideas from their peers.

Not only do students become more comfortable with writing, they also discover how diversity enriches every aspect of our world. Creating a book about diversity inspires a new excitement for differences among people; students begin to realize that we all have the right to be different and unique. While studying diversity, the fifth graders form a bond; a community of learners begins to evolve within their classroom.

Exposing Students to Quality Literature

Samantha and her peers were able to create a beautiful book about diversity because they were exposed to quality literature. Teachers serve a pivotal role in the identification and use of quality literature and authentic multicultural literature. For this reason, Elaine critically evaluates the literature she uses in her classroom, while making informed decisions about her choices.

If we make qualitative decisions, similar to Elaine, our students will begin to see themselves reflected in literature and begin to celebrate their diversity while recognizing similarities between and within cultures. According to Diamond and Moore (1995, p. 44–45) multicultural literature should include the following characteristics:

1. Characters authentically reflect the distinct cultural experiences, realities, and world views of specific groups.
2. Character representations portray characters in a true-to-life and balanced manner, highlighting relationships among people within the culture and with people of different cultures.
3. Settings are representative of an environment within a historical/contemporary time, place, or situation of the specific culture.
4. Themes are consistent with the values and beliefs, customs and traditions, needs, and conflicts of the specific culture.
5. Informational literature is presented in a detailed and accurate manner.
6. Language is characteristic of the vocabulary, style, patterns, and rhythms of speech of the specific cultural group. Dialogue is further culturally authentic with characters using speech that accurately depicts the oral traditions within the culture.
7. Literature is free of stereotypes in language, illustrations, behaviors, or character traits.

8. Language reflects a sensibility to the people of the culture.
9. Gender roles within the culture are accurately and authentically portrayed.

Selecting quality multicultural literature for our language arts curriculum determines whether our youth perceive a multifaceted, richer, clearer, and more accurate view of life (Faltis, 2000; Landt, 2006). As a result of our decisions, multicultural literature becomes a tool to celebrate diversity and equity in education (Cai, 1998).

The use of quality and authentic multicultural literature also provides a model for students' writing and their portrayal of life. According to educators (Calkins, 1994; Graves, 1994; Olness, 2005; Spandel & Stiggins, 1997), writers learn about good writing by hearing and loving books, poems, and essays or articles. Fletcher and Portalupi (1998) further claim that students' writing reflects the classroom literature that surrounds and sustains it. Literature, in fact, is a critical component of a writing curriculum.

Just exposing students to quality literature will not produce quality writing. Calkins (1994) suggests that we need to continuously ask our students authors' questions so they might internalize authors' craft. If a book makes us laugh, she explains that we need to ask, "What did the author do to make us laugh?" "What did you like about the author's lead?" Other authors' questions might include "What kinds of words did the author use to help us see, hear, smell, and taste the setting for this story?" "How did the author help us feel her pain and sorrow?" "What techniques do I want to borrow from this author?"

As Elaine read and reread *People* aloud to her students, she asked them similar questions. As a result, the fifth graders began to transfer these stylistic techniques, as well as the structure and language of the story, to their own writing. According to Olness (2005), authors show us a variety of writing styles; they model the craft of writing. With ongoing exposure to quality literature, as well as authors' questions about their craft, the fifth graders began to learn these stylistic techniques and apply them to their own writing.

Reinforcing Concepts about Diversity through Multicultural Literature

Even though Elaine laid a foundation for understanding diversity and celebrating the right to be unique and different, these concepts need to be continuously extended and developed. To accomplish this goal, Elaine designs numerous literacy experiences to emerge from students' language and cultural experiences. She believes that her literacy curriculum should further reflect the diversity within her classroom.

When people visit Elaine's classroom, they often see students actively engaged in a variety of literacy activities that evolve from multicultural literature. These activities might include choral reading, reader's theater, interactive reading and writing activities, writing responses to literature, interactive discussions and dialogues, mapping and knowledge-generating activities, and creative responses to literature through drama, art, music, or dancing (Moore-Hart, 2004). Infusing multicultural literature with the literacy curriculum simultaneously improves students' reading and writing performance and heightens their awareness of other cultures (Moore-Hart, Knapp, & Diamond, 2003).

Integrating Multicultural Literature with a Thematic Unit on Cinderella Stories

Knowing there are so many versions of the Cinderella story, Elaine follows these activities with a thematic unit on Cinderella stories to reinforce students' appreciation of the rich diversity within their classroom. She believes that the Cinderella stories, as well as other folktales, might stimulate her students to connect with their own cultural traditions, values, and beliefs and learn about those of their peers.

After reading several versions of the Cinderella story from countries around the world (i.e., *Cinderella,* by Perrault; *The Korean Cinderella,* by Climo; *The Rough-Face Girl,* by Martin; *Mufaro's Beautiful Daughters,* by Steptoe; or *The Brocaded Slipper,* by Vuong) aloud to her students, Elaine first helps her students see similarities and differences among the folktales and cultures by having students complete a cultural story map (see Figure 5.2). She uses the cultural map to highlight some differences and similarities among cultural values and beliefs revealed within the folktales. As the class continues to read more stories, her students discover that, no matter what their country of origin, the Cinderella stories seem to have some universal themes, such as good overcomes evil (Buss & Karnowski, 2000).

After reading the Cinderella stories, Elaine often extends the stories by doing interactive reading and writing activities, creative responses to the stories, or mapping and knowledge-generating activities. Other times she merely reads the story interactively, allowing her students to enjoy the stories aesthetically; still other times, she has her students use inquiry to learn more about the countries where the different stories are set (see Chapter 8).

Her major goal, however, is to connect her students to the world and its diversity, helping her students begin to understand and appreciate the diversity among people of the world. The multicultural stories serve as a window to view other cultures and to perceive the great riches that diversity brings to our nation and world (Diamond & Moore, 1995). She further hopes to affirm students' cultural heritages and traditions as they encounter characters and settings that reflect their own cultural background.

Integrating a Cinderella Story with Writing as a Framework for Learning about Characters

As she integrates her unit with her literacy curriculum, Elaine always begins by interactively reading a Cinderella story to her students. Then she follows the read aloud with

Figure 5.2

Cultural Story Map Highlighting Similarities and Differences among Cultural Values and Beliefs in Folktales

Cultural Story Map

Title of Folktales	Culture	Setting of Story	Characters	Character's Traits	Cultural Values/ Beliefs	Message

reflective discussions about the story and its cultural context. Depending on the story and its attributes, Elaine then uses a variety of follow-up activities to reinforce interpretation and understanding of the story. Given current issues of accountability and student performance, Elaine wants to make sure her students perform well on standardized tests, especially in reading comprehension. In fact, her students significantly improved their reading and writing performance on standardized tests (Moore-Hart et al., 2003).

Heightening Understanding of Character. After interactively reading the Cinderella story, *Mufaro's Beautiful Daughters* by Steptoe, for example, Elaine reinforces her students' understanding of character through a writing activity. Consistent with Langer (1995), she wants to help her students "step into" and "move through" the story by heightening their awareness of character and its influence on plot. Elaine realizes that an understanding of characters helps her students perceive relationships between characters and the story elements—the setting, characters, goals or problems, actions, events, and resolutions of a story (Martinez & Roser, 2005),

To help her fifth graders identify with the two sisters in the story—Manyara and Nyasha—Elaine plans a minilesson, which includes both shared writing and guided writing. Using literature as a tool (Rickards & Hawes, 2007) for developing students' awareness of character in *Mufaro's Beautiful Daughters,* Elaine hopes that her fifth graders will then apply these concepts about character when reading future folktales or when writing their own folktales.

Creating a Web of Words about the Characters. To begin the minilesson, Elaine asks her students to think of words to describe Manyara. Brittany shares that she thinks Manyara is sneaky because she left for the village during the night, ahead of her sister. Demario adds that he thinks she is deceitful because she told her father that Nyasha would never want to leave him. As the students randomly describe Manyara, Elaine quickly records their words, forming a web of words (see Figure 5.3). As the fifth graders continue to share their ideas, Elaine has them also explain their reasons for selecting the words. This strategy reinforces comprehension of the story while creating an initial awareness of the role of characters in stories.

Whenever students use vocabulary words that are unfamiliar to some students (for example, Demario's choice of *deceitful*), Elaine asks students to "tell us about your word."

Figure 5.3
Web Showing Manyara's Character Traits

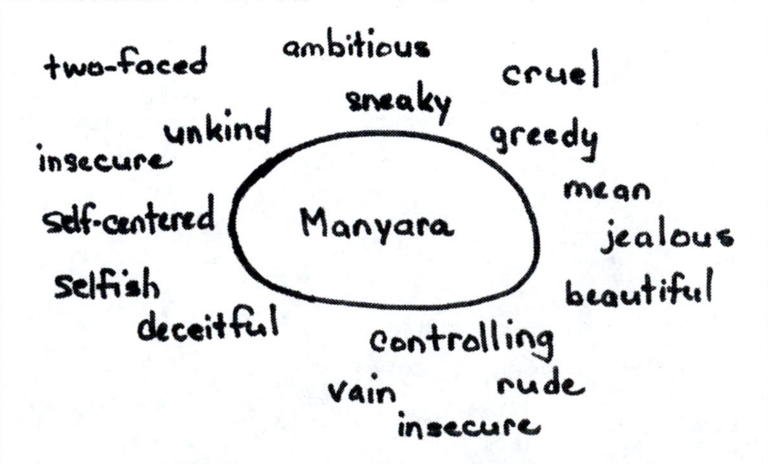

This technique strengthens vocabulary development for some students and provides a form of praise for those who use vibrant, descriptive adjectives. The web in Figure 5.3 shows the fifth graders' web of words for Manyara.

Creating "I AM" Poems about the Characters. Following this shared webbing activity, Elaine explains that they will use the words from the webs to create a poem about one of the characters in the story. Using the formula poem "I AM" (Diamond and Moore, 1995), each student chooses a character and selects words to describe the character from the character's point of view, as in the following poem.

I AM
I am (3 words describing character)
I like (3 words)
(2 words) are important to me
I am good at (3 words)
I am not good at (3 words)
I love (3 words)
I don't like (3 words)
This is me!
I Am
(Name of character)

The completed poems, shown below, demonstrate students' understanding of the characters' intentions, motivations, and feelings.

I AM

I am sweet, thoughtful, and forgiving
I like to pick flowers, sing, and feed my garden
My family and my garden are important to me
I am good at planting flowers and singing
I am not good at being cruel, mean, and selfish
I love flowers, singing, and my garden
I don't like it when my sister teases me and I don't like to tease her back
This is me!
I am
Nyasha

I AM

I am nice, beautiful, and smart
I like my father and having servants
I am good at being ambitious, manipulative, and sneaky
I am not good at being nice and respectful
I would love to be the queen
I don't like small boys, snakes, and headless men
This is me!
I am
Manyara

While working on their poems, students continue to talk about the characters' qualities and their behaviors with their peers. Thus, the social context within her classroom becomes a way for students to think and problem solve as they compose the poems. Writing about Manyara, for example, requires that students make deeper inferences about her thoughts and feelings to determine how she is good. While observing her students as they write the poems, Elaine notices that many of her students incorporate some of the new vocabulary words within their poems. Writing seems to reinforce their understanding of vocabulary (Moore-Hart et al., 2003).

When Demario began writing, he asked if he could write about the Prince instead of Manyara or Nyasha. Without hesitation, Elaine encourages him to write his poem about the Prince. After hearing his poem during the share session, two other boys also decide to write a poem about the Prince. Thus, the writing activity about Africans gave these boys voice in their writing. At the same time, the activity validated the boys' pride in their cultural heritage. Demario's poem is shown below.

I AM

I am kind, helpful, and caring
I like my friends and Nyasha
My friends and family are important to me
I am good at being king
I am not good at being mean or cruel
I love my mother
I don't like people who are deceitful and self-centered
This is me!
I am
King Demetrius

Through this writing activity, the fifth graders gain a heightened awareness of the characters—their names, dialogues, and descriptions; they also begin to perceive the relationship between plot and characters. According to Graves (2005), this understanding will reveal itself later in the students' fictional writing.

Using Multicultural Folktales to Learn about the Literary Elements of Literature

Similar to Elaine, Alexa Holyman uses multicultural folktales at the beginning of her school year. Since folktales emerge from countries around the world, Alexa believes that the multicultural folktales might affirm the rich diversity within her classroom. As students simultaneously encounter ways of thinking different from their own (Grimes, 2005), she feels that the folktales will provide a way to learn about and, on some level, to experience unfamiliar cultures.

Since folktales often reinforce cultural and social mores (Russell, 1997), Alexa highlights the themes of the tales, using this as a context to discuss cultural values and beliefs. She helps them see that qualities like humility, kindness, patience, hard work, or courage are invariably rewarded in folktales, while qualities like greed, selfishness, and excessive pride are punished (Russell, 1997). At the same time she shows her readers that folktales also reveal ways that we are all alike beneath the skin by creating themes that are universal (Grimes, 2005). Thus, as Alexa's students read and talk about the multicultural folktales, they have another lens from which to view ways that people are similar and different.

Reinforcing an Understanding of Elements of Story with Multicultural Folktales. Alexa also realizes that folktales represent a way to simultaneously learn about elements of story. Since folktales follow a patterned beginning, a conflict, a quick resolution, and an ending (Buss & Karnowski, 2000), Alexa reinforces her students' understanding of narrative structures and predictable story elements. As a class, students begin to look for familiar signals for the beginnings and endings of stories like "once upon a time" or "they lived happily ever after." Alexa also guides her students' understanding of authors' craft by asking them authors' questions, as described previously.

To specifically strengthen understanding of the story elements, Alexa reads folktales interactively with her students, asking questions to prompt their thinking and understanding of the story. Sometimes, she frames a few of her questions, using the vocabulary related to elements of a story so that they become familiar with these terms. For example, she might ask

- Where is this story taking place?
- Who is the main character of this story?
- What do you think the problem will be in this story?

Later, she reinforces concepts about the story elements by having students fold a paper into six squares. After labeling each square with a story element, her students then use illustrations to show the story elements. Other times, she has them complete story maps. Staci's story map (see Figure 5.4) reveals her understanding of story elements in the story *Babushka's Doll* by Patricia Polacco. By varying how she supports these concepts, she continues to engage her students' interest in learning about these elements.

Reinforcing Understanding of Theme in Multicultural Folktales. Fostering an understanding of a story's theme is often more complex since it involves inferencing. One of the themes from *Babushka's Doll,* for example, suggests a need for fairness as we interact with others. To highlight understanding of this important theme, Alexa asks her students, "Was it fair for Natasha to treat her Babushka the way she did? Was it fair for Babushka's doll to treat Natasha in such an unkind way?" As her students respond to these questions,

Demario writing an I AM poem about the Prince.

Figure 5.4

Story Map of Babushka's Doll

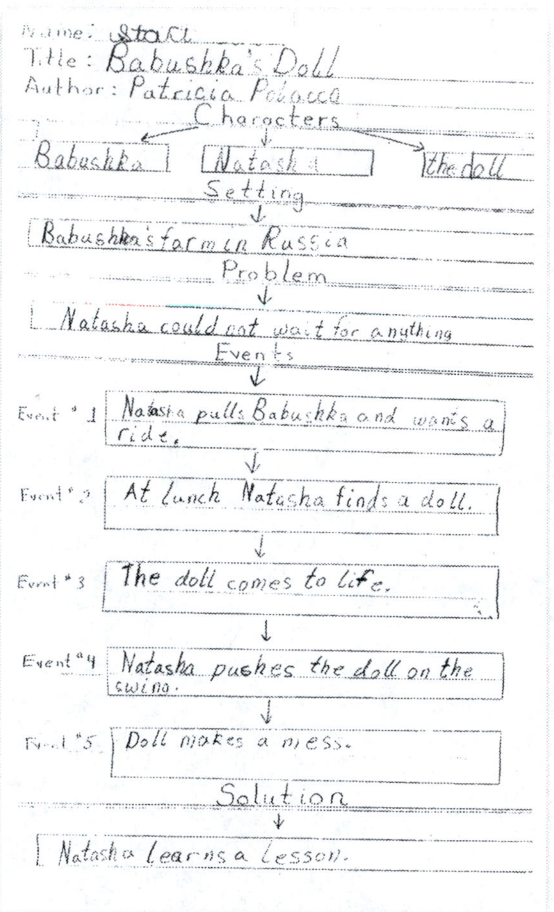

Title: Babushka's Doll
Author: Patricia Polacco
Characters
Babushka
Natasha
the doll
Setting
Babushka's farm in Russia
Problem
Natasha could not wait for anything
Events
Event #1 Natasha pulls Babushka and wants a ride.
Event #2 At lunch Natasha finds a doll.
Event #3 The doll comes to life.
Event #4 Natasha pushes the doll on the swing.
Event #5 Doll makes a mess.
Solution
Natasha learns a lesson.

Alexa encourages them to explain why or why not. Through this interactive discussion, Alexa strengthens her students' understanding of the author's theme about justice and fairness.

Alexa then reinforces the concept of theme by explaining that Patricia Polacco wrote this story to remind us that we need to treat one another fairly. To help her students understand how justice and fairness relate to their own lives, Alexa has them reflect on justice and fairness in their own family life through writing. Ashleigh's story shows us what Natasha's doll would teach her:

What Natasha's Doll Would Teach Me!

If Babushka's doll came alive it would teach me to stop fighting with my brother and my sister. Babushka's doll would teach me and Jessica to keep our stuff on our side of the room. Babushka's doll would help me stay out of my brother's room so he won't hurt me. Babushka's doll could come over to my house and stay there. She would make my mom and dad very happy.

As can be seen, writing helped Ashleigh reflect on her own home life and think about how she might adjust her own behavior. Through reading and writing, students begin to discover how to solve problems and discover solutions to problems in their own lives (Clark, 1995). This writing event further serves to mediate children's social relationships (DeNicola & Franquiz, 2006), helping the third graders consider alternative ways of treating their friends and family. By laying a foundation for discussing these principles, Alexa opens up opportunities to continue these discussions at deeper levels. When her students move to higher grade levels, they will be able to relate these concepts to prejudice and discrimination in our nation and world.

Learning about Authors' Craft through Multicultural Folktales. While reading numerous multicultural folktales, students also begin to discover how to write their own folktales. Using a story map, for example, might become a prewriting strategy for the students to determine what the story elements will be in their own story. Having multiple models of folktales to draw from helps them see how to begin and end stories, how to create settings, and how to determine what a goal or problem may be. Given quality literature, even kindergarten and first grade writers can create their own folktales (Martinez & Roser, 2005). Julia, age 5, demonstrates her understanding of folktales in her story about a grasshopper and a fairy:

The Grasshopper and the Big Kerplop!

Ouns [Once] thar [there] wus a fairy namd Columbine. His best frend was Grashopr. Tha [They] both livd in Nevrlad [Neverland] with thar [their] frends Rose and Lilly. It wus sumr [summer]. It wus Buootiful! Wun [One] sumr day Columbine invited hiss frend out for a piknik. Sudile [Suddenly] the clods trnd [turned] gray Sudile a thandr [thunder] cloud made a bash [bunch] of litng [lightning]. It strtd too ran [rain]. Then Columbine went home to get his umbrella. Rose and Lilly hid undr a lef [leaf]. Grashopr wus hiding undr a gras blad [blade]. A ran [rain] drop fell on grashppr [Grasshopper's] hed [head]. KERPLOP!!!! Columbine retrnd [returned] with his umbrella as the sun shone. Rose and Lilly wr [were] dry. Grashopr was soking [soaking] wet. Rose lookt [looked] at Grashopr. "Lets go swimming." She sed [said]. "Hav a good time stinkpots. I am alredy wet!" brst [burst] out Grashopr.

Consistent with Buss and Karnowski (2000), Julia's story reveals her understanding of patterned beginnings and how to create a setting and conflict for her story. She even uses a sense of humor in her ending.

Using Writing Responses with Literature: A Way to Highlight Understanding of Diversity

Living as we do in a multicultural society and in a global economy, Barb Dykman believes we need to discuss diversity with our students on an ongoing basis. She chooses to use writing as a way to learn about other cultures, traditions, beliefs, and values. Through writing, Barb feels that her students will first begin to learn who they are; second, they will discover who their peers, family, and neighbors are. As a result of these ongoing experiences, Barb hopes that her students will gradually begin to gain more knowledge about the people within their community and their world.

Barb also believes that writing contributes to her third graders' evolving understanding of cultures. Through writing responses to literature, they begin to see beauty in cultural traditions, beliefs, and values; they might also begin to confront issues of racism, discrimination, and prejudice. (See Using Literature Response Journals in Chapter 3.)

When writing responses to literature, many teachers have their students record their ideas in journals, as shown in Chapter 3. Consistent with Tompkins (2004), Barb senses that there is a need for both journaling and focused writing. Through focused writing, Barb helps her students learn more about specific genres; other times, she reinforces various concepts about the writer's craft; sometimes, she heightens attention to social or cultural concepts. Consistent with Calkins (1994) and Graves (1994), Barb's students still have choices in their selections of topics or in their particular interests when using focused writing.

Since reading aloud is part of her daily routine, Barb often uses multicultural literature as a catalyst for gaining a perspective on how others experience life, as well as their cultural traditions, beliefs, and values. She then uses focused writing activities to develop an awareness of social or cultural concepts within the story.

Using Writing Response with Multicultural Biographies

Barb enjoys reading multicultural biographies, which combine elements of expository text writing with narrative writing (Tompkins, 2004). She realizes that students often gain role models for their lives. Rather than read about cultures in a fact-filled textbook, students experience a culture through the life of a leader who has made contributions to the world. Since biographies often take readers into the character's life, Barb finds that her students often relate to the humanized format or story format, which is also compatible with the learning styles of her African American (Ladson-Billings, 1994) and Latino students (Parker, 2001; Ramirez & Castaneda, 1974). This focus on people also helps her students create a link between their lives and experiences and the cultural perspectives, traditions, lifestyles, and experiences of a cultural group.

While reading the story *The Real McCoy: The Life of an African-American Inventor* by Towle, for example, Barb helps her students learn about an African American who was born free when most blacks were still enslaved. As they listen to the story, the third graders discover how Elijah McCoy, through persistence and determination, continued his education by attending a university in England. Students also find out how Elijah overcame challenges in his life to become a scientist and an inventor. His fortitude models how people can bring about change in a proactive way.

To reinforce these concepts about persistence, determination, and courage, Barb has her third graders write a biopoem, which is a type of a formula poem, about Elijah McCoy:

Biopoem
Name
Son of
Lover of (3 things)
Who feels (3 things)
Who gives (3 things)
Who fears (3 things)
Who would like to see (3 things)
Resident of
Last Name

As can be seen in the following poem, writing the biopoem helps her third graders perceive McCoy as a role model in their own lives; students also begin to see how an education can help us achieve our goals and dreams. The writing response further highlights how an African American influences change through his invention; in fact, his legacy continues even today.

Elijah
Who is black, an inventor, a student, and a Canadian
Relative of escaped slaves
Who loves family, education, and inventions
Who needs money, freedom, and family
Who gives peace, kindness, and inventions
Who fears nothing, not a thing, and not a man
Who would like to see kids stay in school
Residing in Detroit
McCoy

Other biographies that similarly portray the contributions and accomplishments of culturally diverse people include *A Weed Is a Flower: The Life of George Washington Carver* by Aliki, *A Young Painter: The Life and Paintings of Wang Yani—China's Extraordinary Young Artist* by Zhensun and Low, *The Double Life of Pocahontas* by Fritz, or *Harvesting Hope: The Story of Cesar Chavez* by Krull. These biographies, which express themes of working hard, struggling for freedom, facing adversity, sharing talents with others, or working together with others to overcome problems, provide role models for students to follow in their own lives. Chapters 7, 8, and 9 reveal additional ways to use writing with biographies.

Using Writing Response with Multicultural Narrative Stories

Barb also uses writing to highlight emotional responses to various traditions, beliefs, or values of a cultural group. After reading *The Talking Cloth* by Rhonda Mitchell to her class, for example, Barb heightens appreciation of cultural traditions and artifacts by having students write about their own story cloth and its colors and symbols. After learning about the adinkra cloth from Ghana—"embroidered in sections and hand printed all over with small black symbols. Like words"—Barb's students become inspired to craft and illustrate their own story cloth and then write about its designs, colors, and symbols.

As a result of this activity, the third graders make connections between this cultural tradition and their everyday lives. Her African American students further receive affirmation of their heritage. Edward's and Mariah's written descriptions are displayed below:

My Story Cloth

I feel like an Ashanti Prince when I war [wear] my story cloth. For me, the colors mean many different things. Green makes me think of St. Patrick's Day. Blue reminds me of "good" stuff, and purple is my favorite color. Gold means to me treasures. This is my story cloth.

My Story Cloth

I feel like an Ashanti Princess when I war my story cloth. Each of the colors mean different things to me. My story cloth means friendship and happiness. Pink represents the love we have for one another. Orange means the warmth of the sunshine. Blue means the life and yellow shows how God watches over us and green shows us the growth that can happen. The hand means friendship and the fish represents freedom. This is my story cloth.

Using Writing Response with Multicultural Poetic Books

To help her third graders appreciate the Native American respect for nature and their belief that man should live in harmony with nature, Barb reads *Giving Thanks: A Native American Good Morning Message* by Swamp and *The Circle of Thanks: Native American Poems and Songs of Thanksgiving* by Bruchac. While reading the books, she hopes that her students might begin to show more respect for nature and realize how our lives are linked with nature.

After reading the two books, she invites her students to compose their own poems, expressing their own love for nature and their own thankfulness for nature in their lives. As can be seen, her students gain an appreciation and respect for nature. They begin to understand that our lives depend on nature and its gifts.

Things That I Am Thankful For

by Antonio

I am thankful for the soil
I am thankful for my ancestors
I am thankful for drums and dancing
I am thankful for the beautiful sun, moon, and stars
I am thankful for the stillness
I am thankful for the waves in the ocean
I am thankful for prayers and for God
I am thankful for animals
I am thankful when the earth meets the stars.

Things That I Am Thankful For

by Sarah

I am thankful for my friends
I am thankful for my family
I am thankful that I have a life to live in
I am thankful for having water to make cool-aid and pop to drink
I am thankful for having food to eat on the table
I am thankful for Mother Earth
For making the trees so we can breathe
So that we can have shade from the sun
I am thankful for having Thanksgiving
Because we can eat all of that delicious food.

Creating Choral Readings from Multicultural Stories

Similarly, to celebrate the rhythm and beat often portrayed in African American poetry, songs, and raps, Shari Simpson reads *Bring on That Beat,* by Rachel Isadora, to her students. Following the read aloud, Shari creates a choral reading, simply defined as students taking turns reading text together (Hoskisson & Tompkins, 1991), of the story. As her students participate in the choral reading—reading selected portions of the text together, they began to internalize the sounds, feelings, and magic of language expressed in *Bring on That Beat.*

Next, Shari extends her students' experiences with sounds and language by having her students create their own choral readings. As can be seen, Aliyah captures the story's rhythm and beat in her own rap, "Bring that Beat in the Street."

Bring that Beat in the Street

A Choral Reading by Aliyah

Hip-Hop
Hip-Hop

Bring on the beat, wake up the feet
Play the noise with your drum and toys
Play a song while I sing along
Drum a song, dance the night along
Shake it like a salt shaker!

Aliyah's feelings about herself as a reader and writer become affirmed through this experience. Seeing herself reflected in the story enhances her self-image and her feeling of belonging. The language of the story further reflects the rhythm and beat of her dialect, which she mimics in her choral reading. As her peers read her choral reading with her, she experiences language as a way of expressing who she is, how she feels, and how she experiences life (Isenbarger & Willis, 2006).

Using Writing Response with Multicultural Informational Books

To foster a deeper understanding of the life of Native Americans when pilgrims first came to America, Diane Burchett reads *Tapenum's Day: A Wampanoag Indian Boy in Pilgrim Times* by Kate Waters to her third graders. Through narration, Kate Waters gives the reader an authentic glimpse into the life of a Wampanoag Indian boy in the 1620s.

After interactively reading the story, Diane rereads the story to her students as they take notes about Tapenum's day. Following strategies for notetaking (see Chapter 4), Diane has her students write down phrases or words that tell about Tapenum's life, home, clothing, or activities during the morning (see Figure 5.5).

While simultaneously taking notes and listening to the story a second time, students become more aware of how Tapenum dresses, how he prepares himself for hunting, and how he trains himself to be strong in body while hunting for food. They also become more aware of the Wampanoag people, their lifestyles, their eating styles, and their desire to be strong in body and spirit.

Following the notetaking activity, Diane invites her students to share what they have learned from their notes. As their peers share information about the Wampanoag people and Tapenum's day, Diane encourages her students to add to their notes, explaining that they

Figure 5.5

Notes about Tapenum's Day Hunting

1. breech cloud) close
2. hunting
3. nife
4. corn) food
5. bow arrow) wepen
6. morning) Start of the day
7. praying
8. animals
9. training
10 waiting
11 hungree
12 branch
13 breeings
14 sicesse) hearing, seeing
15 atenchen
16 consentrate
17 thinking
18 rapit
19 sounds
20 food
21 eat
22 turkey
23 practice
24 stong
25 small
26 big

will use this information to write about Tapenum's day tomorrow. Diane further emphasizes that all writers collect information before they write; notetaking is a tool authors use to gather information for their writing.

The next day her third graders write about Tapenum's day, detailing events about his day and his hunting experience early in the morning. Over the next few days, the students revise and edit their pieces. After revising and editing their work, they use word processing tools to publish their writing. Pharoah's and Kyra's pieces show how this experience helps them learn about the Wampanoag people during the 1620s.

I woke up early. It was very quiet. I put on my stone knife around my neck. I checked my pouch. I got my breechcloth and my Bow and Arrow and went out the door. The sun was shining and I couldn't wait to go hunting. The ground was still wet. I went into the forest and I climbed up the tree. I saw a rabbit and I shot it. I hit the tree but that did not matter at all. I tried it again and I hit a squirrel and a rabbit. I started to head home and I gave them to my mom who was happy.

Hi. My name is Tapenum. I woke early in the morning to go hunting. I grabbed my knife, my arrows and bow, and my pouch full of corn. I headed to the forest. I watched and

Kyra word processes her story about Tapenum.

listened for sudden movement. I aimed my bow, but I messed and hit a tree. I knew I could do better. I tried again and I shot a Rabbit. I tried again and I shot a Squirrel. I went back to the hut. When I got back to the hut mother was pleased.

Using Writing Response to Reinforce Cultural Concepts. To give her students a historical view of different cultures through the motif of walls, Beth Koryzno reads the book *Talking Walls,* by Margy Knight. By exploring walls around the world, Margy Knight shows the impact of walls, which sometimes divide or unify countries, or people in countries around the world. Due to its vibrant illustrations and colorful language, the story offers a glimpse of people from a variety of cultures while simultaneously highlighting their customs, traditions, and historical perspectives.

Similar to Diane, Beth first interactively reads the book aloud to her sixth graders, asking questions to guide their understanding of the wall motif and the impact walls have on various cultures around the world. The following day Beth invites each student to select a wall that they would like to write about.

Once each student chooses one of the walls from the chart, Beth prepares her students to use notetaking as they listen to her read the page about their wall. Since they have not had many experiences with notetaking, she models the process first by having one of her students read a note card about one of the walls while she takes notes. As she takes notes on an overhead slide, she models how to record key words or short phrases about the information; she also emphasizes how to use temporary spelling when she doesn't know how to spell certain words.

teaching TIP 5.1

Notetaking promotes good listening skills. Notetaking also models how writers paraphrase information from other sources.

After modeling notetaking through this minilesson, Beth has her students fold a sheet in half "hamburger style" so they can record notes about their wall. Following her model, her students take their own notes, using key words or short phrases. To be sure that her students have time to record the information, Beth reads slowly, pausing so that students can record the important information in their notes.

The following day, Beth demonstrates how to write a paragraph from her notes. She shows her students how to use the key words and phrases to tell about the wall—its location, its history, its people, and its information.

Once she models the process, students begin to draft their paragraphs about the walls. Rosie wrote about the Great Wall of China; Chrissy wrote about the Western Wall or the Wailing Wall in Jerusalem. The unpublished paragraphs are displayed below:

The Great Wall of China is in the contint [continent] of Asia. It is the only wall that can be seen from Space. Chines [China's] familys love this wall. Some people believe it was bilt [built] to keep the enemy out of China. It is made all out of bricks. Also the biggest wall in the world.

In Jerusalem there's a wall called the Westeren Wall or the Wailing Wall. The people would tuck prayers or letters in the wall. It's called the Wailing Wall because people were sad that there temple was destroyed. More than 2,000 years ago the wall was part of King Salamons Temple.

Using writing response with the story *Talking Walls* gives students a brief glimpse into the lives of people. They begin to see how these walls tell fascinating stories about people. This activity further provides a context for learning more about cultures and people around the world.

Creating New Endings to a Story

Young children love to make predictions as they read stories aloud. Many young readers especially enjoy predicting endings to stories. If we follow a process approach, students may design an ending for the story that includes more than two or three sentences.

First Graders Predict Tiblo's and Tanski's Dream

Marilyn Addy, a first grade teacher, encourages her first graders to predict the ending for the story *Dream Wolf* by Paul Goble. Before reading the story to her first graders, she builds background knowledge by asking them to predict what the story will be about from the cover of the book. In response, Mark volunteers that he thinks that the story will be about two Native American children; Kristen predicts that the story will be about two Indian children and a wolf; Steven adds that he thinks that the two Native American children and the wolf will go for a walk in the country.

Reinforcing their observations, drawn from both the illustrations and the title of the story, Marilyn explains that *Dream Wolf* is about two Native American children, Tiblo and Tanksi, who live in the Plains. As she turns to the first page of the story, she further extends their prior knowledge about the Native Americans by asking them what the illustrations tell them about Tiblo's and Tanksi's home and clothing, the animals, and food. She concludes the discussion about Native American lifestyles by sharing that Paul Goble is both the author of this story and the illustrator. Today, she continues, we will all be authors and illustrators when we continue Goble's story.

Next, Marilyn begins reading the story with her students, asking questions to reinforce understanding of the story. When she comes to the part where Tiblo and Tanksi, who are lost, find "a small cave among the rocks," she stops reading, asking her first graders to close their eyes and pretend they are Tiblo or Tanksi.

Once everyone closes their eyes, she invites them to pretend that they fall asleep and begin to have a dream. After a few seconds, she asks them to think about what they are dreaming as they fall asleep.

After giving them time to think, she asks them to open their eyes, allowing them to share their dreams. Terrence suggests that Tanski might dream about their mother and father finding them the next day. Danielle shares that the two children might dream about a bear whose fur would keep them warm during the night. Sean comments that Tanski might dream about an old man who will help them find their way home, while Ryan decides that a wolf will help them find their way home.

Using Prewriting Strategies to Help First Graders Gather Their Ideas for Writing

To help her students learn more about the writing process and see how authors craft their stories, Marilyn asks her students to return to their tables and begin drawing what they think Tiblo and Tanksi might dream about on their paper.

After about 5 or 6 minutes of drawing, Marilyn asks her students to pause and listen as their peers share their drawings. As various students share their drawings, others begin to get more ideas for their own drawings. When the children begin illustrating their dream this time, they add more details to their drawing. After about 5 or 6 more minutes, Marilyn invites the first graders to share their drawing with partners, telling them what is happening in their dream. Having all students verbalize their ideas with a neighbor becomes another prewriting strategy.

Drafting an Ending to the Story

To reinforce the use of temporary spelling before they begin writing their stories, Marilyn quickly reviews how to write down the letters they hear when they write words like *tepee*. Keisha volunteers that she would write a *t* and a *p*. Matt shares that he would write a *t*, a *p*, and an *e*. Marilyn validates both attempts to use temporary spelling, explaining that she will know that both Keisha and Matt have written the word *tepee* on their papers.

As students begin writing about their dreams, Marilyn observes that all her first graders are using at least the first and last sounds of the words. Many have advanced to the letter–name stage, incorporating vowels in their words. She also observes that many students also use the Word Wall, the charts, or bulletin boards to write words like *boy, find,* or *the*. Figure 5.6 shows an example of how Caitlin became an author and illustrator.

Caitlin's story reveals what first graders can accomplish when they follow a process. Through drawing, talking, and brainstorming, Caitlin discovered how to solve the problem when the children became lost. Through writing, Caitlin better understands how authors craft their stories, using problems and a resolution to the problem. She can apply this new knowledge as she independently reads and writes more stories.

Crafting Personal Narratives with Multicultural Literature

Routman (1994) also reminds us that immersion in literature is an effective way to help students learn how to write in a particular genre. Bev Tyler, a special education teacher, wants her students to learn how to write personal narratives, narratives that incorporate personal experiences with the writing (Calkins, 1994). Through guided writing, Bev hopes to renew fourth graders' confidence in their writing.

Using Guided Writing to Craft a "Fictionalized" Personal Narrative

Using a variety of guided writing activities, Bev helps her students learn how to gather their ideas for writing and apply these ideas as they draft a short personal narrative. Bev begins the sequence of lessons by reading aloud the story *Just Us Women,* by Jeannette Caines.

Figure 5.6
Caitlin Predicts an Ending for *Dream Wolf*

She chooses this story because she feels that the theme and characters reflect the children in her special education class. In Caines's story, Aunt Martha and her niece plan a special outing in their brand new car. The relaxed, companionable journey reflects the importance of family in our lives.

As Bev reads the story, she probes and questions, encouraging her students to predict events within the story from their personal experiences. When she rereads the story the second day, she continues to prompt her fourth graders' thinking through authors' questions, similar to those listed previously.

Collecting Information for the Personal Narrative. After rereading the story, Bev asks her students to take out a clean sheet of paper. Today, she explains, they will be planning their own special outing with a person of their own choosing. First, she asks them to think about three people they might like to take with them on this special outing; then she encourages them to write down these names on their papers. Next, she asks them to list three places they might like to visit. After everyone records their responses, Bev asks them to place a star next to the person and place they prefer to visit. Josalynne chooses her aunt; they are going on a walk. Demaya selects her grandmother; they are planning to make chocolate chip cookies at her grandmother's house. Ulyree chooses his dad; they will be leaving for California.

Once they choose a person and a place to go, Bev asks them to list things they might see or do on their special outing. Demaya decides that she and her grandmother will go shopping, drive around town, visit the park, and stop by their church after making the cookies. Ulyree and his dad will be traveling in a truck to California; they will be playing miniature golf, fishing, hunting, and visiting relatives. As can be seen by the examples, students use their own experiences to determine what they might see or do.

After writing for about 5 minutes, Bev stops the fourth graders and has them share one or two of their ideas. As students listen to one another's ideas, they gain new ideas to place on their own lists. Sharing their lists seems to help everyone gather more information for their writing. Bev explains that this process is called prewriting—a time to gather our ideas for our own story.

teaching TIP 5.2

Students of all ability levels find it easier to write if they spend 80% of their time doing a variety of prewriting strategies.

After writing for a few minutes more, Bev allows more students to share ideas from their list. As she listens, she responds to their ideas with enthusiasm, adding that she knows they are going to have interesting stories with lots of action.

Drafting the Personal Narrative. Once a few more share their ideas, Bev announces that they are ready to begin their stories. Before beginning, she asks them to look at the author's introduction to the story once again. As her students relisten to the beginning of the story, she asks them to think about what the author does to make us want to continue reading the story; what words catch their attention, encouraging them to continue reading the story. After listening, Demaya comments that she likes how the author says, "Saturday morning is jump-off time." Katherine shares that she likes how Aunt Martha says, "No boys and no men, just us women." Ulyree adds that he likes the fact that the characters will be traveling in a new car.

To reinforce the importance of good leads in writing, Bev invites them to think of a way to begin their own stories. Josalynne decides to begin her story in this way: "Jump off time was in the summer at 1:00 in the afternoon. Me and my Aunt Bergen are on our way." Demaya's beginning includes, "Saturday is take off time. Yes! It was just that time. Time to take off for the Big Day." Thus, Jeannette Caine's lead provides a model for the fourth graders' own pieces. As they closely look at her lead, they also learn how to incorporate the five W's—Who, What, Where, When, and Why—in their leads, while using an interesting arrangement of words.

After Demaya and Josalynne share their leads, the others catch on and craft similar leads. Bev then encourages them to return to their lists and use this information to create their own personal narratives. Writing flows for the fourth graders because the ideas for the stories emerge from their own personal experiences. Having choices in their writing is also important. Ulyree's and Demaya's pieces are displayed below:

Just Us Men

by Ulyree

Friday is jump off time. Me and my Dad will go to Calafronia in his new truck. No women or girls. Just us men. Me and my Dad went to Calafronia in his Chevrolet. We will go to putt putt Golf and [play] Games. Me and my dad will go visiting relitivs [relatives] and go hunting and fishing at Odell Lake. Then I will go back home and brag to my sisters.

Jump Off Day

by Demaya

Sunday morning is jump off time and my great grandma and me are going to make her delicious chololate chip cookies. After that we are going to do some fun things like go shopping, or go driving around the town, or go to the park, or church and things. Like I mostly would like to drive around the town and eat cookies too. Then maybe go shopping. By the end of the day we will have our list finished and have the night all to our selfevs [selves].

As can be seen, the special education students learned how to create a lead for their "fictionalized" personal narratives, a lead that is interesting and provocative. They also gained knowledge on how to structure a story. Jeannette Caines' story effectively models the craft of writing for the fourth grade writers.

Using the Writing Process to Craft a "Fictionalized" Personal Narrative

Bette Jesse, a third grade teacher, also wants her students to learn how to write a personal narrative. Different from Bev, Bette wants her third graders to apply the entire writing process for their personal narrative. Her third graders have had many writing experiences in the past; they are comfortable with writing and ready to learn how to shape their writing so that it expresses their ideas clearly, applying the revising and editing stages of writing.

During the prewriting and drafting stages, Bette follows the process described above. Once students complete their drafts, they begin to apply the revising strategies detailed in Chapter 4. As their peers ask them questions about their narratives, they gain a sense of audience and begin to understand what additional information readers may need to understand and enjoy their narratives.

Revising Personal Narratives. As they revise their drafts, some students change their leads. For example, Laureen changes her first sentence from "Monday is jump off day" to "Monday morning is rise and shine day." She takes a risk, experimenting with a different type of beginning. Jamie also experiments with his lead, changing "Today is jump off day" to "It is Friday morning and time to go! In case you're wondering where we are going, It's Los Vegas for a week!" As can be seen, Jamie's new lead adds enthusiasm and excitement to his special journey.

Students also revise their drafts, adding more details and examples to their story. For example, in her first draft Alison shares that she is going to a fancy hotel and a fancy restaurant where she would eat ten ice cream sundaes and banana splits. In her revised draft, Alison explains, "When we get to Paris we are driving to a fancy hotel in a limousine." She adds that everyone will get "dressed up and go see Romeo and Juliet." As she continues her story, she describes how they will also go for a swim at the pool at their hotel tomorrow. They will also buy some souvenirs. By adding additional examples and details to her narrative, Alison helps her readers experience her trip to Paris.

teaching TIP 5.3

Writers begin to gather a sense of audience when their peers ask them questions about their writing. Alison gathered ideas for revising her piece when her peers asked her how they got to the hotel or what she did while staying at the hotel.

Not only does Joshua add more details and examples to his story, Joshua inserts an ending to his narrative—"When we got home we talked about the trip all weekend." Similarly, Cassie adds an ending to her narrative. Using Jeannette Caines's model, she writes, "When we get there if our friends say what took us so long, we'll just say we had some girl talk to do. But there were no boys, no men, just us ladies."

Editing the Narratives. As described in Chapter 4, the third graders edit their pieces by first self-editing for spelling, punctuation, and capitals; then they edit in twos. Bette invites four of her students to become "Assistant Editors," helping her double-check students' narratives for possible edits. If the assistants find any errors, they follow their teacher's model, placing a dot by the sentence as a way of asking their peers to relook at the line, checking for additional errors. If students still have trouble finding the error, they give their friends clues or hints so they can find the error more easily.

Laurie's and Matthew's final drafts are displayed below.

Bonjour! Lots of Fun in Paris!

Today is Wednesday. It is the big day. Me, my mom, and my little sister Brianna are all taking a first class flight to Paris, France. We decided to take first class because my mom just inherited five million bucks. We aren't taking any boys or any men, just us ladies.

Me, my mom, and my adorable little sister, Brianna are all buying new dresses to go dancing in. We plan to go sight seeing at 6 o'clock in the evening also. I want to see the Eiffel Tower first thing. This afternoon we are going to take a limo to eat some fancy French food for our lunch. I can't wait till 8 o'clock because just ladies are going to see the French opera Les Miserables. One of the teachers in my school Mrs. Lund said its good. When we get finished at the opera we are going to see the musical Cats. My favorite cat is Grizzabella, Briannas favorite cat is Tiger. Moms is Gus. I'm sure we are going to spend a ton of cash on our fun! We're definitely going to get our hair done. What's money for! My sister wants ten beautiful French braids. My mom wants a day perm and I want a lively curl! One of the art museums we are going to is the famous Louvre. It's one of the biggest art museums on the globe. It has almost 250,000 drawings, paintings, statues, and other works of art. Before we leave we will go sailing with some fresh French guys. Us three ladies need to go home before we decide to stay.

The Big Day

Today is the day that my friend and I are going to Reno. It's going to be a big day for just us guys. We will see lots of machines and lights. There will be games in the front. I will use the slot machines. We'll go get a snack at the snack bar. Then we will go to another casino and play more games. We will win lots of money. We'll rent a hotel and sleep there all night. In the morning we'll go to a fancy restaurant and eat there. We'll go back to our hotel and watch TV for awhile. We will go get some rest and get up real early. Finally Josh and I will go home and tell everyone about our trip.

Learning to Shape and Develop Writing by Following a Process. By following the writing process, Bette's third graders learn that writing is not magic. They learn that writing takes problem solving, thinking, and taking risks. They also discover that writing can be messy as we cross out words when something doesn't make sense, insert new words and phrases to add interest to a story, or change information to make our message clear. With repeated experiences in revising and editing future drafts, Bette's students will learn how to shape their writing for an audience.

Creating Memoirs through the Use of Multicultural Literature

Many multicultural stories provide both a stimulus for writing ideas and a model of language expression. *Knots on a Counting Rope* by Bill Martin, Jr. and John Archambault, a story that recounts the story of a boy's birth, models the power of metaphors, similes, and descriptive language in writing. The story is also an example of a memoir—a moment in one's life written in a conversational tone (Calkins, 1994).

Using Prewriting Strategies to Facilitate Writing Memoirs

Similar to Bette Jesse, Beth Caldwell wants her students to learn how to craft a memoir by applying the writing process. Heeding the advice of Murray (1985), Beth spends 70 percent of her time on the prewriting stage of writing. To build background knowledge and heighten interest in the story *Knots on a Counting Rope,* Beth begins with a minilesson on the Native American customs of storytelling. Explaining that the Native Americans did not record their stories in books for many years, Beth asks her students how their stories and legends might be preserved. Some students share that the paintings on stone or clothing often tell stories about the lives of Native Americans and that of their ancestors; others explain that the Native Americans learn the stories by listening to their elders tell the stories over and over again.

Beth affirms their knowledge, adding that ancient "Grandfather stories" were similarly passed down to future generations through the storytelling tradition (Lake-Thom, 1997). As

Fourth graders perform a dramatic reading of *Knots on a Counting Rope.*

Beth continues, she explains that these "Grandfather stories" reveal the traditions, beliefs, and values of the Native American people. Many stories, for example, detail their respect for nature and how the Native American people love and care for nature; others describe their direct kinship with all of creation and their relationship with nature (Lake-Thom, 1997). To help their listeners retell the stories, Beth continues, some Native Americans tie a knot in their rope after each retelling, symbolizing the recording of the story.

Following this discussion about Native American traditions and beliefs, Beth shares that she is going to read a story about the birth of a young boy, a story that would be told by the boy's grandfather. As she begins reading the story, she periodically pauses to ask questions and elaborate on the meaning of the story with her fifth graders.

Using Drama as a Prewriting Activity. After interactively reading the story, using discussion, questioning, and dialogue, Beth has her students practice and perform a dramatic interpretation of *Knots on a Counting Rope* the following day (see Diamond & Moore, 1995, Chapter 4). Through this dramatic interpretation, Beth hopes that her fifth graders will be able to experience the storytelling tradition.

Using index cards with one event from the boy's life being retold by the grandfather, each fifth grader reads an event in the grandson's life, using the exact words of the grandfather. To recreate the setting for the dialogue, the students sit in a circle, placed in the order that the events occur in the grandson's life. To further capture the moment, Beth dims the lights and places paper logs and a paper fire in the center of the circle.

Assuming the role of the grandfather, each student reads the grandfather's dialogue; assuming the role of the grandson, Beth reads the grandson's dialogue. At the end of the dramatic reading, Beth ties a knot in the rope to symbolize the recording of the story. Figure 5.7 shows how the dialogue begins.

Using Oral Language and Modeling as a Prewriting Activity. As a result of this experience, the fifth graders also begin to internalize authors' use of dialogue and figurative language to tell a story. To help reinforce this language, on day three, Beth asks her students to retell the beginning of the story during a minilesson. After retelling the beginning, Beth and I explain how our own children love to hear stories about themselves when they were

Figure 5.7

Example of Dialogue between Grandfather and Grandson Taken from *Knots on a Counting Rope* by Bill Martin, Jr. and John Archambault

Tell me the story again, Grandfather.
Tell me who I am.
I have told you many times, Boy.
You know the story by heart.
But it sounds better when you tell it, Grandfather.
It was a dark night.
a strange night . . .

Source: Text from *Knots on a Counting Rope,* by Bill Martin, Jr., and John Archambault. Copyright © 1966, 1987 by Bill Martin, Jr., and John Archambault. Copyright © 2004 by the Estate of Bill Martin, Jr. Reprinted by permission of Henry Holt and Company, LLC.

smaller. I add that one of my own children's favorite stories is about a trip to a fast-food restaurant. To help them see how to use Bill Martin's dialogue format in their own stories, I explain how I wrote about this story using Bill Martin's dialogue format.

As I read my story, I see the students smile and giggle as they remember similar stories from their own childhood. At the same time, I perceive a bond forming between the children and me as they learn more about my life and my experiences through my writing:

Mom, will you tell me the story about going to McDonalds's for dinner?

I think you must know that story by heart, Chris! I've told you the story at least 100 times!

But I like the way you tell the story.

All right! Just one more time! It was a Friday evening and I had just gotten home from work. I was simply exhausted! Cooking dinner was the last thing I wanted to do.

Then what happened, Mom?

Seeing that I was tired, Chad and Tiffany decided to take advantage of the moment. They suggested we go to McDonalds for dinner.

Then, just before we got to McDonalds, I saw the golden arches. What did I say?

Just as soon as you saw the golden arches, you shouted, "McDonalds! McDonalds! I see McDonalds!"

Then you drove up to the stand.

Yes, I drove up and ordered three cheeseburgers, three large fries, and three medium Cokes.

Don't forget the chicken sandwich and diet Coke for you! Right, Mom?

Right! Then we slowly inched to the window. I handed the money to the lady at the window. Then she gave me the change.

Then you just drove off! Didn't you, Mom?

Yes, I was so exhausted that I just drove off. All at once Tiffany and Chad began shouting, "MOM, MOM! You forgot our food!" "Wonderful!" I groaned.

Then you saw the policeman's car in your rear view mirror, didn't you?

Yes, when I glanced through my rear view mirror, I spotted a policeman's car. Chad and Tiffany were mortified.

Then what did you do, Mom?

I parked the car and walked right up to the window to get our food.

Then the policeman waved, didn't he?

Yes, the policeman waved and said, "I did the same thing last night. Have a nice dinner!"

Modeling the Drafting Process

After reading the story to the fifth graders, Beth and I ask them if they remember any family stories they like to hear over and over again. Hands eagerly pop up as many students have their own family stories to share. Once several students share their family stories, we model the process of drafting a story, while displaying the sequence chart in Figure 5.8 on an overhead projector.

As students volunteer how my story began, I record their words in the first box—"Tell me the story again, Mom." Tamika helps us record the dialogue for the second box—"Tell me about the time we went to McDonalds for dinner." After sharing this example, I ask students to share what they will place in the first box if they are telling their story.

Drafting the Memoir. Following these activities, students are now ready to compose their own drafts on the sequence chart. To help all students collect their ideas for writing, Beth

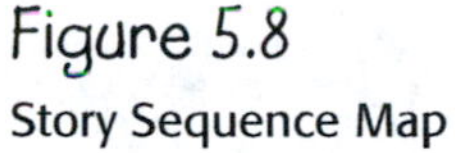

Figure 5.8
Story Sequence Map

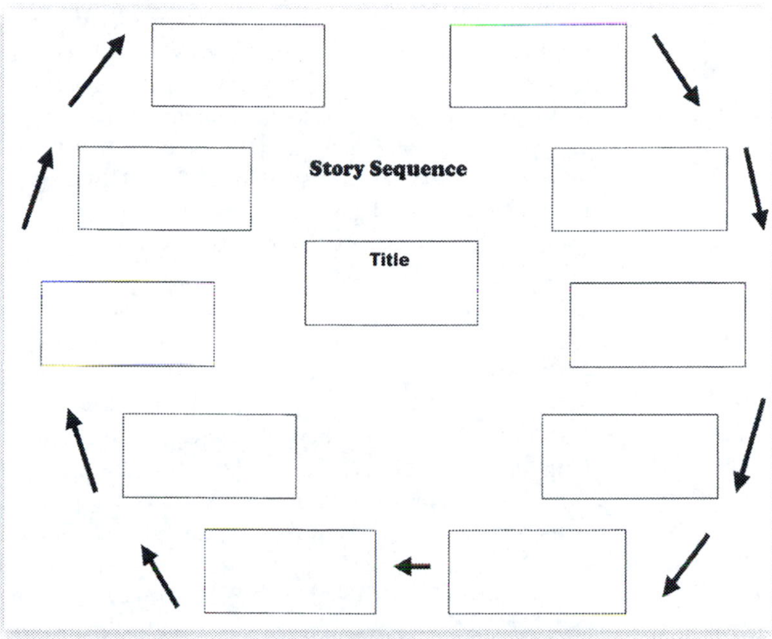

has her students periodically pause to share their drafts (after 5 or 6 minutes). By the end of the 45-minute session, all students complete their drafts, using the dialogue format in *Knots on a Counting Rope.* In fact, many continue their story on the back of the chart.

To culminate the event, several students share their drafts during the share session. Following the session, Beth collects all the sequence charts and the drafts and places them in a folder for safekeeping. This way no one's draft might be misplaced or lost, resulting in frustration.

Using the PQP Process to Revise the Memoirs

About a week later, the class continues the process of writing memoirs by forming writing response groups. Similar to the process described in Chapter 4, Beth divides her class into groups of four students of mixed ability levels. To model the process, she selects one of her groups to apply the PQP formula for the rest of the class, using Bill Martin's story.

Simulating the PQP Process with *Knots on a Counting Rope.* Before she begins the simulation, Beth asks the class to consider how Bill Martin was able to create such a beautiful story. She wants them to realize that authors write and rewrite their stories over and over again—deleting some words or phrases; substituting more colorful, descriptive words for dull, boring words; inserting new information to make the story clearer to the reader; or rearranging parts of the story to follow an appropriate sequence.

Next, Beth points out that authors frequently share their stories with other people. Today, you will be Bill Martin's audience, giving him praise and asking him questions about his story, *Knots on a Counting Rope.* Andrea shares that she liked the boy's name—Boy-Strength-of-Blue-Horses. Mina comments that she likes the way Bill Martin describes the boy's blindness as a "dark curtain before his eyes." Jared explains that he likes the title of the story as it tells about the Native American tradition of tying a knot in the rope.

After sharing their praise for the story, students begin to think of questions they might ask Bill Martin. Nadia wants to know how Martin came up with the grandson's name. Mike wants to know how the boy memorized the trail in his mind. Arif wonders how Martin came up with the name for his story. Akiba questions what the colors—red or orange—might be for the boy. To help students remember these examples of praise and questions, Beth records examples of their questions on chart paper for all to see.

To conclude the process, Beth explains that Bill Martin would share how he might polish or revise his draft after receiving this feedback. Since he is not present, the class predicts some possible ways he might polish or revise his draft. Mike suggests that he might want to explain how the boy learned to memorize the trail in his mind. Mina thinks he might also tell what the color red is, just as he explained what the color blue is.

Modeling the Process with Aaisha's Story. Following this simulation activity, the group applies the same process with Aaisha's writing piece, using the PQP technique. After Aaisha reads her story, her peers give her *praise* and ask her *questions* about her story. Following this process, Aaisha describes how she will *polish* her story. Specifically, she explains that she will insert information about the wall, which was made of plasterboard, in her story. Second, she shares that she will explain how her aunt got ideas for play-acting from watching TV.

After Aaisha shares her ideas for revising her draft, Beth asks her to show where she will insert information about the wall. When Aaisha points to the sentence that tells about the wall, Beth models how to place a small caret in front of the word *wall* and then inserts the word *plasterboard* just above the caret on an overhead slide. Next Beth asks her where she will place information about her aunt getting ideas from TV. When Aaisha points to the correct box, Beth models how to draw an arrow from the box to the center of the page on the overhead slide, showing Aaisha, as well as her peers, where to insert this information.

Applying the Process in Small Groups. The following day all groups practice the PQP process as they work in their writing response groups. After all students have a chance to share their writing and receive feedback, they return to their seats to begin polishing their drafts. Using blue ink pens, the students insert revisions, delete words, or change words.

Figure 5.9
Editing Checklist

Editing Checklist

Author	Peer Editor	
❑	❑	1. I have circled the words that I want to know how to spell.
❑	❑	2. I have checked all sentences to see if they begin with capital letters.
❑	❑	3. I have checked all proper nouns to see if they begin with capital letters.
❑	❑	4. I have checked all sentences to see if they have an ending mark.

Author's Signature: ______________________________

Peer Editor's Signature: ______________________________

Extra Credit:

Author	Peer Editor	
❑	❑	5. I have checked all places where people speak to see if they have quotation marks.

This way the revisions are easily visible for the authors. Beth completes the lesson by collecting all drafts and placing them in a folder.

Using a Checklist to Edit the Memoirs

The next day, students make additional revisions on their drafts, using the blue pens again. Then they begin self-editing their stories, using red ink pens. Working in pairs, students then use the red ink pens to peer edit their writing. To stimulate more editing, Beth uses a checklist that requires that they search for at least three misspelled words and proper use of beginning and ending marks (see Figure 5.9). After each editing team has carefully self-edited and peer edited their stories, they sign the checklists (to show that they carefully edited the drafts) and begin their illustrations. Beth and I continuously circulate, checking to see that each pair has carefully edited their stories. If an error is noted, we place a dot by the sentence so the pair can go back to the sentence and determine what the error is.

Sharing the Memoirs

Beth publishes her students' memoirs by displaying them with their accompanying illustrations on the bulletin board. D'aiShawn wrote the following memoir:

The Robot

Tell me the story about the robot.
I told you many times before.
I want to hear it again.
Ok. I will tell you the story.
Thank you Mom.
Well it all started when I bought you a toy robot for Christmas.
And then I opened my first present. Right?
Yes, son, well it was a robot and you kept on asking me for batteries.
Then I put batteries in it for you and you took it to the back room.
Before you knew it, I was screaming, right?
Yes, you burst out the door and started running. The robot was chasing you.
Then I jumped on the chair and kicked him over.
Yes, you were scared!

Closing Thoughts

Our nation is becoming a rich tapestry, interwoven with people from diverse cultures and ethnic groups. This diversity enriches and strengthens our nation. The literacy curriculum within our schools needs to mirror the beautiful, balanced picture of this tapestry so that all students will view themselves as valued members of society and achieve greater success (Diamond & Moore, 1995).

Various teachers in this chapter modeled ways to develop the lifelong habits of our youth so they might acquire the social and emotional sensibilities needed for cross-cultural work: "empathy and learning with and from others who happen to differ in race; religion; national, linguistic, or social origin; values; and world view" (Suarez-Orozco, 2005, p. 208).

Multicultural literature, combined with writing, represents a tool to help nurture students' evolving understanding about cultures, languages, and perspectives. Acquiring social and emotional sensibilities is a gradual process, shaped by ongoing social encounters and evolving experiences. By using a variety of multicultural books, combined with writing, teachers might help students see a larger picture that includes multiple interpretations and experiences. Multiple experiences with a wide selection of multicultural stories also help students gain a more thorough examination of cultural groups, perceiving differences within and across cultural groups.

Infusing the literacy curriculum with multicultural literature also becomes a way to link students' lives and interests with the curriculum. Through the use of storytelling, drama, art, and language, teachers can tap into students' learning styles so they can generate writing pieces that evolve from their lives and interests. Sometimes the multicultural literature serves as a pattern for learning how to write new genres or how to apply authors' stylistic techniques in their own stories or poems.

Once again the social interactions with teachers and peers, combined with cognitive construction, help students become authors. As teachers, we need to follow a process approach to learning. Specifically, we need to

- Immerse students in quality multicultural literature.
- Link the multicultural literature with students' cultural and linguistic backgrounds and their experiences.
- Engage students in dialogues about the literature and its meaning.
- Mentor students' dialogues about the literature to help them discover similarities and differences among cultures while encountering self within others when they see themselves reflected in diverse cultures, discovering similarities across invented boundaries (Landt, 2006).
- Coach students as they study a genre or author's stylistic techniques through minilessons.
- Tap into students' life experiences and learning styles to gather ideas for writing.
- Support students as they experiment with new crafting techniques.
- Coach and question students to help them shape their writing during revising or editing.
- Celebrate students' accomplishments through sharing or publishing.

Teachers' Questions

1. I teach in a very homogenous school district. Most of the families in my school district are European American. How should I proceed?

When learning to understand and appreciate cultural diversity, we need to begin with the students in our class. Mary Streeter sends a note home to parents before beginning a thematic unit on fairy tales. Using her own family as an example, she shows that her family is Irish, English, and Danish. Then she asks her parents to try and find out what they can about their families' heritages, using both the mother's maiden name and father's name. As students begin to bring back the information, she creates a graph displaying the information by using small photos of the students next to their name and their heritage, whether it be German, Polish, African, Chinese, Japanese, or Vietnamese.

Once the graph is complete, she begins to read fairy tales from the various cultures represented in the class. Students begin to understand and appreciate the diversity within their own class. They can then begin to compare and contrast the fairy tales and the cultural values and beliefs the fairy tales portray on a chart.

As a result of this experience, students are ready to learn about other cultures within their community or state. These concrete experiences help students begin to relate to cultural diversity and its role within our nation.

2. The parents in my community would be upset if we were reading multicultural literature with their children. How should I proceed?

Cultural diversity is a very sensitive topic, one that has been overlooked in the past. Historically, many immigrants have come to America with the attitude that they want to be American, hiding the richness of their cultural heritage. For this reason, there may be a need for a committee of teachers and parents to work together, planning a thematic unit on cultural diversity first. Once a plan is in place, the committee can share the plan and a rationale for the thematic unit on cultural diversity at a parent meeting. By involving parents in the process, they may be less resistant. In addition, this might become a learning experience for parents and children together.

3. I like the PQP process, but I do not think my third graders will be able to ask their peers questions about their writing.

Asking good questions is challenging. Students learn how to ask questions by practicing. Tracey Franklin has her students practice asking questions with one another when they share. Since everyone in her class volunteers to share during share sessions, she has her students listen carefully to their peers as they share their writing pieces. In order for her students to have the next turn sharing, they must give an author praise and then ask one question. By keeping a list of good questions on chart paper, Tracey stimulates her students to ask quality questions. This experience and the chart of good questions help her students ask better and better questions when they meet in writing response groups. She also inspires her students to listen and think carefully about questions that will help the author by circulating among the groups, writing down additional examples of distinctive questions on her clipboard. Once the writing groups finish, she shares these questions with the class. Since all groups want to hear her praise, a friendly competition gradually begins among the groups as they try to outshine their peers.

4. I teach second grade. How can they peer edit one another's writing when they don't know when to use capitals and periods?

You are so right! We can't have students begin to apply these editing skills until they learn the skills. This is why minilessons, Morning News, and shared writing are so important. These are structured times for students to explicitly learn about the conventions of capitals and periods. In particular, Morning News helps students learn about the use of capitals at the beginning of a sentence and at the end of the sentence. Shared writing helps students apply these skills in a larger context. Students acquire these skills more easily within the context of reading and writing.

Similarly, they learn how to apply these skills within the context of their own writing. After modeling the process during a minilesson, students can begin to apply the process in their own writing as they self-edit. Then working in twos (of differing ability levels), students can peer edit. As they practice these skills, however, we must continuously circulate, helping students who need additional assistance.

Children's Literature

Aliki. (1965). *A weed is a flower: The life of George Washington Carver.* Englewood Cliffs, NJ: Prentice Hall.

Bruchac, J. (1996). *The circle of thanks: Native American poems and songs of Thanksgiving.* Mahwah, NJ: BridgeWater Books.

Caines, J. (1982). *Just us women.* New York: Harper & Row.

Climo, S. (1993). *The Korean Cinderella.* New York: HarperCollins Publishers.

Fritz, J. (1983). *The double life of Pocahontas.* New York: Trumpet Club.

Goble, P. (1990). *Dream wolf.* New York: Bradbury Press.

Isadora, R. (2002). *Bring on that beat.* New York: G. P. Putnam's Sons.

Knight, M. (1992). *Talking walls.* Gardiner, ME: Tilbury House.

Krull, K. (2003). *Harvesting hope: The story of Cesar Chavez.* San Diego, CA: Harcourt.

Martin, B., Jr., & Archambault, J. (1987). *Knots on a counting rope.* New York: Henry Holt.

Martin, R. (1992). *The rough-face girl.* New York: G. P. Putnam's Sons.

Mitchell, R. (1997). *The talking cloth.* New York: Orchard Books.

Perrault, C. (1985). *Cinderella.* New York: Dial.

Polacco, P. (1990). *Babushka's doll.* New York: Simon & Schuster.

Spier, P. (1990). *People.* New York: Doubleday.

Steptoe, J. (1988). *Mufaro's beautiful daughters.* New York: Lothrop, Lee & Shepard.

Swamp, C. J. (1995). *Giving thanks: A Native American good morning message.* New York: Lee & Low Books, Inc.

Towle, W. (1993). *The real McCoy: The life of an African-American inventor.* New York: Scholastic.

Vuong, L. (1982). *The brocaded slipper.* New York: J. B. Lippincott.

Waters, K. (1996). *Tapenum's day: A Wampanoag Indian boy in pilgrim times.* New York: Scholastic.

Zhensum, Z., & Low, A. (1991). *A young painter: The life and paintings of Wang Yani—China's extraordinary young artist.* New York: Scholastic Books.

References

Buss, K., & Karnowski, L. (2000). *Reading and writing literary genres.* Newark, DE: International Reading Association.

Cai, M. (1998). Multiple definitions of multicultural literature: Is the debate really just "ivory tower" bickering? *The New Advocate, 11,* 311–324.

Calkins, L. (1994). *The art of teaching writing.* Portsmouth, NH: Heinemann.

Clark, R. (1995). *Free to write.* Portsmouth, NH: Heinemann.

DeNicolo, C., & Franquiz, M. (2006). "Do I have to say it?": Critical encounters with multicultural children's literature. *Language Arts, 84,* 157–169.

Diamond, B., & Moore, M. A. (1995). *Multicultural literacy: Mirroring the reality of the classroom.* New York: Longman.

Faltis, C. (2000). *Joinfostering: Teaching and learning in multilingual classrooms* (3rd ed.). Columbus, OH: Merrill Prentice Hall.

Fletcher, R., & Portalupi, J. (1998). *Craft lessons: Teaching writing K–8.* Portland, ME: Stenhouse.

Graves, D. (1994). *A fresh look at writing.* Portsmouth, NH: Heinemann.

Graves, D. (2005). The centrality of character. In N. Roser & M. Martinez (Eds.), *What a character! Character study as a guide to literary meaning making in grades K–8* (pp. 2–5). Newark, DE: International Reading Association.

Grimes, N. (2005). The common denominator. *English Journal, 94,* 22–24.

Hoskisson, K., & Tompkins, G. (1991). *Language arts: Content and teaching strategies.* Columbus, OH: Merrill.

Isenbarger, L., & Willis, A. (2006). An intersection of theory and practice: Accepting the language a child brings into the classroom. *Language Arts, 84,* 125–135.

Ladson-Billings, G. (1994). *The dreamkeepers: Successful teachers of African American children.* San Francisco: Jossey-Bass.

Lake-Thom, B. (1997). *Spirits of the earth: A guide to Native American nature symbols, stories, and ceremonies.* New York: Penguin.

Landt, S. (2006). Multicultural literature and young adolescents: A kaleidoscope of opportunity. *Journal of Adolescent Literacy, 49,* 690–697.

Langer, J. (1986). *Children reading and writing: Structures and strategies.* Norwood, NJ: Ablex.

Langer, J. (1995). *Envisioning literature: Literary understanding and literature instruction.* New York: Teachers College Press.

Martinez, M., & Roser, N. (2005). Students developing an understanding of character. In *What a character! Character study as a guide to literary meaning making in grades K–8* (pp. 6–12). Newark, DE: International Reading Association.

Moore-Hart, M. (2004). Creating learning environments that invite all students to learn through multicultural literature and information technology. *Childhood Education, 81,* 87–94.

Moore-Hart, M., Knapp, J., & Diamond, B. (2003). The implementation of a multicultural literacy program in fourth- and fifth-grade classrooms. In A. Willis, G. Garcia, R. Barrera, & V. Harris (Eds.), *Multicultural issues in literacy research and practice* (pp. 223–262). Mahwah, NJ: Lawrence Erlbaum.

Murray, D. (1985). *A writer teaches writing.* Boston: Houghton Mifflin.

Olness, R. (2005). *Using literature to enhance writing instruction: A guide for K–5 teachers.* Newark, DE: International Reading Association.

Parker, C. (2001). *What influences shaped the meaning eight Latino adolescents gave to science.* Paper presented at the annual meeting of the American Educational Research Association, Seattle, WA.

Ramirez, M., & Castaneda, A. (1974). *Cultural democracy, bicognitive development, and education.* New York: Academic Press.

Rickards, D., & Hawes, S. (2007). Connecting reading and writing through author's craft. *The Reading Teacher, 60,* 370–372.

Routman, R. (1994). *Invitations: Changing as teachers and learners, K–12.* Portsmouth, NH: Heinemann.

Russell, D. (1997). *Literature for children.* New York: Longman.

Spandel, V., & Stiggins, R. (1997). *Creating writers: Linking writing assessment and instruction* (2nd ed.). New York: Longman.

Suarez-Orozco, M. (2005). Rethinking education in the global era. *Phi Delta Kappan, 87,* 209–212.

Tompkins, G. (2004). *Teaching writing. Balancing process and product.* Upper Saddle River, NJ: Merrill.

chapter SIX

Using Writing in an Integrated, Interdisciplinary Curriculum

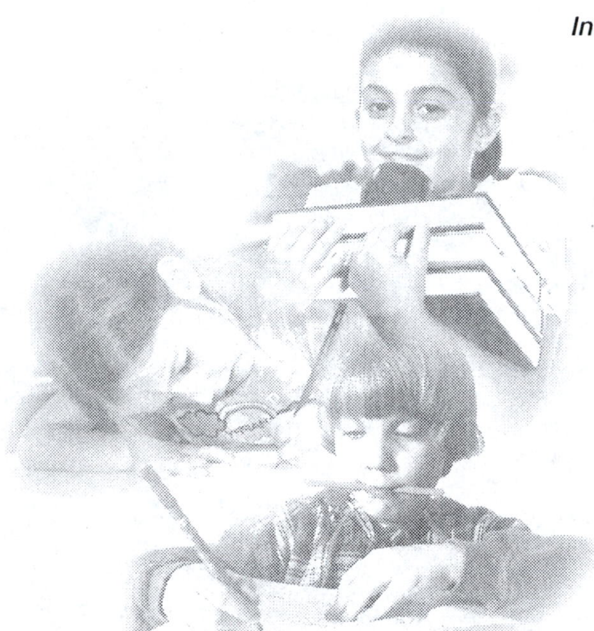

Intro

Sure you have heard of Hawaii or the great state of New York, but have you ever heard of Nebraska? Did you know there is a state where there is a rock shaped like a chimney and where there is a river where you can see 35 feet down? Have you ever heard of a state where there is soil so rich flowers will grow on your rooftops? Have you heard of the state where a pitcher can throw the baseball 105 miles per hour? If not, read on and I will tell you about all of these things from the "Cornhusker State," Nebraska.

Aaron, a seventh grader, has a natural curiosity about the world around him. He tapped into this natural curiosity when given the opportunity to choose a topic for inquiry. He first became interested in Nebraska when his family drove through Nebraska on their family trip to visit relatives. Learning more about the "Cornhusker State" lured his attention when his class began to study regions of the United States.

As he began his inquiry, he discovered that Chimney Rock was an important marker on the Oregon Trail. As a result of this discovery, researching became more than copying facts from books or the Internet; researching became a way to extend his wonder and curiosity about our nation's history and its people (Portalupi & Fletcher, 2001; Rogovin, 1998, 2001).

As can be seen, inquiry became an adventure to Aaron. By tapping into a variety of resources—books, the Internet, and people—Aaron delved deeper into his subject.

There Are Many Landmarks in Nebraska That Attract Tourists

In Nebraska tourists dwell closer to historic sites . . . rather that modern places. One of the historic places than tourists go to is chimney rock. From the name you can probably guess that it is a rock shaped like a chimney. if you guessed that, you were right, so give your self a pat on the back. Anyway, people on the Oregon Trail looked for it as a sign to make sure they were going the right way. If they were low on water supply, they would go a little west to a spring where there was water. Tourists also go to the Elba river, where the water is so clear you can see all the little fishes swimming around. These are just a few of the amazing sites to see in Nebraska.

Voice appears in students' writing when they have choice. Even though Aaron and his peers were all working on nonfiction writing pieces about regions in the United States, they still had choice on their topics—what angle they would take and what would be their areas of focus within the topic (Portalupi & Fletcher, 2001). As a result, Aaron's piece did not reflect a lifeless encyclopedia; his writing showed passion, keen interest, and wonder.

Aaron's piece, however, did not instantly evolve. His piece evolved during Writing Workshop, where Aaron and his peers learned about the process of writing nonfiction texts. Through a variety of minilessons that focused on strategies they could apply with nonfiction texts, Aaron and his peers learned how to research a topic, focus on a topic, take notes from a variety of sources, create a lead or an ending for nonfiction texts, revise and edit nonfiction texts, and complete a bibliography. As students applied these specific strategies to their writing, their teacher invited them to read their piece aloud during share session. In this way, students began to see the process modeled by both teachers and peers. By harnessing a process over time, Aaron shaped his nonfiction text about Nebraska. This is a process that will serve him for the rest of his life.

Integrating Writing and Literature with an Interdisciplinary Curriculum

In an informational world, interdisciplinary learning plays an increasingly important role in the school curriculum. By simultaneously addressing content from several subject areas, teachers make more effective use of classroom time and address content in more depth as they remove artificial divisions among subjects (Freeman & Person, 1998). As a result, students begin to see connections within the content areas; they begin to understand important concepts and ideas more easily (Barton & Smith, 2000; Diamond & Moore, 1995; Fuhler, Farris, & Nelson, 2006; Nuthall, 1999; Wallace & Pugalee, 2001).

Using Theme Teaching or Focused Inquiry in an Integrated, Interdisciplinary Curriculum

By applying a theme, concept, book, or problem, teachers can offer a focus for learning experiences across two or more disciplines (Freeman & Person, 1998). This focus, combined with a variety of learning experiences in the various disciplines, helps students perceive connections within the content areas. Reading, writing, literature, science, social studies, math, the arts, music, and other areas of the curriculum become tools for students to learn about themselves, their lives, and the world (Rogovin, 1998).

Thematic Teaching or Focused Inquiry in an Interdisciplinary Curriculum. Although not a new approach to learning, integrated learning that emphasizes the connections among the disciplines has recently gained more attention. Popular approaches to an integrated curriculum include "theme teaching" (Freeman & Person, 1998; Rogovin, 1998) or "focused inquiry" (Berghoff, Egawa, Harste, & Hoonan, 2000; Short et al., 1996) to explore a topic in interconnected ways. Both theme teaching and focused inquiry emerge from a broad concept that serves as an umbrella for teachers and students to pursue a wide range of topics, themes, and ideas through natural and meaningful learning experiences. The broad concept provides a point of connection for the disciplines. While guiding and facilitating the learning events, teachers weave reading, writing, and oral language into the learning experiences. Informational literature often supports the learning of content-related information or understanding of specific concepts being developed within the various disciplines. Specific characteristics of this interdisciplinary approach to learning (Freeman & Person, 1998, pp. 19–24) include

- Fostering learning through active, hands-on learning experiences.
- Examining a topic through natural and meaningful learning experiences.
- Weaving reading, writing, speaking, listening, viewing, visually representing, and thinking throughout the disciplines.
- Facilitating students' understanding of the interconnectedness of learning across the disciplines.
- Linking language and literacy with curriculum standards in science, math, social studies, and technology.
- Integrating informational literature across the disciplines.
- Using problem solving, prediction, classification, comparison and contrast, collection of data, notetaking, and analysis and synthesis of information in all disciplines.
- Encouraging critical thinking and its application to understand concepts across the disciplines.
- Engaging students in small-group work as they problem solve, dialogue, compute, measure, read, write, or express themselves artistically.
- Applying discipline knowledge to real-world problems and situations.
- Preparing students for a workplace through the use of technology as they locate, analyze, interpret, and evaluate information from a variety of sources.

Using theme teaching or focused inquiry addresses the concerns of many educators who claim that poor academic achievement may be attributed to teaching methods that emphasize rote learning and outdated textbooks and curriculum materials (Saul & Jagusch, 1991). In response to these concerns, teachers place less emphasis on textbook learning and on drill and skill exercises; they place more emphasis on integrated learning experiences that emerge from real-life experiences and the acquisition of critical thinking skills. Both writing and informational literature are integral components for this integrated approach to learning.

Integrating People into the Interdisciplinary Curriculum. Consistent with these theories, Aaron's teacher, Sandy Klein, uses theme teaching as she integrates real-life experiences with her curriculum in the various disciplines. Influenced by *Bring Life into Learning* (Graves, 1999), Sandy also focuses on an integrated, interdisciplinary program that highlights reading, writing, literature, history, science, art, and *people.* According to Graves (1999), students become engaged with the disciplines through people.

If we look at Aaron's writing, we see how an interest in people helped him become more engaged in his inquiry. For example, we see a description of a pitcher who could throw a baseball 105 miles an hour. His interest in people is also reflected in his description of the pioneers on the Oregon Trail. Specifically, a focus on people helped drive his inquiry.

Similarly, studies show that females (Belenky, 1986), Latino students (Parker, 2001; Ramirez & Castaneda, 1974), and African Americans (Ladson-Billings, 1994), in particular, relate to information that is represented in a humanized or story format. This focus on a humanized story format often ignites an interest in the content areas.

Applying Graves's theory (1999) in her teaching, Sandy helps her students begin to relate to information about the history and geography of the United States by integrating novels and biographies about Native Americans, early pioneers, historians, or World War II soldiers with her social studies curriculum. These novels and biographies provide a humanized context for learning about the past.

Integrating Writing with an Integrated, Interdisciplinary Curriculum

Inquiry skills such as communicating, predicting, observing, and classifying are critical components of Sandy's language arts curriculum (Carletti, Girard, & Willing, 1993; Close, Hull, & Langer, 2005). Similarly, they are part of her science, social studies, and math curriculum.

Reading and writing, which naturally employ these inquiry skills, became invaluable tools for Aaron as he pursued his inquiry. He used reading, writing, and inquiry skills to learn content knowledge about Nebraska, as well as to understand various concepts about writing informational text. While reading books and online sources about Nebraska, he learned that people in the field of geography and history often organize their writing around topics. In his own inquiry, he modeled this same process by organizing his paper into sections. Rather than labeling one section as "Landmarks," he added voice and imagination to his writing by labeling his section "There Are Many Landmarks in Nebraska That Attract Tourists."

Just as this inquiry project helped Aaron learn content knowledge, journal writing can be another way to promote active learning. Usually a more informal way to apply inquiry skills in various content areas (see Chapter 3), journals help students think about concepts, generate ideas, make observations, discover questions, and reflect on the information (Baker, 1996; Glenn & Muth, 1994; Holliday, Yore, & Alvermann, 1994; Moore-Hart, Liggit, & Daisey, 2004). In class, Aaron and his peers use journals to write about what they are learning from their sources. This also becomes a prewriting activity to help them think about their topic and the information. As they write in their journals, they explore how they think and feel about a subject. These early emotional connections often influence how they continue their inquiry.

At the same time, formal and informal writing enhances students' understanding of concepts as they integrate, organize, and clarify their prior knowledge with new knowledge (Armbruster, McCarthey, & Cummins, 2005; Fuhler et al., 2006; Glenn & Muth, 1994; Langer & Applebee, 1987). As Aaron gathered information about Nebraska, for example, he reflected on and reacted to the information, integrating his personal experiences of traveling through Nebraska with the new information about Nebraska. As he made connections between his prior knowledge and the new knowledge through his writing, he began to understand the concepts at deeper levels.

As Aaron and his peers continue to use informal and formal writing in their inquiries, they begin to comprehend and retain information over time (Armbruster et al., 2005; Langer & Applebee, 1987; Richardson & Morgan, 1994). Aaron, for example, will remember that early pioneers used Chimney Rock as a marker in their journey westward.

Integrating Informational Literature with an Integrated, Interdisciplinary Curriculum

Nonfiction or informational literature is another critical component of Sandy's language arts curriculum, which is heavily integrated with her science, social studies, and math curriculum. She realizes that informational literature, combined with integrated, interdisciplinary learning, bridges the academic fields (Duke, 2004; Neufeld, 2005) and enhances learning in the content areas (Camp, 2000; Guillaume, 1998; Yopp & Yopp, 2000). To help foster these links, her classroom library includes numerous collections of nonfiction books for her students to read daily. She believes that the wonderful world of informational literature may help her students gain greater familiarity with expository texts. In fact, these books invite her students to discover the excitement and richness of content-area subjects; they often ignite a spark or interest in a subject area.

Written by authors who care deeply and know a great deal about their subjects, informational literature allows students to explore the real world through texts that are inviting and stimulating, as well as accurate and up-to-date (Moss, 2005). By using figurative language, poetic devices, and an engaging writing style, authors of nonfiction books often engage Sandy's students in a topic. These aesthetic features, as well as the illustrations, graphs, and diagrams, provide her readers vicarious experiences, which often provoke new interests in science, math, and social studies. The authors' stylistic techniques also offer her seventh graders a model for writing and illustrating their own informational texts.

By contextualizing disciplinary language and terminology, authors of informational literature help students gain a greater understanding of concepts and vocabulary within a discipline (McClure, 2003; Moss, 2005). The contextualization of information, as well as the vivid illustrations, charts, and graphs, makes it easier for Sandy's students to connect new information with their prior experiences, helping them retain and remember the information over time. The more her students read informational books, the better they will understand other texts, including the more difficult, less interesting content-area textbooks or the more complex informational books (Butzow & Butzow, 1989; Guillaume, 1998).

Sandy especially enjoys using informational books, specifically biographies, because they often provide a more humanized context for learning in the content areas. As stated earlier, this focus on people fosters stronger connections with the disciplines. At the same time, the humanized context facilitates the linkage of background knowledge with new disciplinary knowledge and the acquisition of disciplinary vocabulary. As a result of her efforts, Sandy's students become inspired to learn more about the discipline.

Using Experience-Based Learning with Interdisciplinary Teaching

Just as research advocates the use of writing and literature across the disciplines, current practice also suggests that students, particularly in the elementary grades, should be given opportunities to first learn about math, science, and social studies from direct, hands-on experiences (Guillaume, 1998; Lapp & Flood, 1993; Moore-Hart et al., 2004). As learners observe, describe, and manipulate this world, they begin to experience what scientists, mathematicians,

Shelly learns about pond water life through hands-on experiences.

and historians actually do in the field. Rather than presenting the disciplines as remote, sterile disciplines, far removed from real-life situations, hands-on experiences help students relate the new knowledge to their lives (National Research Council, 1994).

Experience-Based Learning in Mathematics

Reinforcing Concepts about Measurement. Wishing to feed on her second graders' natural curiosity about measurement, Jeanie Lawrence fosters her students' inquiry by beginning with a class discussion on measurement. As students pool their knowledge about measurement, Jeanie records the information on a chart for all to see (see Figure 6.1). Three topics emerge from the discussion: Tools for Measuring, Things to Measure, and Units of Measurement. As a result of this brainstorming activity, students become more familiar with the specialized vocabulary of measurement—rulers, protractors, measuring tape, inches, feet, yards, miles, millimeters, centimeters, or meters. As students brainstorm, they simultaneously pool their knowledge. To extend students' understanding of concepts, Jeanie often invites students to "tell" their peers more about new vocabulary terms (i.e., protractors or millimeters).

Demonstrating Concepts about Measurement. After building background knowledge about measurement, Jeanie holds up a ruler, asking her second graders how she might measure the length of her marker. Tim explains that his dad lays things beside the ruler—next to the end of the ruler, the side where you see the number 1. Continuing, Tim reports that his dad moves his finger to the end of the object and sees what number it's closest to. Following Tim's suggestions, Jeanie lays the marker beside the ruler, placing the end of the marker next to the end of the ruler; then she moves her finger toward the end of the marker and

Figure 6.1
Measurement Brainstorming Chart

Measurement

Tools for Measuring	Things to Measure
ruler yardstick tape measure thermometer protractor	books paper crayons bulletin board window coat rack yourself water bottle paper pencil
Units of Measurement	
feet inches centimeters meters miles yards kilometers degrees	

shows Tim what she finds. "What number do you see?" she inquires. Tim announces that the marker is next to the number 5, or 5 inches long.

To extend the concept of measuring to other objects, she asks her students how she might measure the chart paper, which is longer than the ruler. Katie volunteers that her mother puts her finger next to the end of the ruler, then moves the end of the ruler next to her finger, continuing until she reaches the end of the object. Jeanie invites Katie to show everyone how her mother does this. Moving the ruler across the chart paper, Katie discovers that the paper is 24 inches long.

Next Jeanie holds her pencil next to the ruler. She looks up, noting that her pencil is between the 5 and 6. "What do I do?" she asks. Abdul wonders if it is in the middle of the 5 and 6. Jeanie looks again, saying that it is closest to the 6. Abdul explains you can approximate the length, saying it's 6 inches long because it's closest to the 6. Jeanie agrees, adding that if the pencil is closest to the 5, she would say it is 5 inches long. Then she explains if it is in the middle, she can say the pencil is 5½ inches, recording the number on the board for all to see.

Using Data Sheets to Record Measurements. Following these quick demonstrations, Jeanie explains that now they will measure things at their desk with their rulers. "While some of you measure objects at your desks," she adds, "I will let small groups measure additional objects in the classroom. Once you measure an object, write down the name of the object you measure and then write its length next to the object; we will call this our data sheet—just like mathematicians."

Using a new sheet of chart paper, she models the process for her students, using the examples of things she has just measured with them. Then she reiterates that this is what mathematicians and scientists often do while working—they record data on a data sheet. Tim volunteers that his dad writes down his data in a notebook when he's building things out of wood. As they begin working, Jeanie reminds them to use their temporary spelling if they are not sure how to spell the name of an object.

With eagerness and anticipation, her second graders begin exploring their environment, measuring books, pencils, water bottles, desks, and chairs. Some students also measure their hands, feet, fingers, arms, legs, or head; others measure their shoes, the sleeves of their shirts, or the length of their skirts. At the same time small groups eagerly move around the room, measuring the door, windows, tables, the globe, the whiteboard, or the overhead projector. As the second graders measure objects, Jeanie continuously circulates, helping her students as needed or checking to see that they carefully record the information on their paper. If some have difficulty spelling some of the objects, she stretches out the word, saying it slowly, asking them to write down the letters they hear.

Periodically, Jeanie stops, inviting students to share objects they have measured and their size. This gives her students opportunities to publish their knowledge. At the same time, students gain new ideas for objects to measure. After about fifteen minutes, Jeanie asks everyone to return to their desks and invites more students to share their data with the class. Figure 6.2 shows an example of Marcia's data sheet.

Using Writing to Think about the Learning Experience. To culminate the lesson, Jeanie distributes a new sheet of paper to everyone, explaining that everyone will be writing a letter to a person, sharing what they learned about measurement today. She adds that they may choose

Figure 6.2
Marcia's Data Sheet

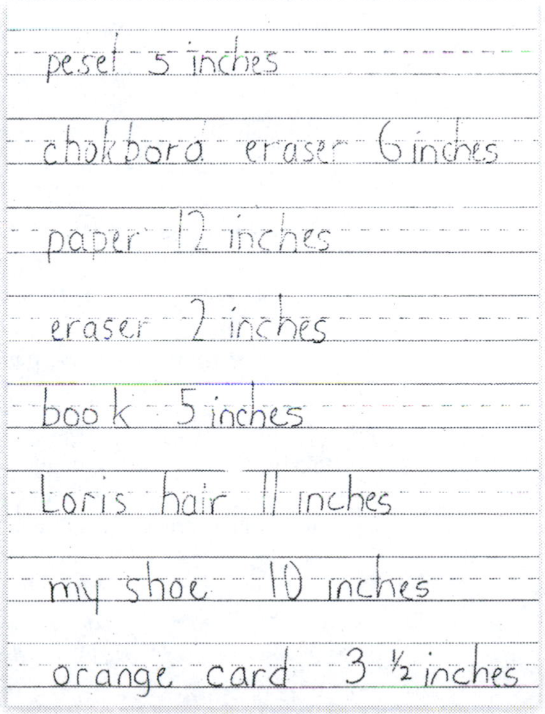

pesel 5 inches
chokboro eraser 6 inches
paper 12 inches
eraser 2 inches
book 5 inches
Loris hair 11 inches
my shoe 10 inches
orange card 3 ½ inches

the audience for their letters, encouraging them to think of people they might write letters to. Darrell volunteers that they could write to their mom or dad; Marcia shares she would like to write a letter to her teacher; Marvin explains that he would like to write to his friend; Kenya announces that she is going to write a letter to the principal.

To further help them gather their ideas for their letters, Jeanie asks them to brainstorm what they learned today. As her second graders share ideas for their letters, some draw on information from the chart; others talk about how to measure objects; still others describe objects they measured and their lengths. Darrell's, Marvin's, and Kenya's letters are shown below:

Dear Mom and Dad,

I am going to rit a note for you. In my clasrom wer [we're] token [talking] abot [about] mishmen [measuring]. I mishien [measured] 17 stuf We had a good time It was fun and she tech us We are going to git [get] bitr [better] at it and she is still going to tech and tech and tech. I catewat [can't wait] for 3 grade I will no [know] evere [every] thag [thing].

Dear Devin,
Today I lurned [learned] when the ruler is to small for what you are meshering [measuring] you could add another ruler and it might be big unuf [enough]. Do you know how long a meter is? I do! But I thik [think] you do. A meter is 3 feet tall. Did you know Dean's hair is 2 inches long.

Dear Mrs. Zokas (principal),
Today I lernd to meager [measure] things at school. I lernd to meager incis [inches]. Did you lern anything today? I meagerd [measured] a lunch box It was 6 inchis.

As can be seen from the writing samples, writing enhanced and supported students' learning. The brainstorming activity and the hands-on experience simultaneously served as prewriting activities for the students, making it easier for the students to write the letters. Having an audience for their writing especially appealed to the second graders, giving them a purpose and meaning for writing.

Rather than having students just write what they had learned in their journals, Jeanie added variety and interest to the activity. Using the genre of letter writing can be engaging for students of all ages, particularly when they can choose the audience for their letter.

Strengthening Students' Understanding of Story Problems in Math. Ellen Hortop's students have trouble with story problems. In particular, they can't determine when they should add or subtract when reading story problems. Knowing that writing helps students understand information, Ellen invites her third graders to create short books of addition and subtraction problems. As they begin drafting the books, her third graders decide that they will share their books with the other third grade class. Once the students in this class solve the problems, they will send them back to Ellen's students, who will check their work. If a student misses a problem, Ellen's students will then help their peers correctly solve the problem.

Prewriting Activities. To reinforce understanding of mathematical vocabulary and to help her students gather ideas for writing story problems, Ellen begins by having her students look at various addition and subtraction problems in their textbooks. As students look over the problems, they begin to notice that certain words often indicate whether they should add or subtract. To highlight this concept, Ellen encourages her students to work in small groups, listing examples of words and phrases that imply addition on one side of the paper and listing words that signify subtraction on the opposite side. Through this experience, the third graders discover that phrases like "How many are there all together?" or "How many in all?" usually signal that one should add. However, phrases like "How many are left?" or "How many are still . . . ?" suggest that one should subtract.

Creating Story Problems. Once her third graders understand the use of signal words, Ellen encourages them to practice writing two addition problems and two subtraction problems as a group. After the groups compose the problems, they trade problems with another group. While solving the problems, students circle the signal words to further strengthen this concept.

After participating in these activities, the third graders are ready to begin creating their own story problems independently. The next day Ellen helps her students organize and plan their problems for their books. First, she encourages her students to think of various topics or settings for their story problems. Brad proposes writing story problems about sports like baseball, football, or basketball. Alexa suggests writing story problems about going shopping for clothes or groceries. Carl explains that he would like to compose story problems about hidden treasures or fish in the ocean, while Cindy offers to write story problems about animals in the zoo, the aquarium, or the wilderness.

Once her students brainstorm several topics and settings for the problems, Ellen asks them to decide what topic or setting they would like to use. After selecting their topic or setting, they begin creating problems on their own, following the model of the story problems in their textbooks. Brad's book includes the following two story problems:

There were 62 brown buck in the dark spooky forest. Then 18 spotted doe came prancing along. They were gong to much [munch] on green grass together. How many deer are there in the herd all together?

There were 48 orders for pizza. Then 21 were diliverd [delivered]. How many pizza are left?

Cindy composed these two story problems:

There were 545 books in the library. 192 new books got put on the shelf. How many books are in the library now?

There were 72 eagles and 35 cardinals flying south. How many birds are flying south?

Carl chose the setting of the school and the soccer field for his story problems:

There were 800 kids in the school. 259 kids were sick. How many kids were in school?

There were 19 soccer players on the soccer field. 5 of them had to go home. How many soccer players were left on the field?

As shown by their writing, Ellen effectively integrated math and language arts to help her students improve in solving story problems. Having a meaning and purpose for writing became motivational to her students; having an audience for their writing helped them carefully construct story problems, following the models in their textbooks. While drafting, revising, and editing their story problems, they become more aware of their audience. They realize that their peers need the problem to be stated clearly and need to be able to read correctly spelled words in sentences with capitals and periods. The authors simultaneously gain an awareness of how math is used in real life.

teaching TIP 6.1

When students have an audience for their writing, they edit their work more carefully, checking for misspelled words or missing capitals and periods.

When they encounter similar problems in the future, the third graders will be more aware of signal words and see how to solve the problems more easily. Writing helped them understand math concepts more clearly; writing will also help them retain the concepts over time.

Reinforcing Math Concepts through Exit Slips or Quickwriting. Similar to journal writing, exit slips or quickwriting are ways for students to have one-on-one conversations with their teachers. They provide a window into what they are learning, what they understand, how they approach ideas, what misconceptions may be present, and how they feel about math learning.

After a hands-on learning experience with estimation, Jamie's class writes exit slips for their teacher, Susan Barry. The students give the exit slips to Susan as they leave for lunch. As shown below, Jamie understands that estimation is something that we use in our daily lives.

> We esetamated [estimated] how many letters in all are names. The shortest name in the class is Ian. The longest names in the class are Stephanie and Elizabeth. The total number of letters in the whole class is 120. I can't wait to see how many the last names are. The most popualor [popular] letter for the class is E.

Similarly, Justin's class uses quickwrites to show what they have learned about story problems. As Justin and his peers informally write about the learning experience for about 10 minutes, they let their thoughts flow. Using quickwrites helps students focus on the content of the math lesson rather than mechanics or spelling.

> Today we did story promblems about the candy bars we had on Friday. We got in groups of two and made story promblems. We traded with another group and did the promblems. We juged [judged] each promblem with stars. 1 star OK, 2 stars good, 3 stars the best. My partener was Reachel. We traded with Mark and Andy.

What's important is that we vary how we use writing during math. Using a combination of writing activities helps students begin to communicate mathematical ideas orally and in writing. Through writing, students clarify their thinking and become engaged in mathematics. Teachers can also use quickwrites to help them make instructional decisions as they informally evaluate their students' understanding or misconceptions about math.

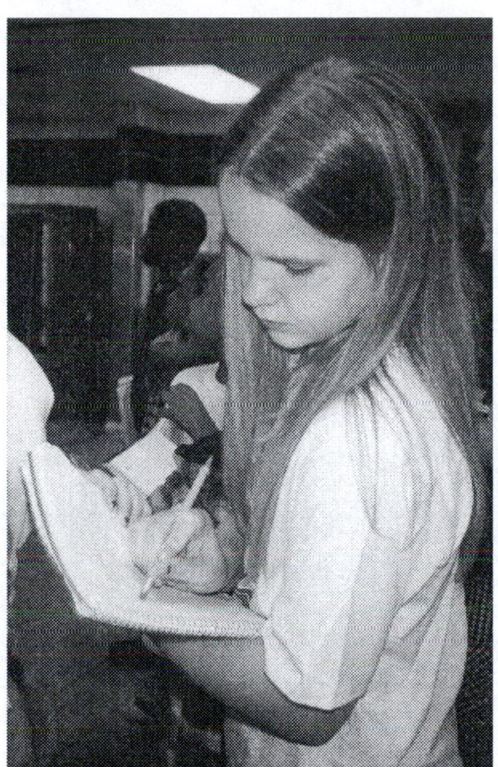

Kerry takes notes about the history of Depot Town.

Experience-Based Learning in Social Studies

Just as students should be given opportunities to learn about math through hands-on experiences, students need direct, hands-on learning experiences in social studies. These experiences help them relate to what historians actually do in the field (Winter & Robbins, 2005).

Experiencing History through Walking Tours. One way to help students experience history firsthand is by going on walking tours, especially in historic areas, within their community. Armed with writers' notebooks, Cathy Bies's sixth and seventh graders take a walking tour of Depot Town to learn about its history. While listening to their tour guide, they record the information in their notebooks. To be sure they gather as much information as possible, they write quickly, using phrases, abbreviations, and temporary spelling whenever needed (see Chapter 4).

The following day, the sixth and seventh graders share their notes in pairs, adding observations or historical information to their notes. To further celebrate their new knowledge, students then share interesting facts or observations about the tour as a class. As they listen to their peers talk about their experiences, students simultaneously insert missing details and facts into their notes.

The sixth and seventh graders become highly motivated to add to their notes because they plan to publish a class book about Depot Town. Creating a book gives them an audience for their writing, as they plan to leave copies of their book at local businesses so people in the community can learn more about Depot Town. When students know their work will be published, they become more motivated to write. Publishing seems to give them a purpose and meaning for learning and writing about Depot Town.

After collecting the information for their articles, Cathy's sixth and seventh graders choose a location that symbolizes the uniqueness of Depot Town to describe. To help them plan and organize their writing, the students first craft a web about the location, using their notes. The notes give them details, facts, or anecdotes to integrate into the web. To help all students see how to gather more ideas for their webs, Cathy encourages some students to share what they are describing and to give examples of facts or details included within their webs. As students share their ideas, Cathy affirms their decisions, emphasizing that these facts and details are what will make their pieces interesting to the reader. As a result of these positive responses to their writing, students begin to learn what information to include in their webs.

Once students complete their webs, Cathy encourages them to relook at their notes, searching for an interesting detail or fact about the location. This, she explains, may be a good way to begin your descriptive piece.

Having collected the information and a possible lead, the students begin drafting an article about their experiences on the historical walking tour. Jessica wrote about Remington Walker Design, a former hotel.

The Legend of Remington Walker

Yesterday we went on a trip to Depot Town and visited many places like Remington Walker Design. Bianca, the lady that works there told us a legend about the place being a hotel and a ballroom on the third floor. Downstairs there is a ghost named Gerard who opens and shuts the doors and knocks over the flower pots and moves things around. I hear Gerard is a good ghost. He was probably a left over guest. Bianca told us when she comes back to the store and the merchandise has been moved around, they blame Gerard. And he gets mad and does something they'll regret.

I like Remington Walker Design because it has pretty home supplies like beds, trunks, flowers, pictures, and a lot of antique furniture. There were beautiful tables and vases, and that's why I like Remington Walker Design.

Her piece captures the history of this former hotel, which continues to be plagued by a ghost. Her article also shows how places change over time. Today the hotel is a home for antique furniture, trunks, flowers, and vases.

Demario's piece, shown below, describes a historical landmark. Before taking the walking tour, Demario was unfamiliar with signal towers and their earlier historical role. His article shows that he has learned how people reconstruct historical landmarks to preserve the town's history.

Depot Town's Signal Tower

The signal tower is a historical landmark. The crossing gates used to be operated by hand from the tower. Signal towers are used for directing trains. The original was probably knocked down by a train, but the foundation is still there. The new signal tower is white with a black roof. It has green lettering which says, "Historic Depot Town." It is near the Peter Rabbit garden. The Norris Thompson building is across the street, where names of Civil War soldiers are carved in the rafters. There are three windows on each side of the tower. There is no door in or out because no one uses it. I wouldn't want to live in there.

Knowing their articles will be published, the sixth and seventh graders carefully revise and edit their drafts, following the process described in Chapter 4. In particular, they revise their pieces to include a good beginning, examples of facts and details about the location, and an interesting ending for the article.

When Cathy later circulates the books at local stores and businesses, the community becomes more familiar with what's happening in the schools. People are impressed with what the students have learned and their ability to communicate their knowledge about Depot Town.

Experiencing History through Museums. Vonnie Taylor takes her students to local museums to learn more about the history of their community. Through the lens of their writing, students begin to view museums as a place where they can learn about history and the life of people in earlier times.

To help her students gather descriptive and detailed observations of the artifacts within the museum, Vonnie has her third graders bring their writers' notebooks to the museums. They have been practicing notetaking, so the third graders know how to gather observations, using words or phrases. They also know how to listen when people are talking, jotting down the important facts and details, using words, phrases, or abbreviations.

As they tour the local museum within their community, the third graders have an opportunity to practice their skills. Returning to school, students review their notes, insert additional information into their notes, generate webs, and then draft an article about the museum. After revising and editing their articles, her third graders use word processing tools to publish the final drafts in a class book. Similar to Cathy, Vonnie left copies of the published books at the museum for visitors to see the writing talents of her third graders. This is Staci's piece about the historical museum:

An Indescribable Trip through History

Our trip to the Ypsilanti Historical Museum was very entertaining. We got a tour of the whole museum. We asked questions and got interesting answers. Ann McCarthy was very nice and helpful. She told us a lot about the clothes, the rooms and what the rooms were used for. We saw old fashion clothes, an antique stove and other furnishings. A formal parlor was used for holidays and other special occasions. Minerva Dow, wife of Asa Dow, died July 14, 1864. After her death, Asa Dow went back to Chicago. On September 23, 1890 he died in Chicago, but was sent back to Ypsilanti to be buried in Highland Cemetery beside his wife. He became the second person to be buried in the newly dedicated Highland Cemetery.

Ann McCarthy said that her favorite thing is the dining room china because she likes the fine china. My favorite room is the bedroom because of the bed and the night gowns. Did you know girls and women wore night caps? They wore the night caps to keep their hair in place, and to keep their ears warm at night.

On a phone interview we spoke to Ann McCarthy and found out that the museum was created "To preserve the town's history." I think the museum was a great idea to establish because it teaches us about Ypsilanti.

If we want our students to experience history, we similarly need to bring writers' notebooks with us when touring museums. Students will be more likely to remember the historical facts and figures when learning is brought to life through pen and paper. Just like professional writers, young writers become collectors of information as they observe, take notes, listen, brainstorm, and journal (Clark, 1995). After having similar hands-on learning experiences, students will also be able to relate to the information in their history textbooks or informational books more easily.

Experiencing World War II through the Yankee Air Museum. To help her students understand U.S. history, in particular World War II, Kelly Newton took her fifth graders to the Yankee Air Museum. Equipped with notebooks, Kelly's students use their observation skills to record descriptions of the artifacts found within the museum; her fifth graders also use their listening skills to chronicle details about life or people in this historical period.

Notetaking opened the door to extensive learning about World War II for Trey, who expressed his knowledge in the format of an acrostic poem.

Yankee Air Museum

Yankee Air Museum started in 1981
Airplanes of all shapes and sizes
No tall tail B-52's are flown in wars now
Kitty Hawk was where the first flight was flown in 1903
Entertainment was listening to a radio in 1944
European conflict was a major part of WW II

Air force was started in the 20th century
International effort to keep the Philippines
Rosey the Riveter made airplanes

Movie theaters gave news of WW II
U.S.A. joined the war in 1941 because of Pearl Harbor
Soldiers protecting America in the wars
Everyone helps with the war effort
United States of America helped end the war
Machine guns were sometimes 45 millimeters in size

His poem illustrates how hearing stories about the war and community efforts to support those fighting in the war gave Trey a humanized context to learn specific facts and dates about the war.

Tanner's piece (below) shows his keen interest in visiting the museum and learning about World War II. His ability to chronicle his observations and knowledge reveals how much students can learn when we explore history through hands-on learning experiences.

Yankee Air Museum

To infinity and beyond! That's how I felt when I walked into the Yankee Air Museum. We saw many different types of planes there. We learned that Henry Ford made a factory that produced B-24s. He also had to make a freeway to Ypsilanti so people could get to the factory.

In 1986, the Yankee Air Museum bought a B-17. It is only one of thirteen B-17s left that can actually fly. The B-17 was once used to put out forest fires. Ten people can lie flat in the B-17. Soldiers wrote names of others that have died in the war, and they were dropped on targets. I found seven oxygen tanks hidden under the plate that you walk over. In the back of the plane there is an area that one person can fit in and shoot the enemy from behind the plane. On the right front wing there is an exhaust pipe. There was a painting on the B-17 that was called "The Yankee Lady."

The B-25 was driven by the Canadian Air Force. It did twelve missions and dropped eight bombs in the summer of 1944. The B-25's weight is 38,000 pounds, but fully loaded its weight is 48,000 pounds.

The C-47 can fit up to two jeeps in it. The C-47 can fit up to 27 people at one time. Two jeeps were actually in it at one point. In the C-47 there were tanks, hoses, fans, switches, and knobs. During WW II, they flew the plane with no radar. After the war, they made radar for the plane.

The gigantic B-52 made over 700 missions. The B-52's wing span is 190 feet. The bombs on the B-52 were over 10 feet long.

These were some of the things I saw at the Yankee Air Museum.

Through authentic experiences, students get in touch with the past. The walking tours and trips to museums represent a way to make history enriching and transformational. At the same time, writing about tours and museums integrates state and national standards of notetaking, listening, interviewing, critical thinking, close reading, and composing as students construct their knowledge about history.

Armed with interesting and important information, students create quality writing pieces. The richness of the details, derived from their observations and enhanced by their imagination and creativity, entertains their readers.

Experiencing History through Interviews. David Wayne, an eighth grade teacher, uses a different approach. He wants his students to experience history, specifically World War II, through people. David believes that his students might understand the issues of war more completely by listening to the stories of people who actually served in the war. Through contacts at the Yankee Air Museum, he invites former World War II veterans to his classroom for his eighth graders to interview. Working in small groups, students interview the veterans, following the process described in Chapter 4.

Interviewee Mrs. Clark shows students a book about her experiences as a pilot in World War II.

Similar to other students, David's eighth graders take notes, generate webs, draft, revise, and edit their articles. Using word processing tools, the students prepare a publication of the interviews, which is then shared with the interviewees and parents at an Author's Celebration. As can be seen, Jonathon learned how committed many World War II veterans remain, even today.

The Brave One

Lloyd Johnson was born in Hazel Park, Michigan, and was an only child. He began playing the harmonica when he was seven years old. In his teenage years, he bought his own business. On December 7, 1941, while Lloyd Johnson was working on his car his dad came out and said, "Lloyd, the Japs (Japanese) are attacking Pearl harbor." Lloyd said, "I've got problems of my own." Soon he found out that his lifelong friend, Bob McIlvride, was the first to die in World War II. Now war became personal. As an only child, Lloyd had the choice of staying home and taking care of his parents, but he wanted to go to war.

When in the air force, his choice was to become a lead bombardier. His job involved dropping bombs on specific targets. As a lead bombardier, the war was a big surprise for him. He fought at Hanover and Berlin, Germany, and several other places. Lloyd Johnson used a technique called an intervelometer, which lets bombs fall every 25 to 30 feet. This killed at least 9000 German soldiers.

Lakeycia's piece shows soldiers' courage while fighting during the war. Using a direct quote from her interviewee, Lakeycia gives power to his words. One can also see that she took careful notes in order to accurately tell Mr. Bodycombe's story.

Mr. Bodycombe, a World War II Pilot

Mr. Bodycombe was a World War II pilot in 1944. Mr. Bodycombe was the only child of his mother and father. In the middle of 1942 Mr. Bodycombe received a draft from the army to come and fight in the war. When he told his mother and father the big news, his mother was scared that he would not come back, and she would not have a son anymore. Dad was okay with it. He knew that he had to do it. At this point and time, Mr. Bodycombe was 20 years old when he decided he was going to be a pilot.

Plane training was 15 months. He trained in Alabama, South Carolina, and Georgia. Within 15 months he was flying the Yankee Lady. Then Mr. Bodycombe went to war in 1943. He flew the Liberator to Italy. The Liberator carried eight 500 lb. Bombs. Every morning he would meet up with the team and he would say, "There's only three things that can happen. We can lose oxygen, get bombed up, or freeze to death. But that's not going to happen to us."

Mr. Bodycombe now has three boys of his own. He is still flying the Yankee lady. I would like to say thank you for taking some time out of your day to talk to us and to tell your great stories.

Viewing World War II within the context of real lives and real aspirations for self, family, and country helps Lakeycia become engaged in history. Her interview gives her a richer understanding of the events of the war and the human emotions that people experienced while fighting in the war.

As a result of this interviewing experience, David's eighth graders begin to learn the facts and dates about World War II much more easily. History becomes accessible and interesting through a story format that gives a meaning and purpose for learning facts. As students begin to see themselves as researchers, they will begin to look everywhere for information (Rogovin, 1998).

Experience-Based Learning in Science

In Sue Bowen's classroom, hands-on learning experiences are a critical component of her science curriculum. The natural wonder and curiosity that emerges when kindergarteners explore and experiment with their environment adds an exciting dimension to the curriculum.

Reinforcing Observational Skills through Shared Writing. In her kindergarten class, Sue Bowen often uses shared writing to help hone her students' observational skills. Similar to many teachers, Sue houses two guinea pigs in her classroom. The guinea pigs become a natural way for her students to observe life and changes as they grow and develop. Linking this hands-on learning experience to science, Sue plans a shared writing lesson to help her students heighten their observation skills.

Prewriting Activities. To begin her lesson, Sue brings the cage to the carpet area and asks her students to think of some words to describe their classroom pets, Bell and Edison. Brian remarks that they are cute and cuddly; Reece shares that Edison has floppy ears. As Sue listens to her kindergarteners describe the guinea pigs, she records their observations on her computer, which is connected to an LCD projector so that all students can see the words as she types. As she records their descriptions, Sue points out that scientists similarly record their observations about animals in a journal just like we are doing right now. In fact, she continues, scientists observe animals in their natural environment, recording notes that describe the animals and their behaviors in a journal or log.

As the kindergarteners continue to share their observations, Sue reinforces their scientific skills, pointing out that they are great scientists, using thoughtful observations and carefully examining the guinea pigs as they describe them. For example, she points out that words like *curvy* ears or *beady* eyes are very effective describing words. Figure 6.3 shows the kindergarteners' list of observations for Bell and Edison.

Drafting a Story about the Guinea Pigs. The following day, Sue shows them their list of observations, reviewing their ideas while some help her read the observations. Following this quick review, she explains that today we are going to write about the guinea pigs so that visitors who come to the classroom might know more about our classroom pets, Bell and Edison. Our list of observations, she adds, will help us write a description of Bell and Edison.

To help guide the process, Sue asks her students to think of things they might want to tell others about Bell and Edison. Caleb thinks they might want to tell others that Bell and Edison are both sisters. Mandy comments that they can tell people what they look like.

After a few others share their ideas, Sue asks them how they should begin. Mike thinks they should begin the story with their names—"Two guinea pigs, one named Bell and the other Edison." Using the word processor, Sue writes down Mike's ideas. Then Caleb adds "Are related as sisters." Again, Sue records Caleb's ideas. As other students share their ideas, Sue uses their exact words. Using the word processor helps her keep a steady pace so that her students remain focused and interested. When the story is finished, Sue and her kindergarteners practice reading the story chorally (see Figure 6.4).

Revising the Story about the Guinea Pigs. To help her young writers learn that many times we go back and revise our writing, she displays the story, triple spaced, on the overhead projector the following day (see Figure 6.4). After the class chorally reads the story, Sue

Figure 6.3

Kindergarteners' Observations of Bell and Edison, the Guinea Pigs

Guinea Pig Observation

Bell	Edison
calm	black
shy	floppy eared
cuddly	cute
colorful	playful
small	jumpy
furry	gurgly
cute	black nailed
not playful	really furry
still	bead-shaped eyed
multi-colored	not scared
afraid	curious
looks around a lot	soft
brown & white	sniffs a lot
curvy eared	long whiskered
long whiskered	straight furred
chubby	girl
nervous	watching everyone
flat eared	skinny
beady eyed	little feet (paws)
pink nosed	twitching
soft	noisy
female	shaky
girl	making squeaky noises
fat	tiny
guinea pig	guinea pig

Figure 6.4

Kindergarteners Write a Story about the Guinea Pigs

All about two Guinea Pigs

Two guinea pigs, one name Bell and the other Edison. Are realated as sisters. Bell is very colorful she has brown, white and black hair. She is kuddly but scared two. She is new to the school so she has to get used to it. Now Edison is kinda the same but she is all black. She has a little bit of white hair in the back. She has black hair, black feet, and black eyes. She is also new to our school so we have to show respect for both guinea pigs.

shares that once she drafts her writing, she usually begins to revise the story. Then she pauses, asking her students if they know what *revise* means. Jamie thinks it might mean *change.* Sue affirms his answer, explaining that sometimes she relooks at the notes she writes to their parents. Sometimes she changes some of the words in the note so that their parents can understand the note more easily. This, Sue explains, is what we're going to do today.

Next, she rereads the first sentence of their descriptive paragraph and asks if anyone has any suggestions for changing it. Julie recommends that they begin the first sentence with, "There are two new guinea pigs in Mrs. Bowen's class." That way, she explains, people will know where the guinea pigs are. Following Julie's suggestion, Sue inserts the words *There are* in front of the word *two,* using a green transparency pen. Since the first word of my sentence is *There,* she explains, I will make the *T* in *two* a lowercase *t.* She models the change. Then she draws a caret on the overhead and inserts the phrase "in Mrs. Bowen's class." This, she continues, is revising; we make changes in our writing so the reader can understand our story. Sometimes we insert words; sometimes we cross out words.

Continuing the process, Sue revisits each of the sentences, listening to her students' suggestions and then making the changes. She wants her students to understand that writing changes; sometimes writing is even messy. She emphasizes that we revise so that others can understand our message. Scientists, she adds, want others to understand what they write, too. After writing about their observations, sometimes they revise their writing.

By modeling the process of revising to her kindergarteners, Sue helps them begin to understand more about the writing process. Simultaneously, she integrates information about using capitals, periods, or other mechanics of writing. Figure 6.5 shows the revisions the young writers made. The final draft is displayed next.

Figure 6.5

Kindergarteners Revise Their Story about the Guinea Pigs

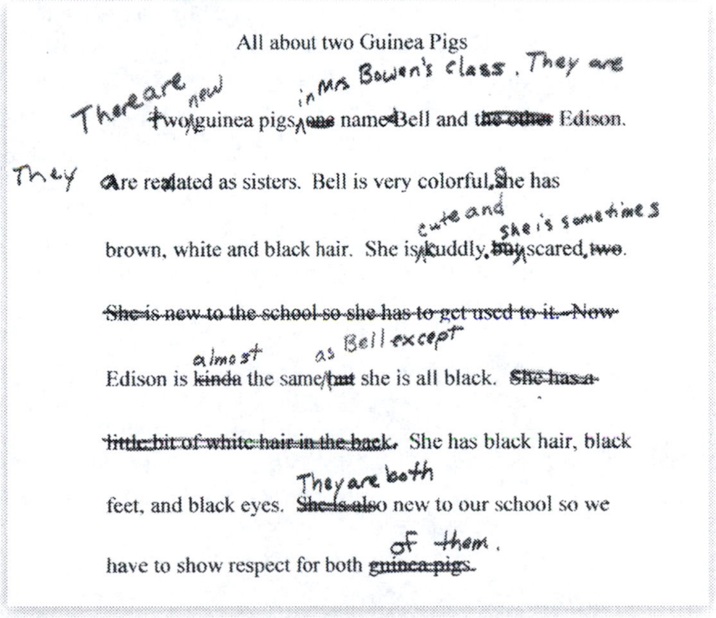

All about two Guinea Pigs

There are ~~T~~two new guinea pigs in Mrs. Bowen's class. They are ~~one~~ name~~d~~ Bell and ~~the other~~ Edison.

They ~~Are~~ are re~~a~~lated as sisters. Bell is very colorful. She has

brown, white and black hair. She is cute and cuddly. ~~but~~ She is sometimes scared. ~~two~~.

~~She is new to the school so she has to get used to it. Now~~

Edison is ~~kinda~~ almost the same as Bell except ~~but~~ she is all black. ~~She has a~~

~~little bit of white hair in the back.~~ She has black hair, black

feet, and black eyes. ~~She is also~~ They are both new to our school so we

have to show respect for both ~~guinea pigs.~~ of them.

All About Two Guinea Pigs

There are two new guinea pigs in Mrs. Bowen's class. They are named Bell and Edison. They are related as sisters. Bell is very colorful. She has brown, white and black hair. She is cute and cuddly. She is sometimes scared. Edison is almost the same as Bell except she is all black. She has black hair, black feet, and black eyes. They are both new to our school so we have to show respect for both of them.

Learning about the Writing Process through Shared Writing. As a result of this shared writing experience, Sue's young writers learn how to make observations and how to write about their observations, using details and examples. Her students will use this same process as they continue to write about their science observations or their experiences in journals.

At the same time, the kindergarteners gain knowledge about the importance of revising so that our message is clearly delivered to the audience. Through shared writing, the young authors discover that writing requires careful thought and an investment of time.

Reinforcing First Graders' Understanding about Magnets. As her first graders use inquiry to learn about science, Pam often begins by having her first graders explore and experiment with science-related materials. Calling her students to the carpeted area, she asks them what they know about magnets. As they talk about their experiences with magnets, Pam creates a web about magnets on chart paper for all her students to see. Justin remembers that some things like nails stick to magnets. Ceslie explains that wooden blocks won't stick to magnets. As they share their ideas about magnets, Pam also models what they describe with a large magnet so that everyone can see how magnets work.

Modeling Concepts about Magnets. Once her students brainstorm what they know about magnets, Pam holds up a plastic bag filled with a variety of objects. She explains that they are going to be scientists today, experimenting with the magnets to see what types of items are "attracted" to the magnets. She points out that scientists use the word *attract* rather than *stick.* Just like scientists, she continues, we will list items that are attracted to the magnets on one side of our paper; on the other side, we will list items that are not attracted to the magnets. Modeling the process, she folds her chart paper the "hot dog" way and labels one side *Attract* and the other side *Not Attract.* Then she asks her first graders to tell her where to write *nails.* Carletta shares that we should put it on the side that says *Attract,* because it sticks to the magnet. Similarly, Erin explains that we would write *wooden block* on the side that says *Not Attract.* Just before sending them back to their seats to experiment with their magnets, Pam reminds them to use their temporary spelling as they write down the objects on their data sheets.

Using Data Sheets to Discover Concepts about Magnets. The first graders eagerly return to their seats, preparing their data sheets while Pam distributes the plastic bags. Once they label their data sheets, they begin exploring the objects, testing them to see if they are attracted to the magnet. While her students experiment with the objects at their desks, Pam allows small groups to also experiment with various items in the classroom. Tarrey's list is shown in Figure 6.6.

> ***teaching* TIP 6.2**
>
> As can be seen, young authors apply concepts about phonics in their writing. Writing reinforces these concepts so that eventually the symbols and sounds become internalized.

Periodically, Pam has her students stop their explorations for a few minutes while students share their discoveries with the class. She also praises her first graders for using their temporary spelling as they

Figure 6.6
Tarrey's Magnet Data Sheet

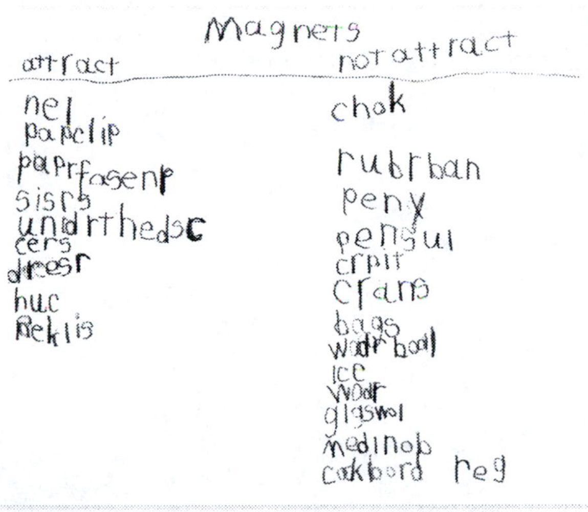

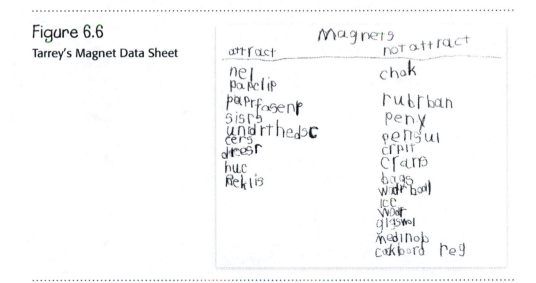

record the information on their data sheets. Pam realizes that notetaking is developmental; pictures, letters, and temporary spelling are all valid forms of notetaking (Rogovin, 1998). Her praise validates these attempts.

After about 15 minutes, the first graders collect all the objects and place them back in the plastic bags. Then Pam invites more students to share items that are attracted to the magnets and items that are not attracted to the magnets.

Using Writing to Think about the Learning Experience. After several students have shared their findings, Pam distributes a new sheet of paper for them to draw what they have learned in science today. After drawing for about 6 or 7 minutes, students share their drawings with a partner, explaining what they have learned. Then Pam encourages them to continue drawing about their experiences for a few more minutes.

Once students finish their drawings, she invites them to tell her what they might write on their papers. After three or four first graders share what they plan to say, all students begin to write what they have learned about magnets on their papers. Figure 6.7 shows what Kiran learned. Erin's and Brad's writing is shown below.

My Magnet

My magnet attracts to the gloeg [globe]. My magnet does not stik to the dreanking fownten [drinking fountain]. My magnet stiks to the pensl shrpenr [pencil sharpener]. My magnet does not stik to my pensl [pencil].

My Magnet

I am a magnit I stick to a dry erace [erase] board. I am a magnit I do not stick to a glass wall. A magnit sticks to a fiyl cabnit [file cabinet].

Thus, writing became a way to show their understanding of concepts about magnets. Through exploration and experimentation, the first graders discover the emotions scientists experience while studying the world and our environment.

Figure 6.7

Kiran Shows What He Has Learned about Magnets

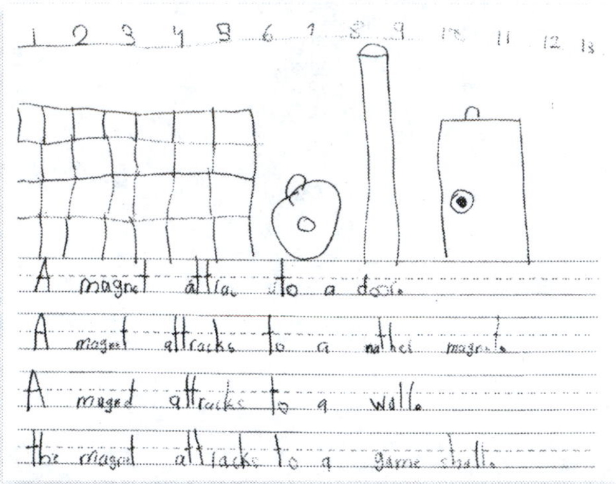

Reinforcing First Graders' Observation Skills. A few months later, Pam has her first graders apply their observation skills as they examine rocks. After inviting her students to the carpeted area, Pam models the process during a minilesson. She shows them a large rock and asks them to look at it carefully, thinking about words to describe the rock.

Modeling how to observe and describe, she shares that her rock is sparkly and writes the word on her chart paper. Diamyn adds that the rock is white with orange stripes; Julie points out that the rock is oval and smooth; Brad notes that the rock has dents in it; Karin observes that the rock has some yellowish and brownish colors in it. As her first graders share their observations, Pam records the words in a list format on chart paper.

After several people have a chance to share their observations, Pam explains that they will be scientists again today. Just like scientists, she explains, you will observe your own rocks and think of words to describe them. After observing your rocks, Pam continues, you will write about your observations, painting a picture of your rock with words.

Once the first graders return to their desks, Pam distributes a rock for each student to observe. Following her model, they list words that describe their rocks. To stimulate their use of descriptive words, Pam periodically has volunteer students share two words from their list with the group.

After about 10 minutes, Pam asks her students to brainstorm what they will write about. By describing our rocks, she explains, we can help others see our rocks through words. After a few brainstorm examples of how they will describe their rocks, Pam encourages them to begin writing. Carley and Rashad gave the following descriptions:

My rock is hard. This rock is flat and it has a dint [dent]. My favriet rock is an oval. My rock is bumpy and it has dots. This rock is smooth. My rock has two sides and my rock is grayish and brownish.

My splshl [special] roik [rock] is a oval. The roik has designs. All roik have a shape. That roik is vaere [very] splishal [special]. The roik is smooth. I like my roik.

Figure 6.8

Tyler's Observations of His Rock

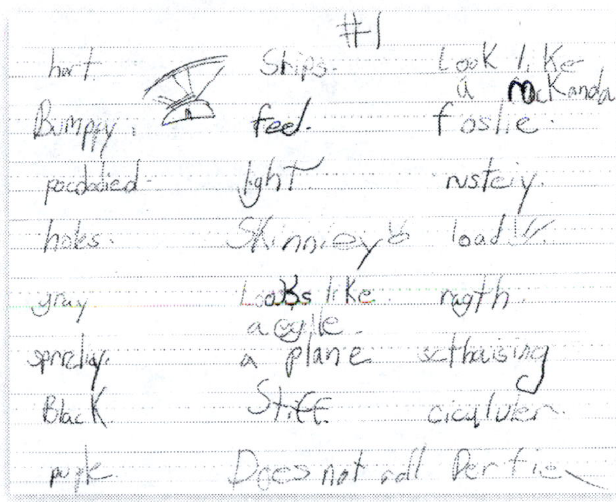

Translation

hard
bumpy
polka-dotted
holes
gray
sparkly
black
purple

stripes
feels light
shiny
looks like eagle
looks like plane
stiff
does not roll

looks like a rock and a fossil
rusty
lead
ragged
?
circular
dirty

Their writing shows us that the first graders know how to observe objects. They are also learning how to write a descriptive piece about their rocks, just as a scientist might write a description of his or her observations in a science journal.

Reinforcing Observation Skills through Poetry in a Second Grade Class. In her second grade class, Margaret Trapp also has her students observe rocks. Similar to Pam, she has them list their observations on paper. As her second graders record their observations, Margaret challenges them to use their senses and carefully examine the rocks. As a result of her questioning and probing, as well as her high expectations, the students' observations gradually become more specific descriptions of the rocks. For example, her second graders begin to use words like *rough, dotted, striped, sparkly, pointy,* or *flat.* Some even use words to describe the sense of smell—Kiara, for example, thinks her rock smells like mud. Figure 6.8 shows Tyler's observations of his rock.

Following the prewriting activities, she explains that they will be using their observations to write poems about the rocks. To help her students see how to transform their observations into a poem, she shares two examples of poems written by her second graders the previous year. After reading the poems to her students, Margaret invites her students to share what they enjoyed about the poems, following the model described in Chapter 4.

Hearing and talking about these poems help Kiara and Wesley see how to create their own poems. Kiara imitates the use of rhythm and beat in her poem, while Wesley begins to experiment with similes in his poem.

My Rock

My rock is pink and it is heavy
It is black and green
My rock is bumpy and hard
Pointy and rough
My rock has stripes on it
It has colors on it
My rock is a little bit orange
My rock smells like mud.

My Rock

Reminds me about a heart
And all so beautiful
It also smells like grass in a nice shiney backyard
That's where it rests–
In the nice smooth grass.

Using the genre of poetry to write about their experiences with rocks brings new discovery and wonder to the learning experience. Writing poems further reemphasizes the use of their senses, an important characteristic of both scientific writing and poetry.

Reinforcing Observation Skills through Poetry in an Eighth Grade Class. To further increase their observation skills, students might also observe shells, plants, fruit, leaves, vegetables, or flowers. For example, Susan Murphy's eighth graders observe, investigate, and examine plants and flowers. Through inquiry, they investigate more information about their plant or flower and integrate this information with their observations as they compose poems. Readers can see, listen, feel, and taste the rose or the mountain glen in Becky's and Steven's poems.

The Blossoms

The tender blossoms
Lustrously layered, shining bright.
Sparkling loosely.
Charcoal-black oak leaves
Still mildly and tenderly indulged.
Brilliantly
Illuminated
Ravishingly elegantly.
Delicate velvet.

A Mountain Glen

A hidden treasure
Enclosed with needles and sap
Morning dew wets it.
A ring of insects appear to dance all around
With orange tails high.
In a mountain glen
Three flowers rise up for life
Protected with care.
This exotic thing
Rare, unlike anything else
In its peak of life.
It lives with nature
And talks with the animals
To tell its great tale.

"Since the dawn of time I have been here," it proclaims,
To see the world change.
Man has come to me
But he has never harmed me
I guess he does care.

Writing about their observations helps both the second graders and eighth graders discover science and learn about its tools—observation and description. This experience opens the door to new questions and learning for the students. The second graders, for example, want to know what type of rock they each have. Then they want to know what type of rock their friends have, which invites opportunities for classification and further inquiry. As can be seen, firsthand experiences bring new life to learning.

Experiencing Science through a Field Trip to a Farm. Just as walking tours can be a way to help students experience history directly, field trips can be a way to experience science firsthand. When Kim Nichol's second grade class takes a field trip to Maybury Farm, they learn how maple syrup is made. Just like Cathy Bies's class, the second graders arrive at Maybury Farm with writers' notebooks to record the process as they listen to Mrs. Norma and Farmer Bemer. Noah's and Caitlyn's pieces, shown below, demonstrate how much they learned from the field trip.

We had a field trip at Mayburg farm. We went to a little cabben [cabin] where Mrs. Norma and Farmer Bemer talked about how to make maple syrup. After that Farmer Bemer took us for a horse ride to the woods. This is how to tap a tree. You take a brace and bit and drill a hole in the tree. The sap will run out of the tree like a waterfall. The sap has 2% of suger. Then you take a spile and stick it in the hole. You take a milk jug on the spile. The sap will run into the jug. Once the jug is full you take the jug to the evaporater.

Maple syruping at our field trip was marvelous. We got to taste sap and what amazed me the most was that the sap has only 2% suger. The sap is mostly water so it is not sweet and each tap can yield 2 gallons of sap. But the most fun part was when the horses galloped to make the wagon move.

By writing about the experience, the second graders are able to review the process of making maple sugar, a process that they will remember in years to come. As one reads the pieces, one feels the second graders' excitement and passion for learning.

These pieces evolved through the use of multiple prewriting activities, which helped the students remember the sequence of steps and specific details about the trip—for example, the actual tools required to make maple syrup. Similar to Cathy, Kim has her students talk about their notes, use their notes to create webs, write a rough draft, revise the piece, and edit the piece. Kim then publishes the students' writing in a class book to be placed in their classroom library for all to read. Figure 6.9 shows Allison's webs, her revised draft, and her final draft.

Allison's prewriting strategies illustrate how the clusters or webs help her plan and organize the ideas in her notes for writing an article. Through her revisions, she also learns more about crafting informational texts and the importance of using transition words in her

Figure 6.9

Allison's Steps to Prepare Her Essay on Maple Syruping

(a) Allison's prewriting web about maple syruping. (b) Allison's prewriting web about maple sap. (c) Allison's revised draft using transition words. (d) Allison's final draft about maple syruping.

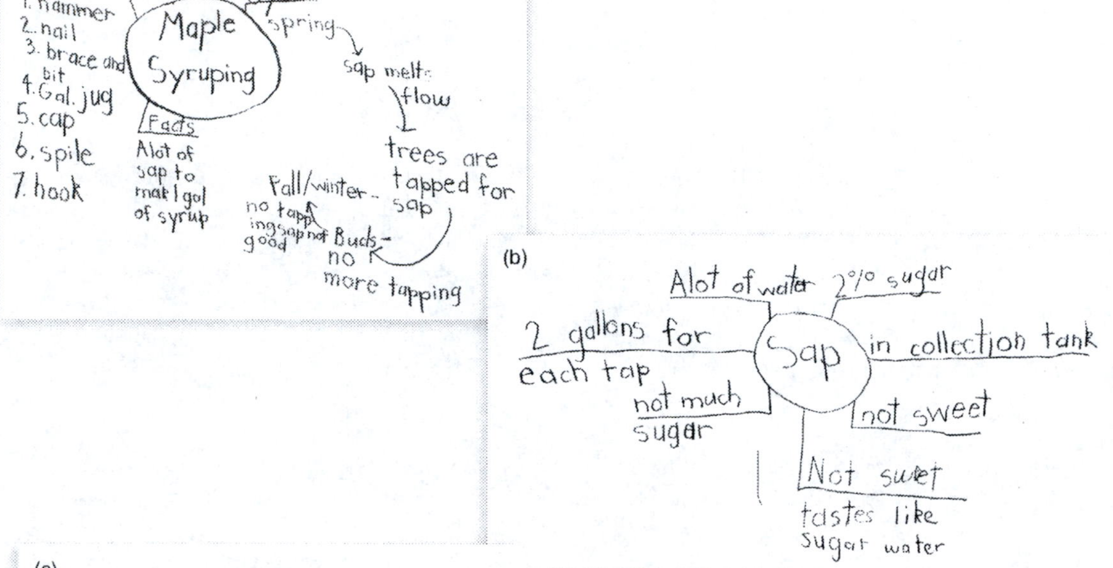

(c)

Maple Syruping is terrifict! ~~We got to drill a hole in the trees~~ First you drill a hole in the tree. Then you have a spile and then you have to hammer the spile in the tree. ~~And then~~ Next you ~~you~~ have a nail and milk jug. You put the milk jug on the spile and you put the nail beneth ~~benthth~~ it.

First
After
Finally
Next
Afterwards

Part 2

I learned that there is 2% sugar in sap. And there is 2 galbns of sap for each tap. Maple Syrup does not have alot of

(d)

Maple Syruping is terrifcet! First you drill a hole in the tree. Then you have a spile and then you have to hammer the spile in the tree. Next you have nail and a milk jug. You put the milk jug on the spile and you put the nail beneth it.

Part 2

I learned that there is 2% sugar in sap. And there is 2 gallons of sap for each tap. Maple Syrup does not have alot.

writing. Specifically, Allison learns how to use transitions in her writing from Kim's minilesson on transitional words, a lesson demonstrating how to craft informational writing. Her decision to implement this minilesson emerged from her observations of students' drafts. These observations revealed that her second graders needed to learn how to use transition words when describing a sequence of events.

Experiencing Science through a Field Trip to the Botanical Gardens. Beth Ramsey wants her sixth graders to experience the mystery and awe of plant and animal life within the Botanical Gardens. As her class tours the gardens, they learn many fascinating facts about plant and animal life in various geographic regions around the world, as well as within their own community. Derick shows his fascination with the Venus Flytrap:

Are you tired of swiping flies? On Thursday, I went to the Botanical Gardens and I saw a Venus Flytrapper. A Venus Flytrapper is very exciting to see in the State of North Carolina. It looks like a mouth, actually it is a mouth! It's a snap trap and it makes it snap. It feeds on insects and some plants.

And did you know they're a relative of the Venus Flytrapper called Tharipod? It can pull a car several hundred feet. The Venus Flytrapper is an amazing plant.

So watch out you pesky flies. The Venus Flytrapper is going to get you.

As Katie tours the gardens, she feels like she can't write fast enough. There are so many amazing plants and animals all around her. Through her writing, we experience the magic of plant and animal life in the gardens.

Plants and Animals at the Matthaei Botanical Gardens

Have you ever seen a huge snapping turtle at the bottom of a pond? Well, I did on Thursday, at the Matthaei Botanical Gardens.

I saw many animals in the pond. Underneath the duckweed and algae there were many types of frogs such as: the bull frog, the leopard frog, and the green frog. The sound of the birds chirping was everywhere, letting you know that at the pond you are not alone. Everywhere you looked you could see insects flying left and right, up and down. Looking down near the bridge you could see crayfish hiding underneath rocks.

The pond had many plants that made living our everyday life easier, like some plants make medicine, food, fossil fuels, clothes, and some even clean the water.

There are many species of flowers there, like the Golden Rods, St. John Wort, Blue Vervain, and Purple Loosestrife. The many different colors of flowers made the pond look like a beautiful rainbow. The pond gave off a wet, musty, earthy type smell, but the beautiful scents given off by the flowers covered most of the smell up, making it seem like you were in a room full of sweet smelling perfume.

There are not just flowers growing in the pond, there are grasses of all different lengths and shades of green all around the pond and in it, making the "rainbow" complete.

The trip to the Botanical Gardens was a great experience because I was able to see many plants and animals that I have never seen before. I recommend going to the pond so you can see all the plants and animals that I had an opportunity to see.

Upon returning to school, the sixth graders share their notes in pairs and with the whole class. They also bring back several brochures from the gardens to help them learn the correct spelling of the plants and animals. Derick notices the brochure has additional information about the Tharipod, so he inserts this information into his notes. Katie uses the brochure to help her list the specific names of the flowers alongside the pond. Many students also go online to the website about the gardens to gather more information about the plants or animals. Similar to Derick, they insert the information into their notes. As a result of this experience, Beth's students learn that we can gather information from several sources when we draft articles.

As they compose their articles, the sixth graders take pride in their work, which Beth will compile into a book to be distributed at the gardens for visitors to see. Knowing that their writing will be published, the sixth graders think about their audience. First, they want to grab the reader's attention by having a good lead. Second, they hope to keep the reader reading by using describing words and by adding interesting details and examples that will help readers see a picture of the plants and animals in the gardens. Finally, they think about a way to end their article; Derick, for example, used a clever ending that included a play on words.

To add interest to the published book, Beth uses her digital camera to take pictures of her authors while touring the gardens. Once students finish their articles, they apply word processing tools to integrate the pictures with the text for their class book.

Using Interviews to Spark Interest in Science. Consistent with Graves (1999), Nathan Dolbert believes that a focus on people might make science more accessible and interesting to his fourth graders, especially if they have contact with people in the field of science. To accomplish his goal, his class visits the community hospital and interviews doctors and nurses. Through her interview, Porsha learns how science can be used to help patients with cancer.

All About Radiation Oncology

Have you ever wondered how people get cancer? No one knows all of the ways, but Lenore Andres knows most of them. Lenore is a radiation Oncology specialist at St. Joseph Mercy Hospital.

With cancer, you have to make a pinpoint of a tattoo on the spot where the patients have cancer and Lenore, with some help from other people, makes lines with a felt marker on the patient's body. The worst part about it is the tattoo doesn't come off and it hurts! The felt marker comes off. That's a relief!

Many people mistake chemotherapy for being a part of radiation oncology, but it's not. Radiation is a big machine that kills the cancer cells, but chemo is a liquid that drips into your bloodstream from an I.V.

Lenore helps take care of people suffering with cancer. We think she really likes her job.

As a result of interviewing Lenore, Porsha is more motivated to study science; she sees a purpose and reason for studying cells and chemistry—one day she might be able to help patients who are sick. Due to her focus, Porsha's readers also learn more about cancer treatment and how radiation treatment differs from chemotherapy.

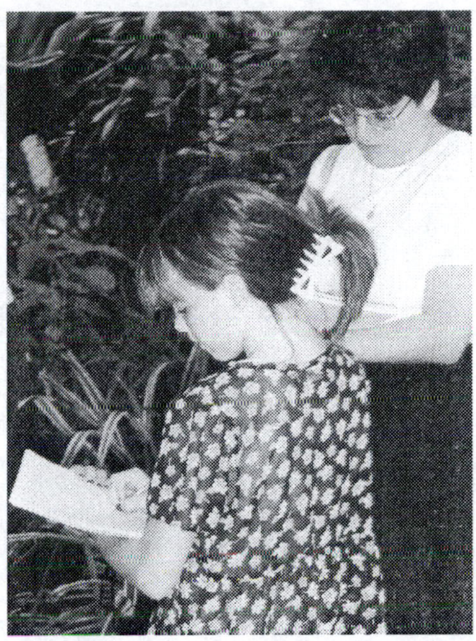

Marcy takes notes about the tropical plants at the Botanical Gardens.

Kayla interviewed a pediatrician at the hospital. Not only does she learn more about the role of a pediatrician in the hospital, she also learns about the importance of safety in our lives.

An Interview at St. Joseph Mercy Hospital

Me? Yes, me! I got to interview Dr. Eerrol Soskolne! He is a pediatrician. What does that mean? Well, it means some one that takes care of children. I asked him, what is the best part of his job, and he said the best part is seeing someone really sick and knowing that they get better. Many people help him with his job, for example, nurses, respiratory therapists (people that help with your breathing), pharmacists and social workers (people that help you with your family). He told me that the children stay 1 or 2 days.

I asked him what was the worst injury he has ever dealt with and he told me what it was. It was a child that had a broken spinal cord. The child was paralyzed for life and it was broken because the child was not wearing a seat belt. That is why you should wear one.

He also told me how many years that he went to school and I guess I will tell you. He's gone 13 years to regular school, then 4 years of college, 3 medical years and 3 residency years. He also has to go to school for the rest of his life to keep up with all the medicine and procedures that he might need to know. I thought he was very nice and it was a good interview. If I were hurt I would want him to be my doctor.

Kayla also learns that education is a lifelong process. If we want to pursue a career and to keep up with change, we, too, will need to go to school for the rest of our lives. Encountering an adult who is passionate about science helps her realize the importance of science and education in our lives.

Using Informational Literature with Interdisciplinary Teaching

There are times when hands-on learning experiences are not practical, nor possible. Informational literature is one way students can vicariously experience the subject areas of math, social studies, and science.

Experiencing Math through Informational Literature

Using Poetry to Foster Positive Attitudes about Math. In her book *Math Talk: Mathematical Ideas in Poems for Two Voices,* Theoni Pappas adds a new twist to mathematical learning. Her poems, which are designed to be read aloud, help students view math in a magical, playful way. After reading selected poems aloud to her fourth graders, Erin Minnis invites her students to form groups to read various poems chorally and then perform them for the class (see Chapter 5).

After listening to the poems and chorally reading them, her fourth graders begin to internalize Pappas's stylistic techniques. They are ready to create their own mathematical poems. Once they select a topic or number for their poems, they first create a web about the topic or number. Kevin's and Raquel's unpublished poems are displayed below:

Squares

Four sides
Four angles
Angles equal to ninety degrees
Four sides
Four angles
Squares

Zero

I am nothing I have no value
Yet I am essential
I am the origin of the number line
With positive numbers on my left
And negative numbers on my right
I'm neither positive nor negative
I am essential
I am the origin of the number line
I am zero

As Erin's students read and write poetry about math, some students begin to become more positive about it. They realize that math relates to the arts, music, and language; they discover that math is relevant to their lives in many ways.

Learning to Value Math through Biography. While reading the story *Dear Benjamin Banneker* by Andrea Davis Pinkney, Barb Dykman helps her students gain a humanistic, affective connection to mathematics. The biography portrays an African American who was born free when most blacks were still enslaved, making Benjamin Banneker a role model for her African American students.

As they listen to the story, her third graders discover how Benjamin Banneker, through persistence and determination, became an accomplished mathematician and astronomer. By applying his knowledge of math and astronomy and by plotting the cycles of the moon, Benjamin published the first almanac by a black man. To their amazement, students also find out that Benjamin took a stand against slavery by writing to Thomas Jefferson. This courageous act models how people can bring about change in a proactive way.

To reinforce these concepts about persistence, determination, and mathematics, Barb has her third graders write a biopoem about Benjamin Banneker. As can be seen below, writing the biopoem helps the third graders see Banneker as a role model for their own lives. Students also begin to see the relationships connecting math, science, and writing when they discover that Benjamin Banneker integrated his knowledge from several disciplines to publish a book. Writing helps students begin to realize that we use mathematics to solve problems in agriculture, weather, and astronomy.

Benjamin
Who is both a free and smart author, a mathematician, and an astronomer
Relative of Mary and Robert
Who loves freedom, looking at the stars, and his parents
Who needs to publish a book and take a stand on slavery
Who gives information, maps, and the weather to others
Residing in Maryland
Banneker

Experiencing Social Studies through Informational Literature

Informational literature also provides an avenue for learning about faraway places, past times, and current times (Freeman & Person, 1998; Fresch, 2004). Sometimes the literature stimulates students' imagination; other times it invites them to see connections between their lives and the lives of people in another time or place. Diverse in subject matter and depth of coverage, informational literature allows us to supplement the curriculum and transform students' interest in social studies.

Learning about Life in a South African Village. If you've never been to South Africa, Maya Angelou takes you there in her book *My Painted House, My Friendly Chicken, and Me.* Through the eyes of a Ndebele girl named Thandi, we learn about the life of children in this South African village. Thandi greets her readers on the very first page, saying, "Hello Stranger-friend."

Margaret Trapp's second graders visit Thandi's village as she reads the story aloud to her students. They learn how Thandi and the women in her village paint their homes with multicolored designs; how Thandi and the women sit under shaded trees, stringing and sewing beaded aprons, necklaces, and bracelets; and how Thandi and her friends play with penny whistles and ride bikes.

As Margaret reads the story to her second graders, they write a list of things Thandi does during the day. Once she finishes the story, the second graders talk about Thandi and ways that her life is similar and different from their lives. Then Margaret invites them to write a letter to someone, telling them what they learned about life in the South African village. Eboni's letter, which is written to his parents, is shown below:

Dear Mom and Dad,

Today we read a story about a girl in Africa. The girl liked to paint and she had a chicken for a pet. The girl had to wear a uniform when she went to school. In Africa, the houses are all made out of clay. The people wear different clothes than we do.

As a result of this writing experience, Margaret's second graders learn what life is like in another country. Learning about countries in faraway places is often abstract. Through writing, however, the students begin to make connections between their lives and the lives of children in other countries. They learn that people around the world often have different homes and ways of dressing, but they also enjoy playing games and riding bikes—just like them.

Appreciating the Bravery and Courage of People Living during the Time of Slavery. Biographies can also be wonderful ways for students to learn about the past. The humanized story format invites readers to experience life during a particular time period. Kelly Wood, a special education teacher at a middle school, shares the story *Molly Bannaky* by Alice McGill to her seventh graders so that they might experience life during the time of slavery.

After reading the story aloud to her seventh graders, Kelly invites her students to dramatize parts of Molly's life, helping them to see, hear, and experience life in this time period. Following the dramatization, Kelly invites her seventh graders to write a formula poem about Molly Bannaky's life. As they write the I AM poem (Lambert, 2005), Kelly's students begin to experience Molly's life more vividly while painting a picture of her life through words. Lillian's and Dillon's poems are displayed below:

Molly Bannaky

I am (Molly Bannaky). I am brave, thoughtful of others, loving.
I saw slaves being pushed out of ships and I heard people crying of leaving there [their] loved ones.
I knew that something had to change.
I did not know how bad people treated them.
I wonder when there will be no more slaves.
I believe that no one should be owned by another human.
This is me standing up for people that can't or get killed.
It symbolizes that I have a good heart and care for others.
I wish everyone could be free.
I am Molly Bannaky.

Molly Bannaky

I am Molly Bannaky
I saw rushing onto the east coast.
I heard screaming coming from houses, banging from the ship.
I knew I was in a volcano of trouble.

I did not know I was all ready a slave.
I wonder if I will ever be free again.
I believe that everyone is free if their heart is free.
This is a good thing to think at a bad time.
It symbolizes that you are being brave for those who are not.
I wish I will be free yet again.
I am Molly Bannaky.

When Lillian and Dillon share their poems with their peers, listeners begin to visualize Molly's life. Through the combined experiences of reading, drama, and writing, history comes alive for Kelly's students. In particular, writing helps the seventh graders interpret, evaluate, and analyze issues related to slavery.

Using Informational Books to Learn about Countries around the World. Seeking ways to honor the traditions and cultural heritages of people around the world, Charlotte Anderson invites members from the community to her fifth grade class. When Seyam Kim arrives, he greets the children in Korean.

Following his brief introduction, he continues his lesson by building background knowledge about Korea. Knowing that students are often interested in learning how to count in another language, he demonstrates how to count in Korean while displaying the numbers in Korean for all to see. The fifth graders become so enthralled with the experience that they begin taking notes. However, their notes are in "temporary Korean" so they will remember how to pronounce the numbers in Korean after he leaves (see Figures 6.10 and 6.11).

To continue building background knowledge about Korea, Seyam also shares examples of Korean clothing and various artifacts from his country (see Figure 6.11). The fifth graders maintain their notetaking in "temporary Korean" as Seyam shares the Korean artifacts and clothing with them, even though no one has mentioned taking notes.

After building background knowledge about Korea in these ways, Seyam reads the book *Count Your Way through Korea* by Jim Haskins to the fifth graders. As he reads the story, he shares additional information about his country and its food, clothing, language, and recreational activities. Working in twos, students take notes on one of the numbers in the book (Charlotte has preassigned the numbers and has explained the notetaking process for this portion of the lesson prior to the guest's arrival) to help them remember the information.

The next day, students collaborate with their partners, writing about their assigned number, which tells about a Korean custom, tradition, or artifact. Working in pairs, the students then revise and edit their pages, creating their own version of *Count Your Way through Korea.* They plan to give the class book to Seyam when he returns the following week. This will be their gift to him for his kindness and generosity while visiting their class. Claire and Noni wrote about the number 3; Eric and Steven wrote about the number 9.

In Korean, three is pronounced like set. There is something unique about every number in Korea. Set, or three, is unique because of the see-saw that requires three people. This see-saw is used with one person in the middle holding it in balance while the second person jumps on it and the third is thrown into the air. This Korean see-saw is called Neal.

Figure 6.10

Ben Uses "Temporary Korean Spelling" to Take Notes about Korea

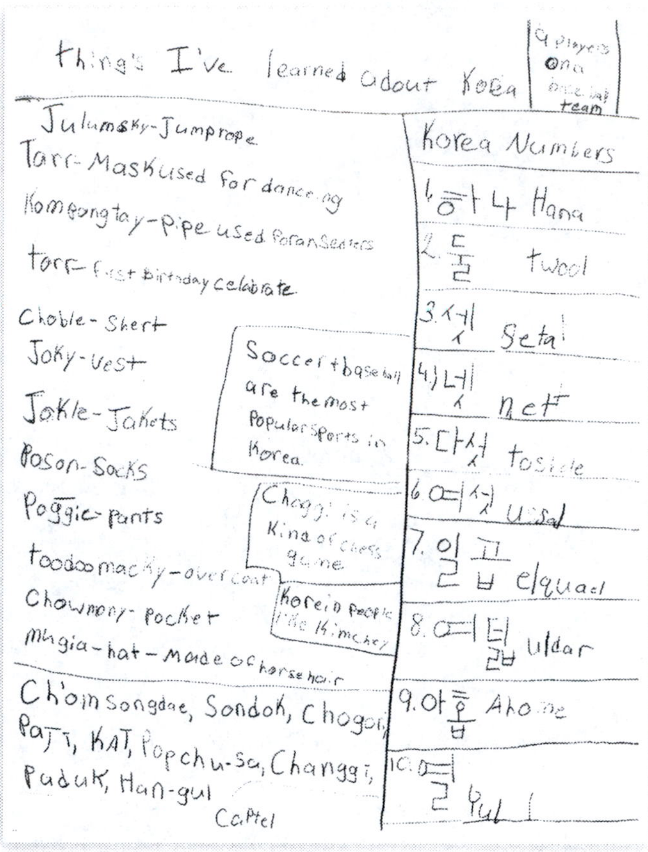

Nine. Baseball is almost as popular in Korea as it is in America. There are nine players on a team. It was introduced by the YMCA in 1906. Then in 1982 the first professional baseball team in Korea was organized. Then a while later they won the 27th World Baseball championship.

Learning about Korea becomes personalized when we invite a guest to the classroom from the community. The students' keen interest in learning about Korea is shown as they spontaneously begin taking notes, using "temporary Korean" to write the Korean numbers and words. Both Seyam and the students will remember this experience due to the creation of a class book, written and illustrated by the fifth graders.

Experiencing Science through Informational Literature

Similarly, science comes alive through informational literature. Frequently nonfiction books about science communicate a sense of wonder that attracts students to the book over and over again. Science informational literature also provides a model of how to write about the world around them. In order for students to learn to write nonfiction texts, Kletzien and Dreher (2003) emphasize that they need many experiences with literature; they also need guidance in how to create nonfiction texts.

Figure 6.11

Ben's Drawings and Notes about Korean Clothing

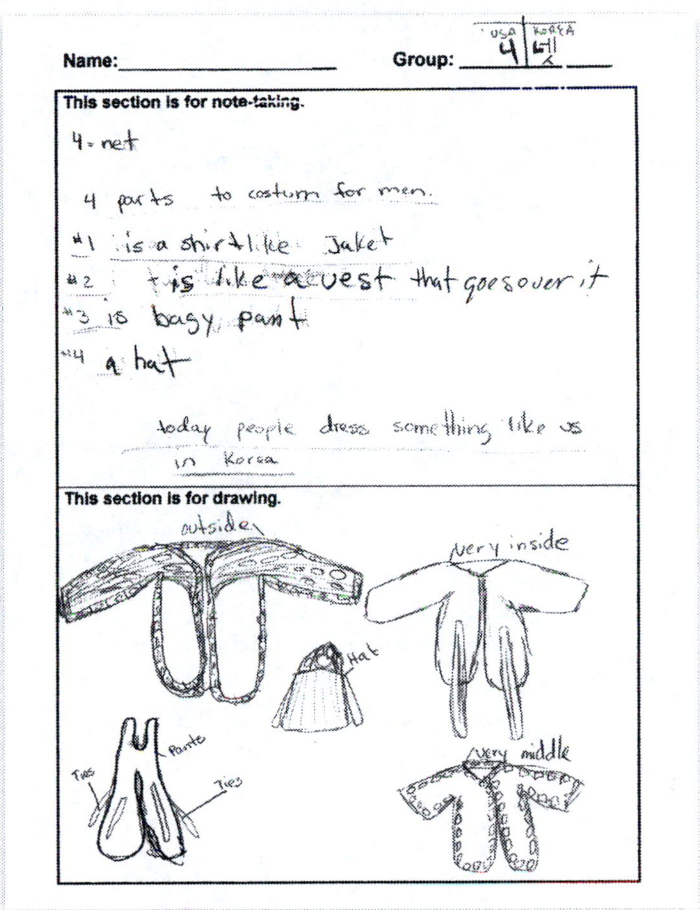
Name: ______ Group: USA 4 | KOREA 4

This section is for note-taking.

4 = net

4 parts to costum for men.

#1 is a shirt like Jaket

#2 is like a vest that goes over it

#3 is bagy pant

#4 a hat

today people dress something like us in Korea

This section is for drawing.

Using Informational Literature to Describe and Observe Animals. As stated before, students are naturally curious about their world. In particular, animals fascinate many young children. Tapping into this natural curiosity, Jeanie Lawrence reads the book *Welcome to the World of Beavers* by Diane Swanson. The opening line, "Using strong jaw muscles, the beaver can chomp through a trunk more than half a meter (1½ feet) thick," draws the reader to the beaver pond where beavers gnaw down tall trees.

As Jeanie reads the story to her second graders, they learn many amazing facts about the beaver. The next day, Jeanie rereads the story as students take notes, pretending they are scientists observing a beaver at the pond. As they record their notes about the beaver they concentrate on what the beaver looks like and his behaviors or what he did. To help them take notes (see Figure 6.12), Jeanie has them fold their papers in half, the "hamburger way," and label one side of the paper *Looks Like* and the other side *Can Do.*

After listening to the story, the second graders relook at the first page to examine how the author, Diane Swanson, captured their interest in this story. Using this as a model, the second graders brainstorm ways to begin their own story about the beaver. After talking about

> ***teaching* TIP 6.3**
>
> Literature provides a model for students' writing. Using literature to model how to create interesting leads or endings helps students begin to apply these techniques in their own writing.

Figure 6.12
Sarah's Notes about Beavers

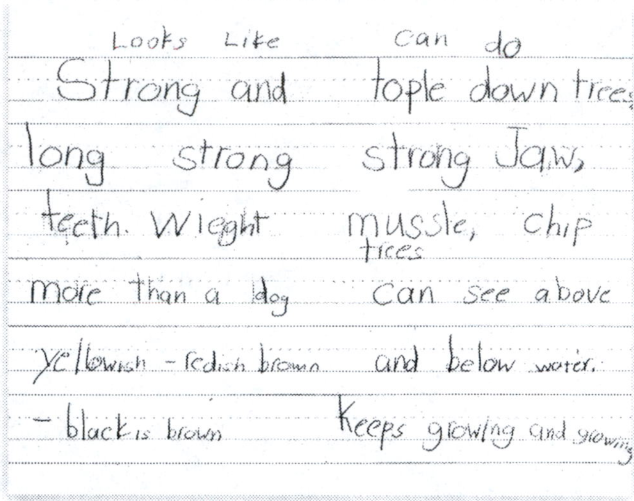

special leads for their own stories, the students return to their notes and place stars next to the information they want to include in their story and then begin drafting their stories. After revising and editing, they publish their stories using word processing tools. Sarah's revised draft is shown in Figure 6.13. Timmy's final draft is shown below:

Beavers

Beavers can do many things. Their teeth can grow on forever. They have to chip bark so their teeth won't grow super big! They can topple down trees one and a half feet thick. They can use their tails like a boats rudder. Beavers are amazing!

As shown through his writing, Timmy learns how to write about his observations, following the model of the author. By following a process, he discovers how to create an interesting lead for his piece, as well as an ending. He also incorporates Swanson's use of active verbs like *chip* and *topple* to describe the beaver's behavior. Consistent with Stead (2002), Timmy begins to detect what writers do when they write to inform others.

Exploring Terrestrial Biomes through Informational Literature. Informational literature can also be a way for students to learn about the natural homes, or biomes, of our planet. *Cactus Hotel* by Brenda Guiberson tempts us to put on our hiking shoes and grab a back-pack as we explore the desert, the home of the saguaro cactus, which can become a hotel for birds and other animals. To help her third graders relate to this biome, which her students had never seen, Diane Heiss reads the story first. To help them remember the characteristics of this natural home and its plant and animal life, she too has her students take notes in three categories: the desert, the plants, and the animals.

After listening to the story and taking notes, Diane encourages her students to share their notes in pairs and talk about the notes with one another. While discussing and sharing their notes, they also add information to their notes. To reinforce these concepts, she invites them to illustrate the desert, displaying the animals and plants one might find in the desert.

Figure 6.13

Sarah's Revisions for Her Story about Beavers

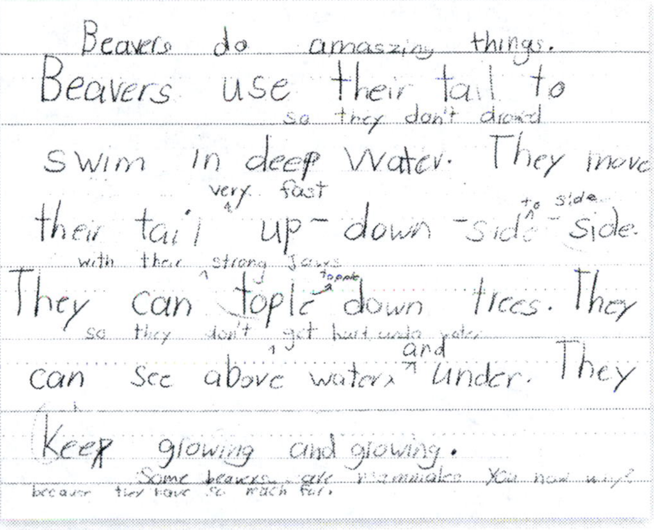

Beavers do amazing things.
Beavers use their tail to
so they don't drown
swim in deep water. They move
very fast to side
their tail up-down-side-side.
with their strong jaws topple
They can tople down trees. They
so they don't get hurt under water and
can see above water under. They
Keep glowing and glowing.
Some beavers are [illegible] You now why?
because they have so much fat.

Once they complete these prewriting activities, the students write a description of the desert. Samantha's paragraph shows how much she has learned about the fragile ecosystem of the desert.

The Desert

Did you know the desert is very dry and hot and it has a lot of sunshine? It's sandy there too. The cactus grows a lot of flowers on top of it. The birds come on top of the cactus. The hummingbirds get nectar from the cactus. Then the hummingbirds go away. The cactus is fat with water and skinny without water. The animals make holes in the cactus and one animal moves out and finds a different hole and lives in it. Other animals move in the cactus.

The combined activities of drawing and writing about the desert help Samantha understand its features, plant life, and animal life in more detail. As she reads more books about the desert, her knowledge and understanding will continue to grow and develop.

Journeying with a Seed through Informational Literature. Just as students are naturally curious about animals, plants also intrigue them. Tapping into this natural interest, Linda Roslin reads *The Dandelion Seed* by Joseph Anthony to her second graders.

The story begins in the autumn as the dandelion dies and drops its seeds. At this point, one seed begins its journey, filled with wonder and beauty, across the country and across the seasons. After reading this mesmerizing account of a dandelion's journey, Linda rereads the story to her second graders as they take notes about the seed's journey. To help her students organize their notes, she has them divide their paper in fourths, the "hamburger way," labeling one side *Fall;* the second, *Winter;* the third, *Spring;* and the fourth, *Summer.* Using phrases or words, the students chronicle the seed's journey, recording their notes in the appropriate column.

Next, students create a diary about the sunflower seed. To help her students write a diary, Linda first reads *Diary of a Sunflower* by Carol Pugliano, which models the process of how to write a diary. Pretending to be a dandelion seed, the second graders use personification in their writing as they create diary entries from their notes about the seed's journey.

Students compose four diary entries, one for each season of the year. Through this reading and writing experience, the second graders begin to understand change in science and life. Deidre's diary entries for *Fall* and *Winter* are displayed below:

Dear Diary,

Today is fall and all of the flowers are dying. I am the last seed. I am holding on tight! A strong wind is blowing though [through] me. I am about to let go. I have to. I did [died]. Now I am blowing away with the wind.

Your friend,
Dandy

Dear Diary,

It is winter. Who thought it would be this cold? Brrrrr. The wind carried me through the air. I saw that the earth was big. Then I landed on the ground. Snow fell on me.

Your friend,
Dandy

Using the humanized format of diary entries helps the young writers relate to the science concepts of growth and change over time. Students also have an opportunity to creatively show how the seed changes.

Closing Thoughts

"My best friend is my notebook. When I hold it in my hand it reminds me to collect details through observation and to write them down. If I use all my senses and channel stimuli to my hand and into my notebook, the writing will come alive" (Clark, 1995, p. 92). This quote symbolizes the role of writing in interdisciplinary learning. Writing helps us interpret our world and our experiences; writing transforms information into memory for longer retention.

In this chapter, we discovered how teachers integrated interdisciplinary learning in their school curriculum through theme teaching or focused inquiry. Writing, which naturally applies the tools of inquiry, became a valuable learning tool in the integrated, interdisciplinary learning environment as young writers collected information from people, informational literature, or their environment. Using observation, notetaking, and interviewing, students collected descriptive details, quotations, and anecdotes from these sources, making their writing and knowledge about history, science, math, and language arts come alive.

As teachers, we can stimulate life learning in all subject areas when we link personal experiences and hands-on learning experiences with the tools of observation, notetaking, and interviewing. Once students see themselves as researchers, they begin to look everywhere for information—in their lives, the school, community, nation, or world. As students begin to progress through these circles of learning, interdisciplinary learning continuously gains depth and breadth.

When we are unable to use hands-on learning events, informational literature becomes another way for students to vicariously experience science, math, and social studies. If informational literature is inviting and stimulating, as well as accurate and up-to-date, the text provokes readers to savor the wonder of science, math, and social studies. Linking literature with the tools of observation and notetaking helps reinforce concept knowledge and strengthen retention of these concepts.

Learning and inquiry become an adventure when students experience reading and writing as a process. By harnessing this process and investing time in learning, we offer our students opportunities to encounter the curiosity and wonder of learning.

Teachers' Questions

1. My first graders primarily write in their personal journals or write personal narratives. Are they too young to write biographies, letters, or expository texts?

Students of all ages need to learn how to write a variety of genres. Writing is a part of our daily lives. We all send emails or write thank-you notes, letters, or lists. People often have to write brief reports or newsletters. Others enjoy writing stories or poems.

Students see their parents and you writing in all these ways, too. Just as Tiffany in Chapter 1 wanted to learn how to write her name, students also want to learn how to write letters or send emails. Building lessons around these needs and interests makes learning fun and exciting for students of all ages.

2. At what grade level can students begin to take notes?

Notetaking is an important strategy that we all use throughout our lives. As shown in this chapter, even second graders can take notes, especially if we limit the categories to one or two topics. I have even had first graders take notes while listening to a poem, using only one category (descriptive words, for example). What's important is to emphasize that students use their temporary spelling. Then, as we read, we need to remember to read slowly, pausing whenever they might need to take notes. This pause initially becomes a clue for students to record something in their notes, but this is something that good speakers naturally do to emphasize a point. In addition, taking time for students to share their notes helps students add to their notes if information is missing.

3. I like the idea of having students take notes while on a field trip. How do we make sure they don't lose their pencils and notebooks?

I'm so glad that you are thinking about trying this! After placing her students in groups of four so they can easily be monitored, Barb Dykman has her parents keep the pencils and notebooks until they are needed. She also gives each parent a few extra pencils and notebooks in case there is an accident or the lead in the pencil breaks. So far, she's never had a problem!

4. Many of these ideas sound very time-consuming. I just don't have time to teach writing in social studies, science, or math.

You are right! Many of these activities require an investment of time, especially if we plan to publish students' writing. Mary Streeter and Kathy Micallef share that when they invest time, they get better quality from the students. However, as emphasized, we can experience burnout if we publish more than two pieces per marking period.

Mary and Kathy also believe that integrating writing with social studies, science, or math actually frees up time in their busy schedule. They also add that writing seems to help students learn the concepts more easily in these subjects. Consistent with research, they have discovered that their students seem to perform better on the unit tests in these subject areas whenever they integrate writing with the subject areas.

Children's Literature

Angelou, M. (1994). *My painted house, my friendly chicken, and me.* New York: Clarkson Potter.

Anthony, J. (1997). *The dandelion seed.* Nevada City, CA: Dawn.

Guiberson, B. Z. (1991). *Cactus hotel.* New York: Henry Holt and Company.

Haskins, J. (1989). *Count your way through Korea.* Minneapolis, MN: CarolRhoda.

McGill, A. (1999). *Molly Bannaky.* Boston: Houghton Mifflin.

Pappas, T. (1991). *Math talk: Mathematical ideas in poems for two voices.* San Carlos, CA: Wide World Publishing.

Pinkney, B. (1994). *Dear Benjamin Banneker.* New York: Harcourt Brace.

Pugliano, C. (1996). *Diary of a sunflower.* New York: Scholastic.

Swanson, D. (1999). *Welcome to the world of beavers.* Toronto: Whitecap Books.

References

Armbruster, B., McCarthey, S., & Cummins, S. (2005). Writing to learn in elementary classrooms. In R. Indrisano & J. Paratore (Eds.), *Learning to write, writing to learn: Theory and research in practice* (pp. 71–96). Newark, DE: International Reading Association.

Baker, D. (1996). It's write for science. *Science and Children, 33,* 24–28.

Barton, K., & Smith, L. (2000). Themes or motifs: Aiming for coherence through interdisciplinary outlines. *The Reading Teacher, 54,* 54–63.

Belenky, M. (1986). *Women's ways of knowing: The development of self, voice, and mind.* New York: Basic Books.

Berghoff, B., Egawa, K., Harste, J., & Hoonan, B. (2000). *Beyond reading and writing: Inquiry, curriculum, and multiple ways of knowing.* Urbana, IL: National Council of Teachers of English.

Butzow, C., & Butzow, J. (1989). *Science through children's literature.* Englewood, CO: Libraries Unlimited.

Camp, D. (2000). It takes two: Teaching with twin texts of fact and fiction. *The Reading Teacher, 53,* 400–408.

Carletti, B., Girard, S., & Willing, K. (1993). *Sign-out science: Simple hands-on experiments using everyday materials.* Markham, Canada: Pembroke Publishers.

Clark, R. (1995). *Free to write.* Portsmouth, NH: Heinemann.

Close, E., Hull, M., & Langer, J. (2005). Writing and reading relationships in literacy learning. In R. Indrisano & J. Paratore (Eds.), *Learning to write, writing to learn: Theory and research in practice* (pp. 176–193). Newark, DE: International Reading Association.

Diamond, B., & Moore, M. A. (1995). *Multicultural literacy: Mirroring the reality of the classroom.* New York: Longman.

Duke, N. (2004). The case for informational text. *Educational Leadership, 61,* 40–44.

Freeman, E., & Person, D. (1998). *Connecting informational children's books with content area learning.* Boston: Allyn & Bacon.

Fresch, E. (2004). *Connecting children with children: Past and present.* Portsmouth, NH: Heinemann.

Fuhler, C., Farris, P., & Nelson, P. (2006). Building literacy skills across the curriculum: Forging connections with the past through artifacts. *The Reading Teacher, 59,* 646–658.

Glenn, S., & Muth, K. (1994). Reading and writing to learn science: Achieving scientific literacy. *Journal of Research in Science Teaching, 31,* 1057–1073.

Graves, D. (1999). *Bring life into learning.* Portsmouth, NH: Heinemann.

Guillaume, A. (1998). Learning with text in primary grades. *The Reading Teacher, 51,* 476–486.

Holliday, W., Yore, L., & Alvermann, D. (1994). The reading-science learning-writing connection: Breakthroughs, barriers, and promises. *Journal of Research in Science Teaching, 31,* 877–893.

Kletzien, S., & Dreher, M. (2003). *Informational text in K–3 classrooms: Helping children read and write.* Newark, DE: International Reading Association.

Ladson-Billings, G. (1994). *The dreamkeepers: Successful teachers of African American children.* San Francisco: Jossey-Bass.

Lambert, B. (2005). Setting the stage for historical fiction. In D. Winter & S. Robbins (Eds.), *Writing our communities: Local learning and public culture* (pp. 45–50). Urbana, IL: National Council of Teachers of English.

Langer, J., & Applebee, A. (1987). *How writing shapes thinking: A study of teaching and learning* (NCTE Research Report No. 22). Urbana, IL: National Council of Teachers of English.

Lapp, D., & Flood, J. (1993). Literature in the science program. In B. Cullinan (Ed.), *Fact and fiction: Literature across the curriculum* (pp. 68–79). Newark, DE: International Reading Association.

McClure, A. (2003). Choosing quality nonfiction literature: Examining aspects of writing style. In R. A. Bamford & J. Kristo (Eds.), *Making facts come alive: Choosing quality nonfiction literature K–8* (pp. 79–96). Norwood, MA: Christopher-Gordon Publishers.

Moore-Hart, M., Liggit, P., & Daisey, P. (2004). Making the science literacy connection: After-school science clubs. *Childhood Education, 80,* 180–186.

Moss, B. (2005). Making a case and a place for effective content area literacy instruction in the elementary grades. *The Reading Teacher, 59,* 46–55.

National Research Council. (1994). *National science education standards: An enhanced sampler.* Washington, DC: National Academy of Sciences.

Neufeld, P. (2005). Comprehension instruction in content area classes. *The Reading Teacher, 59,* 302–312.

Nuthall, G. (1999). The way students learn: Acquiring knowledge from an integrated science and social studies unit. *The Elementary School Journal, 99,* 303–341.

Parker, C. (2001). *What influences shaped the meaning eight Latino adolescents gave to science.* Paper presented at the annual meeting of the American Educational Research Association, Seattle, WA.

Portalupi, J., & Fletcher, R. (2001). *Nonfiction craft lessons: Teaching information writing K–8.* Portland, ME: Stenhouse.

Richardson, J., & Morgan, R. (1994). *Reading to learn in the content areas.* Belmont, CA: Wadsworth.

Rogovin, P. (1998). *Classroom interviews: A world of learning.* Portsmouth, NH: Heinemann.

Rogovin, P. (2001). *The research workshop: Bringing the world into your classroom.* Portsmouth, NH: Heinemann.

Saul, W., & Jagusch, S. (1991). *Vital connections: Children, science, and books.* Portsmouth, NH: Heinemann.

Short, K., Schroeder, J., Laird, J., Kauffman, G., Ferguson, M., & Crawford, K. (1996). *Learning together through inquiry: From Columbus to integrated curriculum.* York, ME: Stenhouse.

Stead, T. (2002). *Is that a fact? Teaching nonfiction writing K–3.* Portland, ME: Stenhouse.

Tompkins, G. (2004). *Teaching writing: Balancing process and product.* Upper Saddle River, NJ: Merrill.

Wallace, J., & Pugalee, D. (2001). *Examining instructional practices of elementary science teachers for mathematics and literacy integration.* Paper presented at the annual meeting of the American Educational Research Association, Seattle, WA.

Winter, D., & Robbins, S. (2005). *Writing our communities: Local learning and public culture.* Urbana, IL: National Council of Teachers of English.

Yopp, R., & Yopp, H. (2000). Sharing informational text with young children. *The Reading Teacher, 53,* 410–423.

chapter SEVEN

Using Information and Communication Technology Tools in an Integrated, Interdisciplinary Curriculum

Our Welcome Poem

Welcome to Ardis School
And to our celebration
Our Home Page can be seen
Throughout the nation.
We're all very proud.
Now that's no lie.
Please listen, and we will tell you why.

This poem was written by Troy, a third grade student in Barb Dykeman's class. In celebration of her school's twenty-fifth anniversary, Barb's class, along with the third grade classes of Venetia Sims and Connie Williams, created a home page on the World Wide Web about themselves, their school, and the community. The project illustrates how technology can be integrated with the language arts and social studies curriculum in a meaningful, purposeful context. Through the use of information and communication technology tools, students collected, organized, analyzed, and synthesized information about themselves, their school, and the community.

Using Technology Tools to Enhance Learning about Our Community

Computers and the Internet, emerging tools that enhance learning, offered an array of enriched learning opportunities for Troy and his peers. They became engaged in reading, writing, and publishing as they communicated their evolving knowledge about changes in their school and community. Technology became both a tool to increase learning and a tool to communicate their knowledge with others.

Many exciting adventures awaited Troy and his peers as they explored the Internet. Realizing that technology was an integral part of society and their individual lives, the team of teachers helped the third graders acquire the new literacy skills—for example, reading electronic texts and writing with electronic-based tools—that new forms of technology demand (Castek, Bevans-Mangelston, & Goldstone, 2006; Henry, 2006; Leu, 2001; Sutherland-Smith, 2002; Wepner & Tao, 2002).

Using a medium that was exciting to them and to the entire community, Troy and his peers became inspired to compose writing pieces about their learning experiences for a large audience on the Web. While the creation of their own home page served as a teaching tool and a source of pride for Troy and his peers, it also became a powerful model and inspiration available to students and teachers around the world.

Specifically, integrating technology with the curriculum gave Troy and his peers opportunities to read, write, and publish with real-life purposes. Technology became a tool for students to construct their knowledge about change.

To help them construct their own home page, the third graders first viewed other student-created Web pages. While viewing other websites, the third graders simultaneously learned how to navigate the Internet. Later they used the Internet to publish their writing using electronic-based tools. Having a purpose and meaning for learning, Troy and his peers continuously explored new ways to read and write with technology.

Over time, they became familiar with the new literacies that technology requires. Specifically, they learned how to locate, critically evaluate, and synthesize information on the Internet as well as communicate online (Henry, 2006; Leu, Kinzer, Coiro, & Cammack, 2004; Owens, Hester, & Teale, 2002).

As new technologies for information and communication relentlessly emerge, Troy and his peers will be better prepared to make use of future developments and to acquire the new forms of literacy that future formats require. Just like Troy's teachers, we all need to embrace technology as a tool for learning. Integrating technology with the literacy curriculum often inspires a lifelong love for reading, writing, and learning for students. According to Becker (2000), using technology increases students' motivation to read, write, and learn.

Getting Started with Technology

In response to parents' requests that technology receive an increased emphasis in the curriculum, a team of teachers—Judy Benns, Barb Dykeman, Venetia Sims, and Connie Williams, with the assistance of professor emeritus Martha Irwin—decide to use technology as a communication medium within an integrated language arts and social studies project. They determine that the theme of their project, which integrates nicely with the third grade social studies curriculum on the local community, will be the twenty-fifth anniversary of Ardis Elementary School.

In honor of the school's anniversary celebration, the third grade teachers specifically work as a team to develop a home page on the World Wide Web. They also decide to extend the social studies curriculum to include *changes* in their school building and education over the years. A small state grant provides funding for the field trips and a digital camera, which will be used in the development of the home page.

As technology becomes an integral part of the curriculum, students learn word processing, explore the Internet in a purposeful way, and become familiar with the scanner and digital camera. Throughout the process, students are actively involved in the development of the home page.

Students Learning about Themselves

To help the third graders perceive their relationship to Ardis School and the community, the teachers begin the project by having students learn about one another. Using the biopoem format displayed in Chapter 5, students write biopoems about themselves. Not only will the third graders learn about one another as they read each other's poems, they can also introduce themselves to others on the Internet. After writing the biopoems, they extend this introductory experience by writing a short paragraph about themselves and their families. Christine's paragraph and biopoem are displayed below.

Christine

My name is Christine. I am named after my grandmother. You can call me by my first name. My mom and dad call me Cherries. My brothers call me Christine. I like them both but I would rather have you call me by my first name but I think I can live with the other name too.

Biopoem

Christine
Likes cake and candy
Relative of Mom, Dad, and brother,
Lover of school, birthday, and playing,
Who needs love, a house, and food,
Who fears drowning, stabbing, and dying.,
Who would like to see Disney World, and my Dad,
Who lives in Ypsilanti, Michigan.

Following the writing process, the third graders draft their paragraphs and biopoems, word process their drafts on the computer, and then revise and edit their writing using word processing tools. Once the students complete their pieces, Dr. Irwin, professor emeritus from Eastern Michigan University, converts the writing pieces into HTML (the language used to create the pages on the World Wide Web) files and then transfers the files to the server.

As they create the home page, teachers organize students' writing so they can be found based on their classes. This way, all students can read one another's biopoems just by clicking on the name of their peers' teacher, which will then show a class list with their friends' names. Using the LCD projector, the four teachers demonstrate that the third graders are now linked together online through their classes, just as people are linked together within a community through their neighborhoods. After seeing the process modeled, the third graders access information about their peers by clicking on these links.

Marsalis explores the Ardis website.

Using Field Trips to Understand Change over Time

To help students understand how school life has changed over the years, the teachers begin the next phase of the project by planning a field trip to a one-room school at Greenfield Village. After viewing slides about Greenfield Village and its two historic schools—the Miller School and the McGuffey School—students, many of whom are dressed in period clothing, visit the village and the schools. While visiting the school, they experience what it was like to attend a one-room school by participating in a variety of activities that simulate early school life—they sit at the wooden desks, write on the slates with slate pencils, read stories from the McGuffey readers, and use Webster's Blue Back Spellers.

As they tour Greenfield Village and the two schools, students take notes about their observations and experiences in their writer's notebook. The following day, they talk about their field trip and then use their notes to write about their experiences. Barb's students write about their impressions of Greenfield Village; Venetia's students write poems about what school life was like 100 years ago; and Connie's class write about things to see and do in Greenfield Village.

Judy Benns, Title One teacher (teacher of at-risk students in reading performance), collaborates with the three teachers during all stages of the writing process. In particular, she facilitates the revising and editing stages of writing (see Chapter 4) and demonstrates how to use word processing and navigate the Internet to both teachers and students. Sometimes Judy works with the teachers in the classroom settings; sometimes she works with small groups in her resource classroom. Throughout the process, students assume the responsibility of revising and editing their writing on the computer under the guidance of Judy or their teacher. In fact, the students become more motivated to revise and edit their writing as they know that people around the world will read their writing pieces once they are put online.

Once students complete the writing pieces, Dr. Irwin again converts the writing pieces into HTML files and then transfers the files to the server. As the home page continues to emerge, Dr. Irwin links the students' writing pieces about Greenfield Village with their biopoems. Just by clicking on the name of their peers' teacher, students can easily read one another's writing by clicking on "My Greenfield Village Report," displayed just below the biopoem. As they read one another's writing and explore their home page, the third graders simultaneously begin to learn how information is linked together on the Internet. While reading one another's biopoems, paragraphs, and other writing about Greenfield Village, students gain more practice in reading, improving their fluency, and comprehension skills.

Salman and Jennifer, students in Connie's class, write about their experiences in Greenfield Village.

My Visit to Greenfield Village

I saw Thomas Edison's laboratory today and went to some stores like Mrs. Cohen's Hat Shop. We saw bicycles in the store. We saw the Wright brothers' house and walked to Miller School. Inside the school there was a stove. Long ago boys and girls had to carry wood to school to burn in the stove. The fire kept them warm. We saw the train. The train was carrying people to another side of Greenfield Village. We had lunch at Miller school and we wrote about what we saw in Miller School and we played outside for recess. When our teacher rang the bell it was time to come in. We had fun. We ate lunch at Miller School.

My Visit to Greenfield Village

We went to Miller School. I went in Thomas Edison's lab and home. I went in Henry Ford's birthplace and home. In Miller School we used slates and slate pencils. I had lunch like back in the 1850s. We used blue books for spelling and reading. We had spelling lessons. There was another school. It was called McGuffey School. I dressed up like an old fashion girl. I had a blue dress with purple and pink flowers on it. My teacher dressed up too. She had a white blouse and a black skirt. We saw the Wright brother's house. We also went in it. The Wright Cycle Co. was interesting. It had an airplane in it. It had a bicycle with two wheels on it. We had lots of fun at Greenfield Village. When we got back from the field trip it was time to go home. The best part was Miller School I want to go there again.

Gabby and Delane, whose poems are displayed below, write poems about school life 100 years ago.

Walking to school,
Teacher ringing the bell,
Boys lining up on the left side,
Girls lining up on the right side,
Writing on slates,
Toeing the line to recite lessons,
Back in the old days.

Many years ago,
Wearing a dunce cap in school,
Feeling bad,
Swatted with a switch,
Feeling bad,
Walking a long way to school,
Feeling tired,
Carrying wood for the stove,
Feeling tired.
Many years ago.

Students in Barb's class write about their impressions of Greenfield Village, such as those by Amanda and Jay found below.

On September 28, I rode with my mom to Greenfield Village. Greenfield Village is a place where you can learn about how people lived long ago. My mom and I were dressed up old fashioned and were wearing long dresses and bonnets. A lot of other people were dressed up too. The class wrote on slates instead of paper. Then we went to a lot of houses. We saw some slave houses. After lunch we played a game called, A Tisket, a Tasket. As we walked along we saw geese everywhere! Instead of cars there were a lot of horses and carriages. We had to watch where we stepped because there was a lot of horse manure. The School was cool and it was a lot of fun to be in a one room schoolhouse. My friend Catherine said to me, "I wish it was our school." In October there was a fire in Greenfield Village. The fire was at Henry Ford's birthplace, but its ok now.

I went to McGuffey School. We wrote with the slate pencils on slates and wrote math problems. At lunch time we sat on the grass in the school yard. We ate a sandwich. After lunch we played a game A Tisket, A Tasket. After A Tisket, A Tasket we went back to the school and wrote in our copy books. After that we rode the bus back to Ardis School. Our homework assignment was to tell someone about our trip to Greenfield Village. I told my mom I had a good time.

Through these hands-on learning experiences, students begin to understand that patterns of living change over time. The simulated experience in the one-room schoolhouse helps them "see" what school was like for children in the past. Writing about the experiences gives them time to think and ponder about a time when children wrote on slates, played games like "A Tisket, A Tasket," or carried wood to keep them warm in their schoolhouse.

Using Interviews to Learn about Changes in Their School over Time

While visiting and writing about schools from the past, the third graders gradually begin to compare and contrast past and present school practices, using their school as a contemporary model. To extend students' concepts about the past, the teachers decide to use interviews as a version of oral history within their own school. Specifically, interviews become a tool to learn about the school, the history of the school, and important people who helped the school emerge within the community.

As they interview Mrs. Fillmore, a teacher who had been at the school since it opened; Mrs. Fehrenbaker, the first secretary of the school; and Dr. Ardis, the superintendent for whom the school was named, the third graders begin to gain a picture of their school in the past. By comparing these interviews with interviews of newer teachers, the current secretary, and the current principal, the students discover how their own school has transformed over the years.

Modeling the Questioning Process. To help her students learn how to interview others, Barb prepares a series of minilessons on the process so her students can later implement the interviews independently in groups. Barb and her class begin the process by brainstorming questions they might want to ask a teacher at the school, using shared writing. As her third graders brainstorm questions, Barb lists them on chart paper for all to view.

Once they compile a list of questions, Barb and her students revisit the questions, deciding if there are any questions they should omit. For example, they decide as a class that they should eliminate the question "How old are you?" as this might embarrass the teacher. Through this process, students begin to consider their audience more carefully while creating a list of questions.

On the following day, Barb and her students relook at the list of questions to determine what order to ask the questions. Barb shares that reporters suggest we begin an interview with a question that will help them become at ease. She adds that this can be a question related to them, their family, or their life. Similarly, Barb explains that reporters suggest that we end the interview with the most challenging questions and then conclude the list with an open-ended question, like, "Is there anything else you would like to share with us?" This way, Barb continues, the interviewees can insert information that they feel is important to know or understand into the interview. As the class continues to relook at the questions and their order, she guides the process, making sure they do the following:

- Help the guest feel at ease.
- Formulate open-ended questions to help them gather information. (Yes/no questions limit the interviewee's response.)
- Plan an appropriate sequence to the questions, keeping related questions together.
- End the interview with more challenging questions.
- End the interview by inviting them to share any additional information.
- End the interview with a thank you!

Once the class determines the sequence of questions, Barb places numbers next to these questions. Next, they decide who will ask each question and finally rehearse the process by asking the questions together. That afternoon Barb revises and publishes the chart, which will be displayed at the front of the room.

Modeling the Notetaking Process. The next minilesson models how to take notes while interviewing a teacher. As her students ask the questions, Barb models how to take notes on the whiteboard as the teacher responds. As highlighted before, she models how to work quickly, using phrases and words. Barb also models the process of using abbreviations and temporary spelling whenever needed.

While she demonstrates the process, her third graders also take notes in their notebooks. Following the interview, Barb and her students share their notes together. Sometimes her students gather information that she missed. To help them understand the process of adding new information, she inserts this information into her notes.

In addition, Barb tapes the interview, so the class can relisten to the interview to see whether there are quotes or anecdotes they might want to add to their notes. Through this process, the third graders learn about the importance of listening carefully and the importance of writing quickly, using words and phrases instead of entire sentences. They also learn that we need to go back to our notes, inserting additional information from memory or from our peers, to provide additional interesting details, quotes, or anecdotes for an article about the person.

Modeling the Drafting, Revising, and Editing Processes. To help her students learn how to organize their writing, look for leads, develop their ideas for an article, and determine interesting endings for their pieces, Barb uses a shared writing lesson to model this process. Working together as a class, the third graders create a draft about the teacher, revise the draft, and edit the draft.

Interviewing in Small Groups. Once the third graders experience the interviewing process, they apply the process in small groups as they interview teachers, secretaries, and principals. Working in groups, students collaborate as they determine questions to ask; conduct the interviews; gather notes from the process; compose, revise, and edit their interviews; and finally share the finished products with their peers. Throughout the activity, interviewers share their notes, drafts, and published pieces with their class. In this way, interviews become a way to learn about the history of their school. Interviews from two of the groups are displayed below.

Mrs. Brooks
by Amy, Jackie, Sequetta, and Brandon

Mrs. Brooks is the school secretary. She loves to work at Ardis School. She says it is hard for her to learn new things. This is the first time she has ever worked in a school. Her last job was being a secretary at St. Joseph Hospital.

When Mrs. Brooks was a child she went to Lincoln School. She loved to go to music class, and loved to do English. Her third grade teacher's name was Ms. Yanackahshee from Hawaii.

When Mrs. Brooks is at her house she likes to draw pictures, to paint, and to read. One of her favorite books is *Alaska* by James Michener. She likes Chinese food and likes to go fishing and boating. She has a cat named Max and a dog named Bosley. She walks her dog and she likes to ride her bike.

Mrs. Brooks has 3 children. Ashleigh is in the sixth grade. Jessica is in the ninth grade, and Dave is in the tenth grade. Mrs. Brooks lives in Ypsilanti and her birthday is March 29th.

Mrs. Taylor
by Jessica, Robert, and Rusty

Mrs. Taylor is a reading recovery teacher and teaches first grade students how to read. Mrs. Taylor thinks it's wonderful at Ardis school and feels welcome here.

Mrs. Taylor grew up in Ypsilanti and went to Ypsilanti schools. When she was a little girl she loved to do multiplication. Mrs. Taylor's ninth grade teacher, Mrs. Mary Louise Mays, was an inspiration and inspired her to become a teacher.

Mrs. Taylor collects books and loves to read. She likes to browse in book stores. She likes to go to craft shows and likes stuffed animals. She collects wood, crystal, and ceramic elephants.

Once students complete the final drafts, Dr. Irwin again converts the writing pieces into HTML files and then transfers the files to the server. By linking the students' writing pieces with their writing about Greenfield Village and the biopoems, Dr. Irwin helps the third graders gain a deeper understanding of how information is linked together on the Internet. Just by clicking on the name of their peers' teacher and then the name of their peers, students easily access their articles. At the same time, students discover a purpose and a meaning for reading and writing.

According to Rogovin (2001), students need to find themselves in history in order to understand the past. By interviewing people from the past and the present, students begin to find connections to history. Starting with what they know, they interview current teachers, the principal, and the secretary to gain a sense of present history. Moving from the known to people who are part of the school's past history, students then begin interviewing teachers, secretaries, and principals from the past. In this way, interviews bridge an understanding of the past and present.

Interviewing Dr. Ardis. The culminating experience for students' journey into the history of their school becomes a teleconference with Dr. Ardis. First Barb, Connie, and Venetia contact Dr. Ardis, who had moved to the state of California, inviting him to participate in a teleconference interview with the third graders. Having multiple experiences with interviewing local people, the students are now prepared to interview Dr. Ardis. All three classes collaborate, determining the questions for the interview prior to the teleconference. Similarly, all three classes work together as they ask the interview questions during the teleconference, which takes place at a local university. After interviewing Dr. Ardis, each class writes their own version of the interview.

Asking questions and finding answers becomes an essential aspect of these third graders' learning experiences. While writing about interviews, they explore patterns and relationships about people who are part of their school's history; then they reflect on these experiences as they collaboratively write articles about the interview.

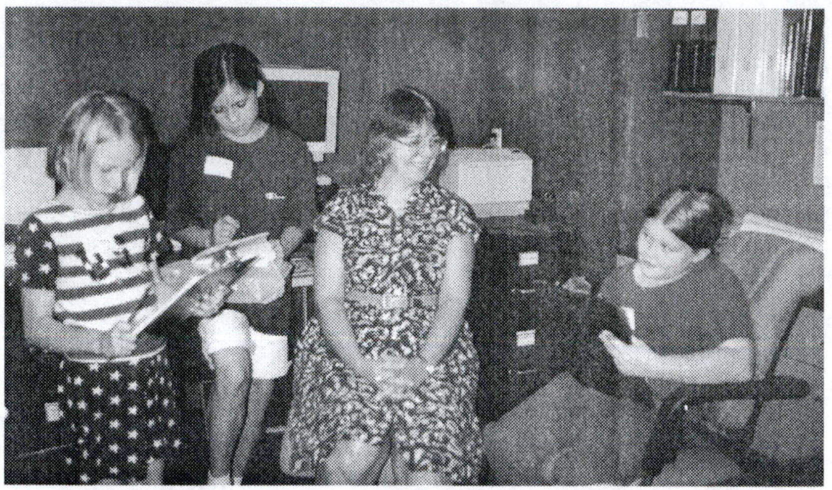

Third graders interview the school secretary.

Celebrating the school's twenty-fifth anniversary provides an opportunity to study their school and how school buildings and education change over time. As a result of this dynamic learning experience, students gain an understanding of history and how it emerges from people with differing interests, points of view, and values. Through the interviewing process, students take ownership of their learning.

Using Interviews and Observation to Learn about the Community

Similar to Cathy Bies's students in Chapter 6, the third graders extend their learning about history by studying how their city has changed over the last 100 years. In preparation for a field trip to view various historic sites in their city, the third graders view slides about the city; look at various artifacts—photos, diaries, postcards, and signs; and listen to various anecdotes from primary source materials presented by Rickie Balkam, the social studies coordinator for their district.

After exploring their city from these primary sources, the third graders take a walking tour to view various sites in the community. Similar to Cathy Bies's class, the third graders take their writers' notebooks with them to record their observations and to collect information about the historical sites.

Returning to the school site, students work in collaborative groups to compile information and write articles about the historic sites. Working together, students determine a lead for their article, the order in which information will be presented, the details and examples from their notes to be integrated into the text, and a conclusion for the article. Once they complete their drafts, students revise and edit their pieces, preparing them to be published on the Web. Knowing their work will be published, the students seem inspired to revise and edit their pieces. Muriel shares, "I want my family and friends to be proud of my work." Figure 7.1 displays one group's piece about the Water Tower, a landmark in their city.

To continue their investigation of their city's past, the third graders also interview various members of the community. Figure 7.2 (see p. 190) shows another group's piece about Dr. Marshall, a local historian.

Publishing their work on the Web gives students new audiences for their writing. The third graders are no longer writing just for their teacher or friends; they are writing for members of their community, the nation, and the world. Receiving emails about the website

Figure 7.1
Ardis Webpage for the Water Tower

The Water Tower

The water tower is an important landmark in Ypsilanti. William R. Coats designed the water tower in 1889. The water tower is one hundred forty-seven feet tall with two small round windows. It holds two hundred fifty thousand gallons of water. Three crosses were built on the water tower. One cross is above the west door of the tower and two crosses are inside the tower. The workers believed that the crosses would protect them while they worked on the tower.

People in Ypsilanti started using the water from the tower in 1891. Water is still stored in the tower today for a fire emergency use. The water tower is on Cross Street in front of Welch Hall on Eastern Michigan University's campus. Our class visited the water tower and took a tour of the inside. There are over one hundred steps to the top. We enjoyed walking around the top of the tower which is called the catwalk. From the catwalk we could see most of the city. It is fun to walk on the catwalk if you like being up high.

Return to "Ypsilanti, Michigan"

Return to Ardis Home Page

intensifies the students' sense of authorship. An email from a local principal is an example of the positive feedback they receive.

> Finally, I am hooked up to the Internet and get to see firsthand the excellent job done by the staff and Ardis students. I am so impressed with what you have done. Great job! It is so very exciting to witness this type of excellence from our students. Congratulations to you all! Keep up the fantastic job! From an alumni all star—Tulani Smith!

However, the ultimate reward came the day the school received special recognition for their website. They took fourth place in the International Cyberfair competition, in which students in kindergarten through twelfth grade showcase a unique aspect of their community by designing a website.

Using Technology as an Information and Communication Tool to Learn about the State of Michigan

Motivated by parents' and students' responses to this unique learning experience, the team of teachers decide to extend students' learning experiences the following year. Linking with the fourth grade curriculum, the team determines they will use "cybercars" to help visitors tour the state of Michigan at their website. Specifically, animated cybercars, which students design themselves, invite readers to move from one Michigan city, town, or tourist site to the next while navigating the website.

To help students construct texts for the website, the teachers begin by inviting students to view a variety of student-generated webpages on the Internet. While viewing these websites, the fourth graders review how to navigate the Internet. After this introductory experience, students use technology as an information tool while exploring various websites about Michigan cities, towns, or tourist sites. To be sure that the students view quality websites, the teachers always preview them before downloading them for students to view.

Building on the fourth graders' online experiences the previous year, the teachers continuously facilitate their students' exploration of the Internet. Through guided explorations, students begin to learn how to locate information online and gain a deeper understanding

Figure 7.2
Ardis Webpage about Dr. Marshall

Dr. A. P. Marshall, Historian

Dr. A. P. Marshall is an historian in Ypsilanti who shares his knowledge and research of African American history with people. He is a favorite storyteller to children who enjoy hearing stories of the struggles about African Americans before and after the Civil War.

When Dr. Marshall was a boy he lived in Arkansas and the schools were segregated. He remembers getting used books and discarded materials from white schools to use in the black schools. Dr. Marshall's first jobs as a boy were cutting grass and raising chickens. In high school and college he worked in a library. He loved books so much that he decided to become a librarian. He also likes to write. He has written several children's books. Two of the favorite ones he has written are *Four Horsemen* and *The Real McCoy*. He is retired now but when he worked at Eastern Michigan University he was the Dean of Academic Services.

Dr. Marshall told us many interesting historical stories about Ypsilanti history. This is what he told us about the Underground Railroad. When slaves started leaving the southern states and running away to the northern states to freedom they traveled the Underground Railroad. They traveled by night and used the North star to guide them. The Underground Railroad was a secret way of traveling. Some slaves hid in barns in the woods or in special hiding places in people's homes. The places the slaves hid in along the way were called "stations". The people that helped the slaves were very careful not to get caught. If people got caught they had to pay fines and some people lost their farms when they got caught helping runaway slaves. Slave hunters were people who received money when they caught slaves and returned them to the families in the southern states who had owned them.

Many escaped to freedom and lived in cities like Ypsilanti, Ann Arbor, Marshall, and Plymouth. Mr. Woodward who founded Ypsilanti didn't want slavery. Ypsilanti was a part of the Underground Railroad system that helped slaves escape to Detroit and then go to Canada. There are two houses in Ypsilanti still standing that were used as underground railroad stations.

Return to "Ypsilanti, Michigan"

Return to Ardis Home Page

of how information is linked together on the Internet. At the same time, students become more interested in the state of Michigan, ready to begin their own inquiries about its cities, towns, and tourist sights.

Similar to the previous year, the team of teachers decides to have students work in small groups as they pursue their inquiries. This year, however, they offer opportunities for students to investigate a city, town, or site independently, as well as in groups. Working in groups, students begin their inquiries by selecting a city, town, or site they want to research. Naturally, many groups' selections reflect their prior experiences—they often choose a place they have visited; other times, they select a place because they have friends or relatives living there; still other times, they choose a place because of their interest in learning more about the city, town, or site.

Modeling the Process of Notetaking and Paraphrasing

Once they choose their topics, students begin their inquiries. To model the process of taking notes when reading informational texts, Barb uses the LCD projector during a minilesson. After she quickly reviews how to navigate to the Ardis website, she models how to click on a link to the Water Tower where they find an article written by their peers last year. Using this article as an example of informational text, Barb asks the class to help her determine important facts and information to record in their notes. She reminds them that we only use words and phrases when taking notes; we do not want to copy the information word for word or use sentences in our notes. If we copy the information word for word, Barb explains, this would be plagiarism, failing to give our friends, or any author for that matter, credit for their hard work. For this reason, we merely take notes and then use this information to write our own article or paragraph about the topic. To give credit to our friends' hard work, she continues, we acknowledge where we find the information in a bibliography. Working together as they gather the notes, Barb and her students come up with the following list of phrases and words:

- William R. Coats, 1889
- 147 feet tall
- three crosses and two windows
- 100 steps to the top
- catwalk around top of tower
- crosses protect workers
- holds 150,000 gallons of water for emergencies or fires
- first used in 1891
- located in front of EMU, Welch Hall

Next Barb reemphasizes that we gathered the information about the Water Tower from Ardis's website, which is our source for this information. When we gather information from another source, we want to give the authors credit for their work, so we write down the source: www.microstore.com/ardis and the authors' names in our notes.

After closing the connection, Barb invites her students to relook at their notes and think about what they would like to say in a paragraph about the Water Tower. Specifically, she asks them to think about a lead for their paragraph. Then, she continues, we will think of sentences to write about the tower, deciding what we will discuss first, second, and third. Finally, she concludes, we will think of a way to end our paragraph.

Brian volunteers, suggesting that they begin with a sentence like "If you ever visit Ypsilanti, Michigan, you will notice the Water Tower, which is over one hundred forty-seven feet tall, located on Cross Street right in front of Welch Hall on Eastern Michigan University's campus." Everyone immediately agrees, so Barb, with Brian's help, records his sentence on chart paper. Charity recommends that they mention who designed the tower and what the tower is used for next. Using her words, Barb writes, "Designed by William R. Coats in 1889, the Water Tower holds over two hundred fifty thousand gallons of water for emergency uses." Then Ian suggests that they describe the tower next. Using his own knowledge and information from the source, he shares, "The Water Tower is a long, perpendicular structure with a curved top. There are one hundred steps leading to the top of the tower, or the catwalk." To conclude the paragraph, Jennifer urges the class to write, "If you ever visit the Water Tower, you will be able to see most of the city."

The minilesson modeled how to paraphrase information from a source. The fourth graders will now be able to apply this skill as they use the Internet to access information about their own topics, analyze and synthesize the information using notetaking strategies, and then link the information with other sources as they write about their topics.

Modeling the Process of Writing Business Letters

In addition to gathering information about their topics from the Internet, students also gather information about their topics by writing letters to the chamber of commerce for their city or town or by writing letters to friends or relatives residing in the town or city. Knowing that her students have had limited experiences writing business letters, Barb also models this process to her class before they begin writing the letters.

Through a shared writing lesson, Barb begins this minilesson by explaining that we need to change the friendly format of our previous letters to a more formal format in the

teaching TIP 7.1

Using a shared writing lesson to demonstrate proper punctuation and capitalization techniques helps students acquire these concepts more easily. Specifically, they learn the concepts in the context of writing.

business letters we write to the chamber of commerce or to a tourist agency. For example, she explains that we begin our letters by writing down the address of our school in the upper right-hand corner, followed by the date. As she shares this information, Barb records the information on chart paper for all to see. Next, she continues, we move to the left-hand margin and write the address of the business. In our case, she shares, we will write to the Ypsilanti Chamber of Commerce so we can receive more information about our city. After modeling how to record this information, emphasizing the appropriate punctuation and capitalization strategies as she writes, she explains that our greeting will change to "Dear Sir," followed by a colon. Then, she continues, we will write our purpose for writing in the body of our letter. Instead of indenting, she explains, we will skip a line between each paragraph. As Barb demonstrates the process, she and her students compose the body of the letter together. She concludes with the closing, again modeling this process. Figure 7.3 shows the format for a business letter.

Investigating Their Topics in Small Groups

Similar to last year, students work in small groups to investigate their topics. They follow a process over several weeks, beginning with the prewriting activities of gathering notes about their topic from the Internet, writing letters, and collecting brochures and pamphlets about their topic.

After gathering the information from several sources, the students collaborate to form a web about their topic, draft an article about their topic, revise their draft, and then edit it.

Figure 7.3
Form for Business Letter

Ardis Renaissance Academy

2100 Ellsworth Rd.
Ypsilanti, MI 48197
Date

Person's Name
Company Name
Street
City, State ZIP

Dear ____________:

____
____
____
____
____
____
____
____

Thank you,

Sincerely,

____
____

Throughout the process, the fourth graders continue to share their notes, drafts, and published pieces with their class. As they share their articles, their peers learn more about their home state and its cities, towns, and tourist attractions. At the same time, the authors receive praise and feedback for their ideas, motivating them to continue their inquiry. Troy's article about Houghton is shown below:

If you were born in Houghton you are a Yooper! Bet you didn't know that!

When I go to Houghton I go hiking and exploring in the woods that surrounds my cousin's house. My favorite place in Houghton is a stream that my friend found. We caught a frog there but later let it go.

One interesting fact about Houghton is there is a great university there. There are more students at Michigan Technological University than there are in all of the Houghton Public Schools.

Another interesting fact is there's a lot of snow. You might even see a ten foot snow bank.

As can be seen from Troy's article, the fourth graders have learned more about the craft of writing, and they are refining their writing. For example, students are beginning to try new types of leads. Troy's lead immediately grabs our attention, inviting us to continue reading so that we can learn more about this city where people are called Yoopers (Upper Peninsula residents).

Ashley, Curtis, and Eugene also apply an interesting lead in their article about Mackinac Island, a popular tourist site in Michigan.

No cars allowed! People only ride horses, bikes, wagons, or horse-drawn carriages on Mackinac Island. To get to the island you have to take a ferry from St. Ignace or Mackinaw City.

Here is what Ashley wrote about a visit to the island in July of 1996. "I went there. I ate fudge from one of Ryba's Fudge Shops which has peanut fudge, chocolate fudge, and much much more. I rode in a horse-drawn carriage. I also went to Fort Mackinac and the State Park. I go there every year. One year I rode around the island on a bike. As my brother, mom, and I biked, we saw the gorgeous waters of lake Huron and saw the beautiful trees and flowers."

If you would like to visit some places, you would want to go to the state park to see Arch Rock, British Landing, Devil's Kitchen, Sugar Loaf Rock, Skull Cave, and Ann's Tablet. These six places are natural features.

You're staying on the Island. Right? Well you have to have somewhere to sleep. Here are some hotels: The Grand Hotel, Harbor View Inn, the Lilac Tree Hotel, and Hotel Iroquois. The Grand Hotel is the world's largest summer hotel! Plus the most expensive on the island!

Working as a group, Ashley, Curtis, and Eugene include information they find from a variety of sources, as well as Ashley's personal experiences while visiting the island. When Ashley shared her own experiences while visiting the island, the group gained an additional incentive to learn about Mackinac.

Winning Another Award

This writing adventure became another challenging, stimulating learning experience for the fourth graders at Ardis. When they reenter the International CyberFair competition this year, they place second in the competition. According to Judy Benns, one of their teachers, the students worked very hard as they investigated their topics, gathering information from many sources, reading, writing, and interpreting information. Judy proudly declared, "They deserved the award and the recognition for all the hard work they put into gathering information cooperatively and making it appealing to others." Their superintendent concurred, congratulating them for "forging ahead in technology," setting a pace for the rest of the school district and staff. The other teachers working with the students also agreed, remarking that they, too, have learned "about Ypsilanti, about Michigan, about the writing process, about computers and the Internet, and about the talents and wonderful ideas of elementary school students." As teachers, we all need to remember that whenever we integrate technology, we become learners among learners.

Others also sent words of praise to the fourth graders. The email excerpt below shows how proud people were of their accomplishments:

> Congratulations on your 2nd place award in the International Schools CyberFair. It's nice to know that all of your hard work in gathering information, writing reports, designing an interesting web site, and publishing for a world-wide audience is recognized by other people. All of you deserve much credit for all of the time and effort it takes to make a worthwhile project.

Using Technology as a Publishing Tool

As can be seen from the students' writing samples, using technology as a publishing tool provided the third and fourth graders real-world publishing opportunities. As the students constructed their knowledge about their community and state, they always had a meaningful purpose for writing. They realized that people they value would be reading their writing, helping them acquire a sense of audience. According to Calkins and Parsons (2003, p. 131), "We need to move heaven and earth to be sure every child knows what it is to be a published author." Posting students' writing on the Web gave these third and fourth graders this opportunity to become a published author and to gain a sense of audience.

Publishing, a critical part of the writing process, also gives authors a way to celebrate their writing through feedback and responses to their writing. When given positive feedback and responses to their writing, authors become more motivated to write and inspired to write more (Calkins, 1994; Clark, 1995; Graves, 2004; Routman, 2000, 2005). Specifically, publishing

- Inspires authors to write.
- Encourages peers to imitate their peers' success.
- Gives a meaningful purpose for writing.
- Establishes a real audience one's writing.
- Legitimizes the need for revisions.
- Provides a purpose and meaning for editing (spelling, grammar, and mechanics of writing).
- Motivates students to do their best work.
- Inspires authors to write.
- Promotes a leap into literacy for emergent and struggling writers as this may be their first successful writing.
- Offers opportunities for students to practice reading and rereading their writing.
- Provides a purpose and meaning for reading as students read their own writing and that of their peers.
- Expands the classroom library as these books often become very popular and treasured books.

Third graders experience what it's like to be a published author.

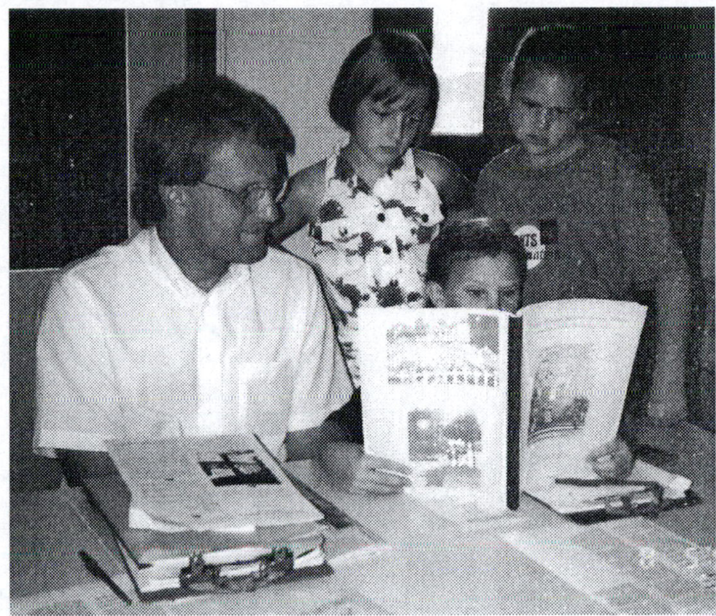

However, not all parents had computers at home; others did not have Internet access. For this reason, Barb, Connie, and Venetia decide that they need to bring the published writing pieces to these parents as well. They believe that all children need to have the opportunity to receive positive feedback and responses about their writing from parents, relatives, and friends.

Authors Publishing School Newsletters

To meet the needs of all families in their community, Barb, Connie, and Venetia decide to publish a quarterly newsletter. The newsletter also gives them another avenue for publishing students' articles about Michigan and an avenue for publishing additional articles about school events and happenings.

Publishing the *Ardis All Star Gazette*. Once the teachers decide to publish their own newsletter, they meet together to determine the process they will follow. Building on their experiences of publishing a home page, they agree to continue having students work in cooperative groups to compile information and write reports for the newsletters, following the writing process. Dr. Irwin volunteers to help transfer articles from the website to the newsletter, and Mrs. Nichols, a parent volunteer, agrees to provide the technical assistance needed for publishing the newsletter.

Using the volunteers from the community, the teachers easily publish the first issues of the *Ardis All Star Gazette,* named by the fourth graders. Since these issues focus on articles about Michigan, which have already been published on their website, the publishing experience becomes another positive experience for everyone in the class.

After hearing the positive responses from parents and the community, the teachers and students become motivated to publish more

***teaching* TIP 7.2**

When we link with parents and community members, we find that we are able to accomplish our goals more easily. At the same time, parents and community members gain new respect for our talents and our contributions to student learning.

issues of the *Gazette;* they decide to publish four issues per year. Students interested in publishing additional articles in the *Gazette* become cub reporters and editors for the newsletter.

Due to high student interest in the newsletter, teachers also encourage the fourth graders to write articles about what's happening in the school and their classrooms. Before long, many new opportunities for writing quickly emerge. For example, when Danny wins first place in a local contest, Andrew writes the following article:

Danny, a fourth grader in Mrs. Williams' class designed a captivating ad for the restaurant, Kenny's Place. He managed to grab the judges' attention and pull out with first place, a pizza party for his class. Over 1000 other kids from several counties entered but only thirty-nine students were winners. It took Danny a few days to do the ad and he looked at ads in books to get an idea. Danny said, "I liked winning first place and I'm very excited about having a pizza party with my class."

In January, the cub reporters interview winners of the school district's Martin Luther King Writing Contest. They also publish the winning pieces in the newsletter. Brianna, a third grader at Ardis, won first place for her article.

Living as Brothers and Sisters

As Martin Luther King, Jr. had a dream, I also have a dream. My dream is for us to live together as brothers and sisters.

How beautiful it would be to call my classmates my brothers and sisters. How wonderful it would be if people realized that skin is only like a pod that protects what is inside. And don't we all have the same thing inside? The only way to make this happen is to think of our neighbors and friends as brothers and sisters.

Would you be mean to your brothers and sisters in your home? Of course not, then why would you be mean to your brothers and sisters outside your home? We must treat each other with respect and love!

I am proud that I have so many sisters and brothers. What a rainbow of colors and minds. Just think how much smarter we would be if we all loved each other. Remember two heads are better than one!

So today when you meet someone, think of them as your brother or sister. You may learn something new from them or they from you. Wouldn't that make you feel good?

When school begins in the fall, the cub reporters decide to interview students who have recently immigrated to America. As a result of this experience, they discover that children at their school speak 16 different languages. As they interview some of these students, they begin to learn more about the rich diversity within their school. This experience also helps them, as well as their readers, learn about the lifestyles and experiences of these students prior to coming to Ardis. Specifically, Tyrone, Jessica, Makeba, JaQuantese, and Kyale learn more about life in Romania.

Lavinia

Lavinia is a third grade student in Mrs. Sims' class. She is from Cluj-Napora, Romania. It is east of Italy and north of Greece. Lavinia's father and uncle came to the United States first. After one year her father called for her and her family because he felt life was better in America.

Lavinia speaks Romanian at home and English at school.

Lavinia's favorite food is cartofi pai which is like a pie that her mom makes. She likes animals. Her dog's name is Pufi. Her family celebrates Christmas and Easter. Easter in Romania is called Pas, ti.

Lavinia felt school was harder in Romania than here. She had to walk to school instead of ride a bus like she does now.

Lavinia played a lot of games with her friends in Romania. Tag and hide and seek were her favorite.

Lavinia misses her friends in Romania sometimes but she like being at Ardis school.

Using Communication Technology Tools across the Curriculum

As the fourth graders at Ardis continue to publish their articles in the newsletter, they discover that their lives and experiences matter; they also realize that their stories matter. Publishing gives them the desire to learn new skills that will help them write well and with passion; they become proud of their work and want to write more. Similarly, students in other schools discover ways to use communication technology as a tool to enhance their writing.

Publishing the *Schryer Press*. Similar to the students at Ardis, fourth graders at Loon Lake publish a quarterly newsletter. The student reporters also work in groups to write the articles. Once the group drafts the article, they meet with other groups who help them revise and edit. Their teachers continuously facilitate the process, helping students brainstorm their ideas for articles, move the pieces through the stages of writing, and finally publish the newsletter. To ensure that the articles are error-free before publication, the teachers use assistant editors, students who are proficient editors, to carefully reedit the articles written, revised, and edited by the groups. Their teachers then serve as top editors, similar to the editor-in-chief of a newspaper. By following this process, the fourth graders gain familiarity with real-life practices. Kelly, Devin, Adam, and Andrew, who interview their principal, write the following article:

Interview with Mrs. Winder

One day we went to interview the principal at Loon Lake Elementary. Her name is Mrs. Winder, but before she was married her last name was Hightower. She was born in Burlington, Iowa on April 11. In school her favorite subject was music, and she played the flute and the viola. When she grew up she became a principal, and she started in 1988.

She was not a principal at any other school, but she was a counselor. Also, she has been principal for eleven years. She has two kids named Kim and Brandt. Last, but not least, she says being a principal is very fun. We think she is a great principal at Loon Lake!

Middle School Students Publish *The Genesis Gazette*. Using publishing software, students in middle school especially enjoy publishing newsletters. The range of topics and types of articles found in newspapers provides a wide range of opportunities for students of all ability levels to participate. Mike, who enjoys sports, writes about skating.

Why Skating Is Better than Most Sports

Skating has grown popular over the years and now about 90% of teens are doing it. When I say skating, I don't mean the fruitbooters that always get in your way, I'm talking about skateboarding. It's better than most sports because of the risk. Every time you go to Vans Skate Park you risk breaking a bone or busting your self up. A pro skater Geoff Rowley says, "It's the agony that makes skating fun." I agree with that because when you try something new you won't get it right the first time. I skate because it's the most enjoyable sport to do on my own time. I would recommend skating to everyone.

Jason takes a different slant in his article. He writes about his feelings and understandings about war, sharing what he thinks about having a brother fight for freedom in Iraq.

When War Gets Personal

Our country has once again crossed the Iraqi border for the second war against a corrupted dictator and his loyal regime. Most of America feels grief for the soldiers overseas fighting Saddam's evil army. Yet, only a small number of Americans know how it feels to worry about the war itself and to worry about having a loved one in the War of Iraqi Freedom. For my family and I, we know how it feels to know that part of our family is in immediate danger. For me, it's like having my best friend in danger and having no way of helping him. My brother is twenty years old. He has been in the Marines for three years. He is a communicator in the war. He joined the Marines because he wants to become a part of the Secret Service.

Even though it's scary to know my brother is in the war, I know he will come back safely. The hardest part about having a family member overseas in Iraq is that you can't be sure if they will come back unharmed. Still my hopes are high. My brother actually calls about twice a week to tell us he's okay. When I talk to him I can hear the exhaustion and anxiousness in his voice. I'm pretty sure that's how most people would sound if they were in his position. My brother isn't even twenty-one years old yet, but he is defending our country, just like thousands of other brothers, sister, sons, and daughters are doing at this exact moment. The one thing we should be thankful for is our freedom, and knowing we have our soldiers to thank for that freedom.

Young Authors Publishing Simulated Newspapers about History

Publishing software invites additional opportunities for students to simulate history. Using the publishing software provides a way to simulate newspapers from the past. By linking information from their textbooks and informational books, Olivia Brown's class creates *The Colonial Observer.*

To generate the articles, the fifth graders first investigate their topics, following note-taking strategies described earlier. After gathering their notes, they devote several weeks to drafting, revising, and editing their pieces. When they circulate the newspaper among their families, the authors receive praise and feedback for their ideas, verifying their efforts. According to Routman (2000, p. 21), publishing "congratulates a writer, affirms the effort, serves as a possible role model for other students, and encourages the student to continue writing." Figure 7.4 displays one page from *The Colonial Observer.*

Young Authors Publishing Magazines

As students explore avenues for publishing their work, new genres often emerge. Students at Ardis received so much affirmation for their writing on their home page and the *Ardis All Star Gazette* that their teachers decide to try another venue for publishing students' writing. After brainstorming several possibilities, students and teachers agree to publish an *All Stars Magazine.*

Figure 7.4

Fifth Graders Use Desktop Publishing Software to Publish *The Colonial Observer*

The Colonial Observer

Vol. 2 **1777**

Declaration of Independence

(1776) On July 4, 1776 The Declaration of Independence was adopted in Pennsylvania. The people who wrote it were Thomas Jefferson and Benjamin Franklin. "The Declaration of Independence" was written because they wanted to let the world know about the war and why they were fighting it. It didn't mean peace because there was still a war to win. Benjamin and Thomas with 53 other men knew that if the patriots didn't win the war they would be put to death by the King. Benjamin said "Men if we don't hang together we will all hang separately." The British General was so upset by this act he sent troops of Red coats to attack the Americans, but General Howe changed direction and the Americans stole supplies and captured a soldier. The soldier said "Washington's a genius." No one told that it was Howe who was the genius one because of his mistake.

Christmas Night, 1776

(1776) On Christmas night, 1776 the Americans crossed the Delaware River. The Americans were led by their leader George Washington. The Americans crossed the Delaware River because they thought the British would not be expecting the Americans to attack on Christmas night. 2,400 people crossed the river that night. When the Americans crossed George Washington fell out of the boat and almost drowned.

After a cold night of traveling, the Americans got to the other side. When the Americans crossed the river was clogged with huge chunks of ice, it was freezing, and the wind went rapidly through the freezing men. The Americans attacked at 4:00 A.M. at Trenton, New Jersey. 900 British surrendered. Finally after a short fight the Americans won!! Only 4 Americans were wounded in the battle.

Revolution

During the war the Americans Continental Army sent a small farmer to spy on British plans. Some of the Loyalists said, "The Declaration of Independence didn't hold the truth." They were wrong. A month or so later Cornwallis had nothing to do but surrender himself, him and his troops were surrounded.

Providing another opportunity to celebrate student writing, the magazine inspires students in all grade levels to write more. While writing articles, students of all ages discover the wide realm of topics for writing within their daily lives. For example, Jonathon, who became fascinated with owl pellets during science, wrote the following piece:

Owl Pellets

We did the owl pellets for three days. When we first got them I didn't know what they were. When I opened mine, I saw bones and I knew it was an animal. When I took the bones out of the owl pellet and picked at it a little, the teacher told us to put the bones into the container. We put them into the container and looked for more bones because there was lots of fur. The next day we got to glue them on a paper with a skeleton on it. Denarus and I found all the bones except one leg bone, so we were able to rebuild one skeleton. I liked playing with the owl pellet; it was fun.

Nate prefers to write poetry. In his poems, Nate shows his feelings about school inside and outside the classroom door. Interspersing his writing with digital pictures, Nate allows the readers to experience his life inside and outside the classroom door.

Outside Door

Outside the door is the place to be
The sky is blue and the sun is yellow
I like to play basketball and play on the tire swing
I like to play with my kite
I like to go fishing
Outside the door is the place to be.

Inside the Door

Inside the doors is a place to be
I like the code book
And I like gym and computers
I like to break words into syllables
Because it is fun
I like to play basketball in the gym
I like to play kidpix on the computer
Inside the doors is a place to be.

Emmet decides to write about her class's overnight trip to Mackinac Island. Through her sense of humor, readers reexperience the adventure of this learning opportunity with her.

Tips for Mackinac Island

Hi! I have some tips for you. Ready to listen? Here we go! While on Mackinac Island be sure to get some fudge especially Rocky Road. Make sure to see the forts in Mackinaw City and on the island.

Now here are my tips for the hotel. Make sure to pick Mission Point. Or try to play with the telephone but don't blame me if you get caught. The Hotel has a nice game room. Take it from a person who knows. The only bad thing about the hotel is the walk my group had to make. Boy were my feet sore! They still are. Take the carriage. That's the smart thing to do.

If you don't like to sit in a car and be bored, I suggest that you bring some music. Make it some good music. Out of all these tips the most important one is to be safe.

Voice, which Graves (1994) describes as an individual and singular expression that precedes writing, emerges as a recognizable and distinguishable quality in these writing pieces. The more students write, the more their voice emerges, changing as it develops through multiple opportunities to write. Publishing students' writing in newsletters and magazines is one way to stimulate the evolution of voice.

Young Authors Publishing Books

Students of all ages also enjoy publishing books written and illustrated by them. Quality informational books become mentor books to teach students the language of words and the language of pictures (Fletcher & Portalupi, 1998).

Publishing a Biography of People in the Community. Jessica Johnson's fourth graders learn about history by interviewing older people, ages 40 to 60, in their community—grandparents, friends, relatives, or people at church or in their neighborhood. First, Jessica and her students determine the interview questions:

- What is your place of birth?
- Where did you grow up?
- Who was in your family?
- What were some things that were different at home when you were growing up?
- What were some things that were different when you went to school?
- What did you do when you had free time?
- What jobs have you done as a grown-up?
- What do you like to do when you have free time?
- What are three things you have done in your life that you are glad you did?
- What is something you would like to do but you haven't had a chance yet?
- What is a good change you have seen?
- What is a change you have seen that you do not think is a good one?
- If you could change something to make the world a better place, what would you change?

After interviewing their person using notetaking strategies, the fourth graders create webs about their person. Following the writing process, students then draft, revise, and edit their writing while planning where pages will begin and end. They also follow a process with their illustrations—drafting, revising, and editing them before beginning their books. Through this process, the fourth graders realize that artists, as well as writers, follow a process to craft their work. Figure 7.5 displays a page from Mackenzie's book.

As Mackenzie and her peers interview people in their families or community, they discover how life was different in the past. They learn that many people grew up in the country in homes with barns, lambs, chickens, and cows; that people watched television with only two

Figure 7.5

Fourth Graders Follow a Process While Writing and Illustrating Their Biographies

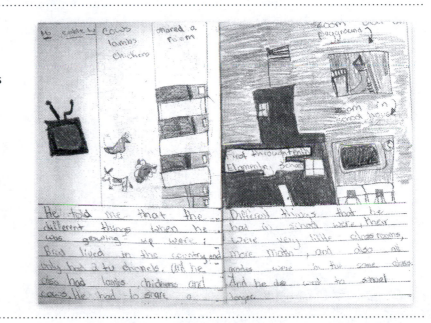

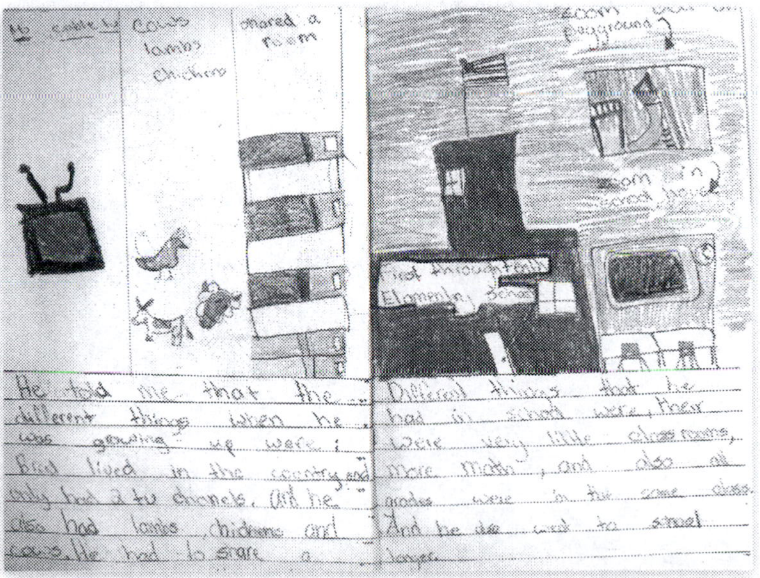

channels to choose from; that schools often housed grades one through twelve in one building; or that people saw changes in education, medicine, air conditioning, and technology. They also notice that people would like to see fewer wars and a safe world for their children. By publishing a biography of these people, students begin to compare and contrast life in the past with life in the present; they begin to appreciate the quality of their lives today.

Publishing a Beary Special Book. Paula Kiser's first graders each write stories about a bear of their choice, following the writing process, to celebrate Bear Day. To help her first graders understand how books are published, the first graders take a field trip to the local printing shop to actually see their book being published. Upon returning from their field trip, the first graders celebrate the experience by reading their story to their friends in the Author's Chair, using a microphone. Figure 7.6 displays Jeremy's page in the book.

Paula, a first-year teacher, is so proud of her first graders that she decides to send a copy of the book to her superintendent. The first graders gain a sense of audience when they receive a letter from him the following week. In his letter, Vance Johnson shares that bears are also one of his favorite animals. He further adds that he didn't realize there were so many kinds of bears until he read their book. In closing, he congratulates the first graders, saying, "I am also pleased to see how well you are doing with your writing skills. Keep up the good work. I look forward to reading your next book."

The superintendent's positive responses spur the first graders' motivation to write more. As they continue to write and publish special projects, their writing will grow and develop.

Figure 7.6

Jeremy Writes about Winnie the Pooh

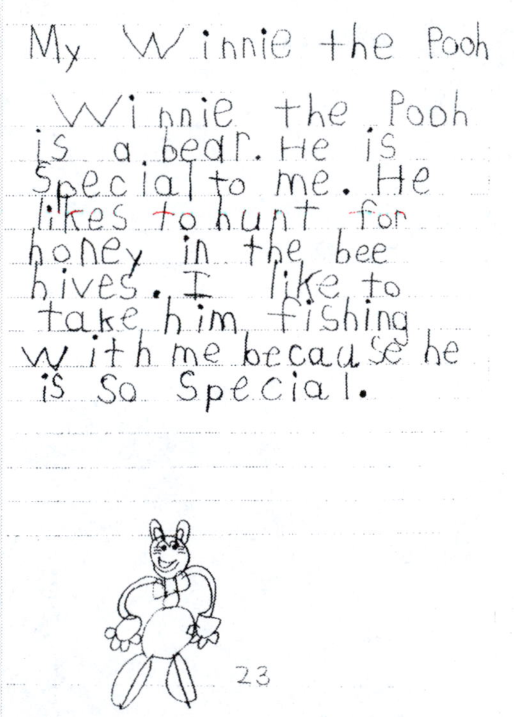

My Winnie the Pooh
Winnie the Pooh
is a bear. He is
Special to me. He
likes to hunt for
honey in the bee
hives. I like to
take him fishing
with me because he
is So Special.
23

Using Technology Tools to Publish Students' Writing

As more and more software becomes available and accessible to classroom teachers, we can also publish books using technology. Combined with the motivation for publishing, technology communication tools add new incentives for authors of all ages to write. These publishing tools often invite students to read and write more, allowing them to practice and hone their reading and writing skills.

Publishing Books about Mom Using Word Processing Tools

Kindergarteners gain a sense of audience when their teacher publishes their book about Moms. Consistent with Graves (1983, p. 54), they began to "envision the appearance of a piece in print, and the teacher, parents, or friends turning the pages" when they see their teacher, Karen Carpenter, hold the book for all to see.

Adapting the biopoem format (see Chapter 5), Karen has her kindergarteners write about their Moms. The young writers begin by using their temporary spelling to describe his or her Mom—what she loves, what she needs, what she gives, what she would like to see, and what she says. After they complete their first drafts, parent volunteers invite each student to come to the writing center, which includes a computer, to type his or her poems. After indicating the words they want to know how to spell, the kindergarteners see how to spell the words when parents type their biopoems for them. The format of the biopoem allows the kindergarteners to type some of the words with the parents, retaining their ownership of the writing. After typing the first draft of the poem for them, the kindergarteners read the poems with the parent volunteers. Since the poems include their words, the kindergarteners can more easily read the poems with the parents' assistance.

Over the next few days, Karen conferences with each of the young writers, rereading his or her poem with the student. She invites each of them to make simple revisions on the poem to change words to better describe Mom or to better indicate what she loves, needs, gives, says, or would like to see. Through this interactive process, the kindergarteners begin to learn about revising and editing their writing. However, the most exciting part of the experience is seeing and reading the published book of poems. Figure 7.7 shows Jenny's poem about her Mom.

Using Graphics to Create "Coloring Books"

Using Graphics to Create a "Coloring Book" for First Graders' Poems. Margaret Trapp uses a different twist to publishing her first graders' poems about animals. Having her young writers work collaboratively in twos, Margaret invites her first graders to write about their favorite animals after listening to several poems in *Eric Carle's Animals Animals.* Following the process described in Chapter 4, the young writers prewrite using webs and then draft, revise, and edit their poems. Margaret celebrates her students' accomplishments by publishing the completed poems in a book. Not only does she feature each pair's poem about an animal, she also includes a box for their peers to illustrate the animal after reading the poem. Figure 7.8 displays Jim and Nanthaly's poem.

Using Graphics to Create a "Coloring Book" for Kindergarteners' Fairy Tales. Similarly, Michelle Cox's kindergarteners publish a "coloring" book of students' fairy tales. After reading many fairy tales, the kindergarteners decide that they want to write their own. After reviewing the story elements found in fairy tales, Michelle models the process of composing one through shared writing.

Figure 7.1

Kindergarteners Use Word Processing Tools to Revise and Edit Poems about Their Moms

MY MOM

My mom is the nicest mom in the world.

She is the mother of Jenny and Kim.

She loves kisses.

She needs love.

She gives kisses.

She would like to see a clean house.

She always says "I love you."

My mom is

She begins her minilesson by having her students create a list of describing words about her stuffed animals, recording the words on chart paper. The following day, they brainstorm the characters (the stuffed animals), the setting for the fairy tale, the problem, and the resolution of the problem. As Michelle records their words using word processing tools and the LCD projector, the kindergarteners view their story on the screen. Writing together, they create the following story about the three stuffed animals:

> Once upon a time there was a fuzzy, white bear who lived with Mrs. Fox. The cute, loveable bear loved her friends, the pink bear with the white heart and the gray and white sea otter. The pink bear, the white bear, and the sea otter played with each other all day. One day they had a sleep over. When they woke up, the white bear was missing. The sea otter and the pink bear went to find the gorgeous white bear. They looked and looked and found her wandering in the black forest. The white bear was lost. They called to her, and she came back. They were so happy, they had a party.

Once the class completes the story, they celebrate the event by reading the story chorally. Then Michelle prints out their story so they can illustrate the story and take it home to read to their parents.

Eager to compose their own fairy tales, the kindergarteners similarly create a list of describing words about their stuffed animals. Then they share their ideas for a fairy tale about their stuffed animal with a partner. Using this strategy helps the young writers orally compose their fairy tales before writing.

Figure 7.8

Jim and Nanthaly's Poem about a Bunny

Bunny

Brown happy bunny
Long ears
Eats carrots and grass
Hops and jumps and runs and hides
Brown happy bunny.

Draw a picture of a bunny.

After drafting their story with paper and pencil, the students go to the computer lab to word process their fairy tales the next day. Having had multiple experiences with word processing on the computer, the young writers easily type their fairy tales. As they word process their stories, they also help one another find letter keys or show one another how to use the delete or insert keys. Michelle also facilitates the process as she circulates among them.

Making a few simple revisions becomes easier for the young writers when they apply word processing tools the following day. They no longer have to recopy their writing. Seeing that most students do not yet have a title, Michelle demonstrates how to insert a title into their fairy tales in the classroom, using the LCD projector, just before they go to the computer lab. Following her model, the kindergarteners insert a title into their story, using capital letters just like they use capital letters in their names.

They also practice simple editing the next day. Before visiting the computer lab, the kindergarteners circle words they want to know how to spell on a printed draft that is triple-spaced. Every student finds at least three words they want to know how to spell. After they find three words, Michelle records the correct spelling for them above the word. Then the kindergarteners correct the spelling of these words on the computer, using the delete and insert keys. To complete the process, all young authors change the print font; some even change the color of the print font, using word processing tools.

teaching **TIP 7.3**

We need to turn spell check off while students draft their writing so that they can concentrate on their ideas. After printing out the draft, students can then find the misspelled words themselves. When we turn spell check back on, students can then see how carefully they edited for misspelled words.

When Michelle publishes their writing in a class book, she also inserts a box for the readers to draw a picture of the fairy tale. The young writers seem to experience little difficulty reading one another's temporary spelling and illustrating one another's fairy tales! Niki's fairy tale is shown in the following "translation."

The Owl (Translation from temporary spelling)
by Niki

Once an adorable owl was born from it's Mother! It was so cute some people took it to be a star! A little girl named Niki bought it. And she took it home! She took real good care of him! But one day it was gone. She looked and looked for him. Then one day she found an owl just like hers! Maybe it was hers?

Young writers can learn about the writing process more easily if they write daily. Although they only use simple revisions and edits with their writing, the kindergarteners begin to learn about the process. When they move to higher grades, they can acquire more sophisticated strategies for revising and editing their writing. Michelle spontaneously remarks that she is amazed at how easily they acquire word processing skills. She also enjoys seeing the children teach one another in the informal environment of the computer lab. Without a doubt, she adds, children love technology. This seems to motivate them to learn word processing skills quickly and easily.

Publishing and Illustrating Children's Writing with KidPix

Once Margaret became comfortable writing with young children, she too began to explore using technology tools with her first graders. She begins by inviting her first graders to use word processing tools to publish their writing. Even though she only has two computers in her classroom, the students take turns word processing their writing in twos. Each pair of students rotates to the computers, following a schedule posted nearby. Once they finish,

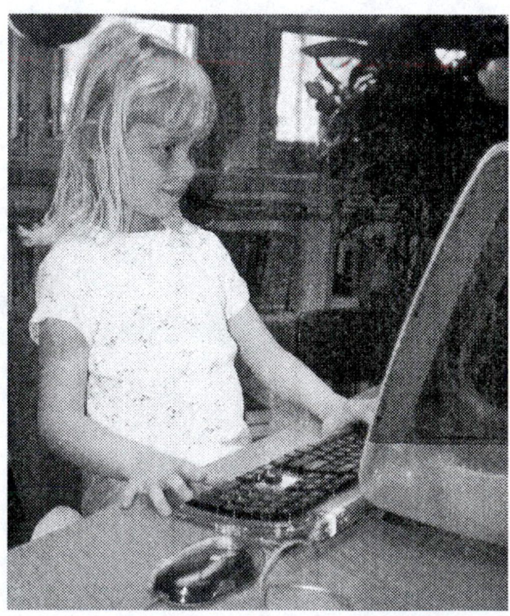

A first grader uses KidPix to illustrate her poems.

Third graders show their parents how to navigate the Internet.

students take ownership of the process by quietly going to the next pair of students to announce that it is their turn to begin word processing.

One of her students, Katherine, who knows how to use KidPix, asks Margaret if she can also illustrate her poem. Fascinated, Margaret encourages her to illustrate the poem. Since Katherine is so skilled at KidPix, Margaret decides to have her show her classmates how to illustrate with KidPix. Figure 7.9 shows the cover for the class book with an illustration by Elizabeth.

When we integrate technology with our curriculum, some students often know how to use technology tools already. Sometimes they have skills that exceed our own skills.

Figure 7.9

Elizabeth Uses KidPix to Illustrate the Cover for the Class Book

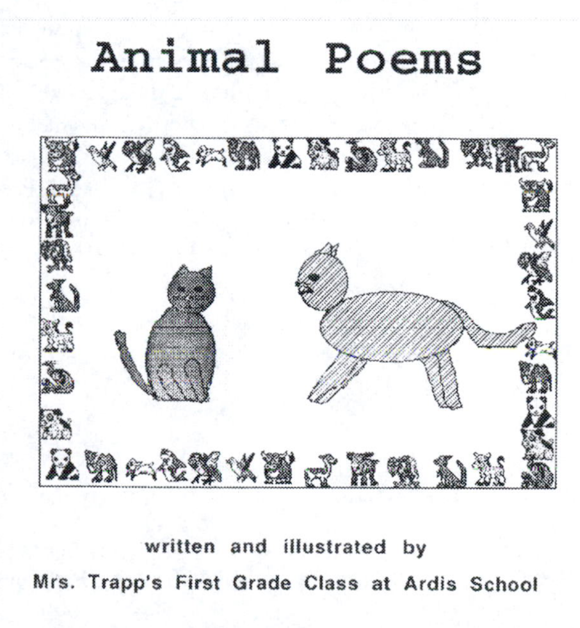

Animal Poems
written and illustrated by
Mrs. Trapp's First Grade Class at Ardis School

Following Margaret's lead, we can let them facilitate the learning of their peers by inviting them to show how to use the technology tools. Students often learn quicker when someone guides them one on one, but as teachers, we seldom have time to do this. However, our students can serve the role of a facilitator as they help their peers acquire new skills and strategies in a one-on-one learning environment.

Closing Thoughts

Technology offers many stimulating and powerful learning opportunities for our students. Living in a world where technology abounds, students seem to acquire these skills quickly and easily.

As shown in Nate's "Inside" poem, computers are an important part of students' learning environment. In fact, some students are so motivated by computers that they are willing to give up their recess so they can continue to explore and experiment with technology. Specifically, 5-year-old Aaron shares, "I'd stay in from recess to use the computer." Chris, a third grader, also shows his natural interest in using technology by stating, "Well, it's sort of like a really good activity. It's something you could do for an hour and type a story and do all those fun things. It's really fun."

As teachers, we need to follow our students' lead. When we do, students move to higher levels of learning just like the third and fourth graders who composed a home page for viewers around the world. While being challenged, our students simultaneously become prepared to make use of future technologies and to acquire the new forms of literacy that future technologies will require. Embracing technology as a tool for learning may inspire students to pursue a lifelong love for reading, writing, and learning.

Following the model of the teachers at Ardis, we can enlist the help of parents and community members to help us accomplish our goals. Similar to Barb, Connie, Venetia, and Judy, we can take risks as we implement our own inquiry projects. By taking risks, we become learners among learners. Since the ever-changing technology environment will continuously challenge us to acquire new skills and strategies in the future, we need to become comfortable taking risks and acquiring these new tools.

At the same time, like the teachers at Ardis, we need to integrate technology with our curriculum and its standards and benchmarks. Once we determine the direction for our curriculum to evolve, technology becomes a tool to enhance and support learning. Technology may even lead students to higher levels of learning as they use the tools to access, analyze and synthesize, and evaluate information.

Technology is also a wonderful tool to publish students' writing, which motivates and inspires them to write more. According to Graves (1999, p. 116), without this emotional attachment to learning, "lasting learning doesn't happen." Authoring with desktop publishing software enriches students' learning experiences as they create new products while using technology in constructive ways.

Teachers' Questions

1. **I am not comfortable with the Internet. How can I help my students successfully learn to use the Internet when I am uncomfortable?**

   Just like you, Barb Dykman, Judy Benns, Venetia Sims, and Connie Williams were not comfortable with the Internet. Their decision to integrate technology with literacy and social studies evolved from parents' requests that technology receive more emphasis in the curriculum. To help them accomplish their goals, they asked Dr. Martha Irwin to help them with the project.

As technology continues to rapidly advance, we must become learners among learners just like this team of teachers, who found that parents, students, and people from the community were more than willing to help them with the project. Just by showing an interest in learning more about technology, they found many people interested in helping them accomplish their goals.

The team first looked at their curriculum, the state standards, and the benchmarks to determine how they would use technology. Once they established their goals for the project and carefully aligned the project with the third grade curriculum, they were ready to begin. Using technology to create a home page became a way to enhance learning for the third graders. Parents and community members then helped them learn how to use technology to accomplish their goals.

Other ways to become more comfortable with the Internet include attending workshops and inservices related to technology or taking classes at the university. This need to know more about technology will be an ongoing process as new forms of technology continue to evolve.

2. The parents in my school are not comfortable with their children using the Internet due to safety issues. How should we proceed?

Many parents and teachers are not comfortable with young children using the Internet. Certainly, we must carefully guide and facilitate young children's use of the Internet. In today's world, there are many ways to limit use of the Internet to safe websites by using bookmarks or limiting the websites students visit through software. Certainly, these decisions should be made in the early planning stages of any project. Technology and media specialists in any school district can help facilitate these decisions. Some school districts have a technology committee comprised of parents, teachers, and administrators to help make these decisions.

Not only do we want to provide a safe learning environment, we also need to prepare our youth for living in a technological society. We do not want to marginalize their learning.

3. Are kindergarteners and first graders too young to create a home page?

Kindergarteners and first graders may be too young to help design and create a home page. However, they certainly enjoy having their writing published online. Therefore, many teachers create a home page for their classrooms, not only to publish student writing, but also as a place where teachers can easily communicate with parents. In addition, parents can view classroom projects, students' writing, or students' work in other content areas. Many teachers also use the home page as a place to share suggestions on how parents can help their children at home. When teachers and parents work together, we can accomplish even more!

4. How often should I publish students' writing pieces?

As mentioned earlier, we should be careful not to publish too frequently as this can cause burnout for both students and teachers. Setting a goal to publish one or two writing pieces per marking period is reasonable. Students who are motivated to publish more frequently can produce their work independently. Having a home page or newsletter to publish students' writing can become an exciting learning venue to support their interests.

Children's Literature

Carle, E. (1989). *Eric Carle's animals animals.* New York: Philomel Books.

References

Becker, H. (2000). Pedagogical motivations for student computer use that lead to student engagement. *Educational Technology, 40,* 5–17.

Calkins, L. (1994). *The art of teaching writing.* Portsmouth, NH: Heinemann.

Calkins, L., & Parsons, S. (2003). *Units of study for primary writing/poetry: Powerful thoughts in tiny packages.* Portsmouth, NH: Heinemann.

Castek, J., Bevans-Mangelston, J., & Goldstone, B. (2006). Reading adventures online: Five ways to introduce the new literacies of the Internet through children's literature. *The Reading Teacher, 59,* 714–727.

Clark, R. (1995). *Free to write.* Portsmouth, NH: Heinemann.

Fletcher, R., & Portalupi, J. (1998). *Craft lessons: Teaching writing K–8.* Portland, ME: Stenhouse.

Graves, D. (1983). *Writing: Teachers and children at work.* Portsmouth, NH: Heinemann.

Graves, D. (1994). *A fresh look at writing.* Portsmouth, NH: Heinemann.

Graves, D. (1999). *Bring life into learning: Create a lasting literacy.* Portsmouth, NH: Heinemann.

Henry, L. (2006). Searching for an answer: The critical role of new literacies while reading on the Internet. *The Reading Teacher, 59,* 614–627.

Leu, D., Jr. (2001). Internet project: Preparing students for new literacies in a global village. *The Reading Teacher, 54,* 568–585.

Leu, D., Jr., Kinzer, C., Coiro, J., & Cammack, D. (2004). Toward a theory of new literacies emerging from the Internet and other information and communication technologies. In R. Ruddell & N. Unrau (Eds.), *Theoretical models and processes of reading* (5th ed., pp. 1570–1613). Newark, DE: International Reading Association.

Owens, R., Hester, J., & Teale, W. (2002). Where do you want to go today? Inquiry-based learning and technology integration. *The Reading Teacher, 55,* 616–626.

Rogovin, P. (2001). *The research workshop: Bringing the world into your classroom.* Portsmouth, NH: Heinemann.

Routman, R. (2000). *Conversations.* Portsmouth, NH: Heinemann.

Routman, R. (2005). *Writing essentials.* Portsmouth, NH: Heinemann.

Sutherland-Smith, W. (2002). Weaving the literacy Web: Changes in reading from page to screen. *The Reading Teacher, 55,* 663–669.

Wepner, S., & Tao, L. (2002). From master teacher to master novice: Shifting responsibilities in technology-fused classrooms. *The Reading Teacher, 55,* 642–651.

Generating Meaning through Electronic Learning

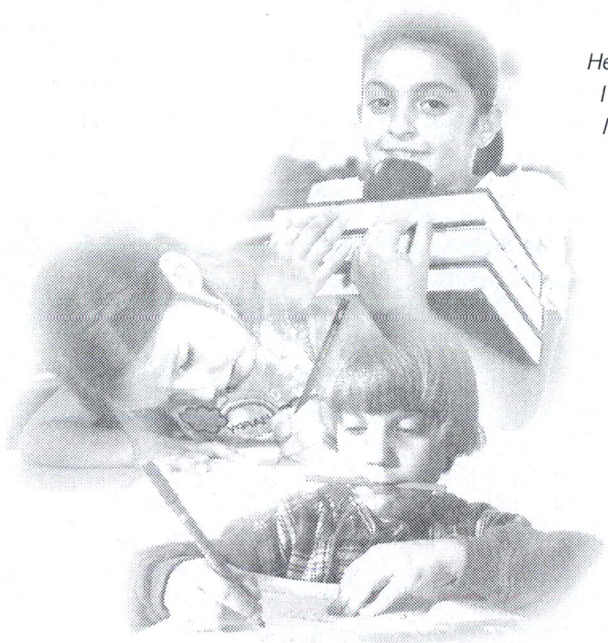

Hello Mrs. Benns,

I wanted you to know that I finished Ramona and her Mother. How did you like the part when Ramona tried to run away? I thought it was OK. I sometimes get mad at my mom and dad because I want to do something and they won't let me. I get sent to my room because of yelling but I don't run away because I wouldn't know where to go and Korea is across the world.

Today in Korean culture Camp I made a placemat for a Korean lunch we'll have on Friday. I saw a Korean dancer do a fan dance and we got to try the dance a little too.

A Joke:
Why is an elephant so wrinkled?
THINK
THINK
THINK
Because it can't fit on the ironing board!!

Bye Bye

Jennifer

This is an email, a way of sharing information over distance, that Jennifer sent to her teacher, Judy Benns. During the summer, Judy communicates with her students via email, hoping to encourage them to continue reading and writing over the summer. The informal nature of email allows Jennifer and her teacher to communicate in a dialogue format, just as one might communicate when using dialogue journals—writing that consists of students' comments about their reading and teachers' responses to their ideas (Moore, 1991; Tashlik, 1987; Wollman-Bonilla, 1989).

Using Electronic Dialogues in Literacy Learning

In viewing Jennifer's email, one sees that the "electronic journal" became a way for her to sharpen her thought processes, predictions, questions, and understandings about the book she was reading, while allowing her voice to be part of her work (Atwell, 1987; Wollman-Bonilla, 1989). Email is an exciting learning tool that enables students to communicate and exchange information across classrooms and even across the globe. Electronic learning creates a meaningful, language-rich environment where students share information, ideas, interests, collaborative projects, or questions with other students, professionals, or experts in a variety of locations.

Instructional Uses of Electronic Dialogues

Blystone (1989) claims that the real educational power of technology lies in its communicative ability—the ability to store and transmit information quickly and easily to any location at any time. Email, the process of electronically sending and receiving information over distances, offered Jennifer a real-life experience with communication and technology. As Jennifer shares her ideas, personal experiences, and information with her teacher, they are no longer constrained by the time limitations of mail.

Fostering Social Interactions between Readers and Writers. Electronic dialogues create social interactions between readers and writers that lead to a social construction of meaning (Daiute, 1985; Howie, 1989; Riel, 1989; Willis, Stephens, & Matthew, 1996). For example, Jennifer explores her understanding of the book she is reading with her teacher. Through this interactive dialogue, she negotiates meaning with Judy, finally constructing her own interpretations of the story. While constructing meaning in this social, interactive way, Jennifer becomes aware of similarities and differences in modes of interpretation. At the same time, she learns how cultural or social experiences influence meaning (Diamond & Moore, 1995; Willis et al., 1996).

Whenever she communicates through email, Jennifer simultaneously begins to develop a sense of audience and a concept of point of view (Moore, 1992). Jennifer is also learning to organize and construct coherent thoughts and ideas in a meaningful context (Daiute, 1985). Since personal appearance, physical handicaps, or special needs are invisible in the network, students who are set apart from their classmates can participate as equals (Forcier, 1996). Forcier also points out that those who are reluctant participants in classrooms often become eager contributors when they write their inquiries and responses through email.

Opening Doors for Global Communications. The capability of storing and transmitting information quickly and easily to new locations, at any time, may open new doors for global learning for Jennifer when she returns to school. For example, she can learn more about Korea by communicating with students who live in Korea through Pitsco's Keypals (www.pitsco.com/p/keypals.html), a place where students can meet others their age around the world. This website, which provides links to other keypal websites, categorizes information according to age, topics of interest, or collaborative project interest (Iannone, 1998) so that teachers can link students with keypals and still meet the goals of their curriculum. Should Jennifer's teacher decide to connect her students with keypals in Korea, Jennifer and her peers will have an opportunity to broaden their knowledge of Korea and its people as they communicate together.

As information expands at exponential rates, electronic learning offers endless opportunities to bring global resources and experiences to all learners (Forcier, 1996; Howie, 1989). Traditional barriers of social and geographic isolation disappear; interactive and cooperative exchanges emerge from all corners of the world (Howie, 1989; Solomon, 1993). While participating in these exchanges, Jennifer and her peers will become more aware of diversity and gain new knowledge that is frequently missing in textbooks. Consistent with Rief (1992), classrooms become enriched with the knowledge and experiences of others:

> We are all different—all bringing our own learning experiences and learning styles into that room. No matter what I present, each student sees it differently and takes his or her own meaning from that experience. It is this diversity that I try to foster in my classroom. I want to hear all the diverse voices of my kids. I want them to hear each other. We are all learners/teachers. (p. 3)

Accessing Current Resources in the Content Areas. Due to the speed at which information is broadcast, Jennifer and her peers can also learn how to access current resources related to information they are studying in science, math, or social studies. Through email, they can communicate directly with prominent scientists, government agents, researchers, or authors to learn more about their field of study. Then they can exchange this newly acquired information with keypals or other students in new locations. Using email to collaborate, discuss, and reflect about information enables students and teachers to become part of the larger world of scholars and scientists (Sheingold, 1991). Schools that are rural, small, or remote are able to enrich the lives and experiences of their students by accessing these resources through computer communications. According to D'Ignazio (1990), email provides a vehicle to the furthest reaches of human knowledge and imagination.

Expanding the scope of data collection also becomes possible in science or social studies. If Jennifer and her peers collaborate with classrooms across the country or world, they can compare and contrast weather, water pollution, soil composition, conservation efforts within a community, or political interests of a community. These cooperative learning projects can evolve into a communal database, which all can easily access and use to explore the relationships between phenomena. Using this data, students can then create hypermedia stacks, publish a global newsletter, or create a PowerPoint presentation to share the findings and implications with others. As a result of these combined experiences, collaborative learning moves beyond the classroom walls, creating new opportunities for literacy to grow and develop over time.

By adapting this way of viewing information within our own classrooms, our students become learners whose voices can be heard through electronic learning. As teachers, we naturally foster the values, skills, and beliefs needed to function in a global society as we engage students in authentic tasks so that they might produce genuine products under our guidance and coaching.

Using Computer Communications as Interpersonal Exchanges

Harris (1994) adapted three general categories for the use of computer communications in education. These categories include interpersonal exchanges, information gathering through inquiry, and problem-solving projects. Interpersonal exchanges, the most prevalent use of computer communications in education to date (Willis et al., 1996), offer exciting learning opportunities for students of all ages.

Educational studies consistently indicate that students are highly motivated as they negotiate meaning with others and extend their personal understandings about information or books they read through computer communications (Montoya, 1992; Moore, 1991; Riel, 1985, 1989). These studies further suggest that students' attitudes toward reading and writing become more positive and that students read and write more when they have an audience for their writing (Crim, 1995; Moore, 1991; Riel, 1989). In fact, students seem to become more motivated to improve their writing when they have a purposeful, meaningful context for practicing their writing (Honey & Henriquez, 1993; Moore, 1992; Moore-Hart, 1995; Riel, 1989).

Knowing how to organize the curriculum and the learning environment to use computer communications, however, may seem challenging. The following vignette shows how

Lynne Raglin, a fifth grade teacher, creates a purposeful, meaningful context for practicing interpersonal exchanges.

Electronic Dialogues between Fifth Graders and Teachers at the University

To provide a real-life context for interpersonal exchanges, Lynne pairs her fifth grade students with teachers taking a graduate class at a local university. Through electronic messages, the "computer pals" communicate with one another about the books the fifth graders are reading in class. During one semester, students exchange their ideas, thoughts, and feelings about the book *Superfudge,* by Judy Blume, with teachers at the university.

Similar to dialogue journals, these electronic dialogues help students gain fluency in their writing. Since students are free to concentrate on what they are saying, they can sharpen their thought processes, predictions, questions, and understandings about *Superfudge* with another teacher in a one-on-one relationship. The added use of computers further motivates students to write longer texts.

Getting Started. To help the computer pals become comfortable with one another, teachers and students begin the electronic dialogues with an informal, personal exchange about themselves. Teachers initiate the dialogue by composing a biopoem about themselves and by sharing some additional information about their hobbies, interests, or activities in paragraph form. To stimulate ongoing communications, they close their first dialogue with a question, asking their computer pal how they liked the book *Superfudge*, adding what they like about the story.

Lynne's students, who are thrilled to find messages from their computer pals, need no prompting to send their computer pals a biopoem about themselves. Courtney's biopoem is found below.

Courtney
sweet, nice, fun, likes piano
Who needs mom, dad, brothers and cat
Who loves family, friends and M.C. Hammer
Who hates war, Sadom Hussian, and dying
Who would like to see Peace, no killing animals
Courtney

Following the model of her teacher, Courtney also adds a sentence or two about her hobbies and interests. In response to her teacher's question about the book *Superfudge,* Courtney, like most of her peers, simply responds, "I like the book because it is funny."

Continuing the Dialogues. As the electronic dialogue continues between the teachers and fifth graders, teachers model the effective communication strategies they hope their computer pals will use. For example, in their second dialogue, teachers might agree that the story is funny. However, they also share which parts of the story are funny to them by referring to specific incidents in the story. When students respond to their second message, they too, share the parts of the story that are amusing to them, reflecting their computer pals' use of specific details or examples from the book. DeJuan comments, "I think Daniel is a nerd because all nerds think there [they're] tough and they talk tough. I think he is weird when he said I don't eat anything with onions and I don't eat peas or lima beans." In his response to his teacher, Michael states, "If I descriped Fudge in one word it woud be risky because he takes so many risks. My favorite part is when he plays hide and seek with Tootsie. I think my brother is a little like Fudge. He's my yougest brother. I'm really enjoying Superfudge."

In the third communication exchange, teachers begin to ask the fifth graders questions. "Who is your favorite character?" "Does Fudge remind you of someone you know or someone in your family?" "How do you suppose Fudge felt about moving?" "Why do you suppose Fudge hid his baby sister in the closet?" Again, teachers provide a model for the students by sharing their own responses to the questions, using details or events from the story to support their ideas, thoughts, or feelings. Reflecting their teachers' responses, students respond to the questions, using details and examples to support their ideas. For example, in response to "What would happen if you called your teacher rat face?" Chih Ping explains:

> I think the teacher would get angry if I called her a rat face because it would be irratating to be called a rat face. If I called a teacher a rat face my friends would say that I did a stupid thing and maybe one of my friends may say "Wow". If my parents found out that I called the teacher a rat face then I would get big trouble and they would take my allowance and they wouldn't let me go out. They wouldn't let me watch T. V. or play my computer at home. The teacher would probably get angry and send me to the office.

Teachers also sprinkle words of encouragement or praise in their responses as the dialogues continue. Tracy, for example, begins her second entry to Mistey by saying, "I am so glad that you have gotten a chance to respond to my first message. You also sound like a very nice person." Similarly, Beverly comments, "I am looking forward to getting to know you. I have a cat too. What's your cat's name?" On one response, Suzanne praises her student's writing, saying, "Akiba, you did such a nice job on your writing." When students read these messages, their self-esteem begins to increase. Before long, Lynne notices that many of her students, who typically write only one or two sentences when using paper and pencil, are beginning to write more and more sentences. Most students, in fact, expand their earlier single or double sentence responses to several sentences, or even a paragraph.

Lynne also observes that her students' understanding of *Superfudge* is enhanced as students begin making comparisons between the characters, the setting, the plot, or the events in the story to their own personal lives. Tasha, for example, explains, "If I was Peter I would not treat my brother or sister like that. I would spend more time with them. I would help them understand things." Josh understands Fudge's embarrassment at his sister, when he shares how his sister embarrasses him. "I remember the first day my mom tried to pottie train my sister. And she came out of the bathroom with all her clothes off in front of my friends. I fainted of shyness in front of all my friends." Through these social interactions, Lynne's students are beginning to discover how stories relate to our own personal experiences and to everyday living.

The teachers' model of correct language use, spelling, and vocabulary further contributes to the growth and refinement of students' communication skills. Even though no one comments about the need to spell correctly, students look for the correct spellings of words like *character, favorite,* or *interesting* within their teachers' responses whenever they write back to their computer pals. Students also begin to use their teachers' vocabulary in their own responses. Brandy spontaneously responds, for example, "I am *impressed* to see that you like the same part of the book I like."

Akiba applies keyboarding and computing skills as she communicates with her computer pal.

Just as their teachers ask them questions, some students start asking their own questions. Aisha, for example, asks, "Did you ever believe in Santa and when did you know that he was make believe?" After Janicton admits that she has read ahead of her teacher and "found out some interesting thinks [things] . . . I know you will find out sooner or later!" she changes course, saying, "So enough about Superfudge, I want to know about you. Do you like animals?"

Benefits to Students. In summary, having a purpose and an audience for their writing seems to inspire these fifth graders to write longer responses and use more examples and details to explain their ideas. Students' responses soon begin to reflect their teachers' way of communicating as they elaborate on their ideas or use details from the story to explain how they feel and why they have certain thoughts about the characters, setting, or plot. Students are never told that their ideas are too general or that their responses lack examples to support their ideas. Students acquire the ability to elaborate on their ideas and use examples to support their ideas or viewpoints by seeing a model of effective communication presented by their teachers.

Similarly, students learn about the correct spellings of words from their computer pals. They discover that the text within their teachers' responses can be a tool for finding correct spellings. Using their teachers' spelling is easier and faster than a dictionary. Students also learn new vocabulary words or new ways of expressing their ideas from their teachers' responses. They spontaneously experiment with these new language forms and patterns. Through joyful, playful experiences with language, the fifth graders increase their communication abilities.

Interestingly, having to learn keyboarding and computing skills does not inhibit their ability to communicate. As students begin to apply and use keyboarding skills, their facility with the keyboard naturally increases with practice. Using computers is motivational. In fact, students remain on-task, concentrating on the communication process while using the computer.

Electronic Dialogues in K–1 Multiage Classrooms

These joyful, playful experiences with language similarly emerge in classrooms with younger children. Michelle Fox's kindergarten and first grade students see their parents, teachers, and relatives using email all the time. Interpersonal computer exchanges are part of their daily lives and experiences. Desiring to tap into her students' natural interests in technology, Michelle decided to show her students how to use email exchanges. She believes that email might become a way to promote her young students' writing development as they send emails to their parents, friends, or teachers.

Learning to Use Email through Peer Coaching. After talking with Michaele Rae, a teacher teaching in a second–third grade multiage classroom, Michelle decides to use peer coaching to help her students acquire the skills necessary for sending emails. Specifically, Michelle pairs each of her students with a second or third grader in Michaele Rae's class. To help their students become acquainted, Michelle and Michaele begin the peer coaching process by having pairs collaboratively string colored beads together, creating necklaces or bracelets.

Once her students have an opportunity to informally work with the kindergarteners and first graders, Michaele discusses peer coaching with her second and third graders, helping them begin to think about how to help another person learn a new skill. Recording their ideas on chart paper, Michaele consistently guides the discussion, helping them distinguish between helping another student and doing the task for them. Through this interactive discussion, the second and third graders decide that they will help by first modeling the process and then by encouraging the kindergarteners and first graders to try the activities themselves. The students also determine that they will need to be patient while giving the younger students lots of time to practice the skills independently, providing assistance only as needed.

After discussing how to effectively peer coach a younger student, the second and third graders simulate the experience by practicing in twos in the computer laboratory. The following day, they implement the ideas. Specifically, they

- Show the younger students their own emails.
- Model how to click on an email and read an email.
- Allow their partners to click on an email and read the email with them.
- Model how to write and send an email to their partner, using their address book.
- Allow their partners to write and send an email to them, using the address book while guiding the process.
- Allow their partners to write and send an email to a person of choice, using the address book.

Similarly, the second and third graders follow the same process during two more sessions. Within two weeks, the kindergarteners and first graders are sending their own emails independently. Circulating among her students, Michelle and Michaele facilitate the process, reviewing and modeling as needed.

Sending Emails to Family and Friends. To specifically help her young writers experience the thrill of receiving emails, Michelle emails all her parents a few days before the class is scheduled to go to the computer lab, encouraging them to send their child an email. When Niki opens her first email from her mother, she reads

Mommy loves you.

Josh models how to send an email for David.

Niki writes back to her mother, saying

Hi!
I love you.

Daniel's dad sends him an email about the snow fort they had made together, saying that he hopes the fort would last a long time. Daniel writes back, saying

I hope so to.
Love you.

Before long, the young writers begin sending emails to one another. Gabrielle's friend, Anika, sends her the following email:

Will you be at Niki's party?
I will
Bye

Aaron sends his computer teacher an email:

I like computer class.

His teacher writes back:

Thank you for the nice compliment. I enjoy teaching computer classes.

Gaining Fluency in Reading and Writing through Email Exchanges. Through these informal writing experiences, the young writers gain more fluency in their writing as they experiment with symbols and sounds to write messages to friends, family, or teachers. Following the model of their communicators, the young students begin to extend their messages, writing more and more. They feel free to write their ideas, thoughts, and feelings, as they are comfortable using temporary spelling. (Michelle turned spell check off so that they will not become frustrated by seeing their temporary spellings highlighted in red.) At the same time, they improve their reading performance as they encounter new words they've never seen before in emails from friends, parents, or relatives. If they don't know a word, they ask their neighbors. If their neighbors don't know the word, they ask Michelle or their computer teacher. Thus, new opportunities to practice reading and writing evolve naturally in the meaningful context of interpersonal computer communications.

> ***teaching* TIP 8.1**
>
> If we want students to become comfortable using their temporary spelling, we need to turn spell check off as they draft their writing. If we don't, we will compromise their ability to record their ideas fluently and their ability to concentrate on the message.

Additional opportunities to extend students' learning emerge naturally. When their computer teacher visits Mexico, she encourages the young writers to send her emails asking her questions about Mexico. When David inquires about the cars in Mexico, Ruth Knoll sends him a picture showing cars and explains how they are different from the cars his parents and relatives drive (Figure 8.1). When Nondi asks about the houses in Mexico, Ruth sends her a picture of the houses in Mexico, sharing how the homes are different from her home. Through these playful experiences, the kindergarteners and first graders gain a glimpse of life in another country.

As the year continues, new ways to use email will evolve from students' own questions and interests. As teachers, we need to tap into the rich sources that lie within our community. Electronic dialogues are one way to facilitate this process.

Virtual Book Clubs in the Middle School

Virtual book clubs, forums for dialoguing about books through email exchanges, provide a way for students to keep in touch with others around the globe. Through these ongoing exchanges, students learn to develop reading, writing, and communication strategies and to appreciate diverse points of view (Castek, Bevans-Mangelston, & Goldstone, 2006).

Figure 8.1
Ruth Emails David a Picture of the Cars in Mexico

Wishing to increase her special education students' interest in reading, Kelly Wood, a seventh grade teacher, decided to participate in the virtual book club at the Spaghetti Book Club website (www.spaghettibookclub.com). She chose this website because students can post book reviews about books they are reading. She believes that her students will become more motivated to read when they hear about favorite books from other students. Kelly also enjoys the website as her students can exchange ideas about their favorite books.

Emily, a seventh grade special education student, wrote the following review:

Is "Report to the Principal's Office" Worth the Paper It Was Printed On?

This is one of the best books I have ever read. It made me laugh. It made me cry. It made me question my place in the Cosmos and made me wonder about my very existence. So if you are interested in reading a book this year that will have you talking for weeks on end, buy this one. You WILL LOVE IT!!!

As she read reviews by other students, Emily began to internalize the writing style to be used when writing book reviews. As seen by her own review, Spinelli's book touched her soul. Knowing her review would be published, she carefully revised and edited the review, frequently conferencing with her teacher. The experience became so motivational that Emily later wrote a second review of Spinelli's book, *Stargirl,* a book she did not enjoy.

Jerry Spinelli: When Was He at His Best?

Jerry Spinelli was at the very height of his literary career when he sat down to pen the immortal classic "Report to the Principal's Office." And, in my humble opinion was on the verge or [of] literary suicide when he dredged the pages of "Star Girl" from the dark and twisted cavern of his mind. It would be a fascinating psychological study for some young or old psychologiphiser to attempt to pry open the seemingly endless complexities of Mr. Spinelli's mind and answer the question: How could such two divergent works come from one mind?

By posting her review on the website, Emily is able to share her viewpoints with others. As readers respond to her review, she will gain new insights into the story and gain multiple perspectives about the book.

Having an audience for her writing inspires Emily, as well as her peers, to read, write, and communicate about books they are reading. The seventh graders, who prefer to write with computers, are eager to publish their reviews of books online. They also enjoy getting ideas for good books to read from students across the globe.

Using Computer Communications to Inquire about Diversity

As previously mentioned (see Chapter 5), Elaine Bortz believes that we all need to identify, clarify, and affirm the cultural heritages of students within our classroom, as well as those of people within our nation. To accomplish her goals, she integrates computer communications, which provide a tool for accessing information about other cultures, with her thematic unit on Cinderella stories.

Elaine's fifth graders begin their own inquiries about diversity by investigating their own identities and then those of their peers. As they explore information about cultures, religions, and languages, the fifth graders become more sensitive to differing beliefs and value systems across the nation and world. Gradually, a community of learners evolves among the students as they begin to share their discoveries. Through ongoing dialogue and discussion, the fifth graders see how people remain tied to one another and the world (Schiller, 1996); their dialogues help them notice that the intermingling of cultures, religions, and languages enriches our lives.

The following vignettes describe how Elaine and Mary Mansfield, a fourth grade teacher, expand the lives of their students through hypermedia technology (Diamond & Moore, 1995). Multiculturalism lays the foundation for their literacy curriculum; the use of hypermedia technology and multicultural literature provide the tools to investigate diversity.

Discovering Deeper Cultural Knowledge about Cinderella Stories with Hypermedia Technology Tools

As illustrated in Chapter 5, Elaine begins the school year by reading fairy tales and folktales about Cinderella around the world. While reading the Cinderella stories, Elaine and her students quickly encounter a need to acquire a deeper knowledge about the ways people live their lives and view the world in the Cinderella stories. Specifically, Elaine realizes a need to penetrate the thin layers of cultures and to discover the deep layers of cultures—the underlying values and beliefs that give uniqueness to ways of thinking and living. Books, resources, and materials related to cultures, however, remain limited; other resources are outdated. Having resources available to access information becomes crucial if her students are to begin to view the world through the eyes of diverse people.

Using Multicultural Links to Gather Information about Cultures. Multicultural Links, a hypermedia program created by Dr. Martha Irwin to support and enhance multicultural literature, provides quick and easy access to information about varied cultures (Irwin, Moore, & Stevenson, 1994). Consistent with other hypermedia (Liu, 1994; Swenson, Young, McGrail, Rozema, & Whitin, 2006), Multicultural Links interconnects information in such a way that a click brings information to the user in the form of graphics, sound, or text. Students and teachers are able to explore the program interactively in nonlinear ways according to their interests, motivations, curiosity, or needs. The versatility of its semantically organized formats further allows students of diverse cultural and linguistic backgrounds, varying abilities, and different learning styles to enter a learning environment compatible with their individual needs (Irwin et al., 1994; Diamond & Moore, 1995). This semantically organized network system, which parallels schema theory (Liu, 1994; Swenson et al., 2006), further supports students' integration of knowledge with preexisting knowledge.

As a resource bank of materials, Multicultural Links includes information about people throughout the world and their cultures, including maps, pictures, music, and familiar phrases from different languages. While navigating through these semantic networks, Elaine's fifth graders begin to construct their own knowledge about cultures by making connections between their own culture and the cultures of others. Access to information through graphics, sounds, images, and icons allows students to learn about geography, history, literature, biographies, and social studies according to their needs and interests. These verbal, audio, and visual elements create new contexts for reading and writing (Bolter, 1992; Schwartz, 1992; Swenson et al., 2006; Wepner & Ray, 2000). The very nature of reading, in fact, changes as students read in nonlinear ways. With hypermedia links, they can integrate new knowledge with their preexisting knowledge according to *their* interests, motivations, curiosity, or needs.

***teaching* TIP 8.2**

Hypermedia software addresses students' different learning styles. Information is displayed in text format as well as through graphics, sounds, images, and icons.

While linking multicultural literature with Multicultural Links, Elaine guides and develops her students' understanding of other peoples, cultures, ideas, and beliefs. As a cultural mediator, Elaine thoughtfully and carefully facilitates her students' knowledge development by cutting through the surface layers of cultural knowledge as her students investigate the people and their cultures themselves. Using the combined tools of multicultural literature and Multicultural Links, she continuously strives to avoid stereotypical viewpoints and misconceptions about others by engaging her students in ongoing dialogues and sensitive discussions about these concepts.

Getting Started with Multicultural Links. To help her students become acquainted with the hypermedia program, Elaine begins the school year with a demonstration of Multicultural Links, using the LCD projector. By first modeling how to access the various features of the hypermedia program, she facilitates students' independent use of the program. Following this demonstration, students begin to find information about various cultures while reading multicultural stories. For example, after reading and talking about *Mufaro's Beautiful Daughters* by John Steptoe, Elaine takes her class to Zimbabwe by clicking on Maps, the continent Africa, and the country Zimbabwe. After looking at the map and its geographical features, she models how to click on the word *More* to explore various topics about Zimbabwe, such as the flag, music, holidays, language, clothing, or housing. As Elaine and her students explore the hypermedia stacks about Zimbabwe together, they learn how to say "hello" and "how are you" in Languages; they see a picture of the soapstone bird, Zimbabwe's national symbol, and information about the carvings of the soapstone bird in Arts and Crafts; they learn about the clothing of the Zimbabwe people in Clothing; and they listen to the national anthem in Music.

Returning to the Main Menu, Elaine then models how to navigate among other topics. For example, students discover the names of other African stories such as *Who's in Rabbit's House?* or *Why Mosquitoes Buzz in People's Ears* by Verna Aardema in Books and Stories; they learn more about the lives of John Steptoe and Verna Aardema when they visit Mini-biographies; and they find out what other important events occurred on September 14, John Steptoe's birthday, while exploring Calendars.

After the demonstration, students are ready to explore the hypermedia program themselves. Since she only has one computer, Elaine encourages her students to work in pairs at the computer station. While navigating together, the pairs remind one another how to maneuver the mouse, where to click, or how to move from one hypermedia stack to the next. They also take turns reading the texts, helping one another with the pronunciation of new or unfamiliar words. When they finish, they eagerly print out a copy of their favorite screen to place in their learning logs, where they also record three things that they have learned. The fifth graders especially enjoy the freedom to browse through the stacks and select which subjects or cultures they want to investigate. Throughout, they make their own decisions according to their own interests, curiosities, or needs.

To help her monitor students who need assistance, Elaine trains three students to become her "computer experts" during a few minutes before or after school. In this way, she minimizes interruptions from students needing help. At the same time, students become empowered to solve problems themselves. Sometimes, Elaine even turns to her computer experts for assistance herself!

Elaine also displays a schedule at the computer station so that everyone has equal access to the computer. The schedule identifies who works together, their scheduled time, and the sequence of who follows whom. A smooth transition from one pair to the next follows as students quietly invite the next pair to report to the computer station once their time is up.

Integrating Multicultural Links with the Thematic Unit on Cinderella in Different Countries. Once all students have had at least two opportunities to explore Multicultural Links and to record what they have learned in their learning logs, Elaine begins integrating the hypermedia program with her thematic unit on Cinderella stories (see Chapter 5). To highlight how culture influences setting, characters, events, and themes in the stories, Elaine invites students to sign up to work in groups of four or five to investigate countries like France, China, Korea, Egypt, or Vietnam in more depth, using Multicultural Links. After gathering information about their "Cinderella Country" and placing their notes in a folder, the cooperative groups then compile the information into a booklet, which will be shared with the class.

To begin their inquiries, students first locate their Cinderella Country on the map and print out a copy of the map for their learning logs. Next, they explore the information about their country according to their individual interests, moving among the five sections of the Main Menu.

According to Elaine, students become highly motivated when they are able to choose the topics they explore. Students also enjoy collaboratively reading the texts, which is facilitated by the user-friendly computer screen that displays the text for both to easily view. Students who need help pronouncing words are no longer embarrassed to ask for help because only their partner is aware of their needs. From repeated exposure to words and phrases, most students soon learn to recognize the words independently. The fifth graders also enjoy the visual and audio formats of the texts as they listen to the spoken language or the national anthems or view children's artwork and other artifacts from their countries.

Once each pair completes their rotation at the computer station, they return to their desks and record three facts they have learned about their Cinderella Country. Before long, the log entries became longer and longer. As shown below, students add many details and facts about their country:

Vietnam

In Vietnam there are four main rivers. Their names are Hongha, Da, Mekong and Mekong Delta rivers. There are four main cities. There names are Hanoi, Haiphong, Hue and Ho Chi Minh city. You should see some of the food they eat like rice and fish. They only eat chicken, ducks and geese on special events or weddings. They love fruits and vegetables. Almost everybody knows that bamboo, soybeans, are popular. They like sweet potatoes, corn and here are some of their favorite fruits: bananas, mangos, and coconuts. In Vietnam they call soup PHO and they love to buy snacks from venders. Their religions are not like ours. Here are some of their religions: Roman Catholic, Protestent, Muslim. Their natures are clouds, trees and rivers. That's all that I can tell you about Vietnam and the rest will be for later.

The fifth graders especially look forward to sharing their log entries at the end of the day. Elaine finds that providing time to share is motivational and encourages students to elaborate their writing by adding more details and examples in their log entries. As their peers share their entries, students learn more about each culture and spontaneously begin to perceive similarities and differences among the cultures. This knowledge also helps them perceive the linkages between cultures and settings, characters, events, or themes of the Cinderella tales. Before long, students begin to understand that many of the themes reflect the beliefs and values of the people.

Once everyone has at least two opportunities to explore their country, each group meets to decide which topics they will investigate for their books. As pairs return to the computer station, they interactively read the information about their topic together and print a copy of the screen to place in their folders. They also continue to write in their learning logs. Interestingly, some students begin to use drawings and labels in their logs; others create lists of information or use examples to illustrate a point. Through these spontaneous responses, they are learning how to read and write about content-related texts and how organizational features facilitate understanding of the texts.

Learning How to Access Information and Paraphrase Information. To help her students learn to paraphrase information and to prevent any students from plagiarizing text, Elaine models how to paraphrase information during a minilesson. With an overhead slide of text about Italy, she begins her minilesson by having volunteers read the text aloud. After reading the text, she leads the class in a discussion about the ideas within the text. Next, she removes the text and replaces it with a blank overhead transparency, asking students to think about ways to tell about the information they have just read. After listening to various students share, she begins to record their sentences on the transparency. "Let's see . . . Alex shared . . . Italy, a peninsula in the continent of Europe, is a small country . . . Vanghai told us . . . Rome is the capital." Soon a new version of the text evolves; students see how they can paraphrase words and create their own version of the text. They also discover that their way of expressing information may be more interesting than the author's.

On the following day, Elaine gives her students an opportunity to apply the process with their own topics. After students read their selection silently, she encourages them to think about the important ideas and to underline the ideas with a colored marker, just as one highlights texts. Next, she asks them to turn their papers over and restate the ideas in their own words, forming a paragraph. Once they are finished, students eagerly share their paragraphs with one another.

Using the Writing Process to Create Informational Writing Pieces for the Cinderella Country. To complete the process, students revise and edit their drafts, using the word processor. Working in their cooperative groups, students share their drafts with their peers. As modeled earlier, the fifth graders give one another praise and then ask questions about the information, showing where there is a need for clarification, description, or expansion of ideas. Next, they edit the revised texts in pairs.

Throughout the process, Elaine coaches and guides her students by probing, offering helpful hints or cues, or modeling the art of praising and questioning. During the process, she shares that she has yet to come across a student who isn't extremely interested in using word processing tools, even if they have limited keyboarding skills. Her observations are affirmed by her students' comments. "It is easy to correct your mistakes; you don't have to erase." "The computer helps me with my spelling and makes my work look neat." Word processing tools eliminate the need to recopy their writing; students merely insert, delete, or cut and paste information when revising and editing.

Knowing that their writing pieces will be published in the Cinderella Book motivates students to revise and edit their writing more carefully. They want to make sure that their pieces are error-free. Creating illustrations to accompany the texts is challenging and motivational, too. As a final step, the group decides on a title for their book and prepares an author's page where everyone shares something about their country and their feelings about studying the country. The books are then bound and published. An example of Alex's writing is shown below.

Chinese Languages

The main language of China is "Putonghua" (Standard Chinese or Mandarin.) It is based on the language that is taught in the school. Other languages are Cantonese, Shangainese, Fujjanece, and Hakka. Chinese is the only modern language that is written entirely in ideographs. In the pinyin system letters are pronounced as they would be in America. The pinya system has been used in street signs and commrical [commercial] signs and in elementary Chinese books.

Discovering Deeper Cultural Knowledge about Japan and China with Hypermedia Technology Tools

Mary Manchester, a fourth grade teacher, also uses Multicultural Links to increase her students' background knowledge about China and Japan as they read a variety of stories from the two cultures (Diamond & Moore, 1995). For example, when reading *Sadako and the Thousand Paper Cranes* by Coerr, the fourth graders use Multicultural Links to gather information about the Japanese culture.

Using Multicultural Links to Gain Cultural Knowledge about Japan. As the fourth graders explore the map of Japan, they quickly recognize the cities of Nagasaki and Hiroshima from the story. When they explore the hypermedia stacks about Japan's housing, arts and crafts, holidays, and religions, they begin to understand the lifestyles of Sadako and her family more easily. Whenever they encounter references to bed quilts, tatami mats, and the celebration of Peace Day, students are able to relate to these cultural concepts more easily. For example, viewing tatami mats or reading about the celebration of Peace Day under Holidays clarifies their questions about these cultural traditions.

Students' interest in learning about Japan and its people is shown by Katie's learning log entry.

Arts and Crafts

In Japan, there are many different art and crafts. Japanese deep love of nature is found in literature and art. An important art in Japan is sculpture. Many temples were decorated with Buddhism figures. Chinese influenced Japanese painting. Flower arranging or Ikabana has a formal set of rules and can be studied in over twenty Ikebana schools. Bonsai is at least 1,000 years old. Bonsai is the art of raising miniate [miniature] trees in pots which makes scenes of nature.

As a culminating project, Mary invites her fourth graders to create informational books about Japan, following the process described above. In her class, students choose three topics about Japan to investigate and write about in their own informational book about Japan. An example of Jason's work is displayed here:

Japanese Languages

Japanese is the main language is Japan. You can go right to left and top to bottom to read in Japanese. There are many dialects but educated people speak Tokyo dialect. When you read a book in Japan, you read it right to left and top to bottom. Nihon is the Japanese word for Japan. There are two charters [characters] in Nihon (shown on cover). "Sun" is the top charter [character] and "origin" is the bottom charter. English letters can also be used to communicate in Japan. Japan is often called "The land of the rising sun."

Since this is their first time using the word processor, Mary only asks the fourth graders to type the author page. The remaining pages are written by hand. Nicole's page is found below:

After reading and studying about Japan, I have learned a lot. I have chosen to write about Japan's geography, languages and arts and crafts. I hope you enjoy my book.

Using Multicultural Links to Gain Cultural Knowledge about China. After reading the stories related to the Japanese culture, Mary introduces her class to the Chinese culture through Multicultural Links. This enables her to build background knowledge for the story *In the Year of the Boar and Jackie Robinson* by Lord. As the fourth graders gather information about Chinese culture, students continue to record what they are learning in their learning logs. Similar to Elaine's class, the fourth graders enjoy sharing their log entries with one another at the end of the day. To reinforce the cultural features of the story, such as the misunderstanding related to Shirley's age (Chinese people consider their children to be 1 year old at birth), Mary elaborates on these features when students share information from their log entries.

Other stories the class reads include *The Five Chinese Brothers* by Bishop, *The Empty Pot* and *Liang and the Magic Paintbrush* by Demi, *Yeh-shen: A Cinderella Story from China* by Louie, *Chasing the Moon to China* by McLean, *The Enchanted Tapestry* by San Souci, *Lion Dancer: Ernie Wan's Chinese New Year* by Waters, or *Lon Po Po: A Red-Riding Hood Story from China* by Young. As Mary reads these stories from Chinese culture aloud to her students, they remember the cultural and factual information from their learning logs. For example, while reading *Chasing the Moon to China* and seeing the picture of the Great Wall, students remember Antone's log entry about the Great Wall of China.

In order that fourth graders move beyond surface features of the Asian culture to its deeper layers, Mary then encourages her students to complete Venn diagrams about a specific topic within both the Japanese and Chinese cultures. As Roman completes the inner portion of his diagram, he learns that both the Chinese and Japanese play basketball, soccer, and volleyball (see Figure 8.2). Specifically, he discovers that the Japanese participate in sumo wrestling, racing miniature sail boats and model airplanes, and sightseeing. Some of their hobbies include weaving, knitting, quilting, and ceramic art. The Chinese, however, participate in calisthenics, badminton, ping-pong, swimming, and shadow boxing. Some of their hobbies include playing cards, chess, or flying kites.

Gradually, the fourth graders discover that there are many similarities and differences between the Japanese and Chinese cultures. They also find out there are many similarities and differences between themselves and the Japanese and Chinese cultures.

As a culminating experience, Mary invites her fourth graders to create a biopoem about China or Japan. Using their learning logs and copies of printed screens from Multicultural

Links, students insert cultural information about their chosen country within the poem. Daniel's poem is displayed below:

Biopoem
Name: China
Country: Asia
Big, Crowded, warm, pretty
Who produces iron, steel, coal and textiles
Who needs more schools, money, and freedom
Where people live, fly kites, play ping pong and soccer
Where I can see the Great Wall of China and the Forbidden City
Another name for this country: The Kite Flying Country

Using Hypermedia Software to Heighten Cultural Knowledge. The combined culture-based projects heighten students' understanding and knowledge about diverse countries as they question, access, negotiate, and interact with their peers. Using computer communications, students participate in purposeful and meaningful reading and writing experiences while gathering information from computer sources. Through this process, they also link their personal and cultural experiences with new subject matter.

Consistent with research studies (Au, 1993, 1995; Cummins, 1986; Moore-Hart, Knapp, & Diamond, 2003), Mary and Elaine increase literacy learning of all students by incorporating language and culture into the curriculum. The two teachers foster the emergence of a socioculturally sensitive environment as students and teachers inquire about their own cultural traditions and histories and those of others. Not only do electronic communications erase the boundaries of time and space, they enhance multiple ways of knowing and living in a global community.

When students share what they have learned at the end of the year, their responses illustrate their knowledge about these multiple ways of knowing and living. In their words,

Figure 8.2
Roman's Venn Diagram about Japanese and Chinese Hobbies

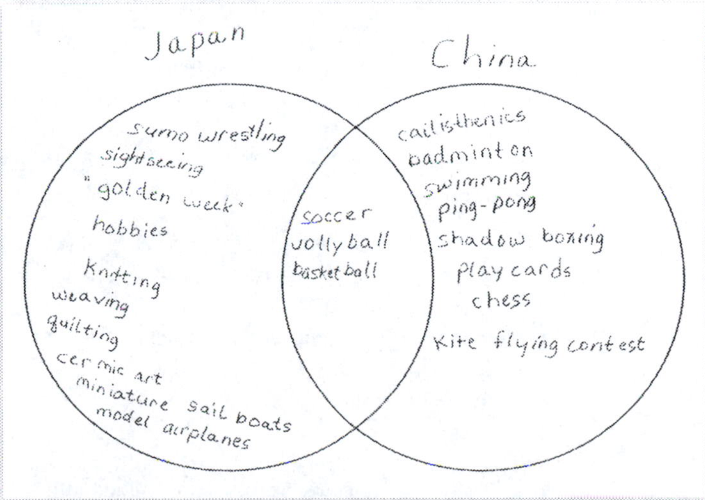

these multiple computer communications help them "experience other people's cultures," as shown in the following examples.

- I learned all about the United States, countries, and cultures of people.
- I learned that the people in Swaziland have poor medication and that people die because they don't have many doctors.
- I learned about the types of transportation people use in China. Most people in China ride bikes.
- I learned how Japanese people eat and live. I learned how African people dress and the colors of their flag.
- I loved reading about African-American inventors. It helps me learn how things were back then; it also showed that blacks were smart and educated.
- I have learned a lot this year; I would like other students to have the same opportunity.

Extending Multicultural Learning Experiences through Hypermedia Software

These multicultural experiences can be extended through other hypermedia and multimedia software as well. Wiggleworks by Scholastic, for example, uses multimedia formats so that students can read, write, take notes, and manipulate texts from various cultures. Through multimedia profiles, for example, students encounter culturally diverse mentors and authors in the workplace or hear music and songs from people around the world. Latino students also have the chance to read, write, and manipulate texts in Spanish, since the program is available in Spanish. Other possibilities for accessing information are available through multimedia software: Compton's Multimedia Encyclopedia, World Book Encyclopedia, Webster's Exploring Nature, or World Atlas (Edwards, 1999).

Multicultural experiences can be expanded through other uses of technology as well. Opportunities for students to find out about themselves and others, to inform, and to tell their stories can evolve through email or the Internet. Students reap the benefits of a multicultural heritage when their teachers operate as cultural mediators, guiding the growth of their students' cultural knowledge.

Teachers Becoming Technology Mediators

Just as we must become cultural mediators, we must also become technology mediators. We must guide and facilitate students' use of technology. When we follow a process approach, our students improve and learn every day. Alan adds that he has learned different techniques on the computer, "like how to load different programs, how to print and to settle the printer. . . . I had lots of fun." Alan's peers have also learned about computers and word processing during the year. The following list depicts what they've learned and why they like computers and word processing:

- It's always ready to use (unlike paper and pencil).
- You can use the keyboard rather than a pencil to write.
- It's easy to use.
- You can use different writing styles.
- You can make letters big or small.
- Typing is very helpful and it saves time.
- It's easy to correct your mistakes; you don't have to erase.
- The computer helps me with my spelling and makes my work look neater.
- You can put files onto a disk and save them.
- It helps you publish your stories and reports.

One can easily see that these students are, in the words of their teacher, "so 'literate' in using the computer, much more than I am." Elaine further adds, "There is no intimidation on their part." The children further feel that "working on the computer was an educational experience." In fact, they hope they can learn more about the computer next year. Hopefully, they and others will continue to have more educational experiences with technology. Once we start, our students energize us to discover new ways to integrate technology with the language arts curriculum.

Using the Internet to Gather Information about Animals

Introducing Students to the Internet

Wishing to create educational learning experiences for her students on the Internet, Kelly Newton takes her third graders on a virtual tour of the San Diego Zoo. Using the LCD projector, Kelly begins the virtual tour at the gates of the zoo. She invites her students to determine where they want to go first. Kelly is not surprised to find that her students select the Monkey Trail first.

Visiting the Monkey Trails on the Internet. After clicking on this exhibit, Kelly lets them visually experience the Monkey Trails by clicking on the Photo and Video Bytes of the mandrill monkey. After enjoying the playful habits of the mandrills, the students are ready to learn more. To help them learn about the mandrills' habitat, Kelly leads them to the map, displayed at the top of the website, where they discover that mandrills live in the western region of Africa in the rain forest.

Then she begins reading about the mandrill as her third graders follow the text on the screen. The students become quickly engaged in learning due to the reader-friendly writing style, which includes interesting facts and information. For example, everyone laughs when they read and view the image of the mandrills who "shake their heads and 'grin' widely as they show their enormous canine teeth, which can be over 2 inches or 5 centimeters long. This may appear scary to us, but it's usually a friendly gesture within the mandrill community" (www.sandiegozoo.org/animalbytes/t-mandrill.html).

Kelly also shows her students how they can easily gather information about the mandrill from Quick Facts and Fun Facts. Encouraging more active participation in the read aloud session, she then invites students to read information about the mandrill's weight, tail length, or weight at birth. The third graders also enjoy taking turns to read the fun facts about the mandrills.

To conclude the virtual tour, Kelly visits the Kid Territory, which includes a story about PJ, a mandrill living with two female companions at the San Diego Zoo. As students listen to the story, they learn about PJ's lifestyle, which includes room service, two gorgeous companions, and a large, spacious home at the zoo.

Visiting the Giant Panda Research Station and the Polar Bear Plunge on the Internet. During the next few days, Kelly and her third graders continue their virtual tour of the San Diego Zoo. Each day the class votes to determine where they will go. When they visit the Giant Panda Research Station, they even get to hear the bleats of the panda bear while viewing Video and Photo Bytes. After viewing videos and photos, the class continues their virtual tour, learning more about China's national treasure, the beloved panda bear. They conclude the tour by visiting the weblogs, also called "blogs," written by the Giant Panda Team, where they learn more about the panda bears living in San Diego Zoo. They also enjoy hearing a story about Panda Pita Pockets.

On the third day of their virtual tour, the third graders enjoy watching the Polar Cam live from the San Diego Zoo, as well as the Video and Photo Bytes. After learning about the polar bear, the tour seems to come alive when they take a self-guided Zoofari Audio Tour to discover how polar bears "keep their cool" in the San Diego Zoo.

Third Graders Use the Internet to Pursue Their Own Inquiries about Animals

After building background knowledge about the Internet, Kelly invites her third graders to pursue their own inquiries about animals of their choice. Similar to Elaine, Kelly allows students to explore the San Diego Zoo in pairs at her computer stations. (She is lucky enough to have three computers in her classroom.) Having seen the process modeled, the third graders easily navigate the website in pairs. If they experience any difficulties or challenges, Kelly also uses "computer experts" to help them solve the problems. After exploring the zoo in pairs, the third graders print out favorite pages and record three facts they have learned about an animal in their logs.

Following these explorations, Kelly has each third grader select a favorite animal to investigate in depth. To help them learn how to gather notes and paraphrase information (see Figure 8.3), Kelly models the process during two minilessons. To help her students in gathering specific information about the animal, she has them record the information on a web, which helps them draft paragraphs about their animal.

Following the writing process, the third graders then revise and edit the paragraphs about their favorite animals. Sian's paragraph is displayed below:

The giant panda is related to the raccoon. They eat like 16 out of every 24 hours. They even eat more than 80 pounds a day! The giant panda has 1 baby. Pandas live in west central china. Pandas are 6 feet tall. When the baby is born it has to be born on August or September. They are very rare Animals. I like learning about Animals! Learning is fun.

Figure 8.3

Animal Notetaking Chart

Animal Notetaking Chart

Characteristics	Habitat
Food	Predators
Prey	Interesting Information

To help her students "enjoy" revising, which they initially resist, Kelly gives her third graders purple pens to use. Since they always use pencils when writing their drafts, Kelly explains they may enjoy revising with a purple pen. She also helps her students understand that we often forget to include information or leave out words by accident on our first drafts. Revising, she adds, gives us the chance to insert the missing information or words.

Her third graders then use red pens to circle words they want to know how to spell and to insert punctuation or capital letters wherever needed. Even though the drafts are not perfect, her students are beginning to learn how to edit their work independently as they self-edit and peer edit their work.

After assessing her third graders' paragraphs, Kelly notices that her students write using very basic sentences. Since this was their first time to follow the writing process, she did not pursue this as they revised. When they apply these skills in another writing piece, however, she plans to include minilessons on using more complex sentences and more descriptive words. Kelly realizes that we need to focus on only one or two points in our minilessons. Her goals for her students are to access information about an animal, paraphrase the information, and record a paragraph about the animal. The more her students write, the more they will learn about shaping their writing during the revision stages. Similarly, the more they edit, the more skilled they will become in finding more of their errors. Focusing on too many elements of revising and editing at once can become overwhelming to students, which may inhibit their ability to convey their ideas.

Using the Internet with the Inquiry Process

Building on her sixth graders' natural interest in animals, Marcia Gelpie similarly creates opportunities for her students to experience technology and its tools as they use the inquiry process to learn about endangered species. Since her students have had some experiences navigating the Internet, Marcia decides to broaden their experiences so they will become more familiar with selecting appropriate websites for their inquiries.

Under the watchful eyes of librarians, Marcia feels that her students access fairly reliable sources (i.e., books, newspapers, encyclopedias) in their inquiries. When using the Internet, however, a huge buffet of information is available, but an amazing amount is inaccurate or biased. As a result, there is a need to analyze and evaluate webpages to determine the reliability of the information (Patterson, 2003; Swenson et al., 2006; Willhelm, 2004).

Initial Experiences with Analyzing and Evaluating Internet Sources

To help her sixth graders begin to analyze and evaluate Internet sources, she begins her sequence of lessons with a minilesson on website evaluation, using ideas from Interactive Demonstrations (http://writing.colostate.edu/demos) and ReadWriteThink (www.readwritethink.org/lessons/lesson_view.asp?id=328). First, she asks her students to list characteristics of Web resources that might be effective on a sheet of paper. After about 5 minutes, she suggests that they share their ideas with a partner, adding or deleting ideas from their lists. After a few minutes, Marcia invites students to share their ideas with the class as she records the information on chart paper. Some of the ideas the sixth graders determine include

- Qualifications of the author.
- Accuracy of information.
- Date of information on website.
- Purpose of the website (advertisement versus educational sources).

To extend their thinking to new levels, Marcia begins to ask her students additional questions, encouraging them to also think of their own questions as well. Together they create a list of questions to help them consider the reliability of the source.

- How can you tell who is the author of a website?
- Is there information about the author? Can you contact the author?
- Does the author provide a list of sources of information? Is the information consistent with other print sources of information?
- How can you tell who publishes the information? What are the differences among .com, .edu, .org, .gov, and .net sites?
- How can you tell who the intended audience of the website may be? Is this a site created for commercial purposes; a site devoted to a particular political cause; or a site developed by a particular organization, educational agency, or government agency?
- Does the publisher have a particular bias?
- How can you tell what the purpose of the site is? What types of websites do we want to access for our inquiries?
- Why does the date of information on the site matter? What does it mean if you find technical issues like broken links?

Through interactive questioning and dialoguing, Marcia helps all her students begin to view information more critically. They begin to realize that some websites are designed for commercial purposes; others are created by individuals who present information that may be inaccurate or biased; still others are developed by organizations or institutions that have established reputations in the field. Through this process, her sixth graders start to realize that we must carefully evaluate our sources if we want to access accurate information.

Critically Analyzing and Evaluating Two Websites. Continuing with her lesson the following day, Marcia distributes an evaluation form (see Figure 8.4) for her students to use as they visit two websites:

Figure 8.4

Website Evaluation Form

Website Evaluation Form

Website: ______________________

Evaluated By: ______________________

1. **Author's Qualifications:** Who is the author of the webpage? Is the person qualified or an authority on the topic? Why did the author publish the information?
2. **Purpose of Webpage:** Who is the publisher of the site? What is the goal of the site? Is the information accurate? Is the presentation of the information unbiased?
3. **Audience:** Who is the intended audience for the webpage? Are you part of this audience? Is the audience appropriate for you as an investigator of information?
4. **Publication:** When was this site published or updated? Is the information current? Are the links up to date? Are all technical aspects of the site up to date?
5. **Overall:** What is your overall opinion about this site? Would you recommend this site to others? Why or why not?

Source: Adapted from Read Write Think (www.readwritethink.org/lessons/lesson_view.asp?id=328)

The UNICEF Website: Information by Country (www.unicef.org/infobycountry/index.html) This website, which is produced by a well-known organization, provides a resource model that is reliable because the publisher is an authority on children around the world.

Flags of All Countries (www.theodora.com/flags) This website uses advertising and dated information. In addition, the site's connection to a company that sells immigration software also raises questions. This site provides a model of a resource that is questionable.

Working in twos, the sixth graders complete the evaluation forms. Next the class discusses what they have learned as they critically view the websites; they compare and contrast their responses on the forms, seeing several viewpoints expressed about the websites.

Applying Analysis and Evaluation Strategies. The following day, students begin to explore websites for endangered species. Working in twos, they use the evaluation forms to critically analyze the sources. If the pair decides that a source can be recommended to others in the class, they post the website on chart paper for all to view.

After completing these activities, Marcia's sixth graders revisit their original list of characteristics for useful resources. They revise the list to include these ideas:

- Qualifications of the author.
- Qualifications of the publisher of the website.
- Audience for website.
- Accuracy of information.
- Presentation of information (biased or unbiased).
- Relevance of information (current or outdated).
- Date of information on website.
- Purpose of the website (advertisement versus educational sources).
- Technical aspects of website.

Using the Internet to Pursue Inquiries about Endangered Species: A Process Approach

Marcia now feels her students are ready to begin their own inquiries. Knowing that many of her students will also explore additional websites at home on their computers, she feels they will be able to access more reliable sources by applying these strategies with their inquiries.

Using Brainstorming to Identify Endangered Species to Investigate. To help her sixth graders identify animals they want to investigate, Marcia encourages her students to brainstorm examples of animals who are endangered. Similar to many teachers, Marcia begins the brainstorming session by having students create a list of endangered animals they might want to investigate. After a few minutes, Marcia invites students to share two examples from their list, while encouraging others to add to their lists if they hear an example they might enjoy studying. In addition to gathering ideas for their inquiries, this brainstorming activity stimulates excitement and interest in the focused inquiry. After the sixth graders place a star next to their favorite example, they are ready to begin their inquiries. To encourage her students to use multiple sources for their inquiries, she asks all students to access at least two websites. However, she challenges them to try and access three websites for their information.

Gathering Information about Endangered Species. Similar to Kelly and Elaine, Marcia encourages her students to work in twos at the computer station. This way, students can help and support one another as they locate websites, read about endangered species, and determine what information they may need to print out for their learning logs.

The first day, students explore websites and determine which websites they will use. Following the model of their teacher on the chart paper, they record their sources in their learning logs. They also record at least three things they learn about their endangered species. Phillipe becomes so intrigued by his topic that he records eight facts in his log.

Fascinating Facts about Penguins

1. Penguins are born in eggs.
2. Penguin babies live in warmer places than adults.
3. Penguins can't fly.
4. There are 17 kinds of penguins.
5. Penguins are expert swimmers.
6. Penguins eat fish.
7. Penguins live in the Arctic and New Zealand.
8. Penguins have dotted eggs.

When students return to the computer station a second time, they continue reading the information about the endangered species with their partner; they also begin recording information about their species, using words and paraphrases, on a chart form designed to facilitate notetaking (see Figure 8.3 on page 230). To maximize time on the computer, students spend time reading the information and talking about the information at the computer station. Then they print out sheets with the required information about their species and complete their forms independently at their desks. This way, all students receive support from their partners while reading the text. Talking about the ideas in pairs further reinforces comprehension of the information, especially as they locate relevant information about the endangered species.

Modeling How to Shape the Writing. Following these prewriting activities, students begin writing their first drafts about the animals. Marcia then looks over the drafts and determines that her students need to improve their leads and endings in their writing.

To help her students improve their ability to craft leads, Marcia models ways to create leads through a minilesson. She begins with a brainstorming session about leads, asking her students to think about ways authors seize their attention at the beginning of a story. As her sixth graders describe methods various authors use, Marcia forms a list of their ideas.

Next, she invites the students to listen to the leads authors use in informational books, encouraging them to think about what the author does to grab their attention and interest in the story. For example, she starts by reading Dee Stuart's lead in *The Astonishing Armadillo* (p. 5): "Slowly, slowly, for the past 150 years, a small army has trundled steadily northward from Mexico. In 1854 the army crossed the Mexican border and invaded Texas. . . . These astonishing creatures were nine-banded armadillos." After listening, Luca exclaims that she likes the way the author creates a mystery for the reader. We want to know what the army is.

Continuing with another example, Marcia reads the lead from *Into the Sea* by Brenda Guiberson: "Tap, tap. Scritch. The tiny sea turtle is the last hatchling to break out of her leathery egg and crawl up the sides of a sandy nest. She is not much bigger than a bottle cap." Liam explains that this lead caught his attention because the author uses sense words and created a setting for the tiny sea turtle.

After listening to several leads, Marcia encourages her students to revisit their list and add more ideas for beginning a writing piece. After revising their list, the sixth graders decide that authors

- *Fashion a picture* of a person, place, thing, or event by describing it in detail.
- *Use sense words* to help the reader see, hear, taste, feel, and smell the person, place, thing, or event.
- *Create a mystery* about the topic by giving bits of information while leaving out other pieces of information.
- *Begin with a startling or unusual piece of information* about the topic.
- *Craft a scene or setting for the topic,* inviting the reader into the topic.
- *Compare the topic* to a person, place, thing, time, or event.
- *Begin with a big or important event* related to the topic.
- *Invite the reader to start predicting* information about the topic by giving the reader hints.

By recording their ideas and posting the chart for all to see, Marcia hopes her students will try one of these techniques in their own writing.

Following this same format, Marcia also helps her students consider alternative ways to conclude their writing pieces about the endangered species. Using actual examples of conclusions from informational literature provides her students a model to consider for their own writing.

As they revise their leads and endings, the sixth graders then begin to apply these techniques. Justin tries to create a mystery about his topic when he revises his lead: "It's a duck! NO! It's a plane! Nope! It's a bird that cannot fly! What is it? It's a penguin." Luca revised her beginning to include a question that sparks interest in her topic.

Wonderful White Polar Bears

Did you know there are many different names for a polar bear? Like the ice bear, or the great white bear, or "sea bear?"

Let me tell you a bunch of facts about the polar bear and its delicious food, cute babies, and cold shelter.

First of all, we live in houses, but polar bears live on seashores of the Arctic. Polar bears' shelter changes all the time, so they move a lot. Some polar bears live under the slushy snow. Under the snow there are chambers, one for the cubs and one for the mom. Some dens have a lower chamber, kind of like a basement.

Next, polar bears have one cute, furry baby at a time because they are mammals like us. Polar bear babies don't eat solid food until they leave the den. Some polar bears live for 25 years, some can grow older.

Last, we eat seal cooked, but polar bears eat seals raw. That is tasty for them, but not for us. Yuck! A polar bear sometimes waits about four hours waiting for the seal to come up the hole. Then it snatches the seal with its humungous jaws. Polar bears would eat penguins, but they can't find them because they live in Antarctica. Polar bears also have predators, like us.

That is my story of the fantastic polar bear and its shelter, food, and babies.

Luca's writing also shows how the models of literature influence her writing style. For example, she uses comparisons to help the reader picture what she is describing. She explains that the chambers are kind of like a basement and shows how the polar bear is similar to humans as we both eat seals, even though humans prefer theirs cooked. Luca also incorporates interesting describing words throughout her piece—"slushy snow," "delicious food," "humungous jaws," or "fantastic polar bear."

By carrying their writing through all the stages, the sixth graders learn how to shape and craft their writing. Marcia is pleased to note that her students are learning to "ask their peers thoughtful questions." Even though they are talkative at times, she further reports, "They are on task." However, learning to ask questions takes time to develop. Just as the more students write, the more their writing improves; the more students participate in revising groups, the more their questioning improves.

Of course, the sixth graders especially enjoy using word processing tools to publish their writing. Happily, Marcia no longer hears groans and moans when they write; now she "sees a group of smiling faces, excited about writing!"

Publishing Multimodal Texts with Inquiry Projects. To help her students realize that we can convey information about topics in other genres, as well as expository texts, Marcia also challenges her students to create "If I Were" poems about their endangered species. After sharing a variety of ways her previous class used poetry to write about their endangered species, her students use their notes and learning logs to compose poems. Trevor, who also investigated polar bears, wrote the following poem:

If I Were A . . .

If I were a pale white polar bear I would give birth to my stupendous cubs
Have up to three little cubs at a time
Have a thick layer of fat called blubber
To keep me as hot as a desert in the Arctic
Run 35 miles an hour to catch my prey that are as fast as lightening
Slip, slip, slip, slip as I walked across the freezing ice
But I wouldn't put myself on the slippery ice and toboggan
Because that's what penguins in "tuxedos" do!

Using the Internet to Write Advice Columns about Animals

Erin Minnis adds a spark of humor to inquiry with her fourth graders. Using the book *Dear Mr. Blueberry* by Simon James, Erin integrates science, literature, and writing to help her students learn specific information about various animals. After reading the comical story, Erin reviews the format of a friendly letter with her students. In particular, she emphasizes the greeting and closing for a friendly letter and its appropriate punctuation marks.

Next, she encourages her fourth graders to write down the names of three animals they might like to investigate. After they jot down a list, Erin has them place a star next to their favorite animal. Using a list format, the fourth graders continue their prewriting activities by recording three or four reasons they would like to have this animal for a pet. After moving through these prewriting activities, the students begin drafting their letters. Using the model of letters from Emily in *Dear Mr. Blueberry,* Logan composes the letter shown in Figure 8.5.

Next, Erin permits her students to choose partners for their inquiries. Together, the partners decide how they will research their animals and how they will give one another

Figure 8.5

Logan's Letter to Her "Pet Pal"

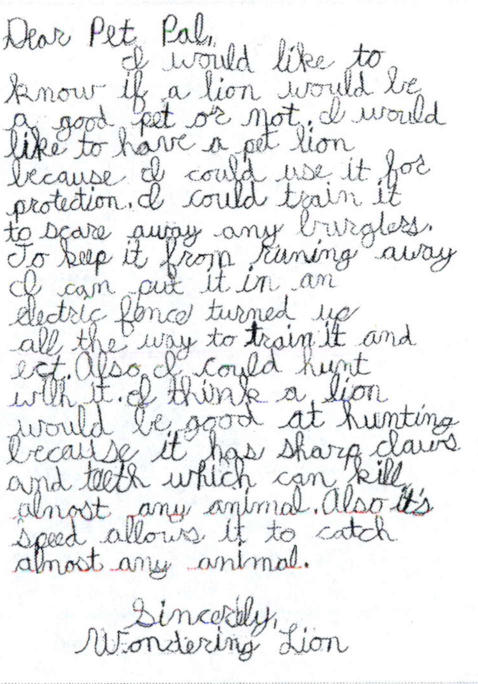

Dear Pet Pal,
I would like to know if a lion would be a good pet or not. I would like to have a pet lion because I could use it for protection. I could train it to scare away any burglers. To keep it from runing away I can put it in an electric fence turned up all the way to train it and ect. Also I could hunt with it. I think a lion would be good at hunting because it has sharp claws and teeth which can kill almost any animal. Also it's speed allows it to catch almost any animal.

Sincerely,
Wondering Lion

advice about having the particular animal for a pet. To research the animal, the fourth graders use the Internet for their inquiry. Since they have used the Internet several times during the year, they understand the process to follow. Using notetaking strategies, the students first gather information about the animal. Because their partners have identified problems and questions, the fourth graders are able to focus their inquiry more easily as they have specific questions to research.

teaching TIP 8.3

Students learn to consider the audience in their writing when they have opportunities to write for a variety of audiences.

Once they collect the information for their letters, Erin rereads examples of Mr. Blueberry's responses to Emily. As she rereads, students realize that Mr. Blueberry does not simply write an answer, but provides background information to explain his response. Following this model, Logan's partner writes the advice shown in Figure 8.6.

Erin and her students particularly enjoy this different approach to inquiry as it allows students to be creative in their research. In particular, students delight in having a choice in their inquiries. This, Erin observes, helps her students remain engaged, interested, and on-task throughout the process. Having a different audience than the teacher or parents also seemed to inspire the fourth graders.

Using the Internet to Investigate a Historical Time Period

Wishing to pique her seventh graders' interest in the Renaissance period, Kellie Wood, a special education teacher, integrates the Internet with her thematic unit. She believes that accessing information about the Renaissance era through graphics, sound, images, and icons matches the diverse learning styles within her classroom. Rather than memorizing lifeless facts, her students might access artifacts from this historical period by reaching outside of the classroom and immersing themselves in virtual learning experiences on the Internet.

Figure 8.6

Logan's Partner Responds to Her Request about a Pet Lion

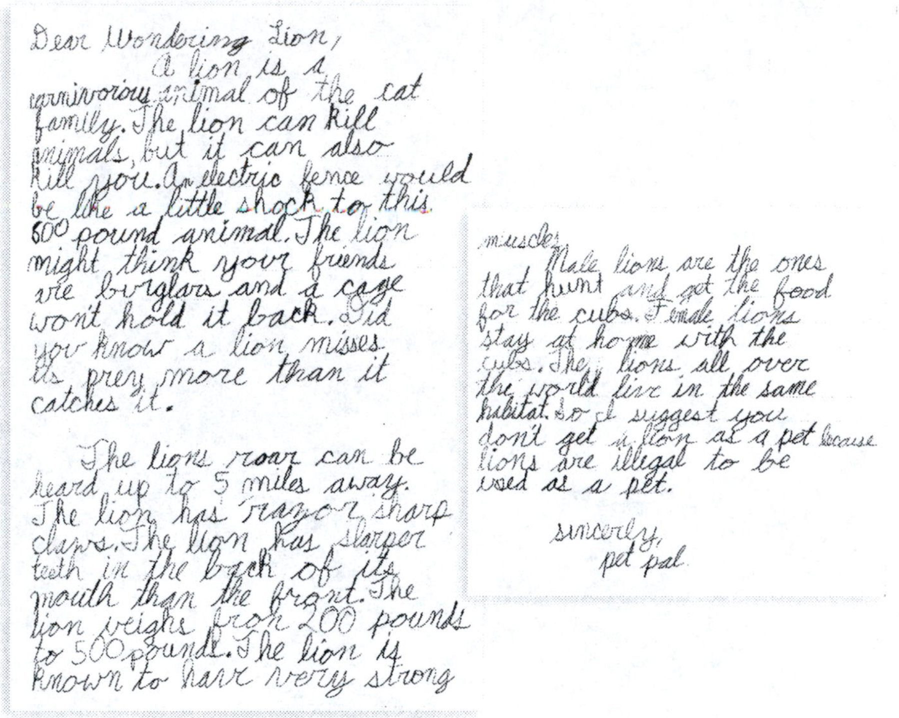

Dear Wondering Lion,

A lion is a carnivorous animal of the cat family. The lion can kill animals, but it can also kill you. An electric fence would be like a little shock to this 500 pound animal. The lion might think your friends are burglars and a cage won't hold it back. Did you know a lion misses its prey more than it catches it.

The lions roar can be heard up to 5 miles away. The lion has razor sharp claws. The lion has sharper teeth in the back of its mouth than the front. The lion weighs from 200 pounds to 500 pounds. The lion is known to have very strong muscles.

Male lions are the ones that hunt and get the food for the cubs. Female lions stay at home with the cubs. The lions all over the world live in the same habitat. So I suggest you don't get a lion as a pet because lions are illegal to be used as a pet.

Sincerely,
pet pal

Tapping into Students' Interests. To begin her thematic unit, Kellie brings in a reproduction of the Mona Lisa for her special education students to examine. As her seventh graders examine the painting, they begin to talk about their reactions to the famous painting. Before long, the discussion turns to the clothing and how it differs from current dress styles.

This focus on a person brings life to the historical period. Picking up on this interest, Kellie transports them to the Renaissance era through a virtual learning experience on the Internet. Using the LCD projector, Kellie and her class navigate the website through verbal, audio, and visual elements. As a result, learning becomes more of a hands-on experience. Gradually, Kellie's students acquire a thirst for learning more about the people within this time period. Questions begin to emerge.

Using the Circle of Questions in Inquiry. The next day, Kellie invites her students to think about questions related to the Renaissance period. She begins this brainstorming event by having her students list a few questions they may have. After a few minutes, Kellie then encourages her students to share their questions as she records them on chart paper. Drawing a circle on the board, Kellie writes students' questions around the circle (Sampson, Sampson, & Linek, 1994). This Circle of Questions, Kellie explains, is how authors begin to write informational texts in picture books or our textbooks; these questions often become a way for authors to organize the concepts and ideas within texts (see Figure 8.7).

Their questions also become a way for students to independently investigate the Renaissance era in more depth. Working in mixed ability groups of three, the seventh graders select questions they want to investigate before navigating the website. Just like Elaine's

Figure 8.7
Circle of Questions

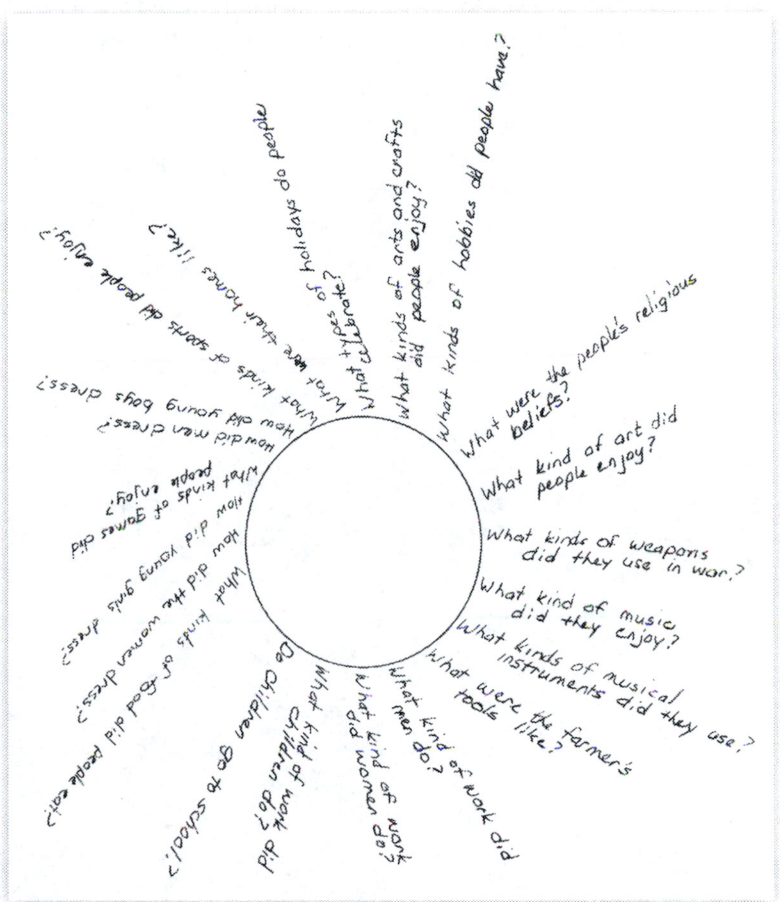

students, the seventh graders first explore the website, using their questions to guide their explorations. At the end of each session, they also record at least three things they learn in their logs. Through these open-ended explorations, Katie learns that boys wore leggings while girls wore woolen dresses; Eddie discovers that the armor was made of extremely heavy metal, so heavy that men could scarcely lift it; Chrissy finds that herbs and plants were often used for medicine and that wormwood was placed in clothing to repel fleas.

Gathering Information about the Renaissance Period. After navigating the website in this way, the group selects specific questions they want to investigate from their own Circle of Questions. Using the web displayed in Figure 8.8, each group then gathers notes about the historical period and its people. Throughout the process, the students retain ownership of their inquiry by selecting the questions they want to pursue.

Using PowerPoint to Publish their Inquiry Projects. Instead of compiling the information into a booklet, Kellie's students compile the information into a PowerPoint presentation. Using graphics, images, sound, and icons, they creatively display the knowledge they have gained about the past. They also experiment with different ways to use text—sometimes they use paragraphs or sentences to share information; other times they list the information, using bullets. Figure 8.9 illustrates one group's PowerPoint presentation.

Figure 8.8

Katie's Group Gathers Notes about People during the Renaissance

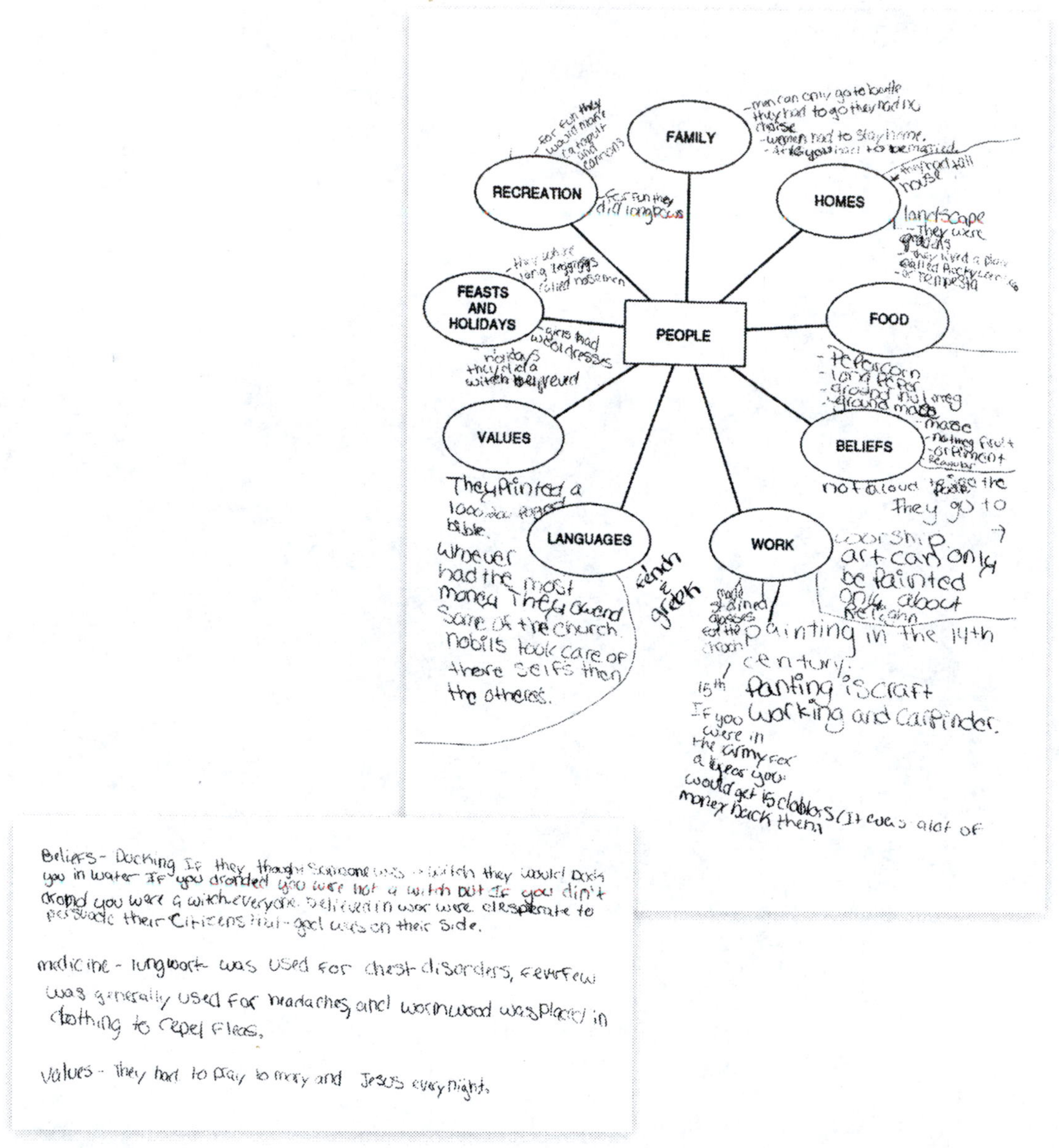

Creating Poems about Historical People in the Renaissance Period. As a culminating experience for the thematic unit, Kellie encourages each of her students to select a historical person from the Renaissance time period to research. Following the process described in Chapter 6, her students gather notes about the historical person and fashion an I AM poem about the person, writing from the perspective of the historical figure. After revising and editing the poems, the seventh graders word process their poems, selecting their favorite print font to publish the poem. Shawn's poem is displayed on the next page.

Figure 8.9

Mike's Group's PowerPoint Presentation about the Renaissance

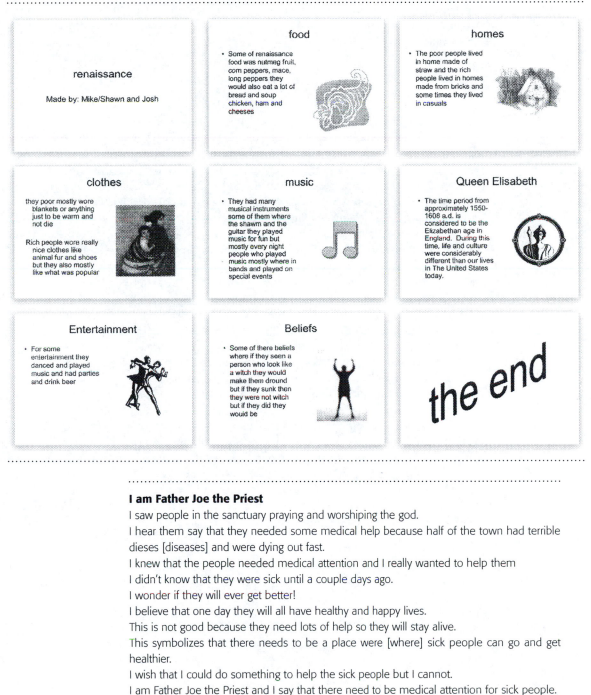

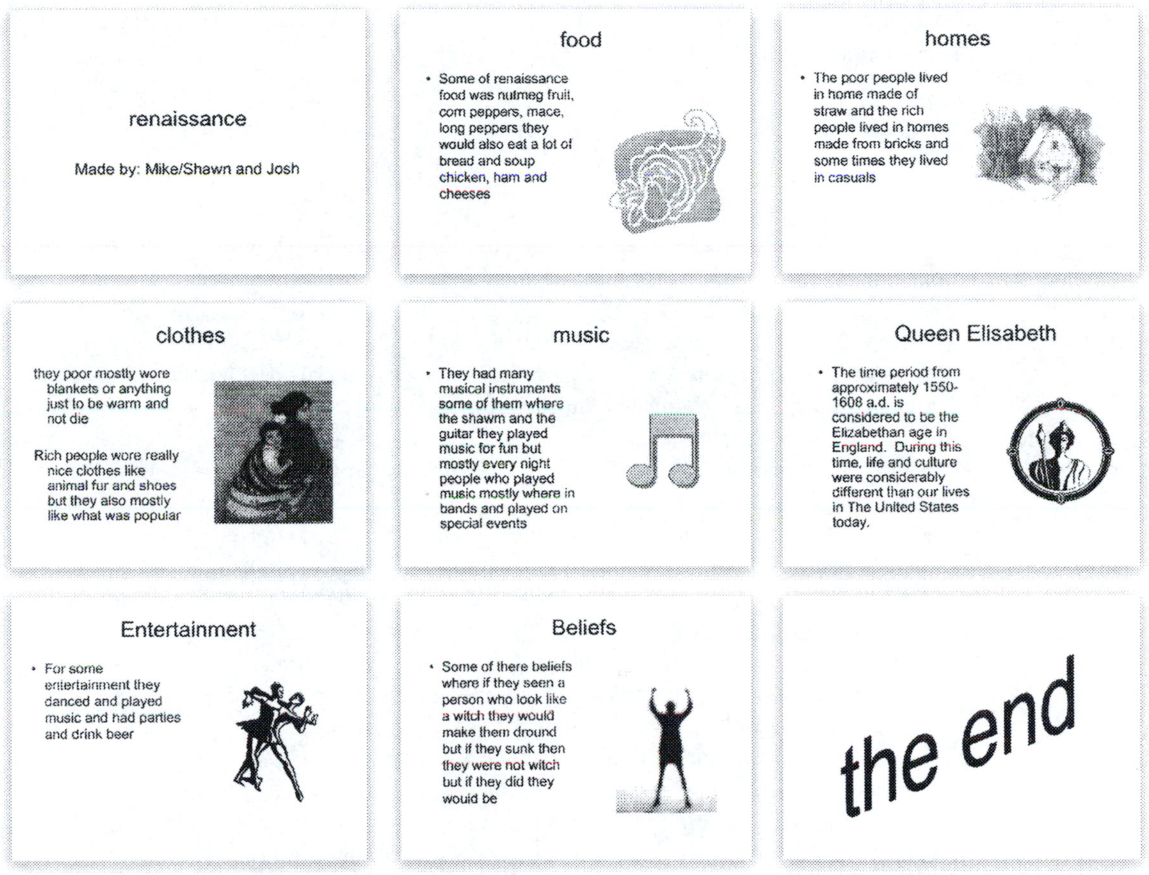

renaissance

Made by: Mike/Shawn and Josh

food

- Some of renaissance food was nutmeg fruit, corn peppers, mace, long peppers they would also eat a lot of bread and soup chicken, ham and cheeses

homes

- The poor people lived in home made of straw and the rich people lived in homes made from bricks and some times they lived in casuals

clothes

they poor mostly wore blankets or anything just to be warm and not die

Rich people wore really nice clothes like animal fur and shoes but they also mostly like what was popular

music

- They had many musical instruments some of them where the shawm and the guitar they played music for fun but mostly every night people who played music mostly where in bands and played on special events

Queen Elisabeth

- The time period from approximately 1550-1608 a.d. is considered to be the Elizabethan age in England. During this time, life and culture were considerably different than our lives in The United States today.

Entertainment

- For some entertainment they danced and played music and had parties and drink beer

Beliefs

- Some of there beliefs where if they seen a person who look like a witch they would make them dround but if they sunk then they were not witch but if they did they would be

the end

I am Father Joe the Priest

I saw people in the sanctuary praying and worshiping the god.
I hear them say that they needed some medical help because half of the town had terrible dieses [diseases] and were dying out fast.
I knew that the people needed medical attention and I really wanted to help them
I didn't know that they were sick until a couple days ago.
I wonder if they will ever get better!
I believe that one day they will all have healthy and happy lives.
This is not good because they need lots of help so they will stay alive.
This symbolizes that there needs to be a place were [where] sick people can go and get healthier.
I wish that I could do something to help the sick people but I cannot.
I am Father Joe the Priest and I say that there need to be medical attention for sick people.

As can be seen, Shawn's poem illustrates that he has gained a perspective on the historical time period. His poem effectively reflects the time, place, and culture of the Renaissance.

Using multiple forms of technology brought excitement and motivation to the learning experience for these special education students, while offering them varied ways to learn about history. Kellie remarks that her students "were actively engaged with each step of this lesson, despite the fact that it centered on topics and activities that don't have much appeal to them." Using technology seemed to bridge the gulf between the past and the present for her seventh graders.

Using Computer Communications to Solve Problems

Another exciting way to link computer communications with the curriculum is through Internet projects, partnerships between students or classes in different locations in order to solve a common problem or explore a common topic (Castek et al., 2006). As students cooperatively work together to solve problems, they acquire skills they will use in the world of work (Leu, 2001; Leu, Leu, & Coiro, 2004).

Similar to many other teachers, Monica Haddock, a media specialist, realizes that children of all ages enjoy learning about animals. Tapping into this natural interest, Monica invites her third graders to select an animal they would like to investigate. Once everyone selects an animal, they visit the Wikipedia website (http://en.wikipedia.org) to gather information about the animals. Using notetaking strategies, the third graders record facts about the animals' weight, length, gestation period, number of young born, and life span (see Figure 8.10).

The following day, each student enters their data on a spreadsheet (see Figure 8.11), which is used to determine how many animals fall within the various categories. After students enter their data on the spreadsheet, Monica shows them how they can use Excel to organize and display data, using the LCD projector. After modeling the process, Monica then shows students how to create a graph to display the findings.

About a week later, Monica shows the third graders how each class in the school similarly entered their data on a spreadsheet. By expanding the scope of data collection, Monica models how students can use this information to compare and contrast animals, using categories like weight, length, or gestation period.

When she displays the findings for the school, the third graders see how data may change when larger numbers of people gather information. Similarly, when Monica graphs the findings for the school, the third graders see how the graph may take a different shape when we gather larger numbers of data.

As a culminating event, Monica compiles the third graders' research into a class book. The students especially enjoy having a published book about their research, which they can all take home to share with their families. Figure 8.12 displays Arnell's page in the class book.

Figure 8.10
Notetaking Sheet

Name of Animal ______________________

By______________________ (your first & last name)

Average weight is ________

Average length is ________

Gestation period is ________

Number of young born (is/are)________

Life span is ________

Figure 8.11

Third Graders Enter Their Data on a Spreadsheet

Weight of Our Animals	Number of Animals
<1 pound–2,000 pounds	
2,001–4,000 pounds	
4,001–6,000 pounds	
6,001–8,000 pounds	
8,001–>10,000 pounds	

Length of Our Animals	Number of Animals
<1 foot–20 foot	
21 foot–40 foot	
41 foot–60 foot	
61 foot–80 foot	
81 foot–>100 foot	

Gestation Period	Number of Animals
<1 month–5 months	
6 month–10 months	
11 month–1 yr 3 months	
1 yr 4 months–1 yr 8 months	
1 yr 9 months–>2 years	

Name ______________________

Room # ________

Life Span	Number of Animals
<1–20 years	
21–40 years	
41–60 years	
61–80 years	
81–>100 years	

Number Young Born	Number of Animals
1–20 born	
21–40 born	
41–60 born	
61–80 born	
81–>100 born	

This cooperative learning experience models how learning projects can evolve into a communal database that all can easily access and use to explore relationships between animals. As a result of this learning experience, the third graders begin to see how technology can be used to solve problems and display information. After having this experience, students might enjoy conducting a survey in their community about ecology or conservation. Based on prior learning, they can then use technology tools to organize and display the findings.

Closing Thoughts

This chapter presents strategies to provide more effective links between technology and reading, writing, social studies, science, and math. As new forms of information and communication technology (ICT) continue to emerge, new avenues for reading and writing simultaneously evolve. These transformations create a lifetime of opportunities for learning, opportunities awaiting our imagination and creativity.

Figure 8.12
Arnell's Page in the Class Book on the Arctic Hare

ARCTIC HARE

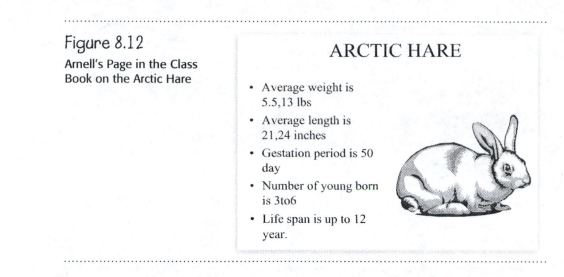

- Average weight is 5.5,13 lbs
- Average length is 21,24 inches
- Gestation period is 50 day
- Number of young born is 3to6
- Life span is up to 12 year.

As we traveled through a variety of classrooms, we saw how technology became a tool for interpersonal exchanges. Reading and writing gained new purposes and meaning as students exchanged emails with teachers, their family, and friends. New opportunities for accessing current information similarly become available as students communicate with educators, scientists, politicians, or historians across the nation and globe. As a result of this interpersonal process, reading and writing become more motivational for many learners.

Continuing with our journey, we visited other classrooms using hypermedia technology. Working in twos, students learned how to navigate hypermedia links through experimentation and delightful learning experiences using hypermedia software. Even though reading required a different approach as students explored various links according to their interests, students embraced this style of reading, which gave them choice according to their interests. Having choice and ownership in their learning invited them to read and write more.

Once students explore these new forms of reading, they apply inquiry to learn about diversity or to access information about topics they wish to investigate in more depth on the Internet. By following a process, students learn to craft informational texts about their inquiry, using desktop publishing tools and PowerPoint. Specifically, students learn to

- Critically analyze and evaluate websites.
- Access and gather information from sources.
- Paraphrase information.
- Create informational texts from their notes, webs, and graphic organizers.
- Shape their informational texts through revising and editing.
- Publish the informational texts, using multiple genres, desktop publishing tools, or PowerPoint.

Through an ongoing process, students extend their knowledge while retaining ownership of their learning. Through the publishing process, they pool their knowledge with larger audiences.

Continuing our journey, we stopped by yet another classroom where a teacher used technology as a tool for cooperative problem solving. After students cooperatively created a communal database, they began to see how they can access the database to explore relationships between phenomena. Following a process, they could also create a website displaying the information, publish a global newsletter, or create a PowerPoint presentation about the findings.

As information and technology continue to expand and develop, we can harness these tools to enrich classroom learning. As teachers, we merely need to tap into these valuable learning opportunities, which are highly stimulating and motivational to all learners (Leu, 2002).

Teachers' Questions

1. **I would like to have my students participate in email exchanges with teachers, but I do not live close to a university. What other options do I have?**

The good news is that your students can participate in email exchanges with teachers even if you live far away from a university. In fact, your students can participate in email exchanges with teachers at a university in another country. You can send an email to personnel in the College of Education at a university, asking if there are any professors who might be interested in participating in a project of this nature.

In addition, email exchanges can similarly occur between elementary students and middle school students or high school students within the same school district. Both the elementary students and middle school or high school students will improve their reading and writing performance as they discuss a book they are reading, for example.

2. **How can first graders and kindergarteners write inquiry reports? They are too young.**

Students of all ages are naturally curious. They have many questions about life and the world around them. When they are able to pursue their own questions, first graders and kindergarteners become motivated to explore the unknown. Sandy Todd, a first grade teacher, involves her parents in the inquiry projects. Once students determine their questions, Sandy, along with the media specialist, helps the first graders find books or other resources to pursue their inquiries. Parents then read the books, pamphlets, or information to the first graders. After reading about their topic (i.e., animals, insects, trees, or flowers) with their parents, the children write about what they have learned and then draw a picture, showing what they have learned.

3. **Should younger children, even first graders, add a bibliography to their inquiry reports?**

Certainly! Students need to learn right away that we must always cite our sources. Forming good habits at a young age may prevent plagiarism later.

Sandy Todd, whom we just mentioned, sends a letter home to parents, explaining the inquiry project to them. In her letter, Sandy shows parents how to help their children cite their sources. She also models this in a minilesson during class. Following this model, students then cite the source or sources they used in their inquiry projects with the help of their parents.

4. **How do you feel about fourth and fifth graders analyzing and evaluating Internet sites?**

If fourth and fifth grade teachers follow Marcia Gelpie's model, they, too, can begin to learn how to analyze and evaluate Internet sites. Media, advertisements, and the Internet are an integral part of our students' lives. They need to learn how to critically think about the information given to them. By analyzing and evaluating these sources, students will learn how to problem solve, think, and make better decisions in their lives.

Children's Literature

Aardema, V. (1975). *Why mosquitoes buzz in people's ears.* New York: Dial.

Aardema, V. (1977). *Who's in rabbit's house?* New York: Dial.

Bishop, C. H. (1938). *The five Chinese brothers.* New York: Coward-McCann.

Blume, J. (1980). *Superfudge.* New York: Puffin Books.

Cleary, B. (1979). *Ramona and her mother.* New York: Avon Books.

Coerr, E. (1977). *Sadako and the thousand paper cranes.* New York: Dell.

Demi. (1980). *Liang and the magic paintbrush.* New York: Henry Holt.

Demi. (1990). *The empty pot.* New York: Henry Holt.

Guiberson, B. Z. (2000). *Into the sea.* New York: Henry Holt and Company.

James, S. (1991). *Dear Mr. Blueberry.* New York: Aladdin Picture Books.

Lord, B. (1984). *In the year of the boar and Jackie Robinson.* New York: Harper & Row.

Louie, A. (1982). *Yeh-shen: A Cinderella story from China.* New York: Philomel.

McLean, V. (1987). *Chasing the moon to China.* New York: Redbird.

San Souci, R. (1987). *The enchanted tapestry.* New York: Dial.

Spinelli, J. (1991). *Report to the principal's office.* New York: Scholastic.

Spinelli, J. (2000). *Stargirl.* New York: Alfred Knopf.

Steptoe, J. (1988). *Mufaro's beautiful daughters.* New York: Lothrop, Lee & Shepard.

Stuart, D. (1993). *The astonishing armadillo.* Minneapolis, MN: Learner.

Waters, K., & Slovenz-Low, M. (1990). *Lion dancer: Ernie Wan's Chinese New Year.* New York: Scholastic.

Young, E. (1989). *Lon Po Po: A red-riding hood story from China.* New York: Philomel.

References

Atwell, N. (1987). *In the middle: Writing, reading, and learning with adolescents.* Upper Montclair, NJ: Boynton/Cook.

Au, K. (1993). *Literacy instruction in multicultural settings.* Fort Worth, TX: Harcourt Brace Jovanovich.

Au, K. (1995). Multicultural perspectives on literacy research. *Journal of Reading Behavior: A Journal of Literacy, 27,* 83–100.

Bolter, J. (1992). Literature in the electronic writing space. In M. Tuman (Ed.), *Literacy on-line: The promise [and peril] of reading and writing with computers* (pp. 19–42). Pittsburgh, PA: University of Pittsburgh Press.

Castek, J., Bevans-Mangelston, J., & Goldstone, B. (2006). Reading adventures online: Five ways to introduce the new literacies of the Internet through children's literature. *The Reading Teacher, 59,* 714–727.

Cummins, J. (1986). Empowering minority students. *Harvard Education Review, 56,* 866–898.

Daiute, C. (1985). *Writing and computers.* Reading, MA: Addison-Wesley.

Diamond, B., & Moore, M. (1995). *Multicultural literacy: Mirroring the reality of the classroom.* New York: Longman.

D'Ignazio, F. (1990). Electronic highways and the classroom of the future. *The Computing Teacher, 17,* 20–24.

Edwards, W. (1999). Making moves with information technology: An information technology center works closely with the resources center in a small school. In J. Hancock (Ed.), *Teaching literacy using information technology* (pp. 31–47). Newark, DE: International Reading Association.

Forcier, R. (1996). *The computer as a productivity tool in education.* Englewood Cliffs, NJ: Merrill.

Harris, J. (1994). A model for integration of telecomputing in precollege curricula. In J. Willis, B. Robin, & D. Wills (Eds.), *Technology and Teacher Education Annual—1994* (pp. 637–642). Boston: Allyn & Bacon.

Honey, M., & Henriquez, A. (1993). *Telecommunications and K–12 educators: Findings from a national study.* New York: Center for Technology in Education.

Howie, S. (1989). *Reading, writing, and computers.* Boston: Allyn & Bacon.

Iannone, P. (1998). Exploring literacy on the Internet. *The Reading Teacher, 51,* 436–443.

Irwin, M., Moore, M., Stevenson, J. (1994). Enhancing a multicultural program through hypertext links. *Computers in the Schools, 10,* 255–280.

Leu, D., Jr. (2001). Internet project: Preparing students for new literacies in a global village. *The Reading Teacher, 54,* 567–585.

Leu, D., Jr. (2002). The new literacies: Research on reading instruction with the Internet. In A. Farstrup & S. Samuels (Eds.), *What research has to say about reading instruction* (pp. 310–336). Newark, DE: International Reading Association.

Leu, D., Jr., Leu, D., & Coiro, J. (2004). *Teaching with the Internet: New literacies for new times* (4th ed.). Norwood, MA: Christopher Gordon.

Liu, M. (1994). Hypermedia assisted instruction and second language learning: A semantic-network-based approach. *Computers in the Schools, 10,* 292–310.

Montoya, I. (1992). Put a star in your classroom. *The Computing Teacher, 20,* 18–19.

Moore, M. (1991). Electronic dialoguing: An avenue to literacy. *The Reading Teacher, 45,* 280–286.

Moore, M. (1992). The effects of computer communications on the reading and writing performance of fifth-grade students. *Computers in Human Behavior, 8,* 27–38.

Moore-Hart, M. (1995). The effects of Multicultural Links on reading and writing performance and cultural awareness of fourth and fifth graders. *Computers in Human Behavior, 11,* 391–410.

Moore-Hart, M., Knapp, J., & Diamond, B. (2003). The implementation of a multicultural literacy program in fourth- and fifth-grade classrooms. In A. Willis, G. Garcia, R. Barrera, & V. Harris (Eds.), *Multicultural issues in literacy research and practice* (pp. 223–262). Mahwah, NJ: Lawrence Erlbaum.

Patterson, N. (2003). Becoming literate in the ways of the web: Evaluating Internet resources. *Voices from the Middle, 10,* 58–59.

Rief, L. (1992). *Seeking diversity: Language arts with adolescents.* Portsmouth, NH: Heinemann.

Riel, M. (1985). The computer chronicles newswire: A functional learning environment for acquiring literacy skills. *Journal of Educational Computing Research, 1,* 317–377.

Riel, M. (1989). The impact of computers in classrooms. *The Journal of Research on Computing in Education, 1,* 180–189.

Sampson, M., Sampson, M., & Linek, W. (1994). Circle of questions. *The Reading Teacher, 48,* 364–365.

Schwartz, H. (1992). "Dominion Everywhere": Computers as cultural artifacts. In M. Tuman (Ed.), *Literacy on-line: The promise [and peril] of reading and writing with computers* (pp. 95–108). Pittsburgh, PA: University of Pittsburgh Press.

Sheingold, K. (1991). Restructuring learning with technology: The potential for synergy. *Phi Delta Kappan,* 17–27.

Solomon, G. (1993). On the nature of pedagogic computer tools. The case of the writing partner. In S. P. LaJoie & S. J. Derry (Eds.), *Computers as cognitive tools.* Hillsdale, NJ: Lawrence Erlbaum.

Swenson, J., Young, C., McGrail, E., Rozema, R., & Whitin, P. (2006). Extending the conversation: New technologies, new literacies, and English education. *English Education, 38,* 351–369.

Tashlik, P. (1987). I hear voices: The text, the journal and me. In T. Fulwiler (Ed.), *The journal book.* Portsmouth, NH: Heinemann.

Wepner, S., & Ray, I. (2000). Using technology for reading development. In S. B. Wepner, W. J. Valmont, & R. Thurlow (Eds.), *Linking literacy and technology: A guide for K–8 classrooms* (pp. 76–105). Newark, DE: International Reading Association.

Willhelm, J. (2004). Inquiring minds use technology. *Voices from the Middle, 11,* 45–46.

Willis, J., Stephens, E., & Matthew, K. (1996). *Technology, reading, and language arts.* Boston: Allyn & Bacon.

Wollman-Bonilla, J. (1989). Reading journals: Invitations to participate in literature. *The Reading Teacher, 43,* 112–120.

chapter NINE

Fostering Respect and Appreciation through the Use of Technology in an Inclusion Environment

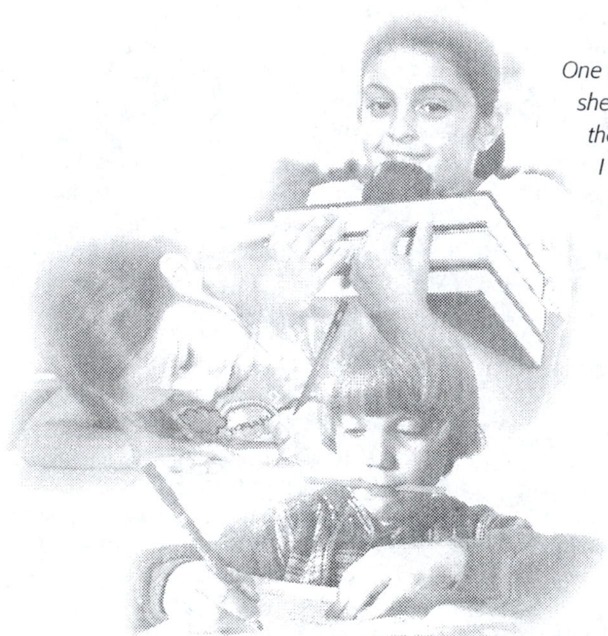

One of the saddest days of my mom's life was when she found out that I had cancer. So they put me in the hospital. I stayed in the hospital for a long time. I was always getting poked and having tests done. I was not even 2 yet. The doctors told my mom that I had cancer. She did not believe them. So she prayed and the next morning the doctors had some great news for her. They could put me on a waiting list for a new liver. After she heard that she jumped with joy. We waited until October 12. That was the day I received my new liver. Right now I am in remission.

Building a Community of Learners through Inclusion

This is a paragraph written by Trina, a Physically and Otherwise Health Impaired (POHI) student, in an inclusion class—a class composed of fifth graders and their POHI peers. Trina and her classmates are learning about writing through the use of technology in meaningful, authentic contexts.

The students in Trina's class feel they are especially lucky because they, different from most students, have *two* teachers, Mary Streeter, a fifth grade teacher, and Kathy Micallef, a special education teacher (see Chapter 4). The two teachers share a vision of building a community of learners where peace, unity, and acceptance for all flourishes. They believe that students with disabilities should be served in inclusive classrooms that acknowledge and respect all individuals. Their classroom is a place where students construct their own knowledge, show ownership of their learning processes, and cooperatively investigate verbal and written language through the use of technology. Not only is this classroom the least restrictive environment for the POHI children, but it is also an enriched environment where all students achieve academically, increase their self-esteem, enhance their social relationships, and become lifelong learners. All students benefit due to the teachers' focus on abilities and strengths rather than disabilities or weaknesses.

As more and more students with disabilities enter general education classrooms, teachers are asking for help in designing models, strategies, and techniques for reaching the diverse needs of their students and creating successful learning experiences. As a team, Mary and Kathy have codeveloped over several years a variety of strategies and techniques to facilitate the learning of their fifth graders and POHI students. Every year, they discover new ways to reach the varying needs and abilities of their students. By remaining flexible and open to new ideas, Kathy and Mary have found that technology, a learning tool that is constantly expanding, opens new doors for learning (Bialo & Sivin, 1989).

What Is Inclusion?

Inclusion is a philosophy—a view of learning—that reflects real life with its challenges and distractions (Scala, 2001). Inclusion occurs when students of differing abilities and strengths learn alongside their age mates with *all necessary supports.* Without these necessary supports, inclusion becomes jeopardized, and the best interests of all students cannot be taken into consideration (Ferguson, 1995; Lipsky & Gartner, 1992; Scala, 2001).

Creating an inclusion classroom takes time to develop. Mary and Kathy began by coteaching lessons and thematic units in a multicultural literacy program implemented within their school district. (For a description of the multicultural program, see Chapter 5.) After experiencing success in their combined teaching efforts, they decided to join their classrooms, following the principles of inclusion.

Using the policy statement of the Council for Exceptional Children (1993) to guide them in constructing their inclusion classroom, the two teachers determined that children, youth, and adults with disabilities should be served in general education classrooms within inclusive communities whenever possible. Consistent with the policy statement, they realize that the classroom setting becomes strengthened and supported by the infusion of POHI students and their specially trained personnel and other appropriate supportive practices.

Even though support services would remain for the POHI students in the inclusion environment, Kathy and Mary realize that additional support may become necessary so

POHI students continue to receive supportive services.

teaching **TIP 9.1**

This model of creating a flexible learning environment applies to all classrooms. There are always students in our classes who may require adaptable curricula, instruction, or resources.

that students will be able to function optimally in the inclusion classroom (Scala, 2001). They are supported by a systemic commitment to directing special education resources so that more students will be appropriately served (McLeskey & Waldron, 1995). Specifically, they believe that all students benefit in this flexible learning environment where adaptable curricula, instruction, and resources become accessible to all (Schirmer & Casbon, 1995; Schrag & Burnette, 1994). In particular, Mary and Kathy perceive that students who are borderline cases will receive the additional support they need and deserve.

Viewing themselves as "one class with two teachers," Mary and Kathy link their talents, expertise, and knowledge. The collaborative effort stimulates their teaching as they share their lessons, teaching tips, instructional techniques, successes, and failures. Co-teaching facilitates deeper reflections about their practice so that they can support the varying characteristics and learning styles of their students while simultaneously fulfilling their assessment, instructional, and curricular needs.

Specifically, the two teachers follow the fifth grade language arts curriculum, individualizing the instruction and making necessary adaptations for "any student in their classroom." They frequently revise and develop lessons to include more hands-on, manipulative activities or more use of technology. They also vary grouping arrangements such as cooperative learning groups, paired groupings, or cross-age and peer tutoring. Students who are having extreme difficulty receive additional in-class instructional support from specialists or support services. To further accomplish their goals for learners, Mary and Kathy constantly pursue professional development opportunities to support the diverse needs of their students.

According to Mary and Kathy, the best part of their program is the true friendships that form between the fifth graders and their POHI peers. Through the broadened range of social contacts, all students discover that everyone brings strengths and needs to every situation. Students gain an awareness and sensitivity to one another, influenced by role modeling from adults; they also learn about conflict resolution and the importance of being responsible (Scala, 2001).

Expanding Learning Opportunities in an Inclusion Classroom through Technology

As one might imagine, meeting the diverse needs and abilities of students in their inclusion classroom often challenges Mary and Kathy. In order to reach the needs of all their students, they move cautiously as there are no simple answers (Ferguson, 1995; Schnorr & Davern, 2005; Thousand & Villa, 1995; Zigmond et al., 1995) and no recipes for success. Technology often offers a way to confront the complex demands of varying learning styles, needs, interests, and abilities. Consistent with research, technology provides an effective means of reaching students of all ability levels, especially at-risk students and students with disabilities (Anderson-Inman & Horney; 2007; Boone & Higgins, 1993; Kulik & Kulik, 1985, 1987, 1991).

teaching **TIP 9.2**

Students of all ability levels need learning experiences that focus on higher-level thinking skills and problem-solving skills. Students become more engaged when we challenge them.

To date, however, the potential impact of technology on academic learning has not been tapped. Low-achieving students are more likely to use computer technology for drill and practice rather than for problem solving or other higher-level thinking activities (Anderson & Speck, 2001; Leu, 1997; Office of Technology Assessment, 1988; Reinking, 1998; Snyder, 1999). In contrast, Mary and Kathy believe that there is a need to concentrate on using technology through cognitively demanding tasks, rather than low-level tasks and skills. In order that all their students will improve academic performance, they specifically use technology to focus on higher-level thinking and problem-solving skills. Moreover, they find that the rich possibilities of video, graphic, and audio representations more closely match the various learning styles of their students.

Knowing how to organize the curriculum and learning environment to use technology often challenges Mary and Kathy. To meet these demands, they attend in-service and professional development programs whenever possible. Through these resources, they learn about technological innovations and ways to integrate technology with their instruction.

Technology as a Communication Tool in an Inclusion Classroom

Primarily, Mary and Kathy use technology as a communication tool. While interacting in a collaborative environment, which fosters spontaneous discussion and the use of language in a variety of ways, the fifth graders and their POHI peers learn about the purpose, forms, and strategies of reading and writing infused with technology. This informal environment, which naturally integrates reading, writing, language, and real-life experiences, sets the stage for effective composing and comprehending (Roach, 1974; Graves, 1983). Mary and Kathy also use assistive technology (AT), defined as any item, equipment, or product system that improves the functional capabilities of students with disabilities (Individuals with Disabilities Act, 2004), to support the POHI students' learning.

Creating a Community of Learners in an Inclusion Environment

To help all their students gain an awareness and sensitivity towards others, Mary and Kathy begin the school year with the patterned writing activity, biopoems. Working in pairs, students interview one another about their relatives, loves, fears, and needs. As interviewees respond to the interview questions, their partners record their responses on the biopoem sheets. Once interviewers complete the poem, partners switch roles and the interviewer becomes the interviewee. If POHI students are unable to use pencils due to physical limitations, Mary and Kathy place an aide, who records the words for them, next to the partners. Once they complete the interviews, students discover they have created poems with their peers.

Continuing to work in pairs, they then type the biopoems on the computer, using word processing. By combining their resources, Mary and Kathy have six computers and three printers for students to use, placed along the side of the classroom for easy access and so the two teachers can simultaneously monitor students' work at the computers and desks.

To further facilitate working in pairs at the computers, the teachers space the computers so that two students can easily work together. Even though Kristin is unable to use pencil and paper, she is able to type the biopoem independently by pressing the keys. Through Kathy's modeling, her partner slowly dictates the words from the biopoem sheet, spelling some of the words for Kristin as she types on the computer. This helps Kristin focus on pressing the keys with minimal distractions. Once Kristin finishes, she discovers that she can "see" the words and letters more clearly on the computer screen. Wisely, Kathy supports Kristin's visual needs by encouraging her to print a copy in large print so that she can easily read the printed page.

On the following day, students edit their poems. After seeing Kathy model the process with the overhead, the students take ownership of their editing by applying the skills of proofreading. Working in pairs at their desks, partners proofread their poems for commas and for capitals at the beginning of each line, in their names, or in proper nouns. There is no need for teachers to use red pens. Students carefully check one another's poems, making sure that there are commas and capitals wherever needed. Mary and Kathy circulate, guiding and coaching their students. If someone has forgotten a capital or comma, the teachers point to the line and ask students what's missing. By merely giving cues or prompts, the two teachers leave the responsibility for proofreading with the students.

Once students complete the editing with the word processing tools, they select their favorite print font to publish their poems. After mounting the published poems on colored paper with photos, Mary and Kathy display them in the hallway for all to see.

By following a process, everyone begins the year as a successful writer. The writing experience further affirms each person's self-identity as students discover that they are all unique individuals who share many similar interests and feelings. Kristin's biopoem is displayed below:

Kristin

Nice, kind, good friend, and cool
Relative of my grandma
Who loves mom and dad and doll
Who feels happy, sad, and mad
Who needs love, food, and a home
Who fears bees, falling out of my wheelchair, and that mom'll get fired
Who gives presents, surprises, and candy
Who would like to see mom, grandma, and dad.

This early learning experience also helps the fifth graders begin to see how they can support their POHI friends. They discover that they can write down information for their friends who are unable to use pencils or help their friends focus while typing by dictating words, phrases, or spellings.

This interviewing and composing experience helps both the fifth graders and their POHI peers begin the school year in a cooperative way. As a result of the evolving social interactions, the POHI students become more familiar with the language associated with writing such as drafting, editing, and interviewing. While reading their biopoems with their partners, they also increase their word recognition skills. Importantly, they are able to read the poems more successfully because they are able to predict words by relating their knowledge and experiences to the written text. When they come to words that they cannot figure out, the fifth graders tell them the word, following the model of their teachers. With practice, the POHI students begin to read more and more of the words independently. Simultaneously, the fifth graders increase their proofreading skills as they help the POHI students find their missing capitals and commas or misspelled words. They also increase their social skills as they follow their teachers' models, patiently supporting their POHI peers and thoughtfully giving them positive feedback along the way.

In order that the fifth graders and POHI students continue to grow and learn together at the beginning of the year, Mary and Kathy invite students to create life-size paper puppets of one another in pairs. As students work together, they trace their bodies on large butcher paper, cut out the puppets, decorate the puppets, and finally stuff the puppets. Charlie creatively helps Michael make wheels for his desk chair, so that it looks just like his wheel chair. Everyone then places the completed puppets at his or her desk for open house.

These combined experiences foster eye–hand coordination and fine and large motor development of the POHI students. The fifth graders simultaneously apply problem-solving strategies to help their partners construct the puppets. Throughout this process, the two teachers model different tasks, such as guiding POHI students as they cut paper, remaining patient and using praise. They model how to ask questions, and ignore certain physical or emotional behaviors the POHI students cannot control. As the fifth graders begin to apply these strategies, Mary and Kathy support their efforts by offering them specific praise, encouragement, and constructive feedback. Gradually, the fifth graders become sensitive to their POHI peers and quite adept at supporting their learning. They even invent their own creative ways to support the needs of their POHI peers.

Extending Scientific Concepts through Poetry

Having established a caring and supportive atmosphere for all learners, Mary and Kathy continue to move forward with the curriculum. As shown in Chapter 4, Writing Workshop is an important part of daily activities. Writing is also an effective tool for learning across the curriculum and for meaningful integration of the core subjects. To conclude their science unit on leaves and trees, for example, they integrate science observation and notetaking activities with writing to create poems about leaves or trees.

Prewriting Activities. Recognizing that students need to learn how to become collectors of information, Mary and Kathy begin this poetry activity by having students work in groups of four or five to observe their environment. Using writing journals to take notes and temporary spelling when needed, the cooperative groups go outdoors to record observations about trees and leaves at various locations on the school grounds. After about 10 minutes, each group moves to a new location to record observations in a new setting.

As students take notes, they share ideas with one another under the guidance of their group leader (i.e., aides, support teachers, or Mary or Kathy). The group leaders encourage students to insert adjectives or verbs to describe what they see. For example, when Charlie sees a caterpillar and records this in his notebook, he adds *squirmy* in response to his group leader's prompting. Jenny adds *colorful* and *wrinkly* next to the word *leaves.*

To help POHI students who cannot use paper and pencil, aides, the group leaders, or fifth grade partners write down their dictations. Hearing others share their ideas helps all POHI students gradually learn what to record in their notes and how to observe their environment.

On returning to the classroom, students take turns sharing two to three of their observations with their classmates. Similar to other teachers, Mary encourages students to add words and ideas to their lists as they listen to their friends. Kathy also stretches students' thinking by frequently asking them to think of words to describe their observations when single words are mentioned. For example, when Andrew shares *branches,* he adds that they look like spiderwebs in response to her prompts. Pencils continuously move across the paper as students integrate these ideas into their notes. While sharing their ideas, both POHI and fifth grade learners contribute to the discussion; everyone adds words to their lists. Consistent with Clark (1995), *all* students simultaneously learn how to collect, organize, and synthesize information for their writing.

During the next few days, the two teachers continue their discussion about adjectives and share examples of poetry that use colorful, descriptive language. The class discusses words authors use to help readers see, hear, feel, smell, or taste the images portrayed in their poems. The teachers also encourage their students to think about and apply the scientific vocabulary from their texts to describe their observations.

Drafting Activities. Students are now ready to draft their own poems about leaves and trees. Once again, Kathy cautions that the poems do not have to rhyme, reminding them to think about the poems they have been reading together during the past two days. Using their writers' notebooks and webs, many students compose three to four lines in less than 5 minutes. After listening to their peers' ideas, others soon begin drafting their poems. Before long, everyone has a first draft.

During the next 2 days, the two teachers have students work in pairs to type their drafts at the computer. (In order that each student can save their writing during the school year, the teachers give each student their own CD to save their work.) To ensure that everyone has an opportunity to work at the computers, Mary and Kathy further post a schedule.

To simulate the process of working with partners at the computer, the teachers ask Marcus and Will to model how they work together. Will reads Marcus's poem slowly while Marcus types it. Sometimes Will spontaneously helps Marcus with spelling or punctuation. After 15 minutes, Kathy explains, the two will exchange roles—the author will become the reader; the reader, the author. Once their assigned time is up, they will save their work and quietly signal that it is the next pair's turn on the computer. By following this routine, students easily move back and forth to the computer station with minimal disruptions.

Similar to other teachers, Kathy and Mary also have three "computer experts" to help students who need assistance with the computer, word processor, or printer. These combined strategies help minimize interruptions for the two teachers while they are working with individuals, groups, or the class.

Revising Activities. Once students word process the poems, Mary and Kathy explain that authors revise their poems several times before they are published. To help their students learn how to revise, Mary conducts a minilesson on the process of revising poetry. After making an overhead transparency of Jonathon's poem, she models the PQP process with the students. First Jonathon reads his poem to the class. Mary then models how to give specific praise about his poem. For example, she comments, "I like the way you framed your poem with a window, using the window to begin each new verse of your poem." Then she invites

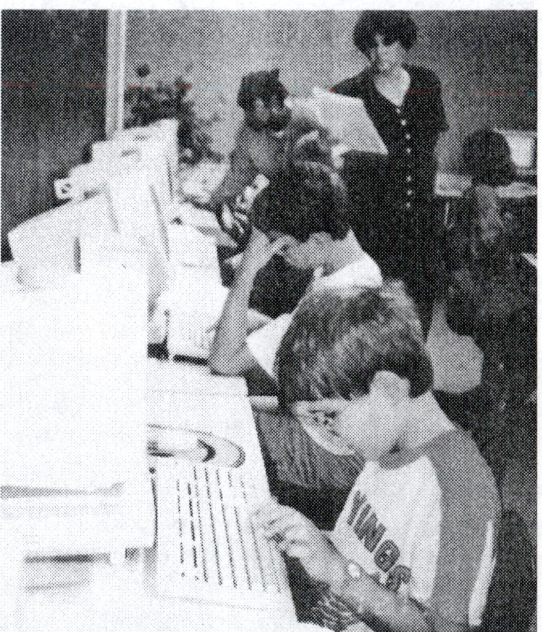

Fifth graders and POHI students type their journals at the computers.

his peers to share what they like about his poem. After students praise him for his ideas, Mary models how to ask the author questions. For example, she asks Jonathon what kind of bird did he hear chirping and how did the flag move. Next, she invites his peers to similarly ask him questions about his poem. She concludes the minilesson by asking Jonathon to share how he will polish his poem.

After modeling these strategies for revising, Mary explains that this is how all authors revise their writing—they think about what people would like about their poem and then they consider what questions people might have about their writing. She further encourages them to reflect about colorful, descriptive words to use in poems. Once she reinforces these concepts, all students try this process with partners, making at least three revisions in their poems. By giving them a goal to achieve, Mary finds that many of her students exceed her expectations.

After students polish their poems, she asks various students to share the first draft of their poem and then the revised draft, so everyone can experience the effect of the revisions on poetry. As students proudly read their new versions aloud to their classmates, everyone begins to see how revisions improve poems. Students gradually begin to understand how revisions help readers see, hear, feel, or smell the images they are conveying. As a result of this process, students begin to acquire a sense of audience.

Editing Activities. On the following day, the two teachers have the students work with their partners to edit their printed drafts. They encourage authors to circle at least three words they want to know how to spell correctly; their partners then help them circle any additional words they might want to check using spell check. The teachers also encourage all students to make sure that the title of their poem has a capital and that the first word of each line in their poem has a capital. If capitals are missing, the teachers show them how to place three lines underneath the letter, using proofreading techniques. While students work with their partners, the teachers guide and praise their efforts. Students whose poems are "top edited" (proofread a final time by the teacher) return to the computers to make revisions and use spell check to finish the editing of their poems.

Once the changes are complete, students decide the font and design to use for publishing their poems and print two copies—one for their writing folder, inserted along with all previous drafts, and a second copy, which will be published in a class book. Jonathon's poem is shown below:

Look out the Window

Look out the window and what do you see,
I see a baby bird chirping at me.
I see a dead fall tree,
And its branches like dragons staring at me.

Look out the window and what do you see,
I see a big brass house smiling at me.
I see rain drops dripping and blue birds dipping,
Flowers dying and lawnmower sighing.

Open the window and what do you hear,
I hear birds singing and flags wrinkling and wringing.
I hear leafs falling and cars sighing.

Open the window and what do you hear,
I hear the sound of peace filling the air,
I hear my fantasies and dreams come to life.
I sit and I wait for the bright happy light.

As Anna Marie, a POHI student, listens to students share their lists of words, descriptive words, and drafts, she acquires an understanding of what a poem is like. Once she acquires this concept, she is able to compose her own poem. To help Anna Marie write her poem, her fifth grade partner records the poem as she dictates it. Anna Marie then types her poem on the computer. After typing her poem, she practices reading her published poem to her partner. As she rereads the poem, she begins to learn how to read the words independently. Writing seems to strengthen her reading and recognition of words.

I see happy days and happy skies
I hear leaves crunching
I see leaves looking at me.

As a result of this experience, students learn how to collect, organize, and synthesize scientific information into a poem. Interestingly, Kristin, also a POHI student, shares, "I'm learning more this year. I love science." Anna Marie similarly comments, "I'm learning to read better this year." With pride, she then reads her poem all by herself. Through her writing, Anna Marie, who is barely reading at a primer level, begins to learn how to read and predict meaning. Her experiences and prior knowledge help her decode meaning.

Extending Social Studies Concepts through Poetry

Just as writing is an effective tool for learning scientific concepts, writing becomes an effective tool for building and extending understanding of the Native American culture. Using a multicultural, thematic approach to learning, Mary and Kathy begin their social studies curriculum with a focus on early American history and the Native American culture.

Native American literature provides the thread that links learning across the curriculum in this thematic unit. By reading stories like *Star Boy* and *Buffalo Woman* by Goble, *The Legend of Scarface* by San Souci, *Where the Buffaloes Begin* by Baker, *Dreamcatcher* by Osofsky, or *When Clay Sings* by Baylor, for example, the two teachers help their students acquire rich, detailed information about the various Native American tribes. Specifically, students learn how climate and geography influence Native American lifestyles and create differences among tribes in different geographical locations. Through the literature, students also gain insight into the dreams, beliefs, and values of Native American people. These experiences provide a context for understanding the Native Americans' experience in this country—a perspective that is frequently overlooked or omitted from social studies textbooks.

Writing further heightens understanding of these concepts. For example, after reading the collection of Native American poems from the book *Dancing Teepees* by Virginia Driving Hawk Sneve, Mary and Kathy invite students to compose their own Native American poems. First, students discuss the poems, highlighting how they reflect Native American beliefs and values. To extend their appreciation of the poems, the class then chorally reads some of the poetry.

Prewriting Activities. Following the principles of choral reading (Diamond & Moore, 1995), the two teachers first model choral reading as they display a poem on the overhead projector. After chorally reading the poem, they ask their students to read one more time, listening for the way they use loudness, stress, and pauses as they read. Then they ask their students:

- Which parts of the poem did we read loudly? Which parts softly? Why?
- Which words did we read with more stress? Why?
- Where did we pause as we read the poem? Why?
- Did we change our voice as we read other parts? Why?

As students respond, Kathy and Mary simultaneously draw attention to the poet's use of descriptive and figurative language and the use of repetition, rather than rhyme, within the poem. The class also discusses how Native Americans recreate the beauty of nature through the language of their poems.

Following these discussions, the teachers divide the class into two groups to read another poem chorally. After distributing copies of the poem, the teachers invite students to practice reading their parts with a partner. To avoid confusion, the two parts are highlighted with colored markers. (For example, Group I might be highlighted in blue; Group II, in yellow.)

After partners practice reading their parts at least three times, the class performs the choral reading of the poem. Having an opportunity to practice reading helps everyone feel successful. In order to reinforce the importance of reading and rereading texts, the two teachers explain that practice is what helped them chorally read the poem so well. In particular, this strategy is helpful for the POHI students and the struggling readers. As they read with their peers, they learn how to use expression, intonation, and pausing from their partners' modeling. Students also learn to recognize new words from the repeated readings. This rewarding, positive experience further heightens students' self-esteem.

> ***teaching* TIP 9.3**
>
> Choral reading is a way to increase students' fluency, expression, and comprehension. Reading and rereading text for a purposeful, meaningful goal gives students time to practice reading. At the same time, choral reading can be an effective prewriting strategy.

Once students are familiar with how to read poems chorally, the teachers organize students into cooperative groups of mixed ability levels to chorally read other poems from *Dancing Teepees.* This challenges students to decide how they will chorally read the poems and to determine the parts they will read in pairs, individually, or as an entire group. To help guide their decisions, Mary reminds them that the entire group might read parts of the poem that are repeated or parts of the poem that have special meaning. Students then apply problem-solving skills as they make decisions and assign parts. Once the decisions are made, with coaching and guidance from the teachers, the groups practice reading their parts. While practicing together, students help one another with difficult words. Through repeated practice, all students soon learn their parts. Some groups also decide to dramatize their parts by using their own invented "sign language" as they read the poem aloud. Using drama seems to help Andrew and Anna Marie remember the words better.

Another group also decides to have Rohina, a POHI student who is only able to communicate with her voice synthesizer, read a line that is repeated throughout the poem—"I rise, I rise." Working with Rohina's aide, the group programs her computer to read her line. Whenever the group comes to the line, "I rise, I rise," Rohina pushes the button on her computer. Through the creative ideas of her classmates, Rohina becomes an active participant, rather than a listener, in her group's choral reading. Rohina now feels that she is part of the class. When her group performs their choral reading before the class, everyone spontaneously claps. This becomes a turning point in Rohina's literacy experiences. Shortly after this event, Mary and Kathy discover that Rohina can read; they discover that even though Rohina is unable to speak, she can point to each of the words, revealing that she recognizes the words independently.

Once the groups are ready to perform their choral readings, the teachers explain that each group will perform their poem before the whole class twice. The first time the group will listen; the second time, the group will write down "delicious" words or nature words they hear from the poems in their notes. Mary demonstrates how to record the words, which will be used later when they compose their poems, by folding a paper in half lengthwise and labeling one side of the paper *Delicious Words* and the second side of the paper *Nature Words* (see Figure 9.1). She also reminds them to write the words as quickly as possible, without concerns for spelling at this point. In fact, she adds, when taking notes, we can use abbreviations.

As each group chorally reads their poems, the fifth graders and POHI students record either "delicious" or nature words in the appropriate columns. POHI students who are unable to use pencil and paper tell their aides which words they want on their lists and where to place the words. To help students who need more time to write, Kathy periodically asks students to share two or three words from their notes after the choral reading is performed. For example, Alicia volunteers *dazzling* and *dancing fringes;* Anna Marie volunteers *I rise, I rise;* Charlie shares *thunder peeled* and *harvest.* Whenever she sees students add to their lists, Kathy praises them, reemphasizing that we all get ideas from our friends and by listening. As the students continue this process with each choral reading, most discover that they have a whole page of notes to use with their own poems. Students then place their notes in their writing folders for the next day.

Figure 9.1

Darren's List of "Delicious" Words and Nature Words

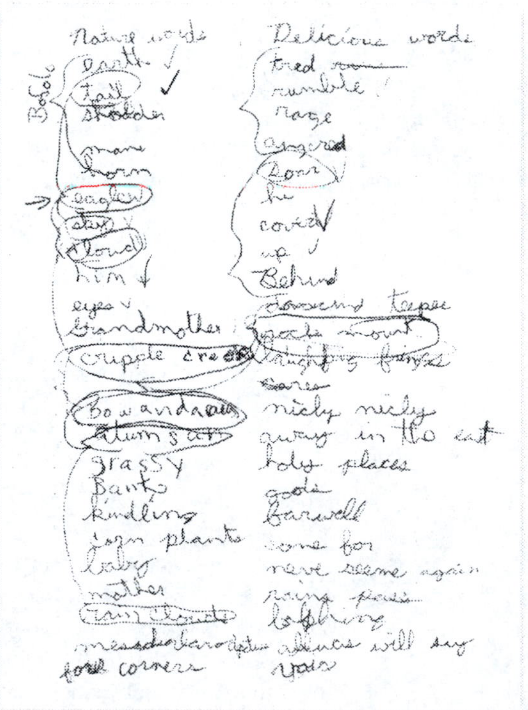

Continuing with prewriting activities, Mary asks students to write a running list of possible topics for their Native American poems. After students jot down possible ideas, they share two or three with the rest of the group. Students suggest topics such as the sun, the moon, thunder, rain, mountains, eagles, harvest, flowers, and rainbows. Next, Mary asks the students to choose one topic from their list and position it in the center of their paper, drawing a circle or other shape around the word. Modeling the process on the board, Mary writes *rainbow.* Then she demonstrates how to take words from her notes and place them around the topic word, forming a web. For example, she records *dew glistened, sparkling sun, dancing fringes,* and *thunder peeled* around *rainbow.*

Following her model, students write down their topics and form their own webs. After about 5 minutes, Mary asks a few students to share their ideas. Once a few have shared ideas, students continue to add more words to their webs for about 5 more minutes.

At this point, students are ready to compose their poems, so the two teachers encourage students to begin writing. Within a few minutes, many students compose four to five lines of their poems. As usual, they are eager to share their beginnings with their peers. By the end of Writing Workshop, everyone has a draft; some students even compose two poems.

Continuing with the Writing Process. During the next few days, students follow the same process they applied with earlier poems. Working with partners, they type a draft on the computer and then revise and edit their poems. Finally, they publish their poems using word processing tools. After selecting different fonts for their published versions, students share that they prefer using the computer to pencil and paper. Alex, for example, explains that his writing is neater and more readable with the computer.

Will's poem, displayed below, shows that he understands the Native American respect for nature; he also perceives that nature shapes how Native Americans view the world.

An Eagle of Light

First nothing, the Eagle and with it, the light
This is the story of an Eagle and of the light.
Long, long ago in a land far away there was darkness,
All of the animals wanted light but all that had tried had to turn back,
The sun was too bright.
Then one day an Eagle was angered because he had bumped into a porcupine while looking for food.
So he decided to make the sun move around the earth.
He set out across the sky, cutting through the clouds.
Up he flies, into the upper part of the sky until he saw the sun
Brighter than anything he had ever seen
But yet he plunged on into the sun, into the heat,
The top of his head feathers begin to burn.
Yet he pushed and pushed until the sun began to move around the earth.
And that is the story of an Eagle of Light.

Similarly, one can see that Andrew and Anna Marie, who collaboratively composed the following poem together, understand many concepts about the Native Americans. Being immersed in this caring, supportive learning environment is clearly advancing their literacy skills. They are discovering how to express their thoughts in written language from the model of their fifth grade peers. As they read what they write, they simultaneously improve their reading performance. Comprehension of what they read is further evident as they form connections between the text and their prior knowledge.

Teepee, Teepee
Dancing Teepees.
In a row or in a circle
Deer and turkey in the forest
Fish in Cripple Creek
It is sunny and warm
In the forest of green trees
I am happy

Extending Learning across the Curriculum through a Thematic Unit

As illustrated in Chapters 5 and 6, using a thematic approach to learning allows Mary and Kathy to address the content of their curriculum from several subject areas, making more effective use of classroom time. Their students simultaneously gain new perspectives on history as they view history from the lens of the Native American people. Integrating both multicultural literature and writing with the social studies curriculum fosters these insights.

Linking the Thematic Unit with Science. As Mary and Kathy continue their thematic unit on Native Americans, they weave connections among social studies, language arts, science, art, and music. After reading *Corn Is Maize* by Aliki, the students learn scientific and historical facts about corn. Specifically, they discover that corn, which belongs to the grain family, was first discovered in Mexico, where the Indians used cornmeal to make tortillas and tamales, and ate misickquatash (cooked corn with beans) and corn on the cob. They also realize that corn is different from many other plants, because corn cannot grow by itself; corn seeds must be planted, weeded, and carefully grown by the help of man.

After learning about corn's history, students discover how corn seeds themselves grow in science. Upon receiving three seeds, a damp paper towel, and a resealable baggie, students place the seeds on the damp paper towel and then insert the towel into their baggie and seal it. Over the next two weeks, the fifth graders and their POHI peers learn about the scientific principles of plant growth as they record their observations about the seeds in a seed journal. The journal includes pictures of the seeds as they grow and develop, labels of the individual parts of the plant (following Aliki's model), and written accounts about the daily changes they observe.

Linking the Thematic Unit with Art. When the class electronically travels to the western regions of the United States, they learn about the Navajos and the art of weaving. To reinforce these concepts, Mary and Kathy invite their students to weave an "Ojos de Dios" (Eyes of God), using twigs and colored yarn. As the students weave, Kathy often reads various multicultural stories about the Navajo people, reinforcing the concept that many Native American weavings, which use multicolored yarns to create intricate designs, tell stories about the life of their nation.

As the class continues its journey across the country, exploring how climate and geography change how the various Native American tribes live and interact with the environment, students begin to learn more about differences and similarities within a cultural group. Through the ongoing use of multicultural literature and writing, students simultaneously grow to appreciate the Native Americans' contributions to our nation's history and our lifestyles today.

Writing Workshop with POHI Students

As the year unfolds, many opportunities for reading and writing evolve within the classroom. Mary and Kathy understand that students learn to write by writing daily and by selecting their own topics for writing. Following these principles, the POHI students, who have not had opportunities to write in the past, become authors.

Watching how their writing grows and develops becomes an amazing experience for both Kathy and Mary. Too often, educators have presumed that writing experiences and instruction are not educationally appropriate for students who have labels such as "mental retardation" (Kleiwer & Biklen, 2001). Kathy and Mary, in contrast, believe that their POHI students can become authors when they benefit from shared interactions and team teaching (Erickson, 2002; Erickson & Koppenhaver, 1998). They have high expectations for all their learners.

Andrew Becomes an Author

To help illustrate this process, we will follow Andrew's development as a writer over the year. Andrew, an autistic learner, began the year with short, structured sentences whenever he wrote. To help him become more comfortable with writing, Kathy encouraged him to do his journal writing at the computer, which seemed to help him remain more focused, with minimal distractions. One of his first entries is shown below:

> Weather. I like the weather. I like the tunderstrms. I like the tunderstroms of the litnen [lightning] storms.

Initially, Andrew only recorded the word *weather* in his journal. To help him extend his writing, Kathy asked questions. For example, when she asked him what he liked about the weather, he replied, "I like the weather." Kathy then encouraged him to write this in his journal, too. After he finished writing, Kathy recirculated to his computer, asking him what was something he liked about the weather. After responding, Andrew wrote this in his journal next. Similarly, Kathy returned to his computer after he finished typing the sentence about the thunderstorms, asking him what he liked about the thunderstorms. This is how his last sentence about the thunderstorms evolved.

Working patiently with Andrew the first few months of school, Kathy helped him begin to extend his thoughts. Within a few weeks, he could type two or three sentences independently. Whenever he finished typing, Kathy recirculated to his computer, asking additional questions to help him elaborate his writing more. The journal entry displayed below shows how his writing progressed the following month.

> Computer. I have a computer at home at my house. I have a computer up into my bedroom. I have a Macintosh. I have games on my computer. I use it after school. I do my homework on my computer.

One can see that Andrew's sentences are beginning to expand slightly. He is also learning that writing is about our lives, adventures, and wonderings. As readers, we have a small glimpse into his life, which is highly influenced by computers. By January, Andrew is able to write independently about his day:

It was snowing today. There was snow on the ground. I went to go to school with my boots on. My shoes were in my bag. The snow was in the air. The snow was on the ground. I went to go to O.T. I went to lunch. I went to go to speech to type on the computer. And I went to go to the library. And I went to go home on the bus. When I got home I threw the snow ball at my mom.

As Andrew continued to explore written language at the computer, he also gained a sense of audience, especially as he shared his writing with his peers. Hearing their praise and interest in his writing motivated Andrew to write more. As can be seen from his journal entries, Andrew enjoys writing so much that he continues writing at home and during speech.

Having the time and opportunity to write helped Andrew learn how to express his ideas in different ways. Not all of his sentences begin with *I* in this journal entry; sometimes he uses the words *It, There, The,* or *And* to begin a sentence. One time he even began his sentence with a clause—"When I got home." Practice, experimentation, questioning, and social interactions with his peers helped him explore new ways to express ideas.

To help him move to a higher level of expression, Kathy decided to have Andrew print out a journal entry that he wrote about the movie *Star Wars:*

I saw Starwars.
I liked the movie.
I went with my mom and dad.
I had popcorn.
I got a Starwars c.d.
I got a light saber.
I liked that movie about Starwars.
I liked the movie alot. Me too said my friends mom and dad
I like it alot.

After reading the journal entry together, Kathy and Andrew looked again at the entry to see ways to revise his story. Working one sentence at a time, Kathy asked Andrew questions about the experience. As he responded to her questions, Kathy modeled how to extend the sentences to include this information by recording his words. Using carets and inserts, she integrated these ideas with his writing as shown in Figure 9.2. Andrew then made the revisions on the computer and proudly published the story.

I saw the movie Starwars and I loved it! I like the movie because it was exciting. It was really loud. I went with my mom and dad. I had popcorn. I ate it all. It was delicious! I got a Starwars cd. I like the music. I got a light saber. It is long and I can turn it on and off. I liked that move about Starwars. I liked the movie alot. Me too, said my friends mom and dad. We all liked it alot.

Throughout this experience, Andrew retained ownership of his writing because the revisions were his words. At the same time, he learned how to elaborate on his message so that

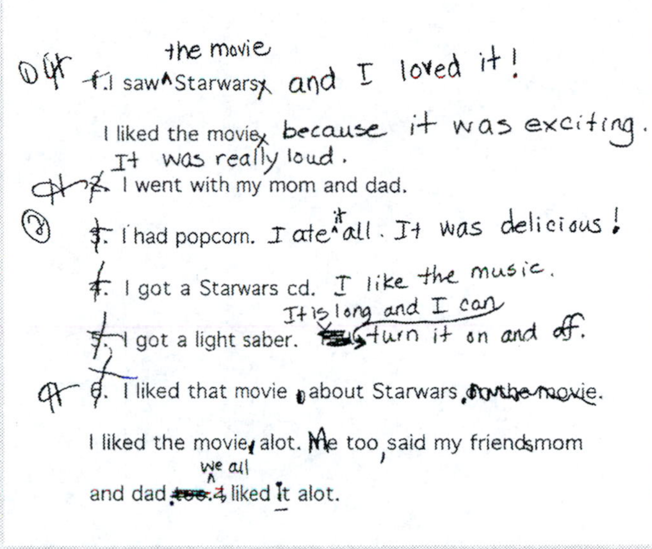

the movie
1. I saw Starwars and I loved it!
I liked the movie because it was exciting.
It was really loud.
2. I went with my mom and dad.
3. I had popcorn. I ate all. It was delicious!
4. I got a Starwars cd. I like the music.
It is long and I can
5. I got a light saber. turn it on and off.
6. I liked that movie about Starwars on the movie.
I liked the movie alot. Me too said my friends mom
we all
and dad too. I liked it alot.

Figure 9.2
Kathy Helps Andrew Elaborate His Writing through Revision

readers might enjoy the experience with him. By observing Andrew's progress over time, Kathy realized that he was now ready to learn more about revising his writing. She used one-on-one conferencing to help him learn more about the process.

Using Focused Writing with Different Genres or Types of Writing

Similarly, the other POHI students gradually improved their writing. What's important is that Kathy and Mary begin where the students are. Once they perceive their students becoming more comfortable with writing, they nudge them to new levels.

Creating Personal Narratives in an Inclusion Environment

When Kathy and Mary notice that the POHI students are gaining some facility with journal writing, they decide to have the fifth graders and their POHI peers create personal narratives, following the writing process. To begin, Kathy explains that personal narratives, similar to their journal entries, are usually about experiences in our lives, often focusing on a special moment (Calkins, 1994).

To help them understand this concept, she invites students to brainstorm possible ideas for a personal narrative. Trina suggests that we can write about a time when we got sick; Jonathon shares that we can write about a basketball or football game; Alicia comments that we can write about going to camp; Anna Marie shares that we can write about our birthday. After acknowledging their ideas, Kathy notes that there are many possibilities.

Once students decide on a topic for their personal narrative, Kathy encourages them to tell a friend about their experience. As students eagerly recount their experience to a friend, they realize that they also enjoy hearing about their friends' experiences. Next, Kathy suggests that they create a web about their experience. Anna Marie and Trina, who have been immersed in the inclusion classroom for 2 years, create the webs shown in Figure 9.3 independently.

Both Trina and Anna Marie are able to generate these webs because they have seen the process modeled by their teachers and the other fifth graders. Having the chance to orally

Figure 9.3

Webs for Personal Narratives

(a) Trina creates a web for her personal narrative. (b) Anna Marie creates a web for her personal narrative.

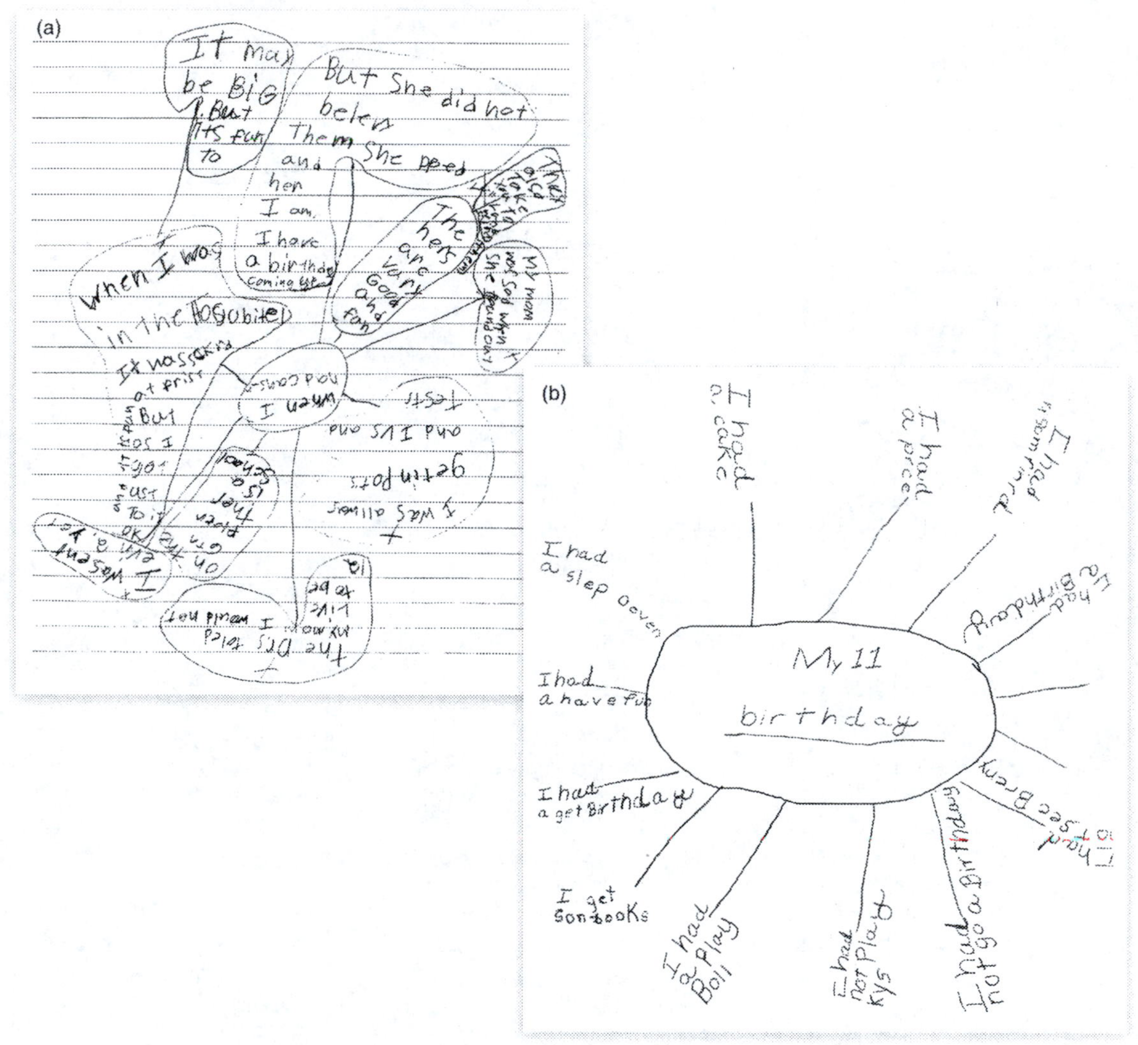

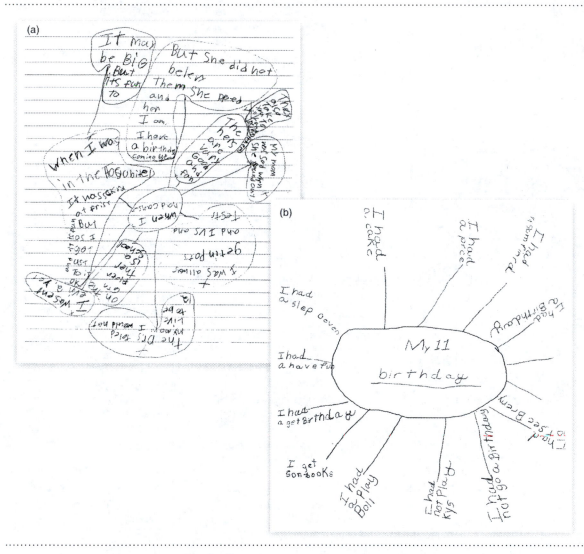

share their experiences before constructing the webs helps them organize their thoughts. Creating the webs helps them arrange their ideas on paper.

After generating the webs, all students share them with a new partner. As they share their webs, many insert additional information, which they initially overlooked. Following these prewriting activities, students begin to draft their personal narratives, using their webs. When Kathy asks them to pause and share their writing, a sea of hands emerges.

Over the next few days, Kathy and Mary have all students word process, revise, and edit their personal narratives. Following the model of their peers, Trina and Anna Marie

Figure 9.4

Revisions of Drafts of Personal Narratives

(a) Trina revises the draft of her personal narrative. (b) Anna Marie revises the draft of her personal narrative.

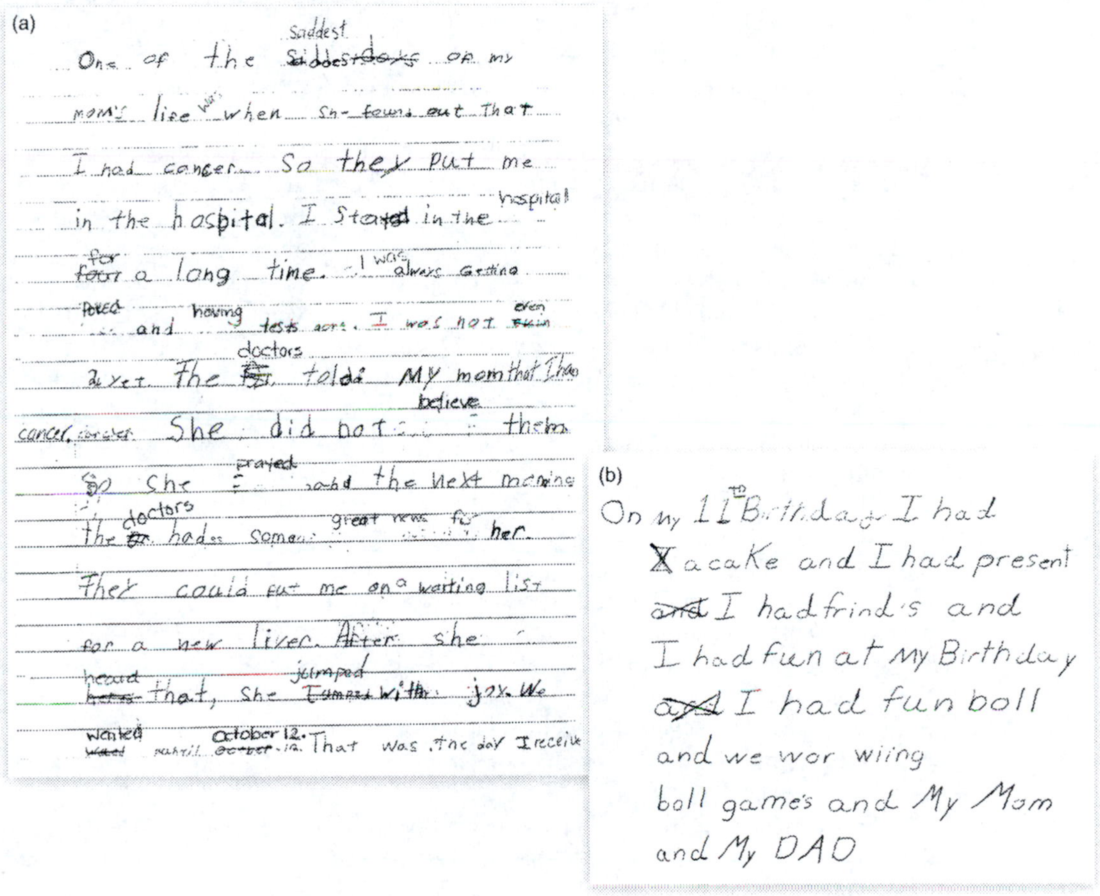

(a)

One of the Saddest ~~days~~ of my
mom's life was when she found out that
I had cancer. So they put me
in the hospital. I ~~Stayed~~ Stayed in the hospital
~~four~~ for a long time. I was always Getting
poked and having tests done. I was not even
3 yet. The doctors told my mom that I had
cancer forever. She did not believe them.
So she prayed and the next morning
the doctors had some great news for her.
They could put me on a waiting list
for a new liver. After she heard
that, she jumped with joy. We
waited until October 12. That was the day I receive

(b)

On my 11th Birthday I had
a caKe and I had present
~~and~~ I had frind's and
I had fun at My Birthday
~~and~~ I had fun boll
and we wor wiing
boll game's and My Mom
and My DAD

revise and edit their narratives, too. Figure 9.4 displays their revised drafts. Trina's final version is displayed at the beginning of the chapter. Her narrative describes how sadness can sometimes turn to joy; Anna Marie's story, displayed below, describes how much fun she had on her 11th birthday.

On my 11th birthday I had a cake and I had presents. I had friends and I had fun at my birthday. I had fun playing basketball. The birthday was at my house and we played games and had fun. We went swimming.

Both Trina and Anna Marie learned how to develop their writing in a new genre. These learning experiences helped them create a personal narrative by following a process.

Learning about Informational Texts in the Fifth Grade Curriculum

Being immersed in an inclusion classroom is an ongoing learning experience for Mary's fifth graders. They continuously hone their own skills as they help their POHI peers on a daily basis. "Teaching" someone else seems to reinforce their understanding of concepts, strategies, and information. Just as the POHI students' writing grew and developed, the fifth graders' writing also improved. To monitor her fifth graders' writing, Mary uses writing folders, which help her continuously evaluate their progress. As she leafs through their writing, she notices that they are becoming more proficient at writing poetry, paragraphs, and personal narratives. She decides they are now ready to create longer pieces, using informational writing.

To help them develop these skills, she decides to apply notetaking strategies to help them gather information for an expository piece. She begins the lesson by interactively reading the biography, *A Weed Is a Flower: The Life of George Washington Carver* by Aliki. After reading and discussing the biography, Mary rereads the story the next day as her students take notes about his life (see Chapters 5 and 6). To help them organize their notes, she has them divide their papers into four sections: George's Early Life, His Later Life, His Beliefs and Values, and His Accomplishments (see Figure 9.5).

A few days later, students return to their notes, sharing them with partners. As they share, students insert information they may have overlooked. Then Mary regroups the students as a class to share what they have learned. The combined activities serve as a way for the fifth graders to review the information about George Washington Carver; now they are ready to create a draft about his life.

At this point, Mary explains that they can easily organize their piece into paragraphs from their notes. For example, they may want to begin their pieces by writing about George's early life. Understanding how the notes progress, Jenny adds that then we can write a paragraph about his later life. Alex agrees, saying that he will write a paragraph about his accomplishments next and then conclude the piece with his values and beliefs. Cathy contributes that she will combine his accomplishments and his values and beliefs into one paragraph. Mary acknowledges their ideas, emphasizing that they are the authors; they need to make their own decisions on how to proceed. Someone may even want to begin with his values and beliefs.

Armed with ideas for organizing their informational piece, the fifth graders begin drafting their ideas. As usual, Mary has students pause periodically to share their writing to support those learners who need more guidance with their writing. Charlie shares his beginning:

He did not ask to be a slave. But he, like millions of other African-Americans, was a slave. George Washington Carver was born to the world in Missouri in 1860. He was sick and weak. He had no father to help raise him. All he had was his mother, Mary, and his brother, James. The Carver in his name stood for his master's last name. His owner was named Moses Carver.

As they continue to write and share their writing, Cathy reads her second paragraph:

As George grew older he was smart and curious. He also asked a lot of questions. George liked plants so much that the neighbors called him the "Plant Doctor." He wanted to go to school but school wasn't open to blacks or negroes. George left the Carver farm to go to school. When he went to Iowa, Iowa had accepted blacks.

Figure 9.5

Alicia's Notes about George Washington Carver

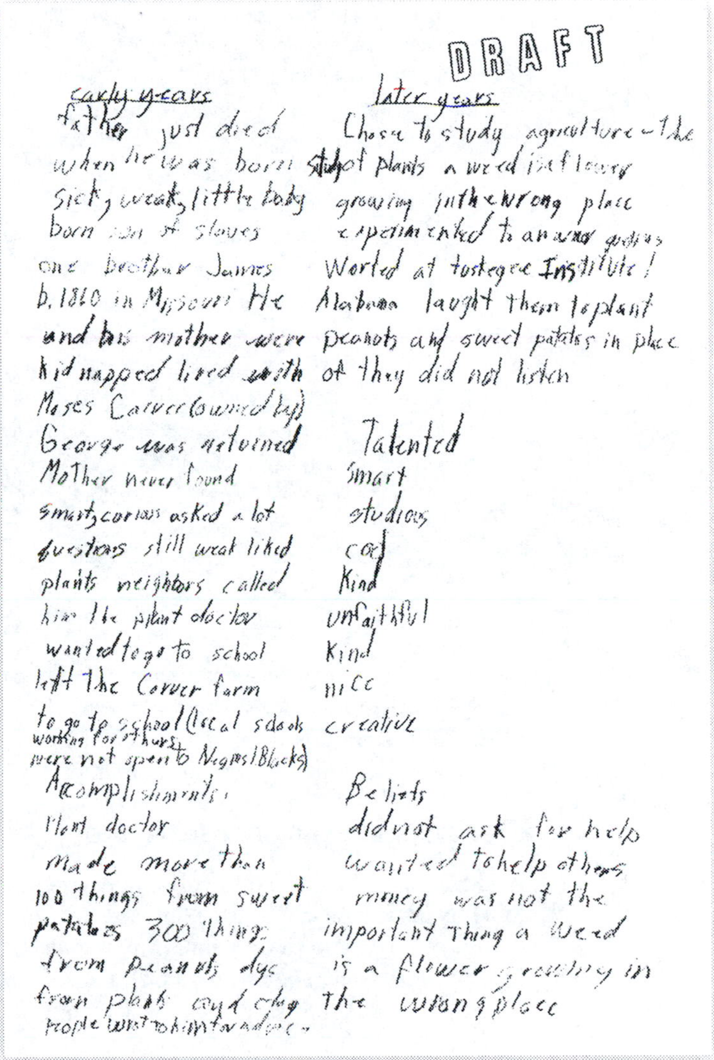

DRAFT

early years

father just died
when he was born
sick, weak, little baby
born son of slaves
one brother James
b. 1860 in Missouri He
and his mother were
kidnapped lived with
Moses Carver (owned by)
George was returned
Mother never found
smart, curious asked a lot
questions still weak liked
plants neighbors called
him the plant doctor
wanted to go to school
left the Carver farm
to go to school (local schools
working for others
were not open to Negros/Blacks)

Accomplishments:
Plant doctor
made more than
100 things from sweet
potatoes 300 things
from peanuts dyes
from plants and clay
people went to him for advice

later years

Chose to study agriculture - the
study of plants a weed is a flower
growing in the wrong place
experimented to answer questions
Worked at Tuskegee Institute!
Alabama taught them to plant
peanuts and sweet potatoes in place
of they did not listen

Talented
smart
studious
cool
kind
unfaithful
kind
nice
creative

Beliefs
did not ask for help
wanted to help others
money was not the
important thing a weed
is a flower growing in
the wrong place

George had chosen to study agriculture, the study of plants. He said, "A weed is a flower growing in the wrong place."

Over the next few days, the fifth graders word process, revise, and edit their pieces, following the writing process. In particular, they work on their leads and their endings; they also shape their writing to include transitions and flow. Jenny's piece shows her ability to combine all these elements into her writing.

George Washington Carver

George Washington Carver was born the son of slaves in Missouri in 1860. When George was born he was sick and frail. When he was a little bit older he and his mother were kidnapped by some bandits. A worker that worked for the Carvers went out to find George and his mother. He found George but he couldn't find George's mother. When he was five or so he was very curious and kept a garden because he liked plants. When he was ten his neighbors called him the plant doctor because he had come up with good techniques for his garden.

His curiosity drove him to want to go to school so much he left the Carvers to find a school that would accept him. The reason he had to leave to find a school was because the schools around them weren't open to blacks. When he found a school he found a family that would house him in exchange for work. When he finished school he had to find a college that would let him in. He finally got into a college when he was about 30.

In his later years he studied agriculture. He learned how to paint, sing, and play the piano. If he couldn't find the answer in a book he would find them out for himself. When he was all the way through college he became a professor in Alabama. One day he was watching the farmers and he said if you rotate the crops the soil will stay fertile. Some of the things you could plant are peanuts and sweet potatoes instead of cotton.

He made many accomplishment and discoveries. He discovered that you can make over 100 things out of sweet potatoes. He also made over 300 things out of peanuts like soap, coffee, candy, shampoo, peanut butter, and many other things. He also discovered how to make dyes out of clay and plants.

George W. Carver believed many things like "A weed is a flower growing in the wrong place." He helped many people but he asked for nothing in return. There were many things that were important to George but money was not one of them. George Washington Carver led a good and prosperous life.

Jenny, similar to her peers, learned many new things about writing by following this process. Most importantly, she discovered that writing takes time. When we give quality time and thought to our writing, we can be proud of our accomplishments. Certainly, this experience will help Jenny as she continues writing in middle school and high school.

Creating Informational Texts about Historical Figures

After learning how to craft informational texts, the fifth graders collaborate with their POHI peers to research historical figures who explored and revolutionized the 20th century through hard work, determination, and friendship. After selecting their historical figure, the fifth graders, each paired with a POHI student, use books and the Internet to research their person. Following the strategies for paraphrasing information, the fifth graders take notes to record important facts and information about their historical figure. The partners then use their notes to compose a biopoem about the person. Following this activity, students compose an informational piece about the person. Charlie and Will compose the following biopoem about Thomas Edison:

Thomas
Persistent, creative, patient, stubborn
Husband of Mina
Who loves Mina, work, inventing
Who feels courageous, optimistic, happy
Who needs his lab, to invent, and to sleep
Who fears failure, death, disaster
Who gives light, sound, movies
Who would like to see computers, CDs, TV
Resident of Menlo Park, New Jersey
Edison

After researching information about Alexis Carrel with her fifth grade partner, Trina independently used the notes to compose the following paragraph about Alexis:

Alexis Carrel was a scientist. He studied transplants to help others live. If it was not for him, I would not be alive today. In the late 1980's, my parents found out that I had cancer, and the doctors said that I would not live to be twelve. Then the doctors signed me up on a waiting list for a live donor. I don't remember how long I waited, but it seemed like a long time. When I did get my liver, I was very scared. My parents kept telling me that it would be O.K., and it was. I am now twelve years old and I am doing fine!

By integrating what she learned about Alexis Carrel with her own experiences, Trina was able to create her paragraph. Learning about someone who played an instrumental role in her life became a motivational experience for her, nudging her to a new level of writing.

As can be seen, the fifth graders and their POHI peers worked in a variety of grouping arrangements. Sometimes students wrote independently; other times they wrote in pairs; still other times they wrote in small groups. Having a variety of grouping arrangements supported the different needs of students as they composed two pieces about their historical figure.

To conclude their study of historical figures during the 20th century, students compiled the information into a database. The database, which revealed the interconnection of the historical people and their lives, became a learning tool to reinforce math concepts as well.

Culminating Experiences with Writing

As the end of the year began to approach, Mary and Kathy decided to revisit the science observation and notetaking activities. Since it was springtime, students would be able to make new observations and take different types of notes about leaves or trees. Due to the similarity of the writing activities, Mary and Kathy would be able to simultaneously look at their students' writing through all stages of the process, evaluating their progress during each stage.

After gathering their observations outside, the fifth graders and POHI students return to the classroom to create a web for a poem about spring. Even though Kathy and Mary guide and facilitate the process, they carefully observe to see how their students demonstrate independence and apply the writing process as they create the poems.

Kathy, for example, observes that her POHI students are able to take more notes outside and create a web for their poem independently. This time Andrew is able to write a poem by himself, rather than writing with a partner. His poem is also beginning to incorporate more adjectives to show what he sees or hears.

Spring

The birds sing in spring
The green grass is good
The sun is warm and bright
I see some sunflowers
I hear cars
I hear birds in the spring

When she compares Trina's fall poem with her spring poem, Kathy notices that Trina is using more descriptive vocabulary in her writing. She is also able to create a more vivid picture of the scene, using different senses. Her fall and spring poems are displayed below:

Leaves

I saw yellow leaves
Red leaves
Different shaped leaves
And Dark purple leaves
I smelled wet leaves
I felt some leaves and they felt crumbly
I heard the wind blowing the leaves.

Spring

Spring is the flowers starting to bloom
And the wind blowing in my hair
I hear the birds singing while they build their nest to lay their eggs
The warm sunshine shines down on the pond to make it twinkling
And the flowers are growing
When I see all the things around me
I see a rainbow around me.

Just as literature provides a model for students' writing, one can see that the fifth graders offered a model for the POHI students' writing. The social interactions that continuously emerged in this inclusion environment stimulated all learners to advance to new levels of writing and thinking. The caring, supportive attitude of teachers and learners further affirmed all learners within the classroom. Learning begins with feeling good about oneself as a learner. Peers and teachers frequently influence how a learner feels about himself or herself.

Celebrating the Power of Teaming

As the year came to an end, Kathy and Mary decided to celebrate the power of teaming by having students write about their experiences in an inclusion environment. Specifically, they invited students to describe how they, and one or two classmates, help and complement one another and how this cooperative friendship is beneficial to the class. Once the students completed their pieces, they compiled the writing in a classroom book for all to take home. The classroom book became a way to celebrate and remember their lifelong friendships.

As one reads the students' pieces, one can truly see how much students learned from this teaming experience. Marquis, for example, shows us that he learned that people can communicate in many ways. He also realizes that friendships often evolve when we reach out to one another.

I've made lots of friends this year like Rohina. She can't talk but she's a friend to all. I help her read, write and sometimes I help her stay on task. She's one of my best friends in the world.

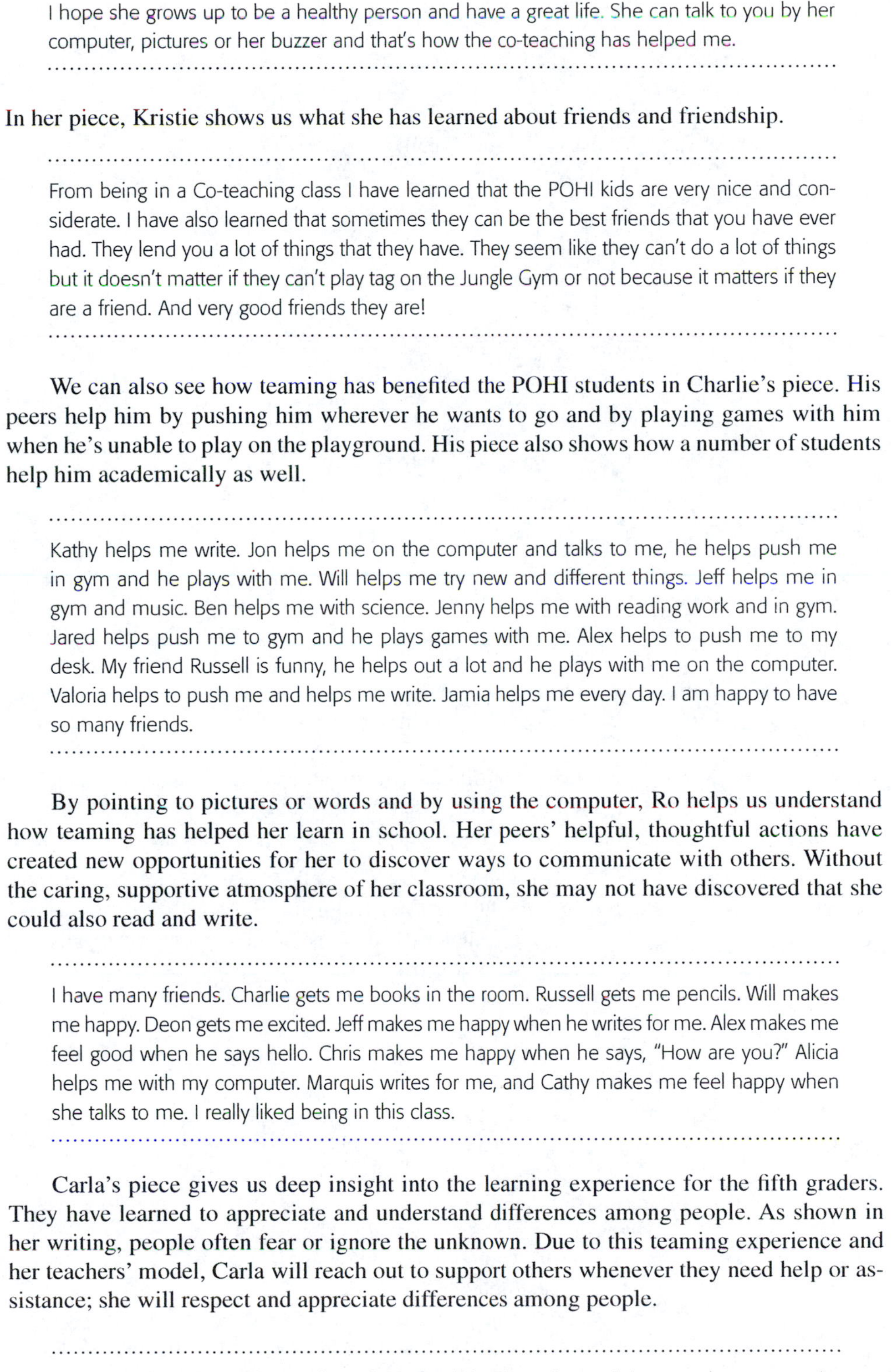

> I hope she grows up to be a healthy person and have a great life. She can talk to you by her computer, pictures or her buzzer and that's how the co-teaching has helped me.

In her piece, Kristie shows us what she has learned about friends and friendship.

> From being in a Co-teaching class I have learned that the POHI kids are very nice and considerate. I have also learned that sometimes they can be the best friends that you have ever had. They lend you a lot of things that they have. They seem like they can't do a lot of things but it doesn't matter if they can't play tag on the Jungle Gym or not because it matters if they are a friend. And very good friends they are!

We can also see how teaming has benefited the POHI students in Charlie's piece. His peers help him by pushing him wherever he wants to go and by playing games with him when he's unable to play on the playground. His piece also shows how a number of students help him academically as well.

> Kathy helps me write. Jon helps me on the computer and talks to me, he helps push me in gym and he plays with me. Will helps me try new and different things. Jeff helps me in gym and music. Ben helps me with science. Jenny helps me with reading work and in gym. Jared helps push me to gym and he plays games with me. Alex helps to push me to my desk. My friend Russell is funny, he helps out a lot and he plays with me on the computer. Valoria helps to push me and helps me write. Jamia helps me every day. I am happy to have so many friends.

By pointing to pictures or words and by using the computer, Ro helps us understand how teaming has helped her learn in school. Her peers' helpful, thoughtful actions have created new opportunities for her to discover ways to communicate with others. Without the caring, supportive atmosphere of her classroom, she may not have discovered that she could also read and write.

> I have many friends. Charlie gets me books in the room. Russell gets me pencils. Will makes me happy. Deon gets me excited. Jeff makes me happy when he writes for me. Alex makes me feel good when he says hello. Chris makes me happy when he says, "How are you?" Alicia helps me with my computer. Marquis writes for me, and Cathy makes me feel happy when she talks to me. I really liked being in this class.

Carla's piece gives us deep insight into the learning experience for the fifth graders. They have learned to appreciate and understand differences among people. As shown in her writing, people often fear or ignore the unknown. Due to this teaming experience and her teachers' model, Carla will reach out to support others whenever they need help or assistance; she will respect and appreciate differences among people.

> This year I have learned a lot about the POHI kids. I have learned that: Just because you're different doesn't mean you have to be hated, feared, or ignored. It just means you have

different needs than other people. You can help people, even if it is only moving a chair out of the way. You can be friends with someone, even if they use a wheelchair.

Even though some us may look and act differently on the outside, Will reminds us that we all have a "good soul" on the inside:

This class has helped me learn about how everyone on the inside has a good soul. I have learned how to communicate with someone who can't talk. Ro can respond with her fingers or pictures or using a computer. She is a good listener and understands a lot. Everyone makes me feel happy.

As one can see, sometimes students know how to express complex thoughts best.

Closing Thoughts

The caring, supportive environment within this inclusion environment is a model for teaching and learning. Once we acknowledge and affirm each person's self-identity, many new possibilities for learning appear for students of all abilities and strengths. There is no need to "water down" the curriculum. We need to expand and enrich the curriculum while responding to the differing interests, needs, and abilities of our students. Students of all ability levels love to be challenged. In fact, students become more motivated when we nudge them to new levels. Ultimately, high expectations ignite and heighten the reading and writing performance of all students.

Many factors contributed to this successful learning environment. First, all support services remained for POHI students; sometimes additional support even becomes necessary. In addition, the following concepts can contribute to successful inclusion classrooms:

- The class becoming one inclusive class, with two teachers who collaboratively construct the curriculum and instructional lessons, reflecting on their practice and refining their teaching to match the needs and interests of their students.
- Adaptable curricula, instruction, and resources within this flexible learning environment that is accessible to all learners, enabling more students to receive the services they need.
- Technology serving as a communication tool to promote higher-level thinking and problem solving.
- Assistive technology improving the functional capabilities of students and supporting the POHI students' learning whenever possible.
- Using a variety of grouping arrangements, including working independently, in pairs, groups, or whole-class arrangements to heighten reading and writing.
- Learning to work cooperatively; using praise, encouragement, and constructive feedback with one another; and following the model of the teachers to create a supportive context for learning.
- Encouraging social interactions within the context of the classroom to stimulate higher-level thinking and foster reading and writing for students of all ability levels.

While working collaboratively and cooperatively, students began to internalize skills and strategies developed as they worked with their peers. Others gained more depth to their knowledge by "teaching" or demonstrating skills and strategies to their peers.

Through the combined efforts of many people, the inclusion process creates a caring community that values the contributions of each individual and builds bonds among its members. We can all learn from this approach to learning as it fosters the ethical, social, and academic development of all students. Students became active learners because the expanded, enriched curriculum responded to their differing interests, needs, and abilities.

Teachers' Questions

1. **Our school does not have POHI students. Could I team with a special education teacher?**

   This sounds like a great idea! Children with special needs should be served in general education classrooms within inclusive communities whenever possible. This way, you will strengthen and support the classroom by the infusion of the special education students and their specially trained personnel or supportive services. Working as a team, you will discover new ways to reach the varying needs and abilities of all students. Certainly, technology may also provide an important instructional tool to open new doors for learning in your classroom.

2. **My special education students seldom write more than one or two sentences. How can I help them write more?**

   Special education students frequently fear the red pen when they write. They must first learn to trust you; they must learn that they can use their temporary spelling when they write. They also need to understand that you value their ideas over the conventions of writing—the use of capitals, ending marks, or appropriate grammar. Hearing praise and encouragement about their ideas helps them slowly become more comfortable with writing.

   In addition, we can begin to ask them questions about their writing similar to the way Kathy asked Andrew questions about thunder. These questions show an interest in their message and model how to expand their ideas.

3. **I have a student who refuses to write. He sits at his desk with a blank page. How can I help him?**

   Whenever Mary and Kathy see students with a blank page in front of them, they quickly circulate to the students in order to determine why the page is blank. Sometimes a student may still be trying to discover a topic for writing. Other times, a student may be uncomfortable writing because their handwriting is poor. Still other times, a student may be uncomfortable because they have trouble spelling. Sometimes the answer may not be readily apparent at first. Through observation, Mary and Kathy begin to gather clues so they can solve the problem. Once they discover the root of the problem, they can facilitate a student's writing by helping with brainstorming or by focusing on the message rather than the handwriting, spelling, or mechanics of writing. They also know that words of sincere encouragement and praise are helpful to these students, who often have low self-esteem.

4. **Why do you have students write so much poetry?**

   When we look at a continuum of writing genres, research tells us that personal narratives and descriptive writing are easier to write than informational writing or persuasive writing. Poetry is an example of descriptive writing. If the poetry evolves from the students' experiences or lives, it also becomes an example of personal narratives. Finally, poems are usually short, so they are easier to publish, following the writing process. I find that poems are ways for students to explore revising and editing without becoming overwhelmed.

5. **How important is it to have students write in pairs, in groups, and independently?**

Varying how students write is one way to address the differing needs and ability levels of our students. If we pair a higher-ability with a lower-ability student, for example, the lower-ability student may have great ideas. Working with the higher-ability student, this student will learn strategies on how to form and shape the ideas into a message. Similarly, if we have students work in mixed ability levels, students begin to learn a variety of strategies to use as they write. As students work in pairs and in groups, they gradually begin to internalize some of these strategies and can begin to apply them as they write independently. In addition, once the writing piece is finished, everyone gains ownership of the writing piece. As a result, some students become more confident in their abilities to write.

Children's Literature

Aliki. (1988). *A weed is a flower: The life of George Washington Carver.* New York: Simon & Schuster.

Aliki. (1988). *Corn is maize.* New York: Harper & Row.

Baker, O. (1988). *Where the buffaloes begin.* New York: Puffin.

Baylor, B. (1972). *When clay sings.* New York: Aladdin Books.

Goble, P. (1983). *Star boy.* New York: Macmillan.

Goble, P. (1984). *Buffalo woman.* New York: Macmillan.

Osofsky, A. (1992). *Dreamcatcher.* New York: Orchard Books.

San Souci, R. (1978). *The legend of Scarface.* New York: Doubleday.

Sneve, V. D. (1989). *Dancing teepees.* New York: Holiday House.

References

Anderson, R., & Speck, B. (2001). *Using technology in K–8 literacy classrooms.* Upper Saddle River, NJ: Merrill.

Anderson-Inman, L., & Horney, M. (2007). Supported eText: Assistive technology through text transformations. *Reading Research Quarterly, 42,* 153–160.

Bialo, E., & Sivin, J. (1989). Computers and at-risk youth. A partial solution to a complex problem. *Classroom Computer Learning, 9,* 34–39.

Boone, R., & Higgins, K. (1993). Hypermedia basal readers: Three years of school-based research. *Journal of Special Education Technology, 12,* 86–106.

Calkins, L. (1994). *The art of teaching writing.* Portsmouth, NH: Heinemann.

Clark, R. (1995). *Free to write.* Portsmouth, NH: Heinemann.

Council for Exceptional Children Delegate Assembly. (1993). *CEC policy on inclusive schools and community settings.* Reston, VA: The Council for Exceptional Children.

Diamond, B., & Moore, M. A. (1995). *Multicultural literacy: Mirroring the reality of the classroom.* New York: Longman.

Erickson, K. (2002). *ALL-Link: Linking adolescents with literacy.* Paper presented at the Annual TASH Conference, Boston, MA.

Erickson, K., & Koppenhaver, D. (1998). Using the "write talk-nology" with Patrik. *Teaching Exceptional Children, 31,* 58–64.

Ferguson, D. (1995). The real challenge of inclusion: Confessions of a "rabid inclusionist." *Phi Delta Kappan, 77,* 281–287.

Graves, D. (1983). *Writing: Teachers and children at work.* Portsmouth, NH: Heinemann.

Individuals with Disabilities Act, Pub. L. No. 108-446 (2004). [Online]. Available at www.ed.gov/policy/speced/guid/idea/idea2004.html [September 20, 2006].

Kleiwer, C., & Biklen, D. (2001). "School's not really a place for reading": A research synthesis of the literate lives of students with severe disabilities. *Journal of the Association for Persons with Severe Handicaps, 26,* 1–11.

Kulik, C., & Kulik, J. (1991). Effectiveness of computer-based instruction: An undated analysis. *Computers in Human Behavior, 7,* 75–94.

Kulik, J., & Kulik, C. (1985). Effectiveness of computer-based education in elementary schools. *Computers in Human Behavior, 1,* 59–74.

Kulik, J., & Kulik, C. (1987). Review of recent research literature on computer-based instruction. *Contemporary Educational Psychology, 12,* 222–230.

Leu, D. (1997). Caity's question: Literacy as deixis on the Internet. *The Reading Teacher, 51,* 62–67.

Lipsky, D., & Gartner, A. (1992). Achieving full inclusion: Placing the student at the center of school reform. In W. Stainback & S. Stainback (Eds.), *Controversial issues confronting special education: Divergent perspectives* (pp. 3–12). Boston: Allyn & Bacon.

McLeskey, J., & Waldron, N. (1995). Inclusive elementary programs: Must they cure students with learning disabilities to be effective? *Phi Delta Kappan, 77,* 300–303.

Office of Technology Assessment. (1988). *Power on! New tools for teaching and learning.* Washington, DC: U.S. Government Printing Office.

Raison, J., Hanson, L., Hall, C., & Reynolds, M. (1995). Another school's reality. *Phi Delta Kappan, 76,* 480–482.

Reinking, D. (1998). Introduction. In D. Reinking, M. McKenna, L. Labbo, & R. Kieffer (Eds.), *Handbook of literacy and technology: Transformations in a post-typographic world* (p. xi). Mahwah, NJ: Lawrence Erlbaum.

Roach, V. (1974). Supporting inclusion: Beyond the rhetoric. *Phi Delta Kappan, 77,* 295–299.

Scala, M. (2001). *Working together: Reading and writing in inclusive classrooms.* Newark, DE: International Reading Association.

Schirmer, B., & Casbon, J. (1995). Diverse learners in the classroom. *The Reading Teacher, 49,* 66–68.

Schnorr, R., & Davern, L. (2005). Creating exemplary literacy classrooms through the power of teaming. *The Reading Teacher, 58,* 494–506.

Schrag, J., & Burnette, J. (1994). Inclusive schools. *Teaching Exceptional Children, 26,* 64–68.

Snyder, I. (1999). Using information technology in language and literacy education: An introduction. In J. Hancock (Ed.), *Teaching literacy using information technology: A collection of articles from the Australian Literacy Educators' Association* (pp. 1–10). Newark, DE: International Reading Association.

Thousand, J., & Villa, R. (1995). Inclusion: Alive and well in the green mountain state. *Phi Delta Kappan, 77,* 288–291.

Zigmond, N., Jenkins, J., Fuchs, L., Deno, S., Fuchs, D., Baker, J., Jenkins, L., & Couthino, M. (1995). Special education in restructured school: Findings from three multi-year studies. *Phi Delta Kappan, 76,* 531–540.

chapter TEN

Organizing and Managing Assessment in a Writing Program

I learned that when you revise you can add in new things that you think of. And when you revise you put in things called caretts [carets] when you want to add something. My teacher taught us about delicious words and organizing your ideas before you start. The way you can get ideas is by taking walks outside to see what you would want to write about. You can make lists of things to put in your poem. You have to have patients [patience] during all of the activitys. Because if you rush, your poem won't sound good.

Alicia, a fourth grader in Tracey Franklin's classroom, wrote this reflective piece in her journal. At Tracey's request, Alicia began writing on what she has learned about writing during the past 6 months. She demonstrates her understanding of writing as a process—she doesn't think writing is magical. As shown by her reflection, she realizes that we gather our ideas for writing by drawing on our experiences and our lives—"taking walks outside to see what you would want to write about" or by creating lists of our ideas. She also perceives the importance of shaping our writing through revising. As she notes, writing takes time and patience if we want to express our ideas well.

Assessment as an Ongoing, Continuous Process

When Tracey reads Alicia's reflective piece, she will begin to form a hypothesis about Alicia as a writer, using information gathered from a variety of sources. Specifically, Tracey will analyze observations of Alicia as she writes, have ongoing conferences with Alicia, and checklists on Alicia's application of the conventions of language (i.e., spelling, grammar, punctuation, capitalization). She will also analyze data like this journal entry, as well as Alicia's writing samples, which are found in her writing folder. As Tracey analyzes the writing samples, she will determine how Alicia applies her knowledge of writing during each stage of the process. Questions she might ask about Alicia include

- How does she gather her ideas for writing?
- How comfortable is she while drafting her writing?
- How does she revise? Does she only change a few words in her writing? Does she move text around while she revises? Does she insert additional phrases and sentences to explain her ideas?
- How does she edit her writing?

Using multiple forms of assessment, Tracey gathers information about her learners on an ongoing basis. As she analyzes the information, she formulates decisions about her writing instruction in order to improve their writing. Tracey then plans her writing instruction—whether the writing is modeled, shared, interactive, guided, or independent—to reflect Alicia's needs, as well as her peers' needs. While providing this instruction, Tracey gains new insight and additional data about her students. Thus, Tracey continuously uses multiple data sources to confirm her analysis or to form new hypotheses about her learners. Periodically, Tracey will validate these inferences and hypotheses by using either formal or informal assessment tools to reassess their writing. Thus, the process begins again.

teaching TIP 10.1

Using multiple assessment tools gives us a more complete "picture" of the student as a writer.

As can be seen, assessment, which is closely linked with instruction, is an ongoing, continuous process always seeking to improve its own reliability, validity, and fairness (NCTE, 2004; Tompkins, 2008). Figure 10.1 illustrates how the process evolves in a continuous way.

To be effective, assessment penetrates the surface to gain a thorough knowledge of students' writing performance and the skills, strategies, and instructional needs sudents require in their writing. Not only does assessment determine how students are progressing, assessment also leads to improved instruction. To accomplish her overarching goals for teaching and learning, Tracey continuously tailors her instruction to meet the needs of her

Figure 10.1

Assessment as an Ongoing Process

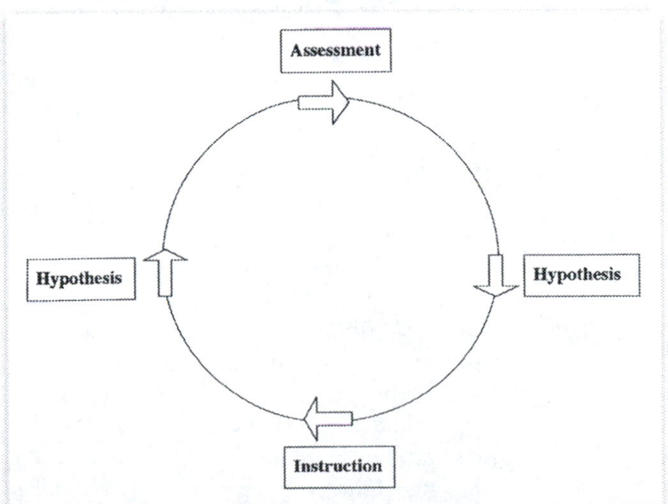

students. This requires ongoing reflection and analysis so that her instructional decisions align with her students' needs. Writing assessment, evaluation, and decision making for writing instruction become the "heart" of teaching and learning for Tracey.

Successfully implementing this model of teaching and learning within the classroom requires that teachers continuously learn about the twin crafts: teaching and writing. Graves (2004) shares that we shape and move toward greater refinement of these crafts by becoming lifelong learners who derive a sense of joy in discovering new learning from students, colleagues, or research. Assessment, which is the key to discovering new learning from students, helps us understand what our students know and what they are able to do. Through assessment, we find clues for effective teaching of writing. Specifically, meaningful and effective writing evolves when we link assessment with our instruction.

Organizing the Curriculum to Reflect Effective Assessment Theory and Research

Consistent with these ideas, Tompkins (2008) suggests that assessment merges with instruction, giving teachers information about two key questions: What do students know about writing? and What can students do with their writing? For example, Alicia's reflection gives us some insight into what she knows about writing; however, the reflection does not show us what she can do with her writing. This is why we must use multiple assessment tools; we need a complete picture of each student as a writer.

Using Observation as a Tool for Assessing Students' Writing

Observation, also referred to as kidwatching (Goodman, 1985), provides a picture of the interactional patterns and routines students follow as they write. Although observation often provides information about what students know about writing, Tracey finds that observation also shows her what her students do with writing. For example, she continuously watches to see how her students gather ideas for writing, locate and handle technology and resource materials, draft their ideas on paper, make use of environmental print, manage their time, interact with peers while writing, revise their writing, and self-edit or peer edit their writing.

Specifically, observation is an ongoing process through all stages of writing. For example, Tracey observes how Justin proficiently uses lists, graphics, or drawings to help him gather information for a writing piece. Gene, in contrast, struggles with prewriting strategies. Some days he sits at his desk for several minutes with a blank page in front of him during journaling. Using this information, Tracey makes sure she is nearby when Gene first begins writing. She may have a miniconference with him, helping him brainstorm ideas for writing in his journal so that he can begin writing more easily. Knowing that Justin quickly gathers ideas for writing, Tracey can postpone circulating by his desk temporarily.

To remain informed about each student's needs, Tracey records short, brief notes about her students as they write. Using a clipboard, she writes on index cards labeled with students' names as she circulates (see Figure 10.2). Later, she places the index cards in student portfolios to track their progress in writing. To keep this process from becoming overwhelming, Tracey only focuses on five students each day. By the end of the week, she will have observed each student at least once. As the year continues, Tracey jots down observations more quickly. More familiar with her students and their patterns of behavior, she may gather running notes on ten students in a day.

Figure 10.2

Using Note Cards to Observe Students as They Write

Katie 11/3 Katie's uncomfortable using temporary spelling. She uses words she knows how to spell.	Kyra 11/3 Kyra wrote a whole page of notes today. She's recording words and phrases rather than sentences!
Ryan 11/3 After we brainstormed, Ryan began writing about basketball—without hesitating.	Tanaka 11/3 Tanaka wrote on the computer during journals—longer journal entry!
Amanda 11/3 Amanda's very motivated to write. She fills up a page quickly.	Sean 11/3 Using interactive writing helps Sean write more. After I write a sentence, he writes a sentence.

Analyzing the Observations. Whenever her observations reveal a pattern or theme developing among her students, Tracey creates a minilesson to address their needs. For example, if she sees that many students are sitting at their desks with a blank page, she may decide to conduct a minilesson on how to select or choose a topic for writing. This minilesson may be for a small group of students or for the whole class, depending on what her observations reveal.

Similarly, her observations may indicate that several students are using dialogue in their writing. To meet their needs, Tracey may plan a minilesson on quotation marks for this group of students. At the same time, she may observe that most of her students use ending marks proficiently in their writing; however, only a few students understand how to use commas. To challenge her class, she will conduct a minilesson on how to use commas with clauses.

Still another pattern may emerge while students are participating in writing response groups. Even though her fourth graders seem to be able to give one another specific praise for their writing, their questions remain superficial and general. Explicitly, the questions do not offer writers precise ideas for shaping and crafting their writing to meet the needs of the reader. Examples of questions Tracey hears include

- How do you feel about your writing?
- Where did you get your ideas for writing?

To help her students move to higher levels of asking questions, she conducts a minilesson on questioning before they meet in revising groups. Working together, the class analyzes a piece about comets on the overhead projector, brainstorming examples of specific questions they would ask the author, including

- What did people originally call comets?
- Who discovered comets? When did they discover the comets?
- How did early scientists study comets? How do scientists study comets today?

- What do comets look like?
- How are comets formed?

Tracey then records these examples on chart paper for all to see. To assess their question-asking behaviors, she records examples of good questions she hears students pose during writing response groups later that day. Later, she will add these questions to the chart, praising her students for their ideas. By consistently linking assessment with instruction, Tracey lifts her students to higher levels of thinking and writing.

Anecdotal Records. Although Tracey maintains brief, ongoing observations of all students in her class, she also uses anecdotal records, notes, and rich details about students' writing to document struggling writers' progress. These notes (see Figure 10.3), which are written in more depth than observation notes, describe specific events without evaluating or interpreting the information (Piazza, 2003). A yearlong collection of these notes provides a picture of the student as a writer, which can be used to document a student's need to receive special services. As Tracey reviews and analyzes the notes, she gains further insight into how a student develops as a writer. By applying this information to her instruction for struggling students, she accommodates their needs more proficiently.

Using Conferencing as a Tool for Assessing Students' Writing

Miniconferences are also an informal way of gathering information about what students can do. Consistent with Clark (1995), these miniconferences last for only a minute or two. Since they are very focused, addressing only one issue at a time, they showcase individualized instruction at its best. To monitor learning most efficiently during miniconferences, teachers need to continuously circulate among their students, pausing briefly to conference with students. These short, focused conferences allow teachers to conference with every student at least once during Writing Workshop.

Sometimes, Tracey uses the miniconference to give her students words of encouragement or specific praise. These supportive comments help her students realize they are on the right track, giving them momentum and motivation to continue writing, revising, or editing.

Other times, Tracey conducts a miniconference to help a student who is struggling with writing. For example, Tracey may help a student brainstorm ideas for topics or decide what

Figure 10.3

Using Anecdotal Records to Observe Students

10/9

Kristin writes at least half a page in her journal. She consistently spells high frequency words correctly. She uses temporary spelling whenever needed, applying the consonant letters to spell the words.

11/9

Kristin's journal entries have increased to a page in length. She continues to spell high frequency words correctly. She's beginning to experiment with the vowels in words, placing her at letter–name stage.

1/9

Kristin is beginning to write fluently, applying her knowledge of vowels and consonants when using temporary spelling. She understands the short vowel sounds, and she's experimenting with the long vowel sounds. Kristin seems to enjoy writing about a number of different topics, including family, friends, and pets.

to write about next. By asking open-ended questions, she helps students continue writing or solve problems that they may encounter in their writing, as in the following examples:

- How is your writing going so far?
- How do you feel about your writing piece?
- What problems do you have with your writing?
- What's your favorite part so far? Why?
- What is the main idea of your piece so far?
- What do you plan to do next?

Tracey also uses miniconferences to help her students during various stages of the writing process. When students begin drafting their ideas, for example, Tracey often uses miniconferences to stimulate their writing or to help them shape their writing more closely.

- How do you feel about your opening line?
- What is the most important thing you are trying to say here?
- Can you tell me more about this part?
- Can you tell me what this part means?
- How can you show the reader what something looks like?
- What did the object look like?
- How did the experience feel?
- What happened next?

These questions also guide students' thinking so that they become more focused or see how to focus their writing more tightly.

Similarly, Tracey uses miniconferences during other phases of the writing process. Figure 10.4 gives examples of questions she uses to stimulate her students' thinking as she conferences with them during these stages.

Throughout the conferencing process, Tracey listens to her students as much as possible (Calkins, 1994). Rather than giving *her* ideas or viewpoints, Tracey asks open-ended questions to stimulate her students' thinking as they write. As a result, Tracey's students retain ownership of their writing. They also become more confident with their writing because they do not feel that someone is criticizing them. They feel that Tracey values their ideas while guiding and supporting them as a writer.

Tracey uses miniconferences to facilitate students' writing during all stages of the writing process.

Figure 10.4

Questions to Stimulate Students' Thinking during the Drafting Stage

Introductory Questions

- Tell me about your piece of writing.
- Why did you choose to write about this topic?
- Why is this topic important to you?
- What surprised you in your draft?
- What problems are you having?
- Do you know what I like the most about your piece?
- Where is this piece of writing taking you?
- Do you have any questions?

Questions That Deal with Meaning

- Do you have more than one story/topic here?
- Can you underline the part that tells what this draft is about?
- What is the most important thing you are trying to say in your piece?
- How does your title fit your draft?

Questions That Deal with Details

- Can you tell me more about this?
- This part isn't clear to me. Can you tell me what you mean?
- How did you feel when this happened?
- How do you feel about your descriptions?
- Did you tell about something, or did you show us by using examples?

Questions That Help a Writer Move On (when a draft is not finished)

- What do you intend to do now?
- What do you think you can do to make this draft better?
- What will you write next?

Questions That Deal with Voice as Students Revise

- How does this draft sound when you read it out loud?
- Can you point to the part that is most exciting?
- Can you show me a place where we hear you speaking?
- How can you bring life to your piece?
- How do you show your personality in your writing?

Questions That Deal with Organization as Students Revise

- How do you feel about your beginning and ending?
- Does the beginning of your piece grab the reader's attention?
- How have you tied your ending to your beginning?
- What kinds of transitions did you use?
- Can you think of some other transition words?
- How can you use sequence of events to tell the story?
- How can you organize your ideas for the reader?

Questions That Deal with Ideas as Students Revise

- Can you be more specific here? (e.g. How did you go into the house?)
- Can you think of a different way to say this?
- What works so well you'd like to try and develop it further?
- What additional details or examples can you include?

Questions That Deal with Sentence Fluency as Students Revise

- How did you vary your sentences?
- How did you use rhythm and flow in your writing?

Questions That Deal with Word Choice as Students Revise

- What are your action words? Can you add others?
- Can you think of another word to use here?
- How can you show the reader what you see, hear, smell, taste, or feel?
- What are some colorful words you used?
- How can you include figurative language in your writing?

Questions That Help Children See Their Growth as Writers

- What did you learn from this piece of writing?
- How does this piece compare to others you have written? Why?
- Can you think of something new you tried in this draft that you've never tried before?
- How are you a better writer now than you were at the beginning of the year?

Using miniconferences through all stages of writing helps Tracey consistently monitor her students' progress. Tracey uses observation to supplement the conferences. This allows her to determine if and how her students move from guided scaffolding to independent writing or if and when they internalize strategies and skills.

Using Checklists as a Tool for Assessing Students' Writing

Along with observations and conferences, checklists provide another way for Tracey to monitor observed writing behaviors. Depending on the purpose, Tracey creates checklists to show how her students move through the writing process, to document how her students apply grammatical or mechanical skills in their writing, or to determine whether students have completed all phases of a writing project. Her instructional goals help her decide when to create and how to use checklists.

Editing and Revising Checklists. In Chapter 5, for example, Beth Caldwell created an editing checklist for her students to use as they self-edited and peer edited their memoirs. To help her keep track of how her students apply punctuation in their writing, Tracey makes a similar checklist to document each punctuation skill they use independently and the date when that skill was consistently applied (see Figure 10.5). This checklist also helps her determine how and when to plan minilessons on punctuation for her students. Whenever small groups of students are ready to learn a new skill, Tracey creates a minilesson for these groups to model how to apply the skill in their writing.

Figure 10.5

Checklist to Monitor Acquisition of Punctuation Skills over Time

Punctuation Checklist
(Indicate Dates When Consistently Applied)

Periods

_____ at end of a sentence
_____ after an initial
_____ after numbers in a list
_____ after abbreviations

Question Marks

_____ at end of a question

Exclamation Marks

_____ after words or sentences showing strong feelings

Commas

_____ to separate words in a series
_____ between day and year
_____ between city and state
_____ after greeting in a friendly letter
_____ after closing of a letter
_____ after an initial yes or no
_____ to separate a quote from a speaker
_____ before the conjunction in compound sentences
_____ after a clause at the beginning of a sentence

Quotation Marks

_____ before and after someone speaks
_____ around a title of a poem, song, story, or TV program

Apostrophes

_____ in contractions
_____ to show possession

Colons

_____ before a list
_____ in writing the time
_____ after the greeting in a business letter

Parentheses

_____ to enclose unimportant information
_____ to enclose stage directions in a play

Hyphens

_____ between parts of a compound number
_____ to divide a word at the end of a line
_____ between parts of some compound words

Source: Adapted from Tompkins, Gail E., *Teaching Writing: Balancing Process and Product,* 5e, p. 81. Published by Allyn and Bacon, Boston, MA.

Checklists help Tracey maintain records for report cards and family conferences. By referring to the checklists during family conferences, Tracey shows the family how their children are progressing in writing. Tracey also conducts student–family conferences where students show their caregivers what skills or strategies they have achieved and what skills or strategies they plan to work on in future writing. Using both the checklist and their writing pieces, students can more easily demonstrate their progress to their family.

Similar to the editing checklist, Tracey often creates revising checklists for her students (see Figure 10.6). Tracey enjoys these checklists because she feels that the checklist not only challenges her students to try more revisions in their writing but also checks their writing piece to see if they followed the predetermined guidelines. When used during family conferences, the revision checklists become a way for students to show caregivers what strategies they apply when revising their writing and what strategies they plan to try in future writing pieces.

In addition to revising checklists, revising strategy checklists (see Figure 10.7) help her students determine what types of revising strategies to apply in their writing. This helps her students begin to see which revision strategies they use most frequently in their writing and which revision strategies they need to try in future writing pieces. Tracey finds that this assessment tool often motivates her students to try more advanced revising strategies when revising future writing pieces.

Using Checklists with Writing Projects. Checklists also help students verify whether they have completed all the requirements for a writing piece. Tracey finds that these checklists help her students become accountable for their work. As students review the checklist, they place a check next to the completed items; peers then review the checklist, determining whether students have completed all the requirements. According to Tracey, following this

Figure 10.6

Example of a Revising Checklist for a Friendly Letter

Revising Checklist for Friendly Letter

Author: ____________________

	Author	**Peer**
I have included a greeting in my letter.	______	______
I have included a closing in my letter.	______	______
I began my letter with an interesting beginning to gain my reader's interest.	______	______
I used examples and details to explain my ideas in the letter.	______	______
I used descriptive adjectives in my letter.	______	______
I used exciting verbs in my letter.	______	______
I varied my sentences in my letter.	______	______
I ended my letter with a thoughtful comment.	______	______
I have included a closing for my letter.	______	______
I revised my letter ______ times.	______	______

Signatures: ____________________ ____________________

Author Peer

Figure 10.7

Revising Strategy Checklist for Students to Show What Types and Numbers of Revisions They Make in Their Writing

Revising Strategy Checklist

Name:

	Additions	Substitutions	Deletions	Moves	Total Changes
Level of Changes					
Word Level					
Phrase/Clause Level					
Sentence Level					
Multi-Sentence/ Paragraph Level					
Total					

Source: Adapted from Tompkins, Gail E., *Teaching Writing: Balancing Process and Product,* 2e, p. 382. Published by Allyn and Bacon, Boston, MA. Copyright © 2008 by Pearson Education. Adapted by permission of the publisher.

process leads to more successful writing experiences. The checklist, which removes subjectivity from the evaluation process, helps her students know how they will be evaluated on their writing. A checklist for biographies is found in Figure 10.8.

Using Checklists to Document Students' Developmental Writing. Melissa Wood, a kindergarten teacher, finds that checklists are an invaluable way to monitor how her students progress through the developmental stages of spelling. Her checklist (see Figure 10.9) gives her insight into her students' knowledge of the symbol–sound system. To help her monitor her students' growth in using the symbol–sound system, she records the date that she observes them advancing to a new stage of spelling. This becomes a way to communicate each student's growth during family conferences. The checklist also helps her decide when to plan minilessons on various concepts related to the symbol–sound system. This way, she continuously nudges her students to new levels of spelling as they demonstrate their readiness.

Using Writing Folders as a Tool for Assessing Students' Writing

Analyzing students' writing pieces on an ongoing basis provides insight into what they can do in writing. To analyze them more easily, as well as keep track of students' writing pieces during all stages of the process, Tracey has her fifth graders keep their writing in folders with pockets. She keeps the writing folders in crates, placed on bookshelves, for easy distribution to further ensure that writing pieces do not get lost. At the end of Writing Workshop, all students routinely place all prewriting activities, drafts, revisions, and edits in their writing folders. Classroom assistants then place the folders back in the crates. By adhering to routines, Tracey finds that her students seldom lose their writing. This eliminates frustrations so that students' feelings about writing will gradually improve.

Figure 10.8

A Checklist to Monitor Students' Implementation of the Writing Process

Biography Checklist

Author: ____________________

	Author	Teacher
Prewriting		
I created a timeline for my biography.	_____	_____
I created a web for my biography.	_____	_____
Drafting		
I created a draft for my biography, writing on every other line.	_____	_____
Revising		
I participated in a writing response group.	_____	_____
My group gave me praise on my biography.	_____	_____
My group asked me questions about my biography.	_____	_____
I made at least three revisions.	_____	_____
Editing		
I proofread my biography, using the editing checklist.	_____	_____
My biography was peer edited, using the editing checklist.	_____	_____
Publishing		
I word processed my biography.	_____	_____
I illustrated my biography.	_____	_____

Source: Adapted from Tompkins, Gail E., *Teaching Writing: Balancing Process and Product,* 5e, p. 148. Published by Allyn and Bacon, Boston, MA. Copyright © 2008 by Pearson Education. Adapted by permission of the publisher.

Having all stages of the writing piece in a folder further helps both Tracey and her students monitor their progress during each stage of the writing process. Specifically, Tracey can more easily determine what strategies and skills each student successfully applies to their writing piece, as well as those strategies and skills that require additional support and guidance in their writing.

In addition, the writing folders provide yet another data source for analyzing and monitoring students' progress. By integrating this information with data from the observations, conferences, and checklists, Tracey feels she can more accurately refine her instruction so that each student becomes a more successful writer—writing to the best of his or her ability.

Whenever her fourth graders publish a writing piece, they then move the prewriting activities, drafts, revisions, edits, and checklists or rubrics—clipped together—from their writing folder to their portfolio. The portfolio, another data source for analyzing and monitoring students' writing progress, provides a picture of students' writing over time. In particular, the portfolios become a valuable resource for family conferences.

Figure 10.9

Checklist for Stages of Emergent Writing

Stages of Emergent Writing
(Dates Indicate When Student's Writing Consistently Shows This Pattern)

Stage 1: Prephonemic Spelling

_____ Uses drawings to record messages
_____ Uses scribbles to record messages
_____ Uses random symbols or shapes to record messages
_____ Uses random letters to record messages
_____ Copies environmental print

Stage 2: Phonemic Spelling

_____ Uses beginning sounds to record messages
_____ Uses beginning and ending sounds to record messages
_____ Uses invented spelling with word labels
_____ Uses invented spelling with phrases
_____ Uses invented spelling with sentences
_____ Uses invented spelling with multiple sentences

Stage 3: Letter–Name Spelling

_____ Uses letter–name spelling with word labels
_____ Uses letter–name spelling with phrases
_____ Uses letter–name spelling with sentences
_____ Uses letter–name spelling with multiple sentences

Stage 4: Transitional Spelling

_____ Uses transitional spelling with phrases
_____ Uses transitional spelling with sentences
_____ Uses transitional spelling with multiple sentences

Stage 5: Conventional Spelling

_____ Uses conventional spelling with sentences
_____ Uses conventional spelling with multiple sentences

Using Writing Samples as a Tool for Assessing Students' Writing

Students' writing samples, placed in portfolios, provide an important tool for assessment. Using these samples for analysis, Tracey begins to see what students can do with their writing.

Holistic Analysis of Writing Samples. One way Tracey analyzes her students' writing pieces is to use a holistic or general impression analysis. When she uses this analysis, Tracey makes sure that she considers every aspect of the writing—both content and mechanical considerations—in order to assign an overall performance score.

In particular, Tracey, who has been trained in holistic analysis, finds that this analysis helps her assess students' writing samples from the beginning and the end of the year. Tracey and her fellow teachers agree that there is a need for this assessment data, not just for accountability, but as part of good teaching. Working together, her principal and co-teachers gather writing samples from all students in the fall and spring, using prompts such as *My best school memory* or *The best thing that happened to me*. As an alternative, they may also use a "typical" writing sample not generated by a prompt (Routman, 2005).

To further make this experience an authentic assessment, Tracey and her co-teachers determine that the prompted writing will be completed in a single day with no teacher interventions. To further ensure that the writing reflects their ability to write, teachers give students time to draft their writing pieces and time later in the day for revising and editing their pieces.

Once students complete their pieces, Tracey and her co-teachers apply holistic analysis to the writing samples. First, they sort students' writing into five piles that range from strongest to weakest. Using a trainer to facilitate the process, teachers then identify anchor

Kristen and her teacher share her writing portfolio with her mother during a family conference.

papers representative of each point on their scale. Once teachers begin to holistically score the writing pieces, they then use the anchor papers to help determine the holistic scores.

Consistent with holistic analysis, two different readers read the same writing pieces (approximately 15 to 20 per person), assigning a score for each piece. After combining the two scores, the trainer then assigns each piece a numerical score, which averages the combined scores. Due to the training process, most scores are the same or contiguous, reflecting the anchor papers. If a discrepancy occurs, the trainer invites a third reader to score the writing pieces.

After holistically scoring her students' writing samples, Tracey places them in portfolios to help her document students' writing improvement during the school year. Specifically, Tracey uses these writing samples, as well as other data sources, to note each student's strengths and weaknesses in writing. At the end of the year, she removes three writing samples—one from the beginning of the year, another from the middle, and a final sample from the end of the year, and places them in each student's academic folder. She then passes the academic folder on to successive teachers.

Primary Trait Scoring. Tracey also uses primary trait scoring, an analysis that determines whether her students incorporate specific traits or qualities in their writing. Tracey especially enjoys this form of analysis because she is more easily able to assess each genre (i.e., letters, narratives, or informational pieces) differently.

Specifically, primary trait scoring considers the specific purpose and audience for a specific genre and judges the writing piece according to situation-specific criteria. Pieces that receive a high score exemplify the primary traits; weak scores, even if they exhibit interesting, well-organized writing, do not (Tompkins, 2008).

By using primary trait scoring, Tracey allows her students to know the criteria used to evaluate their finished compositions. Rather than assigning a subjective grade to their writing, she assigns a grade that reflects whether they follow the requirements for the writing piece. Using primary trait scoring further prevents her from focusing solely on the mechanical aspects of the writing.

In order to promote successful writing, Tracey distributes the scoring guide to her students before they begin writing (see Figure 10.10 for an example of a scoring guide).

Figure 10.10

Example of a Primary Trait Scoring Guide for Learning Logs

Science Learning Log Scoring Guide

Name: ______________________________

Required Criteria:	**Yes**	**No**
List of 20 new science words and their meanings from the text	_____	_____
At least 10 learning logs	_____	_____
Cover for the learning logs, including a title and illustration	_____	_____
Grading Criteria (1 for C; 2 for B, 3–4 for A):		
All entries include information from the text and my thoughts and feelings about the ideas.	_____	_____
Entries include two or more science concepts from text.	_____	_____
Entries show a connection between my experiences and the science concepts.	_____	_____
Entries include graphics or illustrations to show the concepts and ideas visually.	_____	_____

Source: Adapted from Tompkins, Gail E., *Teaching Writing: Balancing Process and Product,* 5e, p. 87. Published by Allyn and Bacon, Boston, MA. Copyright © 2008 by Pearson Education. Adapted by permission of the publisher.

This way, students can use the scoring guide to revise and edit their writing, leading them to a more successful writing experience. At the same time, Tracey remembers that this form of assessment does not reflect interesting, well-organized writing. To look at her students' writing in this way, she usually applies a more holistic analysis.

Nevertheless, Tracey also realizes that she *does not need to score all writing.* If her students constantly have to adhere to strict guidelines, she realizes that she will stifle her students' writing. Understanding that writing is a set of "complex subprocesses that occur interactively as writers work their way from the beginning of a writing to its culmination" (Routman, 2005, p. 243), she frequently allows them to write without evaluating the pieces.

Rubrics. Rubrics, scoring guides that use elements of primary trait scoring (Bratcher, 2004), are another way to analyze students' writing. Specifically, these rubrics often incorporate Spandel's (2004, 2005) six traits or qualities of effective writing: *ideas, organization, voice, word choice, sentence fluency,* and *conventions* (see Figure 10.11). School district personnel in Tracey's district believe that these rubrics, when introduced through minilessons one trait at a time, help students write creatively and communicatively, as well as helping students perform well on standardized tests in writing (Higgins, Miller, & Wegmann, 2007). For these reasons, Tracey often uses these rubrics with her students. However, she realizes that these rubrics are merely an assessment tool. She understands that excellent teaching of writing requires that she teach beyond the rubric or the six traits (Culham, 2003; Routman, 2005).

Similar to primary trait scoring, rubrics use descriptors that are related to the organization, language, and mechanics of the writing project. To support teachers' effective use of rubrics, Tracey's school district designed some general rubrics appropriate for almost any writing. Tracey often incorporates these into the writing curriculum.

Figure 10.11

Using the Six Traits to Create Rubrics for Evaluating and Analyzing Students' Writing

Ideas

- Uses interesting ideas to clearly express messages.
- Applies examples and details to support ideas.
- Uses accurate, logical information to express ideas.
- Draws upon thoughtful or intriguing ideas to present a message.

Organization

- Applies an order or sequence to deliver the message.
- Arranges ideas in proper order.
- Creates a beginning, a middle, and an ending.
- Uses effective lead and ending sentences.
- Applies paragraphs and/or headings.
- Draws upon transitions to organize thoughts.

Voice

- Applies a writing style or personality to convey ideas.
- Creates a connection with the reader.
- Shows a point of view or attitude.
- Brings the topic to life.

Sentence Fluency

- Uses a variety of sentences (simple, compound, complex).
- Varies how sentences begin and end.
- Develops cohesive sentences.
- Creates a rhythm or flow of words.

Word Choice

- Draws upon colorful adjectives, adverbs, and describing words.
- Applies strong verbs and action words.
- Uses quotable or memorable words.

Conventions

- Applies developmental stages of spelling.
- Uses appropriate capitalization and punctuation.
- Applies appropriate grammatical conventions.
- Uses appropriate spelling.
- Applies appropriate language.

Other times, Tracey and her students design student-friendly rubrics to use with specific types of writing assignments (see Figure 10.12). These rubrics, which allow her to evaluate student writing in a variety of genres, encourage creativity and simultaneously incorporate appropriate writing conventions. In addition, students begin to understand and appreciate the value of rubrics because they help construct them.

Regardless of which rubric she uses, Tracey introduces the rubric before students begin writing so they will understand how they will be evaluated. As students begin to apply the rubric during the revising and editing stages of writing, she finds they often improve their writing pieces.

However, as mentioned earlier, Tracey does not evaluate all writing pieces; she does not want to stifle students' creativity. Tracey wants her students to enjoy writing, experimenting and exploring its genres. This creativity and enjoyment cannot be compromised. Specifically, she only evaluates one or two pieces per marking period. She believes her students just need more time to practice writing without being assessed.

Using Self-Assessment as a Tool for Monitoring Students' Writing

To become effective writers, Tracey's students assess their own writing and their use of the writing process. At the beginning of the chapter, Alicia assumed responsibility for her writing by reflecting on what she learned about writing. Through reflection, Alicia discovered more about writing and the writing process. For example, she began to understand that revising improves our writing while requiring patience.

Similarly, Alicia's peers discovered more about writing and the writing process through this reflection exercise. Alex, for example, learned that writing is fun as he puts his thoughts on a sheet of paper. Cathy discovered that she likes using webs as they "help me put my ideas in words." Will, similar to Alicia, learned that revisions improve his writing. He also

Figure 10.12

Student-Friendly Advertisement Rubric

3 Very Persuasive Advertisement

- Focused on the harmful effects of pollutants and the need to preserve wetlands.
- The opening statement captures the attention of the reader.
- The ideas and words are arranged to make persuasive statements.
- Three or more persuasive statements are shown.
- The final conclusion reinforces the ideas and statements within the ad.
- There are minimal spelling or mechanical errors.

2 Persuasive Advertisement

- Focused on the harmful effects of pollutants and the need to preserve wetlands.
- The opening statement interests the reader.
- The ideas and words are arranged to make a statement about pollution.
- Two persuasive statements are shown.
- The final conclusion emphasizes/summarizes ideas and statements within the ad.
- Spelling and mechanics do not get in the way of the message.

1 Emerging Persuasive Advertisement

- The harmful effects of pollutants and the need to preserve wetlands should have more focus.
- The opening statement needs to be interesting or motivational to appeal to the reader.
- The ideas and words need to be arranged to make strong statements.
- Only one persuasive statement is shown.
- The final conclusion is missing or fails to emphasize/summarize the ideas.
- Spelling and mechanics make the ad hard to read and understand.

learned that through writing you can "create your own world." In contrast, Jared warns us, "It takes a few weeks to get the hang of it [writing]. You'll get it sooner or later." Similarly, Krystal cautions us, saying, "It takes a while to figure out what you want to write." As can be seen, these students understand a great deal about writing and the writing process. While sharing their ideas with their peers, all learners gain a deeper knowledge about writing.

Creating a Chart on Students' Concepts about Writing. Similar to Tracey, Mary Streeter and Kathy Micallef (see Chapter 9) asked their students to reflect on what they had learned about writing in January. As the fifth graders and their POHI peers began to share, Mary and Kathy decided to list their students' reflections on chart paper. Within a few seconds, they realized that students' ideas fell into six categories—prewriting, drafting, revising, editing, publishing, and overall feelings about writing, as shown by Figure 10.13.

As a result of this process, Mary and Kathy gained more insight into students' knowledge about writing. They realized that students understand that writing emerges from the writing process. Understanding this basic concept will help their students generate writing pieces in future grades.

After the students reflected on what they know about writing, Mary and Kathy asked them to record at least three goals for their writing. As Mary and Kathy watched, they were amazed to discover that the fifth graders and their POHI peers set realistic goals for themselves. Many students who needed to work on spelling or punctuation listed these as goals; other students who needed to use more descriptive words in their writing listed this goal; still others who needed to work on their beginnings or endings similarly listed these goals.

Figure 10.13

Chart Showing Students' Reflections about Writing

What We Have Learned about Writing

Prewriting

- Do lots of brainstorming.
- Make a web of our ideas.
- Use abbreviations in notetaking.
- Talk about what you're writing to get more ideas.
- Get ideas from books.

Drafting

- Select a topic.
- Look around the room for words and ideas.
- Write about things you like.
- Write about yourself.

Revising

- Check your details and add more details.
- Add adventure.
- Check to see if anything is missing.
- Read to see if it makes sense.
- Make a good lead.
- Use interesting techniques like similes or figurative language.
- Change the words instead of using them over and over.
- Improve your ending.

Revising Groups

- Read it to someone to see if it makes sense.
- Share your stories and leads.
- Think about your audience.
- Encourage the writer.

Editing

- Use capital letters in the correct places.
- Use proper punctuation.
- Use correct spelling.
- Write in paragraphs.

Publishing

- Use good handwriting.
- Share your writing with others.

All the Time

- Do your best!
- Take your time!
- Never quit!

Interestingly, most students listed more than three goals. To help them prioritize, Kathy asked them to place a star next to the three goals that were most important to them. Once again, students placed stars next to the goals that matched their individual needs. Figure 10.14 lists examples of goals students set for themselves.

In the spring, the fifth graders and their POHI peers reflected on their writing once again. They shared these goals with their caregivers during family conferences. After sharing their goals, students then showed how they did or did not achieve their goals in writing.

If we want students to improve their writing, they need to have ownership of their writing. By reflecting on their writing and setting their own goals for learning, students gain ownership of their writing and their learning.

Using Portfolios as a Tool for Assessing Students' Writing

Writing portfolios, a collection of student writing from the beginning to the end of the year, illustrate how each student progresses in writing over time; portfolios show how students apply their knowledge of the writing process. Authenticity of the portfolio emerges from the writing pieces, which include all stages of the writing process, as well as any observation notes, checklists, rubrics, self-assessment items, or reflective writing pieces. To effectively portray a realistic picture of a student's writing, the portfolio may also include a few samples of journal writing or other unpublished writing. What's important is that the portfolios reflect each student's progress during a school year or over several years.

Figure 10.14

Examples of Students' Goals for Their Future Writing

Prewriting

- Walk around and observe.
- Draw pictures.
- Take more notes.
- Make a list of ideas.
- Think of ideas and organize them before writing.
- Do lots of brainstorming.

Drafting

- Remember to double space.
- Be patient with your writing.
- Think before you write.

Revising

- Draw lines through stuff instead of erasing.
- Use carets to add details.
- Revise as many times as possible.
- Read to see if it makes sense.
- Use more description in my writing.
- Use more adventure in my writing.
- Make good leads.
- Make it exciting.
- Use strong words.
- Use interesting words.

Editing

- Use capital letters when they are needed.
- Check my spelling.
- Use proper punctuation.

Publishing

- Use nice handwriting.
- Share my writing with others.
- Publish a book.
- Send my writing to a magazine to be published.

Additional Goals

- Write more.
- Write in my journal at home.
- Write on the computer more.
- Have a super fun time while writing.

Similar to Tracey, Mary and Kathy move students' published writing pieces—including the prewriting activities, drafts, revisions, edits, and checklists or rubrics (clipped together)—from their writing folder to their portfolio. These collections, usually one or two per marking period, reflect what their students know about writing and what they can do with writing. Since the writing pieces include all stages of the writing process, Mary and Kathy easily monitor each student's progress during all phases of the writing process.

In particular, portfolios reveal which strategies and skills students successfully apply to their writing, as well as those strategies and skills that require additional support and guidance. Even though portfolios become a place to collect data and evidence about students' growth and development, their greater purpose evolves from how Kathy and Mary use the data. After carefully examining the data through interpretation, analysis, reflection, and decision making, they use this information to guide their instruction. This process is slow and evolutionary, involving risk taking and ongoing self-examination.

Portfolios also help students and their families gain insight into how their writing grows and develops. For example, as the fifth graders and their POHI peers begin to analyze their writing pieces through all stages of the process, guided by Mary and Kathy, they begin to see how they might improve their own writing. While sharing their analyses with their families, the fifth graders became empowered to set new goals and directions for their own writing.

Combined with all assessment tools, portfolios give an accurate picture of each student's progress over time. Ongoing analysis and interpretation of these data sources increase assessment validity and reliability. Merely using the tools will not result in successful writing. Similar to Kathy and Mary, we must use the analysis and interpretation of the data to inform our instructional practice so that all students, regardless of ability level, move to higher levels of writing performance.

Using Writing Sample Analysis to Help Students Shape and Craft Their Writing

As shown above, ongoing analysis of students' writing helps teachers see how to guide students' writing. Most students' writing needs ongoing shaping so that it improves. Where to begin is often the key question. Culham (2003) suggests that we begin one step at a time. She warns us that students become lost in the process if we overwhelm them by moving too fast or too soon.

Consistent with Culham (2003), Mary Streeter and Kathy Micallef focus on one aspect of writing at a time. For example, in Chapter 9, Kathy helped Andrew, an autistic student, first become comfortable with writing. The process Kathy applied with Andrew models how to begin with preschoolers, kindergarteners, first graders, or struggling students. Similar to Andrew, younger writers need opportunities to explore and experiment with written language through practice and more practice.

As we guide our students at these levels, we need to follow Kathy's example of asking questions, which help students see where to go with their writing. Just as Andrew gradually began to gain a sense of audience through questions, questions can help beginning writers gain a sense of audience. Sharing their writing with their peers helps them further internalize a sense of audience as they write.

Once Andrew became more comfortable with his writing, Kathy showed him how to expand his ideas and language (see Figure 9.2 on page 263). When young writers become more comfortable with their writing, we need to similarly show them how to expand their writing. As we continuously guide students' writing to new levels, however, we only focus on one aspect of their writing. Helping students improve their writing is not dependent on fixing everything at once.

Helping Young Writers Improve the Flow of Their Writing

Realizing that she doesn't have to fix everything at once, Sharon Draper carefully reads over her second graders' drafts about ducks. While reflecting on the drafts, she observes that most of her students begin their sentences with *Ducks* or *They.* Savannah's writing piece illustrates this simplistic flow of language.

Ducks dive 100/300 feet deep. Ducks also fly up to 30/70 miles per hours. Ducks preen their feathers so they don't get wet. Ducks have difrent colors and they are really, really, really pretty.

To help the second graders learn ways to add interest and flow to their writing, Sharon conducts a minilesson on transitional words. After brainstorming a list of ways to begin sentences with transitional words, the class applies the strategy, using a student's writing typed onto an overhead transparency. As the class suggests new ways to begin various sentences, Sharon models how to revise the piece by inserting carets and the new words or phrases on the overhead transparency.

After seeing the process modeled, students make simple revisions on their drafts, inserting words or phrases to change how their sentences begin, similar to Savannah.

A lot of ducks dive 100/300 feet deep. Ducks also fly up to 30/70 miles per hours. Sometimes ducks preen their feathers so they don't get wet. Most ducks have difrent colors and they are really, really, really pretty.

As Savannah continues to draft future writing pieces, she will begin to think about different ways to begin sentences. Sharon will further reinforce this concept during reading. She will ask students to reread sections of a book or story and look for words that authors use to give rhythm and flow to their sentences. Through these interactive experiences, the second graders will also learn that transitions link key points and ideas, providing insight into organizational strategies authors use in their writing.

Helping Young Writers Consider New Leads and Endings for Their Writing Pieces

After looking over her third graders' drafts, Shari Simpson observes that most of her students begin their writing with flat, lifeless sentences. She further notices that her third graders often end their writing pieces without considering an ending that ties up the details, expressing a conclusion, or an ending that leaves the reader with a sense of satisfaction or resolution. Their last sentence usually means that this is all they have to say, leaving the reader hanging in the air!

To help her students move to a higher level of writing, she plans a minilesson on leads and endings. After looking at leads and endings in a variety of informational books (see Chapter 6), Shari asks her students to go back to their prewriting notes to see whether they might craft more exciting leads and more effective endings for their writing pieces about the desert.

In response to this challenge, Jon decides to insert a new sentence for his lead. His first draft began: "There are about 21 animals in the desert." His new lead becomes a question to stimulate interest in his topic: "Do you know how many animals are in the desert?" To create a more effective ending, he experimented with the element of time by showing how the desert changes after 200 years. This is his final draft:

Do you know how many animals are in the desert? There are about 21 animals in the desert. Animals also dig howls [holes] in the ground for there homes. Cidys [Coyotes], ant, rabbits, pack rats, ground scirol [squirrels], mice and snakes live in the ground. Its hot in the day and cold at night. Others live in hole in the cactus like wood peckers, dove, bats, owls, and night birds. After 200 years the cactus falls and animals like scorpeins insecs, bees, lisers, snakes, and milapeds move in.

Through this process, Jon has learned new ways to begin and to conclude his writing pieces. He has learned that these strategies help readers become interested in his message. He has also discovered that beginnings and endings can portray an organizational scheme, demonstrating how the environment changes over time. He will continue to think about these organizational strategies the next time he writes an informational piece.

Helping Young Writers Add More Descriptive Words to Their Writing

Word choice is about using rich, colorful, precise language to communicate a message. In poetry, word choice helps create images in your mind so that you feel that you "see" a picture of what the author describes. To help her students begin to learn more about word choice in descriptive writing, Mandy Church invites her fifth graders to collect notes as she reads poems about color in *Hailstones and Halibut Bones* by Mary O'Neill. As she reads some of the poems aloud, she invites students to keep a list of "delicious" (descriptive) words and phrases they hear in their writing notebooks. When students draft poems about their favorite color, they use the "delicious" words so that readers will "see" a picture of what they are describing.

To further challenge her third graders, she asks them to brainstorm ways to help authors use more description in their poems during a minilesson. After Mandy records their ideas on chart paper, she encourages them to try these questions with their peers during writing response groups. After hearing praise about her poem, Cherise listens carefully to her peers' questions. Then she polishes her poem, adding richer, more colorful words like *rumbling* and *crinkling*.

Crystal Blue Sea

As I walk in the twilight, I see blue all around
When I look in the sky, I notice I have found
A blue fleck flying here and there.
Blue is everywhere.
Slowly, I start my journey home,
Blue is everywhere I roam.
I hear the bark of a hound, and a far off rumbling sound.
As I push away a shrub and look into the distance,
To my surprise I have found a sea of blue.
Blue clouds, blue flowers
Blue lakes, blue bays,
Blue crystals, blue hours,
Blue shadows, blue days.
And in the middle of the meadow
I saw what was making the rumbling sound.
It was a crystal blue waterfall.
So I started off in a run, for the waterfall I was bound.
I dipped my hands in the crystally water.
Then I heard a crinkling sound that was becoming a bother now.
Then I saw a bluish horn stuck out through crystal trees.
Slowly it moved a little forward
And I saw it was attached to a pure white head.
With another thrust forward it revealed a winged body
That I rode above the crystal blue sea
And home to roam another day in my crystal blue hideaway.

As can be seen, Cherise has learned how to show the reader what she sees, hears, and feels; she is beginning to gain a passion for language. By playing with language and word choices in her writing, Cherise is learning how to paint pictures for her readers. The more she experiments with word choices, the better her poetry or descriptive paragraphs will become in the future.

Helping Young Writers Discover Voice in Their Writing

Voice brings personality and tone to writing. Ruth Culham (2003, p. 102) describes it as "the golden thread that runs through a piece of writing." Specifically, authors insert their own personal flavor to a piece so that we know that it is unmistakably theirs.

Sima Thurman, a teacher of second and third graders, believes that journal writing helps students discover their voice. She finds that students explore and experiment more with their writing during journal writing because they have choice and ownership of their writing. Through choice, each student becomes a person who is speaking to the reader, a person who cares about his or her message. As her students experiment and practice writing daily, the magic, wit, feeling, or spirit gradually begins to evolve. In a journal entry, Tim, a second grader, describes his feelings about having his grandparents move closer to his home.

A Bitter Sweet Story

Today my grandpa is in the hostipal [hospital] here in Idaho. My grandma and grandpa moved here about one year ago. He used to live in Crowel [Crowell], Texas. If he still lived there he would propply [probably] be dead right now because they lived in the middle of no where. He has been in the hospital for about one month or two. So I am really happy that he is being taken care of.

By writing about his feelings in his journal, Tim begins to discover his voice, showing us the importance of family in his life.

Azira's voice, which emerges from her poem, soars in a journal entry.

The Yelling Breeze

Can you feel the yelling breeze?
Can you hear the yelling breeze?
Well, I can!
My hands start-a wrinkl'n,
My feet start-a slipp'n,
As I scramble to a scarred tree trunk.
Do you see the picture I am trying to paint?
I smell the scent like sweet pumpin' apple jam pie!
I see the lonely baseball diamond as
I hold on to that tree trunk like white on rice.
Can you feel the yelling breeze?
Can you hear the yelling breeze?

As readers, we see magic and wit flowing from the poem composed by Azira, a third grader. Once students discover their voice, their language begins to flash, giving life and breath to their writing.

Helping Young Writers Become Aware of Focus in Their Writing

Organization, the internal structure of a writing piece, weaves meaning into the piece, helping the reader see the "complete picture." Prewriting activities often help writers showcase their thoughts and ideas about a topic, giving the writing piece its structure. There are no recipes to follow; each writing piece must fit with the author's purpose for writing.

To help her fourth graders gather focus in their writing, Andrea Brace invites her students to practice writing in their journals; she also has them write personal narratives at least twice a year. Journaling gives her students time to experiment and explore ways to discover their ideas for writing while using a variety of genres. In his journal entry, Alex focuses on his sister. By using an interesting lead, sequencing, and a conclusion, Alex effectively organizes his piece.

Do you know why a sister is nice? Well I do. A sister is nice because she takes you places like beaches, restaurants, and stuff like that. She also gives love and plays volleyball and tennis with me! My sister's hair is dirty blond, she has sparkly blue eyes and has pretty long hair. Her name is Jennifer. A sister usually makes you feel excited and special. My sisters are from Michigan. Where are yours from? My sister is important because if I didn't have one I'd be super duper bored. That's why a sister is nice.

As Andrea circulates among her students, she notices that Alex experimented with his lead by asking a question. During her minilesson yesterday, the class searched through a variety of picture books in order to see how authors create leads for stories. Alex remembered how one author used a question to capture the interest of the reader. Experimenting with this technique, he used a question to begin a piece about his sister. Before moving on to another student, Andrea compliments him on his lead.

Using a combination of minilessons, focused writing, and journaling, Andrea supports her students' exploration of ideas in their writing. Because there is not a single right way to focus one's writing, she realizes that students should learn a variety of strategies. These strategies, often gleaned from reading memoirs and literature aloud to her students, become tools to apply as they craft their writing. Discussing how authors focus their writing, elaborate on the details of memories, create effective leads for a memoir, or sequence events and ideas initiates an awareness of these strategies. Alex and his peers later experiment with them in their journals or personal narratives.

Helping Young Writers Apply Writing Conventions

Conventions are a polite way to guide the reader through the text and make ideas readable (Culham, 2003; Routman, 2005). Different from previous examples, which evolve as we craft and shape our writing, conventions relate to editing and preparing the text for the reader. Editing for spelling, mechanics, and grammar is the final touch, a touch that makes the text clear to the reader.

Tracey Franklin does not want to present a distorted view of writing to her students. She does not prioritize the conventions. She strives to create a balance between creating interesting, imaginative, informative texts and edited texts. Helping her students see the difference between revising and editing is one way she creates this balance. As shown previously, Tracey promotes this understanding by showing her students that we craft and shape our writing through revision. She further shows her students that, as authors, we must showcase our good manners. Out of politeness, we must carefully edit our writing so that the message is easily readable.

***teaching* TIP 10.2**

In order for students to learn how to effectively revise and edit their writing, we must first help them understand the difference between revising and editing. Revising is reshaping the meaning of a writing piece. Editing is changing the mechanics, grammar, or spelling in a writing piece.

Marquis's teacher focuses on all stages of the writing process as she monitors his writing progress.

To accomplish her goals related to the conventions, Tracey engages her students in the editing process. First, she reads through her students' drafts, looking for the editing skills they use proficiently and those they do not use proficiently. Using minilessons or workshops, she addresses one or two editing skills that will improve their understanding of the conventions in their writing.

When her students begin to self-edit and peer edit their writing, they use an editing checklist (see Figure 10.15) and apply the newly acquired skills to their own writing. After self-editing and peer editing their writing using the checklist, students give their drafts to assistant editors—students who are proficient editors. Whenever a convention has been overlooked, the assistant editors place dots in the margin next to the error. Then the fourth graders reedit their writing, seeking additional assistance as necessary. By the time the writing reaches Tracey, who serves as the top editor, there is little editing left to do. Whatever

Figure 10.15

Example of an Editing Checklist for a Persuasive Paragraph

	Author	Peer	Teacher
1. I have checked my writing for spelling errors.			
2. I have indented my persuasive paragraph.			
3. I have correctly used punctuation at the ends of my sentences.			
4. I have correctly used commas in my paragraph.			
5. I have used capitals at the beginnings of all my sentences.			
6. I have capitalized proper nouns.			

editing has been overlooked can usually be addressed through a miniconference with the particular student.

By following a process, Tracey's students gradually become skilled editors. They learn the relevant conventions and know how to apply them to their own writing. Using editing checklists further helps them learn to prioritize the conventions according to the genre.

Using Formal Assessment with Our Writing Curriculum

Formal assessments (standardized assessments) provide a quantitative index of writing performance. They include state and national norm-referenced texts, which compare students' performance to a cross section of students in other regions of the state or nation. Historically, standardized assessments dominated the evaluation of writing. Used as measures of educational effectiveness, standardized tests became a way for state or national programs to evaluate program effectiveness.

Today standardized tests have become part of high school exit exams in some states. Many educators (Au, 1993, 2002; Valencia, 1990), however, suggest that the findings from standardized assessment should be used cautiously with students of diverse backgrounds because of possible cultural bias. Others criticize these tests because the tests measure students' ability to write rough drafts rather than their ability to use the writing process to craft a piece of writing. According to Hillocks (2002), we administer these tests in an hour or two even though real writing takes longer.

The format for these formal assessments usually includes a prompt, which includes two parts—the writing topic and the directions for writing. The first sentence usually introduces the topic; the second presents the directions for writing. To perform well, students should have something to say about the topic and recognize the specific genre (personal narratives, fictional stories, informative writing, or persuasive essays) so they can apply what they know about the genre. Students must also know information about the topic and how to generate ideas in order to respond to the prompt quickly.

In large-scale writing assessments, evaluators usually use holistic analysis to assess the writing. Professional readers, trained in holistic analysis, evaluate national and state assessments; trained teachers often evaluate district assessments.

Preparing Students for Standardized Tests

According to Routman (2005), the best preparation for standardized tests is quality writing instruction. Specifically, she reports that high test scores reflect a challenging writing curriculum; high test scores emerge when what is tested is woven into daily teaching.

Too often, we take the joy out of writing while trying to prepare our students for standardized tests. Classrooms across the nation have been spending endless hours preparing for tests, only to discover the time invested yields disappointing results. These classrooms spend hours practicing prompts, going through testing procedures, and applying the six traits. In spite of these efforts, students often perform worse due to the overemphasis on test preparation and skills.

Focusing on skills does not usually result in higher test scores. Focusing on aligning the standards with the curriculum does not usually bring about higher test scores. What is needed is a focus on writing, revising, and editing. Daily writing, extensive writing across the curriculum, and extensive reading of literature will translate into higher test performance.

Strategies to Improve Performance on Standardized Tests

Even though we should avoid overemphasizing test performance, we do need to help our students take testing seriously. Well-constructed tests that provide time for planning, drafting, revising, and editing give insight on how our students are performing in comparison to others. Students need to understand this and value the testing experience as a way to inform others about their school's progress. If they believe that this is a way to showcase their school, students might try their best.

To help students take pride in their school, some schools have student rallies where students perform songs and chants about achieving excellence and reaching for the stars. Sometimes cheerleaders perform at the event, boosting patriotic feelings about the school and its goal to achieve excellence. These rallies often create an audience and purpose for everyone to try their best.

teaching TIP 10.3

If we want our students to perform well on standardized tests, we must invest *time* in quality instruction. This is far more important than trying to teach to the test a few weeks or months prior to a standardized test.

Another way to help students respond to writing prompts is by planning lessons where students have to write on demand. According to Routman (2005), writing on demand is part of life. Test taking, completing job applications, or quickly writing a letter or memo are all demands that we must respond to in life. What's important is moderation. Practicing these types of writing events once every six weeks is sufficient.

Just before the standardized test, Tompkins (2008) suggests that we spend a week or two reviewing the language and format of the test. For example, students need to know how to follow the directions carefully, the parts of a prompt, how to respond to a prompt, and how the writing tests will be scored. Suggested topics include the following:

- Review that there are two parts in a prompt—the topic and the directions.
- Explain that the genre for the writing sample is inferred from words like *explain, describe, argue,* or *tell.*
- Remind them to apply the writing process as they respond to the prompt, using prewriting, drafting, revising, and editing strategies.
- Discuss the importance of pacing themselves as they write.

Some additional teaching strategies (Routman, 2005) that will help prepare students include the following:

- Have students take a practice test and analyze their writing, using the state rubric or a kid-friendly rubric.
- Ask state personnel for exemplary writing samples and analyze these as a class and in small groups, using the state rubric.
- Review specialized vocabulary students may need to know.
- Review how to read directions.

Just as quality teaching leads to higher test performance in writing, quality assessment helps us monitor our teaching so that we can modify and refine our instruction to help students improve their writing throughout the school year. As shown in Figure 10.1, instruction is linked to the assessment process we follow on an ongoing basis. If we carefully analyze our students' writing, using multiple sources of data, we become better informed on how to provide quality instruction for students. If we focus on skills in isolation—spelling, mechanics, word choice, or sentence fluency—students' writing may remain lifeless and homogenized. However, if we effectively link quality teaching with quality assessment, students' writing will begin to improve.

Closing Thoughts

To be effective, assessment and evaluation cannot be divorced from "classroom organization, from the relationship between teacher and student, from continuous learning experiences and activities" (Goodman, 1989, p. 4). If we revisit the various classrooms described in this chapter, we continuously see teachers weaving assessment into their teaching instruction. Without assessment, quality instruction cannot exist. Assessment helps us determine whether quality instruction is occurring.

Specifically, we see teachers using a variety of tools to learn what their students know and what they are able to do. Using observation, checklists, writing folders, writing sample analysis, and portfolios, teachers continuously gather information about their students and their writing. They use this information to hypothesize how they will plan their instruction and implement an effective writing curriculum. Through ongoing and continuous assessments, they determine whether their instruction is effective and how to make the instruction even more effective.

As we revisit the various classrooms, we also see teachers using ongoing analysis of students' writing in order to help students shape and craft their writing. We see students improve their writing by applying the same strategies and techniques authors draw upon in their writing. Using rubrics, revising and editing checklists, or the six traits, we gain a lens on what students are able to do with their writing. Designing minilessons to guide students' writing is one way to facilitate how they shape their writing. Students also learn about writing through experimentation and play in their journals. Reading literature aloud stimulates students to try the authors' crafts and stylistic techniques in their own writing.

Accomplishing our goals for quality teaching is a never-ending, lifelong process. If we continuously link assessment with instruction, we come closer to reaching our goals. Careful reflection, research, and ongoing education enhance our ability to achieve these goals.

Final Thoughts

Successful writing evolves in effective classrooms where teachers pursue excellence in teaching and writing. Is it easy to promote successful writing? No. Achieving excellence is tremendously challenging, yet enormously exhilarating. When we are successful, a sea of smiling faces energizes us. Through careful reflection, research, and ongoing education, we will find the path that leads us to quality teaching and writing.

As we traveled through a variety of classrooms in this text, we caught glimpses of teachers seeking excellence. Revisiting their classrooms may provide a lens through which to view quality teaching. Our own path, however, may differ slightly; there are no blueprints. Each of us must continue to reflect, research, and pursue lifelong learning to realize excellence.

Teachers Helping Students Feel Welcome

If we retrace our steps into classrooms throughout the text, we see models of effective teaching. First, we continuously see teachers implementing a writing curriculum within the social and cultural contexts of their community and personal lives. Recognizing the legitimacy of children's social existence becomes the classroom organization for curriculum and instruction. When we, like these teachers, embrace students' family and cultural styles, school becomes a more natural extension of home practices (Au, 1993, 2002; Diamond

& Moore, 1995; Taylor & Strickland, 1989). Celebrating diversity and its richness further helps all students begin to feel welcome in the classroom community. When writers feel welcome, writing gradually begins to flow.

Teachers Applying the Principles of Quality Teaching

Once teachers lay the foundation for literacy learning, we see them organizing and managing their writing curriculum to reflect effective teaching. The vignettes reveal four major patterns related to effective teaching. First, we see teachers who follow the writing process, using a balanced literacy approach and guided by a multicultural perspective. We also view teachers nurturing and supporting writing that emerges from real-life experiences, literature, and the cultural experiences of students. Third, we observe teachers integrating writing across the curriculum. As they integrate their curriculum, teachers find time to write daily and time to give students choices in their writing. Fourth, we view teachers embracing technology. Using technology as a tool to enhance writing, teachers guide and shape students' writing. They further challenge students to apply problem-solving and thinking skills.

Teachers Acting as Informed Educators

Continuing with our journey, we consistently catch glimpses of teachers who are thinking and acting as informed educators, continuously refining their teaching practice by asking questions and by reflecting. Influenced by their interactions with students and colleagues and by professional development, their understanding of writing theory is always changing. They keep their minds open to ways they might improve and polish their instruction through evolving knowledge.

Becoming a teacher of writing requires risk taking, explorations, decisions, and modifications of one's teaching practices to reflect both a global society and the information technology age. There are no recipes to follow. Shortcuts or simplistic solutions to problems do not exist. Rather, effective literacy draws on research and practice, which are both dynamic and evolving. As emphasized in Chapter 2, we need to continuously question our practice to see whether we

- Refine and shape our teaching through reflection.
- Believe in our students' ability to write.
- Retain high expectations for our students.

When we use research to guide our practice, we discover our own path for promoting writing so that we can help all students succeed. Even though the paths may differ according to the context of our classroom, our overarching goal is to shape, improve, and refine instruction so that *all* students grow and develop as authors.

Teachers Taking One Step at a Time

The struggle in teaching is inherent. For this reason, we need to be gentle with ourselves. We can't struggle with everything; we need to focus and take small steps as we modify our instruction (Routman, 1994). Once we become comfortable with a change, we can refocus and consider another change. At the same time, we need to remember that teaching and learning are an ever-changing, lifelong process.

Teachers' Questions

1. I feel overwhelmed. There are so many ways to assess students' writing. Where do I begin?

Many teachers share your sense of being overwhelmed by assessment. If we can find an entry point, a place where we feel comfortable, this is where we should begin. Many teachers find that observations are an easy place to begin. Most of us use observation naturally as we teach. If we record some of our observations on a regular basis, we can begin to show students' progress over time (see examples in figures).

As we become comfortable with one form of informal assessment, then we can gradually move to a second form and add this to our repertoire. Collecting at least three writing samples from every student might be another strategy to begin implementing. If we collect a writing sample from the beginning of the year, a second writing sample around January, and a final writing sample in April or May, we should be able to document students' progress in writing during the year. Of course, the writing sample should include each stage of writing—prewriting, drafting, revising, editing, and publishing. This way we can document progress during each stage of the process.

2. I feel like my students won't try their best unless I grade everything they write.

You are not alone. Many other teachers feel this way, too. Do you have students share their writing? Tracey Franklin finds that students become motivated to write when they hear her praise and encouragement as well as that of their peers whenever they share. She makes sure that peers explain what they like about each authors' writing. This way her students begin to learn what's working in their writing. When they author new pieces, they continue to use the same strategies or techniques in their writing. Tracey also has her students publish at least two writing pieces per semester. She finds that publishing her students' writing instills a sense of pride in their work and inspires them to write more. In fact, publishing is more motivational than receiving a grade. Grades can cause some students to become discouraged about their writing. For this reason, Tracey evaluates her students' writing on the process (how they use prewriting, drafting, revising, and editing) rather than the product or final draft. This way students can experience more success with their writing efforts.

3. If I don't correct students' editing and grammar errors, how will they learn to write well?

Students learn how to write well by finding their *own* editing and grammar errors. The red ink marks from *our* corrections only remind students about what they can't do. They begin to think that they are not good writers; many even give up trying to write.

If we instead teach *them* how to find the misspelled words, the missing capitals or ending marks, the missing commas or apostrophes, the incorrect tense, or the incorrect use of grammar, they will become writers who know how to shape their writing so that it follows the appropriate conventions of language. Teaching students how to find editing and grammar errors begins one step at a time. Using minilessons, we can begin teaching them how to find misspelled words. Good spellers know which words are misspelled. Even kindergarteners know which words are written in temporary spelling. Similarly, all writers can find their temporary spellings with some nudging. This is the beginning of becoming an editor of one's own writing. As students master one skill, we need to plan new minilessons to teach new editing skills. Looking at the students' writing, we can determine whether they are ready to learn about capitalizing a name, the word *I,* or certain types of proper nouns, for example. Our minilesson then addresses the needs of our writers. Future minilessons are structured to help students learn additional skills they need.

Teaching editing and grammar skills within the context of writing helps students remember and retain these strategies and skills over time. After the minilesson, students then apply the skill as they self-edit their own writing and then peer edit another student's writing. If they do not find a misspelled word or a missing capital or ending mark, we place a dot by that line. Students can go back to the line and find the error themselves. If they need additional clues, we can provide these clues to help *them* find the editing and grammar errors themselves.

What's important is teaching students the editing and grammar skills one at a time, as they are ready to learn these skills. The minilessons then provide students the knowledge and understanding of skills they can apply to their own writing and that of their peers. However, we don't want to overwhelm them with too many skills to apply at once.

4. How do I know where to begin when helping my students improve their writing? They need help on everything!

We need to read over students' writing pieces to determine which strategies will help the students improve their writing the most. Mary Streeter looks at the class holistically first, deciding which strategies will best help her students improve their writing. Then she plans a minilesson on one or two of these strategies, after which students go back to their writing pieces and revise their writing while applying this strategy. For example, at the beginning of the year, Mary often notices that her students seldom use an effective beginning or lead for their writing. After discussing effective leads and sharing examples of leads authors use in various textbooks, her students revise their writing pieces to include a stronger lead.

As Mary circulates, she may also have a miniconference with some students, addressing another strategy they might easily apply to their writing pieces. By asking a question, she helps them begin to think about experimenting with their writing. For example, she may ask a student, "Can you think of another way to end your writing piece?" After the two brainstorm possibilities, she leaves the student, allowing him or her to select an alternative ending.

By using a combination of minilessons and miniconferences Mary addresses the needs of her students. She realizes she cannot address everything at once; this would overwhelm and discourage her writers. Instead, she attempts to address the problems one step at a time.

5. Portfolios require too much time. How should we make portfolios more manageable?

You are not alone. Many teachers feel that portfolios are overwhelming. Making portfolios manageable and practical is important. When Jeanie Lawrence first began using portfolios, she collected three writing samples from her first and second graders' journals—one in October, one in January, and one in May. Then she collected three writing samples from her first and second graders that included all stages of the writing process at these same time intervals. She found that these writing samples gave her a "picture" of her students' writing growth while using both informal writing and more formal writing where they apply the writing process. Jeanie also discovered that the writing samples were very helpful for the parents. During family conferences, she was able to show caregivers how their children were progressing in their writing.

As Jeanie became more comfortable with portfolios, she began to gradually include other helpful informal assessment items. For example, the next year she added a checklist on students' stages of spelling. By placing the date next to the stages of spelling her students had mastered, she could document whether her students were advancing through the stages of spelling over time.

Each teacher needs to find his or her own comfort level with portfolios. Similar to Jeanie, we might begin with collecting writing samples from our students. Gradually, we can insert additional informal assessment items that may help us form a more complete picture of our students' writing growth.

Children's Literature

O'Neill, M. (1961). *Hailstones and halibut bones: Adventures in color.* New York: Doubleday.

References

Au, K. (1993). *Literacy instruction in multicultural settings.* Fort Worth, TX: Harcourt Brace Jovanovich College Publishers.

Au, K. (2002). Multicultural factors and the effective instruction of students of diverse backgrounds. In A. Farstrup & J. Samuels (Eds.), *What research has to say about reading instruction* (pp. 392–413). Newark, DE: International Reading Association.

Bratcher, S. (2004). *Evaluating children's writing: A handbook of communication choices for classroom teachers.* Mahwah, NJ: Lawrence Erlbaum.

Calkins, L. (1994). *The art of teaching writing.* Portsmouth, NH: Heinemann.

Clark, R. (1995). *Free to write.* Portsmouth, NH: Heinemann.

Culham, R. (2003). *6+1 traits of writing: The complete guide (Grades 3 and up).* New York: Scholastic Professional Books.

Diamond, B., & Moore, M. A. (1995). *Multicultural literacy: Mirroring the reality of the classroom.* New York: Longman.

Graves, D. (2004). What I've learned from teachers of writing. *Language Arts, 82,* 88–94.

Goodman, Y. (1985). Kidwatching: Observing children in the classroom. In A. Jaggar & M. T. Smith Burke (Eds.), *Observing the language learner* (pp. 9–18). Urbana, IL: National Council of Teachers of English.

Goodman, Y. (1989). Evaluation of students: Evaluation to teachers. In K. Goodman, Y. Goodman, & W. Hood (Eds.), *The whole language evaluation book* (pp. 3–14). Portsmouth, NH: Heinemann.

Higgins, B., Miller, B., & Wegmann, S. (2007). Teaching to the test . . . not! Balancing best practice and testing requirements in writing. *The Reading Teacher, 60,* 310–319.

Hillocks, G. (2002). *The testing trap: How state assessments of writing control learning.* New York: Guilford.

NCTE. (2004). *NCTE beliefs about the teaching of writing.* [Online]. Available at www.ncte.org/about/over/positions/category/write/118876.htm [June 13, 2005].

Piazza, C. (2003). *Journeys: The teaching of writing in elementary classrooms.* Upper Saddle River, NJ: Merrill Prentice Hall.

Routman, R. (1994). *Invitations: Changing as teachers and learners, K–12.* Portsmouth, NH: Heinemann.

Routman, R. (2005). *Writing essentials.* Portsmouth, NH: Heinemann.

Spandel, V. (2004). *Creating young writers: Using the six traits to enrich writing process in primary classrooms.* Boston: Allyn & Bacon.

Spandel, V. (2005). *Creating writers through 6-trait writing assessment and instruction.* Boston: Allyn & Bacon.

Taylor, D., & Strickland, D. (1989). Learning from families: Implications for educators and policy. In J. B. Allen & J. M. Mason (Eds.), *Risk makers, risk takers, risk breakers* (pp. 251–280). Portsmouth, NH: Heinemann.

Tompkins, G. (2000). *Teaching writing: Balancing process and product* (3rd ed.). New York: Macmillan College Publishing.

Tompkins, G. (2008). *Teaching writing: Balancing process and product* (5th ed.). New York: Macmillan College Publishing.

Valencia, S. (1990). Assessment: A portfolio approach to classroom reading assessment: The whys, whats, and how. *The Reading Teacher, 43,* 338–340.

Index

Text Credits

pp. 51, 58, 59, 111, Children's writing from *Multicultural Literacy: Mirroring the Reality of the Classroom* (1st ed.), by Diamond, Barbara J. & Margaret A. Moore. Published by Allyn and Bacon, Boston, MA. Copyright © 2008 by Pearson Education. Reprinted by permission of the publisher.

p. 60, Excerpt from Moore, Margaret A. (1991, December). "Electronic dialoguing: An avenue to literacy." *The Reading Teacher, 45*(4), 280–286. Copyright © 1991 by the International Reading Association.

p. 81, Excerpt from Moore-Hart, Margaret A. (2005, December). "A writer's camp in action: A community of readers and writers." *The Reading Teacher, 59*(4), 326–338. Copyright © 2005 by the International Reading Association.

p. 105, Excerpt from *People,* by Peter Spier. Copyright © 1991. Used by permission of Random House Children's Books, a division of Random House, Inc.

p. 116, Biopoem from *Multicultural Literacy: Mirroring the Reality of the Classroom* (1st ed.), by Diamond, Barbara J. & Margaret A. Moore. Published by Allyn and Bacon, Boston, MA. Copyright © 2008 by Pearson Education. Reprinted by permission of the publisher.

p. 117, Excerpt from *The Talking Cloth,* by Rhonda Mitchell. Copyright © 1997 Orchard Books, an imprint of Scholastic Inc. Used by permission.

p. 173, Reprinted with the permission of Whitecap Books Ltd. From *Welcome to the World of Beavers,* by Diane Swanson. Copyright © Diane Swanson 1999.

p. 234, Excerpt from *The Astonishing Armadillo,* by Dee Stuart. Copyright © 1993 by Carolrhoda Books. Reprinted with the permission of Carolrhoda Books, a division of Lerner Publishing Group, Inc. All rights reserved. No part of this text excerpt may be used or reproduced in any manner whatsoever without the prior written permission of Lerner Publishing Group, Inc.

pp. 234–235, Excerpt from *Into the Sea,* by Brenda Z. Guiberson. Copyright 1996 by Brenda Z. Guiberson. Reprinted by permission of Henry Holt and Company, LLC.